Americanism, Inc.

HEADQUARTERS.

NATIONAL WORKERS

AMERICA FIRST COMMITTEE
MEMBERSHIP AND CONTRIBUTION CARD

Please enroll me as a member of the AMERICA FIRST COMMITTEE. As
a patriotic American citizen, I am not affiliated in any way with any
foreign power. I wish to support the America First Comm...

NAME   GEORGE PAGNANELLI

ADDRESS   100 West 96 nd St CITY N

I enclose $ 1.00 to be used in furthering the c
the America First Committee is fighting.
(The America First Committee is supported entirely by voluntary
of time and money, but you need not contribute to become

Send this card to
AMERICA FIRST COMMITTEE, NEW YORK CHA
515 MADISON AVENUE

ship Card

Pagnanelli

L.C.

Past 46th St

pt. 15, 1914

Westphal

Secretary.

DEFEND
AMERICA
FIRST

to certify

PAGNANKLL

bes to the a
(see back) and

The ULTRA-AMERICAN

AMERICANISM
HONEST MONEY

The Symbol of a Crusade

COMMITTEE OF
1,000,000

PAUL REVERE SENTINELS, Inc.
An All American Patriotic Non-Profit Membership Corporation

PATRIOTS

unism

Christian Mobilizers
George Pagnanelli
737
7/20/39

The above pictured insignia ha...
of symbolizing the p...
1,000,000."

Address all commun...
Gerald L. K. Smith, Nat...

Literature having to do...
upon request.

See next pag...

MEMBERSHIP CARD
AMERICAN NATIONALIST PARTY
DEDICATED TO CHRISTIAN CONSTITUTIONAL GOVERNMENT

GEORGE PAGNANELLI
159 EAST 46TH STREET NEW YORK
NO   DATE   1/29/1929

eekly

Bulletin

on Federation of America
NATIONAL HEADQUARTERS   5373
DETROIT MICHIGAN

th that George Pagnanelli
New York has paid the Annual Fee
or Regular Membership in the
**ANGLO-SAXON FEDERATION
OF AMERICA**
or Year ending September 1942
Howard B. Rand

NO
FOREIGN
WAR!

Amerikadeutscher
GERMAN AMERICA

ORTSGRUPPE: NEW Y

194   1942

WE THE FATHERS
AUXILIARY
WE THE MOTHERS MOBILIZE
FOR AMERICA

SUITE   UREN ST.

This cert...
AN AMERICAN ... EVE ... THE CONSTI-
TUTIONAL GOVERNMENT OF THE ... TES OF AMER-
ICA, IS A MEMBER ... IZATION, PLEDGED TO
SUPPORT THE ... SET FORTH IN ... CHARTER.

SECRETARY

N.G.L.

Fördererkarte Nr.

TIZENS PROTECTIVE LEAGUE

★★★   NO FOREIGN WAR
★★★   CONTRIBUTION CARD

I believe that in order to preserve the America we all love, we must keep
out of foreign war. Therefore I am contributing   1.00
to support the work of the No Foreign War Committee.

Name   George Pagnanelli
(PLEASE PRINT)

Herr
Frau   GEORG PAG
Frl.

Wohnort   New York, N

Strasse

UNDER COVER

My Four Years in the Nazi Underworld of America—
*The Amazing Revelation of How Axis Agents
and Our Enemies Within Are Now Plotting
to Destroy the United States*

By JOHN ROY CARLSON

BOOKS, INC.

—

Distributed by
E. P. DUTTON & CO., INC.
NEW YORK   1943

AMERICAN BOOK—STRATFORD PRESS, INC., NEW YORK

Dedicated to SAM and STEVE, ROY and JOHN
and to those other official under cover men and women who,
unnamed and unsung, are fighting the
common enemy of Democracy on
the military front abroad
and the psychological
front at home

As investigator of subversive activity, the author joined or became affiliated with many self-styled "patriotic" groups, some of which are listed below. The endpaper pattern was based on his membership cards and buttons.

American National-Socialist Party
German-American Bund
Christian Front
The Ultra-American
Nationalist Party
American Nationalist Party
American Women Against Communism
The Gray Shirts
America First Committee
No Foreign War Committee
Christian Mobilizers
American Destiny Party
American Brotherhood of Christians Congress
The Ethiopian Pacific Movement
Citizens Protective League
Social Justice Distributors Club
The American Defense Society
Anglo-Saxon Federation of America
Paul Revere Sentinels
Ra-Con Klub
Crusaders for Americanism, Inc.
We the Fathers, Auxiliary to We the Mothers Mobilize for
   America
The Christian Mobilizer
Phalanx, PAX (secret gun club)
National Workers League
Yankee Freemen
Cross and the Flag
Committee of One Million
Flanders Hall, Nazi publishers
American Patriots
American Bulletin
National Gentile League

CONTENTS

AUTHOR'S PREFACE

"Thunder on! stride on, Democracy!
Strike with vengeful stroke!"

WALT WHITMAN

"UNDER COVER" is not so much an exposé of the work of alien Nazi or Fascist agents as it is, ultimately, a warning to America of those factors which have led to the development of a nativist, nationalist, American Nazi or American Fascist movement which, like a spearhead, is poised to stab at Democracy.

Defeatist and dissensionist propaganda continues while our country is at war, despite the arrest of nearly all the known foreign agents. This is not surprising. The Kuhns and Vierecks turned the torch over to the Pelleys and Laura Ingallses, and these American-born operatives of a foreign power symbolically relayed it to the thirty-three men and women indicted on charges of sedition.

Unfortunately, the trail that may lead to the destruction of Democracy does not end, but actually begins with these thirty-three men and women. Their missionary efforts and the misguided zeal of a thousand others like them still at large, have permeated deep into the American mind. And after many refining processes, the viewpoints originally promoted by the Kuhns and Vierecks and Shishmarovas have become palatable to many Americans whenever mouthed by neighbors without an accent.

In the course of my investigations, I found that many otherwise fine Americans were propagating the lies and the "party line" originally advanced by Hitler's agents and doing it sincerely in what they believed to be good Americanism.

This state of mind—the most dangerous obstacle to America's future Democracy—could become a fatal issue when we are seated around the peace table, and be a factor in influenc-

9

ing us to lose the peace after winning the war. It was to help illustrate the many facets of this "clear and present" danger of Nazified "Americanism" that I undertook to live, then write *Under Cover*. I want my fellow Americans to learn to recognize the American Fascist whenever he drapes the flag around himself, and to detect his Nazi mouthings regardless of how subtle his approach.

I have applied the terms fascist, fascist-minded, nationalist, American Fascist and American Nazi to those who, according to the record, have subverted Democracy by morally or financially supporting the racial, political or social doctrines of Hitler's National-Socialism, Mussolini's corporate-state Fascism or Franco's clericalist-Falangism; and have promoted an American species of Axis ideology in the name of super "patriotism" and super "Americanism." Actual membership in authoritarian regimes is not necessary for an American, native-born or naturalized, to qualify as fascist-minded.

I regard as blasphemy the stunt of those "super-patriots" who seek to whitewash their native Nazism by falling back on ancestors who died in order that Democracy might live. One need only recall that Major Vidkun Quisling was a "pure-blooded" Norwegian, and Pierre Laval was a "pure-blooded" Frenchman from the heart of Auvergne, to realize that "Democracy" like "fascism" is a state of mind, not of physical boundaries or hallowed ancestry.

My criterion for true patriotism is found in Elihu Root's definition:

True love of country is not mere blind partisanship. It is regard for the people of one's country and all of them; it is a feeling of fellowship and brotherhood for all of them; it is a desire for the prosperity and happiness of all of them; it is kindly and considerate judgment toward all of them. The essential condition of true progress is that it shall be based upon grounds of reason, and not of prejudice.

This definition differs so radically from the "patriotism" of American Fascists that if I know them at all, I am certain they will eventually brand Elihu Root either as a Jew, a Communist, or both. They will manage it somehow. I anticipate the same compliment myself.

"Under Cover" went through many adventures before it was ready to see the light in the form of printer's ink. I began writing it almost as soon as I started my investigations, since it was with a book in mind that I continued in my work. In nearly four and a half years I estimate that I've written about five million words. My files on the Christian Mobilizers alone contain more than 175 individual reports totalling 250,000 words. It was inevitable that this mass outpouring "in the heat of battle," should have affected my writing. Consequently I tried to work with a collaborator in the preparation of *Under Cover*, but after a few weeks we parted company and once again I started out from scratch.

I've had many offers of help on the part of groups and individuals who, while well-meaning and engaged in the democratic cause, each had an obvious axe to grind. All extraneous "advice" and "suggestions"—one of which included the deletion of three consecutive chapters now in Book II—were politely rejected, and the independence of the writing maintained. For better or worse, this book is the author's own work, though of course it has gone through a certain amount of editorial trimming and pruning.

I am grateful for the moral support and foresight of a number of friends, who I hope will remain my friends after reading *Under Cover*. I am indebted to the publishers of *Fortune* magazine, and in particular to Russell W. Davenport, then its managing editor, for engaging me early in 1939 to make a preliminary survey of the New York fascist scene. That is how I happened to get my start.

I am indebted to the patient and kindly Reverend L. M. Birkhead for his permission to use the extensive and orderly files of his militant organization, Friends of Democracy, for some of my background material. I am indebted to Joseph Roos of Los Angeles for information on West Coast Nazis; to Kenneth M. Birkhead (now in the army), Mrs. Marion Hart and Miss Anne Simmons.

I wish also to pay my grateful respects to E. G. Morris for his zealous and untiring efforts in my behalf over a period of two years. He has been my friend as well as my literary agent.

And, finally, I wish to pay tribute to the loving inspiration of Marie and Robert, without which this book would never have been realized nor, indeed, could I have survived the experience of living it.

John RoyCarlson

April 9, 1943

BOOK ONE

BEFORE PEARL HARBOR

"*We National Socialists have never maintained that we were representatives of a democratic viewpoint, but we have openly declared that we only made use of democratic means in order to gain power, and that after the seizure of power we would ruthlessly deny to our opponents all those means which they had granted to us during the time of our opposition.*"—PROPAGANDA MINISTER DR. PAUL JOSEPH GOEBBELS

Chapter I

A BLACK CHRISTMAS

"The evil that men do lives after them;
The good is oft interred with their bones."
WILLIAM SHAKESPEARE

MY STORY actually begins in December, 1933, with an episode that blazed across newspaper headlines for months thereafter. On the morning of Christmas Sunday, 1933, Archbishop Leon Tourian, Primate of the Armenian Church in North and South America, was scheduled to celebrate Holy Mass in the Holy Cross Church on West 187th Street, New York.

The tiny church was filled with devout worshippers. The altar was gayly decorated with flowers. Candles were lighted. The pungent odor of incense filled the air and all morning a vested choir had sung of "Peace on earth, good will to men . . ." The congregation stood up reverently when a stately figure in the full magnificence of ecclesiastical dress emerged from the vestry room at the rear of the church and remained poised at the end of the aisle. In his left hand the Archbishop carried a crozier of gold. With his right hand, holding a jewel-studded crucifix, he blessed the bowed parishioners.

Bound for the altar, the procession was led by a censer bearer, followed by twelve members of the choir abreast in couples. Then came the resplendent figure of the Primate. Two acolytes brought up the rear of the processional. Organ music filled the air, and the choir chanted softly as it started from the aisle. The devout crossed themselves. The candle lights flickered. . . .

Suddenly from the right side of the aisle, a swarthy, pock-marked figure jumped into the aisle and stooped low. In his right hand was a two-edged butcher knife six inches long and whetted to razor sharpness. Simultaneously from an adjoining pew, a second assailant threw himself on the Primate and pinned back his arms, while the first one, with a pumping motion stabbed four times through the sacred roves at the Archbishop's vital section.

Carried out with thoroughly practiced savagery committed in the presence of a stupefied crowd, the murder was over in a few seconds. The figure of the Prelate lurched forward, then fell prostrate the full length of the aisle. The screaming, bewildered congregation stampeded to the door.

Thomas E. Dewey—now Governor of New York—was engaged to prepare the case against the assassins. Nine men were eventually convicted of the murder. All were found to be members and officers of the Armenian Revolutionary Federation, a secretive political gang also known as the Dashnag—the Dashnag whose methods anticipated those of the Gestapo. I had, of course, known of the existence of the Dashnag and had heard of their international program of terrorism, but the murder of Archbishop Tourian and what became known of their organization during the trial, brought to light the formidable power which this small but sinister fascistic clique wielded not only in America but wherever Armenians lived. It was thoroughly hated by the overwhelming majority of Armenians—but they could do little about it.

Our family had known Archbishop Tourian in the Old World. While still a priest, he had baptized my little brother Steven in the Armenian Church at Sofia, Bulgaria. As Archbishop, he had had dinner with us in our home in Long Island. I adored him as a person and literally worshipped him as a man of God. It was nearly impossible for me to conceive that this frightful murder had occurred in my adopted America.

I am an Armenian by parentage and our history as a Christian people goes back to Biblical days. It was on Mount Ararat, in the land of Armenia, that tradition tells Noah's Ark rested. Some people have their religion or their nationality thrust upon them by the accident of birth. I am an American by choice. It was in this country that my family, after countless generations of persecution, saw hope of a reality of freedom and Democracy.

I was born on Good Friday in Alexandropolis—a city founded by Alexander the Great on the shores of the Aegean

Sea in Southern Greece. Our home, the largest in the shipping
port, was located on Governor Street and overlooked the
busy wharves. Father was district manager for the Singer
Sewing Machine Company. Grandfather on mother's side
had been an architect to the Sultan in Constantinople. Other
uncles and grandparents had been jewelers, translators and
right-hand men to various Turkish Sultans.

I used to ask questions about America of the fishermen and
hamals—stevedores—unloading cargo boats. My uncle Arthur
had sailed to the United States three years after my birth. My
companion, Christo, a youth of fourteen years, knew less
about America than the stevedores. Together with *Aydz*, a
goat my parents maintained for its milk, Christo and I spent
most of our afternoons in the peaceful valleys surrounding
Alexandropolis.

Hitler and Himmler now rule it.

Soon after I was born, in 1909, the Greek Army was defeated at Alexandropolis and the Bulgarian Army occupied
our city. They didn't stay long. The Turks came back and
drove them out. Then the Greeks returned with reinforcements and with some Italian help, drove out the Turks. The
inhabitants of Alexandropolis being of Greek, Bulgarian, Armenian and Turkish descent, each marauding army plundered
the homes of the nationals it was fighting. The invading Bulgarians pillaged Greek and Turkish homes. Then the Turkish
soldiers plundered the Greeks, the Bulgarians and the Armenians. Alexandropolis was truly a cosmopolitan city—it
was plundered by each and every Balkan Army.

A portion of the civilian population took to the safety of
the hills whenever one or another army entered the city. People unable to flee lived in the cellars of their homes while
street fighting raged among Turks, Bulgarians and Greeks.

The defenseless Armenians were the prey of all the armies
all the time. The cellar of our home was completely furnished
to withstand months of siege. We lived as refugees in our
own home while the battle went on furiously. At night we
ventured for fresh air into the back yard surrounded with a
high stone fence, and studded on top with broken glass. Our
valuables, which were placed in an urn, were buried beneath
the roots of the grapevine.

Once, when a raiding party was systematically looting homes, piling the booty in waiting carts, father sought protection under the American flag. He hung it from the balcony of our home, and shouted: "I represent an American company. Don't you dare break down the door." The ruffians took father for an American Consul and passed us up.

I was four years old when we were warned that a horde of wild Turkish bandits—*bashibozouks*—were about to raid the town and set it afire. Father and mother piled bread and cheese, bundles, mattresses, blankets and their two children into an old bullock cart and took to the hills. Behind and ahead of us were hundreds of other carts of Armenian families fleeing the terrible Turks.

When it was safe to do so we fled to Bulgaria. I remember the bread line that formed daily in front of the government warehouse in Sofia, the capital of Bulgaria. The line, a long queue of aged peasant women wrapped in shawls, of bent old men, of children bawling from hunger, of young girls with sunken eyes and waxlike pallor, began to form at dawn. There were no young men or middle-aged men in that line. All were off to war. But there were young mothers, their faces pinched, huddling emaciated little infants, waiting hour after hour; waiting eternally, it seemed, for rations of coarse rye bread. Nothing else. It seems odd to hear a people complain today about rationing.

An ally of Imperial Germany, the tyrannous Turk determined to exterminate the Armenians in Turkey who had traditionally sided and volunteered for service with the Allies. Turk nationalists embarked on a Moslem "holy war" of massacre, starvation, brutality and mass deportations which up to that time had been unparalleled among the so-called civilized nations. Hundreds of thousands of innocent Armenians perished. But tens of thousands more would have perished if the Near East Relief, the Foreign Missions and the Red Cross had not established orphanages, hospitals, schools and food kitchens. The unstinting manner with which Americans during those tragic war years gave of their savings left an unforgettable imprint on our family, on all Armenians—and particularly on me. We looked to America with reverence.

My family spent the war years in Sofia and the next two

following the Armistice in Constantinople. In due time, we sailed for America aboard the Greek ship *Meghali Hellas* with several hundred other Armenians and arrived in the New World on April 2, 1921.

I remember our first Sunday here. Mother, father, my brothers John, Steven and I walked up trim, arbored, sun-spotted Willis Avenue in Mineola, Long Island, a suburb of New York. Uncle Arthur was proudly leading the way to our new home. No Turks lurked around the corner. No corpses littered the streets. There was no need to hide in warehouses or cellars, to bolt the doors or talk in whispers. This was America! I was a gawky boy of twelve, and so terrorized by past experiences I could hardly believe that one could live in one place any length of time without having to flee for safety.

Our new home was far removed from the "nationality islands" of New York City. Stern and strong-willed, father insisted that we enroll in school immediately and become Americans. "We have come to a New World," he said, "we must learn new ways of living. Forget Europe."

Mother was a graduate of the American Women's College at Constantinople and spoke English well, in addition to French, Greek, Turkish, Bulgarian and Armenian. She enrolled John and me in school the week after we had landed here. That same week father, accompanied by our uncle, went to the Nassau County Courthouse to register his intention of becoming an American citizen. In the wholesome atmosphere of a pretty little suburb, surrounded by friendly, native-born Americans our own Americanization got off to a flying start.

Father was a linguist who spoke six languages. He learned the seventh, English, very rapidly by reading newspapers. Uncle knew seven languages, including some Chinese. I spoke Armenian, Greek, Bulgarian, Turkish and French and also a smattering of Italian—which I had learned from the Pascualis, the childless couple who were our neighbors in Alexandropolis—but I knew no English.

My first teacher in America, a short, plump, red-cheeked little bundle of sympathy and kindness, kept me after school and patiently tutored me in English and spelling night after night. Miss A. Canning was representative of many Americans I've met since then.

In the meanwhile, father had established himself in business as importer of cheese, fish, honey, rose-petal jam, caviar and other delicacies. Mother spent her evenings helping us with our American history lessons. In May, 1926, the family celebrated our official recognition as American citizens. We invited all the neighbors to a sumptuous Armenian dinner which lasted five hours.

In June, 1928, I was graduated from Mineola High School with honors. America was good to us! We were treated as equals by our neighbors, as fellow Americans. We were given no cause to side, then or in years to come, with alien political movements which thrive on hate and social frustration. We joined the American blood stream and were swept past the painful period of maladjustment which plague many newcomers. Democracy became my ideal of a way of life.

Four years later I was graduated from the New York University School of Journalism, having worked my way through as reporter for a string of Long Island newspapers. I decided to travel throughout the United States—hitchhiking and working at what I could get to do. I was not driven to travel by necessity but by a desire to get acquainted with my adopted country and its people. I returned home in November, 1933.

And it was just after this trip, where I had been learning what my adopted country was like, that I received the terrific shock of Old World politics and terrorism. I had no conception at that time of the forces of evil already at work to undermine the tolerance and freedom which had been the peculiar heritage of America. The murder of the Armenian Primate made me sense that even here there was the danger of the same feelings of perverted nationalism which had plagued Europe for generations.

It is difficult to express in words the effect the brutal murder of Archbishop Tourian by Dashnag henchmen had on me. For a long time I was bewildered and then gradually I began to learn that the Dashnags, while they represented a vicious political clique of terrorists, were not the only fascistic organization then engaged in violating the principles of our

Democracy. Five years later the second incident occurred which was to crystallize for me the certainty that a concerted attempt was being made to destroy Democracy in the United States.

CHAPTER II

SCHOOL AT STAHRENBERG'S

"My religion is National-Socialism. That's the
only religion I believe in. Christianity is the bunk."
PETER STAHRENBERG

IN THE FALL of 1938 while riding in a New York subway, I
picked up a leaflet entitled *Why Are Jews Persecuted for
Their Religion?* It was printed on cheap, gray newsprint
and included four pages of bitterly anti-Semitic quotations
and distorted passages from American history. The leaflet
urged "American patriots" to "rise up as one man and clean
house politically and economically." It bore the imprint of
the Nationalist Press Association, 147 East 116th Street, New
York. Pricked by curiosity I decided to look up these headquarters of "Americanism."

At about eight o'clock on the evening of October 14, 1938,
I went to the address on 116th Street. The building was an
old tenement, with a barber shop in the ground floor and the
headquarters of the American Labor Party on the floor above.
I walked past a series of garbage cans in the hallway until I
came to another door, locked. Taking a deep breath I knocked
on the door of the Nationalist Press Association.

There was no answer but I could hear someone moving inside. Suddenly the door was flung open. With the light glaring in my eyes I could barely make out the form of the man
standing before me. I told him I would like to buy some leaflets on the Jews. Without answering, the man turned and motioned me in. We walked along a narrow hall room and I
noticed on my left a sign: "French and Italian haircuts—25¢."
I could make out the dim forms of barber chairs and hair
tonic bottles on the shelves.

I followed my guide along the hallway into an inner room
—a small, shabby, dim-lit place, cluttered with scraps of paper,
pamphlets, books, twine. There were four men in the room.
Cigarette butts littered the floor. In one corner stood a bat-

tered steel cabinet piled high with magazines and newspapers
and in another corner, a ruddy-cheeked blond with an owlish
face sat scribbling in a ledger under a banner on the wall
reading "America for the Americans." A thin Italian, with
sharp eyes, rodent-featured, folded printed newspaper sheets.
The other two men were standing near by wrapping packages in brown paper.

"I'd like some pamphlets on the Jews," I said.

The Italian dropped his work, went into an inner room
and soon returned followed by a tall, blond man in his late
twenties, with blunt features and a coarse-lipped, brutal
mouth. He wore a khaki army shirt and a black tie. His tie
pin was a pearl-studded swastika.

"Who are you? Where do you come from? What are you
doing here? Who sent you?" he demanded.

As calmly as I could I told him that I was a student at
Columbia University—that I had seen one of his pamphlets
and had liked some of the things in it. I explained that I was
interested in the "patriotic movement," and wanted to know

Stahrenberg's letterhead and issue of the *National American*
devoted to the "sterilization speech" of General Moseley, retired.

more about it. He listened intently, then without a word, turned and disappeared into the inner room.

I stood there watched by the four men who said nothing, but barred my exit. In a moment the tall blond came back into the room.

"Are there a lot of Jews at Columbia?" he asked.

I started to answer, but was relieved when he kept right on talking. "We tried getting into City College but the students fought back. We had better luck at New York University; got some leaflets into the student lockers and the men's toilets."

As he was speaking, he handed me a dozen leaflets. I asked if there was any other literature I ought to read to familiarize myself with the subject.

"You ought to read the *Protocols*.[1] It'll give you the truth on what's really going on today."

"You can get that book at the Germania Bookstore over on Thoid Avenue," the little Italian volunteered. His name was Joe.

"You know, fella," Joe said, "we gotta do something to save this Goddam country from the Communists. It's the duty of every fella what calls himself a patriot. Take Roosevelt, he's a Jew. The Cabinet, the Supreme Court, the Post Office—they're all Jewish."

I smiled disbelief.

"Sure thing," Joe continued eagerly. "Cordell Hull, John Lewis, J. P. Morgan, Wallace, Perkins—they're all Jews. People don't know it. They ain't been woke up. They ain't all read our educational literature."

[1] The *Protocols of the Learned Elders of Zion* purported to be the minutes of a meeting of Jewish leaders allegedly held in 1897, at which they were supposed to have outlined a plot for world domination. Actually the *Protocols* were copies of the political diatribe by Maurice Joly, a Frenchman, entitled *Dialogues in Hell Between Machiavelli and Montesquieu* and first published in 1864.

Casting about for Jew-baiting literature, Sergius Nilus, a briefless and obscure lawyer of Moscow "discovered" the *Protocols* and by adding the word Jew to Joly's diatribe published it in 1905 as an authentic Jewish document. It gave rise to many pogroms in Russia of Czarist days. In more recent years the brazen fraud has been propagated as "truth" in the interests of Nazi propaganda, and has served as the "Bible" of Nazis to disrupt Democracy the world over.

The big blond turned and handed me three copies of *National American*, a newspaper in tabloid size. "That's my newspaper," he said, "I am Pete Stahrenberg. I'm editor and publisher. This is the official organ of the American National-Socialist Party. We are pro-American. We're publishing a paper for real one hundred per cent Americans."

"Are you the head of the American National-Socialist Party?"

"Yes."

I glanced at the paper. Two black swastikas were printed under the title. The Party emblem was an American Indian, arm outstretched in salute, poised against a black swastika.

"Say, what's your name and address?" Stahrenberg asked suddenly. "Write it down on this card."

"George Pagnanelli," I said and wrote down an address somewhere in Brooklyn, I had decided to pose as an Italian mainly because Italy was a partner to the Axis. The few words I still remembered from our neighbors, the Pascualis in Alexandropolis and my pleasant associations with Italians since then prompted me to assume the role of an Italian American.

"There you are. George Pagnanelli; and here's my address," I said, handing him the brown card.

"Whereabouts in Brooklyn is that?" the owlish-faced German asked, after glancing at the address I had given.

"It's right near the subway station," I managed to stammer and started for the door.

"Well, good-bye, Mr. Stahrenberg," I said nervously as I walked out into the passage.

"Come again," he urged after I had turned to go. But I found the door to the outside locked. I stood paralyzed for a moment, twisting the knob, imagining all sorts of things and expecting to be grabbed from behind. After a few moments I took a deep breath, turned and walked back into the room.

"The door won't open," I said casually.

Stahrenberg laughed. "We have a special way of locking it," then he walked with me through the hallway and unlocked the door. His pearl-studded swastika tie pin gleamed in the half-light of the hallway. His ugly features high lighted.

"Good night," I murmured. The door clicked quietly behind me. A wave of relief flooded through me, as I walked out into the lighted street, convinced that my hunch had been a good one. As I rounded the first corner I felt myself followed.

Having given a false address I hesitated between going home and thus leading Stahrenberg's men straight to my parents or going to the address I had given in Brooklyn and managing the best way I could from then on. In the end I decided to take the subway to Brooklyn. Two men who got on the same car with me watched me furtively all the way to Brooklyn. As luck would have it, the address I had given was a residential building and the front door was open. Instead of going up the staircase I hid under it. A little later I heard the door open and heavy footsteps on the staircase. I tiptoed out into the street and hid in an areaway next door. In a few minutes the two men came out of the apartment house and headed for the subway.

I had no intention of making another visit to the offices of the American National-Socialist Party, but a few months after my original visit I happened to meet Joe, the Italian I had met there, and he was so cordial I concluded my ruse had worked.

Until now I had worked for small national magazines and was eager to become associated with one of the large national publications. I had heard that *Time, Life* and *Fortune* paid good salaries and were on the lookout for experienced editorial workers. I applied for a position on *Fortune*. I was granted an interview with one of the editors, and although I did not get a job, he became very friendly and seemed particularly interested when I told him of my experiences with Stahrenberg.

I tried several of the larger magazines without success and had just about given up hope of making a good editorial connection when I received a telegram from *Fortune* asking me to come to their office. They were contemplating a survey on subversive activity and asked if I'd be interested in a job as an investigating reporter. Already my visit to Stahrenberg was paying dividends in a chance to help America.

That was in the winter of 1939. That February saw an episode so alien to America, and so alarming, that it plunged me into a career as an investigator of Nazi activity. I was about to witness star-spangled murder with American Democracy as the corpse. When I visited Pete Stahrenberg for the second time he had given me a red-white-and-blue leaflet addressed "To all American Patriots" which read:

GEORGE WASHINGTON BIRTHDAY EXERCISES

Mass Demonstration for True Americanism

Madison Square Garden
February 20, 1939

GERMAN-AMERICAN BUND

That "Mass Demonstration for True Americanism" turned out to be the wildest Nazi demonstration so far staged on this side of the Rhine. The great hall was jammed with 20,000 men, women and many children. High above the speakers' platform towered a huge figure of George Washington, flanked by giant black swastikas. From somewhere in the rear of the hall came the muffled sound of drum beats as a uniformed Nazi legion, 1200 strong, marched in behind the swastika flags and the banners of the German National-Socialist Party! Twelve hundred brown-shirted arms smartly raised in a Hitler salute!

The first speaker who stepped to the platform was short, sandy-haired James Wheeler-Hill, Russian-born national secretary of the Bund, followed by the "Goebbels" of the Bund, Gerhard Wilhelm Kunze, Rudolf Markmann, Georg Froboese, Reverend S. G. von Bosse. Wheeler-Hill began:

"We stand before you loyal and law-abiding, to be here dedicated together with you to the task of national and social reconstruction, and resolved as you are resolved to restore America to the true Americans . . ."

Hitler, Mussolini, Franco and to my amazement, the mention of the Reverend Charles E. Coughlin's name received ear-splitting applause, while the President was booed and hissed and our officials slandered as, one after another, high Bund officials paraded to the speaker's stand. But they were merely "warmer-uppers" for Fritz Kuhn. The crowd went wild as *Der Bundesführer* rose to speak. Bowlegged, bull-

necked, he acknowledged the applause with the Nazi salute
and then spoke with a thick German accent:

"We now know that it vas the Joos who were responsible
for America's entering the World War through pressure
brought upon President Wilson. It vas the Joos who. . . ."

Suddenly, unable to listen to Kuhn's gospel of hate any
longer, a youth leaped from his chair and rushed toward
the platform. But before he could reach it the O.D. men
(*Ordnungs Dienst*), the storm troopers in uniform along the
aisles, had gone into action . . . I heard in the roar of the
mob the sinister cry of Turkish *bashibozouks* in action. A
moment later the battered body of the beaten youth was
carried out.

I was fascinated by the idea of investigating these people
who seemed intent upon destroying every vestige of freedom
in America. Doing my research work for *Fortune* in the late
afternoon and night and my editorial work for the magazine
during the day, I plunged into the opportunity to repay
America in a humble way, for her kindness and generosity.

My first step was to become a convincing actor. I took a
room near Mulberry Street and lived for a week in the heart
of New York's Italian section under the name of George
Pagnanelli. I ate Italian food and went to Italian movies. I
listened to Italian music and watched Italian housewives bargain with pushcart peddlers. At night, alone in my tiny room
in a smelly tenement, I listened to family quarrels—in Italian.
I modeled my dress after those I had seen. My "Pagnanelli
suit" was dark reddish-brown. My "Pagnanelli shoes" were
pointed, with fancy designs, dark maroon in color. The rest
of my Pagnanelli wardrobe was modeled after that of Tony,
an Italian youth of my own age and complexion. I studied
the manners of speech and gestures and modeled mine after
them. And even though I could not read Italian, I carried
a copy of *Il Progresso Italo-Americano* in my pocket. I was
determined to become the finest synthetic Italian-American
in New York.

My second step was to offer myself as volunteer worker
to Pete Stahrenberg. He was suspicious at first and we talked
in generalities. Then Joe breezed in and I decided to test my
acquired abilities under fire. Apparently I passed every test

except that of fluent diction. I explained this failure by saying that I was born in America and had not picked it up because my parents had raised me in a non-Italian neighborhood.

"Hey, Pete," Joe called out, "this guy is a good *paisano*. He's of my kind and he's willing to work. Why don't you let him help around here?"

"If you say he's okay, Joe, it's all right with me. We can sure use a couple more volunteers, the way the orders are rushing in."

After Joe had left Pete introduced me to his two associates, Carl Halder, a tall, taciturn man with brushy hair; and Gus Hettler—a round-faced German. Gus operated the printing press when Pete was away while Carl looked after the shop.

While he talked, Stahrenberg sat down with Carl and me and started to fold leaflets. At about midnight the printing press stopped. Gus and Carl left, and I remained alone with Stahrenberg. I looked at his powerful biceps and huge bony hands. Fearing that I might say the wrong thing, or make a wrong move, I listened, speaking as little as possible.

I worked at assembling leaflets into bundles of two hundred. These propaganda packages, Pete told me, sold for one dollar apiece. Sitting at the next desk Pete took the bundles from me, placed a few copies of the *National American* on top of each, wrapped them in heavy brown paper, put "Buy Christian" stickers all over the packages and filled out an American Railway Express receipt for each bundle about to be sent away.

He called my attention to the stickers. "The post office won't let us use 'em," he said.

We worked long into the night. And Pete talked. He told me that a certain "nationalist" actor in Hollywood was drilling a large mounted force and "getting ready for the revolution." He informed me that he was getting orders for his literature from all over the nation, particularly from Florida, Philadelphia and Chicago. During a short rest he showed me a letter from the Franklin Institute of the State of Pennsylvania which branded the anti-Semitic statements attributed to Benjamin Franklin as outright forgeries.

"That letter lies," Pete said savagely. "That letter lies!

Stick around with me and you'll find out all about the lies of these people."

I didn't leave until early morning.

Stahrenberg seemed pleased to see me again a few nights later and was even more talkative. He told me how anxious he was to form a youth group in the colleges throughout the country.

"You got to catch them young," he repeated again and again.

He discussed this and other things while we folded leaflets and tied bundles and made them ready for shipping. Those dingy rooms behind the barber shop were the clearing house for a multifold quantity of Nazi propaganda. Gradually I began to learn the catch-words and became familiar with subversive publications. Stahrenberg received material from a hundred different sources then redistributed it to his own mailing list. Off the Nationalist Press Association printing press rolled hundreds of thousands of pamphlets, newspapers and throw-away leaflets. In addition to his own printing, Stahrenberg was doing work for many important anti-American propagandists in the New York area, and he was associated with all these incipient Nazi movements in one way or another.

A large part of the material came to him from *U. Bodung-Verlag*, at Erfurt, Germany, Goebbels' main propaganda mill grinding out Nazi literature in thirteen different languages. From Erfurt also came a "news" bulletin called *World Service*—published by Lieutenant-Colonel Ulrich Fleischhauer. Enormous quantities of leaflets defaming Jews and Democracy with fantastic lies and distortions of truth bore the imprint *Deutscher Fichte-Bund*, Hamburg. It called itself "a union for world veracity." Frequent shipments came from the *Terramare* office, the *Reichsdruckerei*, the *Amerika Institut* which specialized in propagandizing America, and countless other Nazi agencies striving to tear down Democracy wherever it existed in the world.

Stahrenberg showed me copies of the Bund organ, *Deutscher Weckruf und Beobachter*. Half the contents of the scurrilous sheet were in English. In the March 31, 1938 issue was an article by the anti-Catholic editor, Severin Winterscheidt stating that Nazi persecution of Catholic priests for "immorality" was entirely justified. Just two months before Winterscheidt wrote it, I read of his arrest for indecent exposure in New York's Pennsylvania Station. That July he was sentenced to an indefinite term in prison for attempting to attack a little girl in a Brooklyn movie house.

Our conversation turned to the Bund and to my surprise, Pete criticized it sharply, insisting that it was riding for a fall.

"They ain't handling their propaganda the right way. They ought to go easy on the swastikas and the military uniforms because the American people ain't ready for it yet. You don't see us doing things that way around here. We're all for Americanism."

I was being educated in the ways of Nationalist Americanism at the rear of that barber shop.

On subsequent visits I saw copies of *Action* whose slogan was "Britain First," and which was published by Sir Oswald Mosley, leader of the British Black Shirts. Other booklets were branded with a large black swastika above the words "Imperial Fascist League, London." *Aftermath*, a magazine published by the Christian Aryan Syndicate in England, as well as the official fascist party newspapers from Canada, Rome and Paris, arrived regularly at Pete's office.

The American "patriotic" press was represented by *The American Vindicator*, published by North Carolina's Senator Robert Rice Reynolds; *Liberation*, published by Silver Shirt Leader William Dudley Pelley; Father Coughlin's *Social Justice;* Reverend Gerald B. Winrod's *Defender;* James True's *Industrial Control Reports;* Robert Edward Edmondson's *Vigilante Bulletin;* Colonel E. N. Sanctuary's, Merwin K. Hart's and Mrs. Elizabeth Dilling's leaflets.

At Pete's office I became familiar with most of the names that were to come to life within the next four years, many of them of old stock American ancestry. I realized with a shock that fascism could be produced by any nation—under proper "educational" guidance.

In order to learn a smattering of German, I took a room with a Mrs. Meyer, at 100 West 86th Street, who soon proved herself an ardent Nazi sympathizer. One of her sons was in the German Army. The other two spent their time glorifying the *Reichswehr*. When I saw Stahrenberg again he asked me, casually, where I lived. I was not caught unawares. The casual tone had not deceived me. I gave him just as casually, the address of the rooming house kept by the Nazi landlady and remarked that I had moved recently and was living alone in order to better carry on my "patriotic" work.

On an errand for Stahrenberg one day I met a mild, benevolent-looking man named James McGee who ran a small printshop with his son a few blocks away from Pete. Most of McGee's business was in religious literature, but the same press that turned out bereavement cards was used to print anti-Semitic stickers designed in Berlin. This pious, white-haired man held membership in one of the most vicious secret organizations in the country—a Christian Front "Sport Club" known as the Phalanx. Its membership blanks were printed on his press, free of charge. His printshop served as a hide-out and clearing house for subversive literature, and also housed a short-wave set and a recording apparatus. McGee's son, Arthur, used to record songs and speeches from German radio programs and pass them along to fellow "patriots."

Stahrenberg's offices served as a hang-out for *Social Justice* salesmen and men selling *Liberation* and *Deutscher Weckruf*. Among the salesmen were Paul Lucenti and Dan Walker. Walker was a thin scarecrow of a youth with a sharp, pimply face. From Lucenti I got my first information about the Coughlin-inspired terrorism on the sidewalks of New York.

"You got to create terror to get somewhere," he repeated as he recounted his exploits. "You got to terrorize the Jews." Lucenti used to hawk his papers in the Times Square district and his sales technique was modeled after the best Brownshirt traditions. To create a scene and attract attention he would insult passers-by who appeared to be Jewish. A half dozen hoodlums would be standing by, waiting to pitch in.

"I guess I've been arrested a dozen times," Lucenti told me proudly. "I wrote Father Coughlin and told him they'd probably throw me in the jug, and look what he sent me." Beaming, Lucenti unfolded a telegram from E. Perrin Schwartz, managing editor of *Social Justice*, who instructed him to telephone the magazine and reverse the charges if he got into trouble!

"I'm safe now," he gloated. "Father will get me out of trouble."

In the course of conversation I learned several of the quaint sales devices used by *Social Justice* salesmen. One of them was used frequently by young children. A child would stand on a street corner weeping bitterly. When someone stopped to ask what was wrong, he would sob: "A big Jew hit me for selling *Social Justice*." When a crowd had collected, such a scene would frequently end with a collection being taken up to buy the child's magazines. That scene over, the little salesman would hustle to another corner and repeat the routine.

As Stahrenberg and I were discussing selling magazines and circularizing customers one day, our talk turned to secret lists. I asked if he kept one. "And how!" he answered quickly. "Have I got a list of big shot Jews and some of your tolerant Christians! Wait till the time comes to use it!

"Here's the guy who gave me the idea," Pete said as he walked across the room to his desk and tossed me a card. It showed a red-white-and-blue swastika beneath a Christmas tree and was signed "Adrian Arcand." I learned that Arcand was leader of the Canadian Fascist Party. Pete had met him in 1937 as guest speaker at a New York Bund rally. The Canadian Fuehrer was one of Stahrenberg's idols. First among Pete's list of great men stood Adolf Hitler. Then came Rudolf Hess, Benito Mussolini, Sir Oswald Mosley, and the late Huey Long. Pete felt that Huey had been a great man and that there was no one in the United States who could replace him.

One day Pete showed me a stack of petitions he had printed, titled "Ford for President to Restore Americanism."

"Ford is a good man," Pete said. "He'd make a good president."

I couldn't reconcile the relation between Henry Ford's name and the implication that he was approved by the Nazis. But in those early days as investigator, I knew little and had a lot to learn. On Pete's bookshelves I saw my first copy of *The International Jew*, a collection of anti-Semitic articles reprinted from Henry Ford's newspaper, *The Dearborn Independent*. I regarded it as coincidence and didn't think further of it at the time.

"I remember reading about Ford's Peace Ship in the last

war," I said. "Do you think America will have to fight another war?"

Pete whirled around and said savagely: "That is the last thing we want to see because it won't help the nationalist cause any. America must not fight a war in Europe. It's our job to see that she doesn't. Pretty soon I'm going to print a lot of anti-war stuff and send it all over the country. America must remain neutral. She's gotta . . . You gotta help, George. We all gotta help keep America out of war."

Not long after this Pete came into the shop in a particularly surly mood. As he came in he took off his hat and coat without a word, threw them on the chair.

"What's the matter, Pete?" I asked cautiously, hoping he hadn't learned I was an investigator. Pete didn't answer. He sat on the desk, crossed his legs and relieved himself with a volley of oaths at the way "things are going."

"We'll have to have a revolution, that's all. There is no other way out."

"What do you mean?" I asked.

"I mean a revolution, that's what I mean," he yelled. "We got to clean up this Goddam Democracy."

With this he went into the press room and started work. I went on folding leaflets, anxious to learn more but not daring to go near him. After a while I ventured to ask him how long it would take to stage a successful "revolution" in America.

"About ten years," he said.

"That's too long a time," I said, "aren't there any short cuts?"

"This country is too big and there are too many people. Takes a long time to educate them in all classes of society."

"After the people are educated," I asked, "how can we swing it?"

"Easy enough. Once the groundwork is laid, all we do is work up a counter-revolution against the Communists. That'll get us going. Then we get a man like George Van Horn Moseley, the retired United States General, and build up a militant revolutionary machine made up mostly of World War veterans who want to fight Communism. With that as a base," Pete resumed, "we organize a political party to take over the

Emblem of the American National-Socialist Party and samples of hate literature printed on Stahrenberg's presses.

government legally—by one hundred per cent constitutional means. That's how we can chuck out Democracy and turn nationalist."

Nationalism was synonymous with fascism.

To the offices of the Nationalist Press trooped a steady stream of fascist-minded people of all sorts. Pamphleteers, crackpots, petty politicians and racketeers in patriotism. Many of them remembered seeing me there and later on vouched for me at Nazi meetings. But not all of Stahrenberg's acquaintances were shoddy and frustrated. Many who came were well-dressed and respectable. They paid cash for Pete's poison-pen writings and departed without leaving their name.

Pete carried on an extensive correspondence and his leaflets went as far as England, Holland and Australia. His mailing lists included physicians, attorneys, professors and many churchmen throughout the country. There were many German, Italian, Irish and old stock American names. One of Pete's best customers was Reverend John C. Fitting, New Jersey Bundist leader who once hailed Washington as "the first fascist."

When Father Coughlin, in the summer of 1938, threw overboard his pretensions to Democracy and ominous strains of anti-Semitism began to echo from the Shrine of the Little Flower, Stahrenberg rejoiced. Coughlin started off with a series of articles by Nazi agent George Sylvester Viereck, followed by reprinting sections of the *Protocols*.

"The demand for my stuff has jumped sky-high," Pete said. "Since Father Coughlin went to work on the Jews, I'm getting orders from everywhere. I've printed almost a million leaflets already. Coughlin always uses my stuff," he boasted. "I send him a copy of everything I print."

The April 10, 1939 issue of *Social Justice* printed this paragraph:

We sort of liked the frankness of the *National American* which comes to the exchange editor's desk occasionally: "We are not connected with the Associated Press, United Press, International News Service, or the American Newspaper Guild," declares the masthead. This should seem to be something of a start toward becoming a Free Press.

The masthead of Pete's sheet carried the line: "Our foreign news is supplied by the following news services: World Service, Bombay Press Service, Anti-Bolshevism." The first two press agencies were official Nazi bureaus and the last was an Italian agency.

As Father Coughlin became more ambitious politically, Pete turned on the Royal Oak priest: "It's all right for him to talk Americanism, but you can't let him go too far. There are other plans for America; political plans, by people who know how to make them. Religion and politics don't mix.

"I'll turn against him and go after his blood. This business of Christianity is nothing but Jewish propaganda. My religion is National-Socialism. That's the only religion I believe in. Christianity is the bunk."

I had some urgent work to do which compelled me to stay away from Pete's shop for several weeks. When I next saw him he told me that he was planning a change of tactics. He was to go "underground." Shortly afterwards he stopped publishing the *National American* and moved to the rear of a building at 205 East 12th Street. There Pete installed a large press and bought a lot of new type and equipment. Behind locked doors and known only to his intimate friends, he stealthily continued his vicious "educational" activity and specialized in the printing of "anti-war stuff." One of his best customers was a retired officer in the United States Army, Colonel E. N. Sanctuary.

CHAPTER III

CHAPTER III

THE HATE CRUSADE

"Our idea is to sell nationalism to the people first. It's easier that way. Once we sell it to the mob then the big boys will swing around."

AFTER A FEW MONTHS at Pete's I felt ready to go around and enlarge my circle of "friends." With my answers, in case I was questioned, prepared ahead of time, I walked up the dirty staircase of Innisfail Ballroom on Third Avenue to attend a meeting of the American Nationalist Party. Innisfail Ballroom occupied the third floor of a derelict building on New York's East Side. The plaster on the walls had begun to peel and crack, the windows were grey and crusted, the draperies were faded and grimy with city dirt. At one end of the ballroom hung rusty lithographs of Washington and Lincoln and a faded American flag. Light bulbs cast a sickly yellow glow.

I walked into the hall just as the meeting was about to start. Beside the door were several tables loaded with literature. The *National American* was there and *Social Justice*. Also *The Blackshirt*, "Official Organ of the American Fascist Party," and the publications of Edmondson, Pelley, True, Winrod, Colonel Sanctuary and the Bund. Lucenti was on the job as salesman. There were about 400 people in the place, and by far the largest part of the crowd was well past middle age. Most of them were thin-faced Irish folk and chubby German *hausfrauen* who had brought children. Working people. I spotted Dan Walker.

"Hi, George. Sit down." He smiled. "First time you've ever been to one of these, ain't it? Stick around, you'll hear the real dope. Those boys don't pull their punches."

The meeting opened with the singing of the national anthem. The figure which held the flag on the platform interested me. He was grimy. His shirt was filthy, open at the neck. His trousers were baggy. He seemed to be a tavern habitué, with florid face and most of his upper teeth knocked out. He seemed transplanted from the Bowery gutter to the platform of Innisfail Ballroom.

The Chairman, a man named Smith, came up on the platform and led the crowd in the singing of the national anthem. Up to that point nothing significant had happened. Then Smith stepped to the edge of the platform. He stood there for a long moment, his face grim, his lower lip curled with contempt. The crowd waited, hushed.

"All those present are here by invitation," Smith suddenly burst out. "No Jews are privileged to attend, and if any are found in the audience they will be thrown out of the window." He paused to survey the Aryan toughs leaning against the walls. "This here meeting is for Americans—one hundred per cent Christian patriotic Americans."

There was loud applause and some cheering. The Aryan hoodlums, popularly known as the goon squad, looked around for signs of dissent. The speaker held up his hand. When he spoke again it was through gritted teeth.

"In such a room as this the Boston Tea Party met. Wake up, Christians. Look around you. See what is happening to America. The whole country is overrun with foreigners, niggers, Jews. Is this the white America of our fathers? Is this a land of Christian patriots or blood-sucking Communists?" Smith glared at the mob. "This here country has been stolen from us Christians by a bunch of conniving rats. What are we going to do about it?"

The crowd went wild. Next to me Dan was on his feet, his face twisted with rage.

"We'll go to work on the Jews. That's what we'll do!"

"Kill the Jews! Hang them from lamp-posts!"

I looked at him with amazement. His voice rang with fanatical passion. His face, quiet a moment ago, was livid.

"Hang the Jews!"

"Send them back in leaky boats!"

On all sides people were on their feet, screaming. Behind me a woman shouted: "There's foreigners everywhere. My son can't get a job, but the damn foreigners get jobs!"

A few rows in front of me a little bald-headed man turned around, his visage distorted with rage.

"Let's wipe every atheistic Communist off the face of the earth. Let's show 'em real Christian power!"

Eugene Daniels, an associate of the late Huey Long, spoke next. "This is a pro-American, Christian, patriotic meeting," he began in a mild sort of way. Then bit by bit his voice caught the fanaticism of the crowd. "There was only one Christ and in Father Coughlin you have such a savior. There should be a dozen like him."

"A thousand!" screamed out a woman's voice.

"Ten thousand!"

The crowd screamed approval. Daniels went on: "Nationalism is Americanism. It was the Americanism of Washington and Lincoln. What was good enough for them is good enough for us. And no one is going to deny us our rights!"

"America for the Americans."

"To hell with everybody else."

Howls of applause for Father Coughlin, Hitler and Franco.

Another speaker took the stand. Henry George Curtiss, a lean, bespectacled, fanatic young man with Nordic features and twitching gestures. He stood with his hands on his hips, shoulders hunched forward.

"Democracy, Democracy, Democracy!" Curtiss howled. "They throw it in our faces. You hear it on all sides till you get sick of it. What is this Democracy? It is a rotten form of weakness, a defeatist and pacifist attitude that only can mean defeat. I say to hell with Democracy and up with the banner of American nationalism! America for the white, Christian Americans! And it's about time we stopped this absurd propaganda against Germany."

The crowd roared approval.

"We have been looking for a national leader we can all look up to," Curtiss resumed. "I propose the name of General George Van Horn Moseley."

The crowd went wild with thunderous cheering.

"I'll put this demonstration in the form of a resolution and let the General know," Curtiss announced.

He was followed by a thin, pale-faced woman in black brim hat and black dress. She was introduced by Smith as "our distinguished lady patriot" but he withheld her name. In a piping voice she protested that the display of the American flag in a downtown shop was unpatriotic and urged the mob to "bombard that store" with letters.

The last speaker, a round barrel of a man named Russell Dunn, spoke with a fluid eloquence that whipped the crowd into a fury. The place rocked with noise. Whistling, cheering, stamping feet. Dunn stood watching the demonstration for a moment, then abruptly turned and sat down. The meeting was over.

Dan turned to me, his face red from yelling. "What did you think of it?" he shouted hoarsely.

I nodded.

"Wonderful, hey? Puts the Goddam Jews in their place, hey?" We started up the aisle, Dan still talking excitedly. "These boys got the right idea. What we need is action. We got to show the damned foreigners who's boss. They think they own the country. I ought to know. I used to work for a Jew. I come in drunk and he fires me. A couple of lousy drinks—and he tosses me out on my ear. That sure opened my eyes!"

"What about the Communists?"

"Same thing. The Jews invented Communism." Dan tapped me on the shoulder to emphasize his remarks. "All Jews are Communists."

"Where do you get all this dope?" I asked.

"I got it straight from a Berlin office that sends stuff to Pete. They ought to know in Berlin. Them guys there are patriotic."

In the bar after the meeting, I fell into conversation with a short man with cropped hair and military bearing.

"By the way," I asked, "what was the name of the chairman?"

"His name is Smith," the man said. "Stanley Smith. He's good all right."

Without thinking, I took a slip of paper out of my pocket and scribbled down a note. A sudden change came over the man. His eyes narrowed with suspicion.

"What are you writing it down for?" he asked. "Who are you?"

"I just attend meetings," I said. "I'm interested in the movement."

"Why are you interested?" he persisted. "The F.B.I. is interested in these meetings. The cops is interested. Why are *you* interested?" He stood facing me. I had my back to the bar.

"Are you a Jew?" he said loudly. "Well, tell me what you want here?" Three or four of the men who had lined the walls during the meeting put down their beers and edged toward me.

I faced my accuser, speaking with pretended annoyance.

"My name's Pagnanelli, George Pagnanelli. I'm a Christian and I attend these meetings as a patriot. I want to protect Christianity." The ring of hard-looking toughs on the goon squad had gathered closer around me by this time.

"Listen, you guys," I said quickly. "I'm for America for Americans just like you. That's why I'm here."

No one said anything. They just stood there, staring at me. "Look," I said, "you can ask Dan Walker about me. Ask Pete Stahrenberg. They'll tell you I'm okay. They know me."

For a long minute no one said anything. Then one of the gang drawled: "Hell, leave the guy alone. He don't look like no Jew to me. He must be okay if he knows Pete."

The gang broke up.

"You be careful next time you get information," said the man at the bar. "Don't take out pencil and paper like a reporter. We don't like reporters around here." He motioned over his shoulder to the bartender.

"Nick, tell this guy here what happened to the last fella we found woiked for a newspaper."

I attended many other meetings of the American Nationalist Party, but none proved to be as vivid as the first. I heard an assortment of speakers: John Cecil, who headed the anti-Semitic American Immigration Conference Board and boasted of collaboration with Senator Reynolds; William Meyer, a speaker for the Bund; Charles Hudson, the Omaha fascist; Joseph McWilliams who later organized his own American Nazi group.

The American Nationalist Party, however, was more than a mere local "patriotic" group. It had a dozen branches in three outlying states. It was a training school for a score of potential anti-American leaders. Besides holding meetings, the

Party organized a storm trooper's unit which trained regularly in a Yorkville gymnasium. The curriculum consisted of military drills, jiujitsu, rioting tactics. Instruction was given in the manual of arms and the use of clubs, blackjacks, brass knuckles and alley-fighting.

I learned that different types of fascist organizations were designed to operate on each level of society. You hated the Jews, sabotaged Democracy and best served the cause of Hitlerism in America with those of your own social, economic, and cultural level. As the groups grew more respectable, anti-Semitism was carried on in more respectable tones.

Groups like the American Nationalist Party catered to the "mob" and its speakers were rabble-rousers of the lowest order. One step higher and more conservative were organizations like the Citizens Protective League. It met regularly Monday nights at the Turn Halle in the heart of Yorkville and was attended by Americans and Germans alike. "Americanism" was doled out by Kurt Mertig, a fat-jowled, heavily accented employee of the Hamburg-American Line. Mertig was assisted by Louis Zahne, a brusque Prussian and former member of the Friends of the New Germany, which preceded the Bund. As to Mertig's sentiments, he told me:

"We agree with the policies of the Bund, but of course we cannot come out with it at our meetings. We want to be different."

A distinctive note at the League meetings was the free literature: propaganda bearing the imprint of the German Library of Information and a weekly in German, *Die Neue Woche* (*The New Weekly*). Mertig-Zahne spoke on "The Declaration of the Rights of Man" in one breath, and in the next of "Immigration and the Jews"—based on the speech of Senator Reynolds, publisher of *The American Vindicator*. Horse and buggy Americanism was their theme. The meetings were conservative only to the extent that they were less noisy than those of the Nationalist Party. The same atmosphere of virulent hate and defamation of Democracy prevailed.

Zahne ridiculed charges that Germany was preparing for war. "It's Jewish propaganda. Germany has no intention of asking for Danzig. She cares nothing for Poland. All this talk about arming Guam and Hawaii and of national defense is war hysteria. Why does America want to arm and spend millions of dollars of your tax money when no one is going to attack us? We have oceans on each side. Who is going to cross them if we mind our own business . . . and remain friends with everybody?"

I was leaving the hall after making the acquaintance of Mertig when I was attracted to a circle of women gathered around a central figure. It was the woman in the black dress and hat I had seen at the American Nationalist Party meeting.

"Pope Pius is a Jew, I tell you," she was saying. "He and the Jews pooled $5,000,000 to stop Hitler." [This was the time when the Papal encyclical condemning the self-deification of Hitler as "Jesus Christ as well as Holy Ghost of the Fatherland" aroused Nazi ire.] "You think the Pope was elected by the College of Cardinals? Nonsense. The Pope was put there by the international Jewish bankers. They hold a $15,000,000 mortgage on the Vatican!"

I turned to Mertig. "Who's the lady?"

"Her name's Schuyler and she's a big shot in the D.A.R. She always comes to these meetings. She's a fine patriot."

Mrs. Schuyler was waving a newspaper clipping.

"That's from the *New York Sun*," she was yelling. "It looks like a letter to the editor, but it's not. It's a secret code message for all the New York Jews." She snorted triumphantly. "When you learn about Jewish symbols you can understand these things."

It wasn't until later that I found that Mrs. Leonora St. George Rogers Schuyler was more than a comic figure. She was a former officer of the Daughters of the American Revolution and her ancestors had come here in 1682. She was in close touch with many important anti-Americans and spread her propaganda in respectable circles. Mrs. Schuyler was also chairman of the Mrs. Simon Baruch University Prize Committee, which under the auspices of the United Daughters of the Confederacy, awarded a biennial prize of $1,000 for the best essay "bearing on the causes that led to the War between the States." The Prize had been established through an original donation by Bernard Baruch. Mrs. Schuyler told me she had solicited the sum personally and boasted about having taken

money from a Jewish philanthropist. On my May 3, 1940 visit
to her home Mrs. Schuyler gave me copies of propaganda she
had received from the Nazi *Fichte-Bund* and the German
Library of Information.

I was eager to be at the next meeting of Crusaders for
Americanism, Inc. to hear Fritz Kuhn speak. I went early to
the Tri-Boro Palace in the Bronx on the night of June 27,
1939 and got a ringside seat. The crowd, more than 500, was
coarse and boorish, composed mainly of swarthy Italian-Amer-
icans and stern-faced Germans. Women were few, but sitting
two rows in front of me was Mrs. Leonora St. George Rogers
Schuyler. The Crusaders served merely as a "front" for the
Bund. Bund literature was on sale; Bundists in uniform thickly
dotted the crowd; uniformed ushers stood at their posts.

George A. Van Nosdall, fuehrer of the Crusaders, nodded
as I entered. I had made his acquaintance at the American
Nationalist Party. Van Nosdall was a huge man with a prominent paunch, several double chins, bombastic and boastful.
The membership button of the German-American Bund was
prominent on the lapel of his coat.

"I just saw your friend, Jim McGee," I said by way of approach.

"Not mine," Van Nosdall said contemptuously. "That
dirty lousy Irish Catholic ain't my friend any more."

The attitude was typical of many Bundists toward Catholicism.

Applause shook the house. I turned around to see *Bundesführer* Fritz Kuhn poised at the doorway, flanked by Gerhard

Van Nosdall's check to the Bund and endorsement by Fritz Kuhn.

Wilhelm Kunze and James Wheeler-Hill, of the Bund hierarchy. Kuhn marched down the middle aisle in a tumult of cheering, followed by a corps of storm troopers dressed in grey uniforms, military belts, marching boots. *Der Bundesführer* took a seat on the front row, directly in front of Mrs. Schuyler and an elderly friend she had brought along.

Van Nosdall mounted the platform as *The Star-Spangled Banner* was played on a portable phonograph; he smoked a cigarette while the music droned. He took two more hurried puffs somewhere in the middle of the anthem, threw it on the floor, stamped on it then resumed his posture. As the music died down, Van Nosdall shot out his right hand to shoulder level, palm down.

"Free America," he said.

"Free America!" the audience returned.

"Free America" was the battle cry of the German-American Bund. From that time on I was to hear it many times.

I listened impatiently to several speakers attack the Neutrality Bill. Van Nosdall then took the stand and with sickening monotony repeated that his group was pledged to "fight for Americanism." After several rounds of Jew-baiting, he introduced Kunze. Kunze's title of "the Goebbels of the Bund" was well earned. He was shrewd and calculating, suave and cunning. Dressed in the regulation grey shirt and black tie, Kunze chose his words carefully, and expertly fired his propaganda darts. He denounced the "persecution" of Fritz Kuhn and General Moseley and denied that the Bund uniforms were "foreign-inspired."

"They are made in this country, right here in New York," he said. "They are American uniforms. The swastika is not foreign but one hundred per cent American. The Indians always used it. And our salute," Kunze laughed it off lightly, "is the symbol of free men everywhere. We're one hundred per cent American. The only purpose of the Bund is to make better Americans of those of German blood."

As he closed in a burst of cheering, Van Nosdall took the platform. "It is a pleasure to serve as chairman tonight, but I will make my introduction short. You know my Americanism. You know I look upon Hitler as the greatest man since the time of Christ. I now present . . . the greatest living Christian American in the country—our own Fritz Kuhn . . ."

The mob jumped to its feet with one accord as a thunderous ovation broke loose. It whistled and yelled deliriously. All around me hands shot out in the Hitler salute in a wild demonstration of hero worship. And in front of me—just two rows ahead—Mrs. Schuyler and her friend jumped to their feet, waving their hands joyously as Kuhn, bow-legged and pigeon-toed, leaned against the speaker's table and drank in the noise.

I had been unable to edge up to Kuhn in the Madison Square Garden meeting, but tonight I was only a few feet away and I studied him closely. Fritz had a sinister face; a face coarse as burlap, forbidding and fanatic, square-jawed and fleshy, with a bulbous nose and cold grey eyes which were deep-set and vindictive. It was a face which had smoldered in hate so long that it had become hateful and frightening in its intensity. Kuhn was short, squat, with a fat rump and massive frame. His mouth was unusual. His upper lip covered the lower completely so that there was nothing but a wide and flexible slit which screwed itself into all sorts of grimaces as *der führer* tried to say in English what his mind evolved in German. His accent was abominable and, when excited, his English became unrecognizable.

"De Joos, they are persecuting me again. Eleven times I have been to court and eleven times I have returned a free man. But I am glad to see that Amerika is waking up. Ve shall have it yet—a Free Amerika."

Kuhn did not speak long but his delivery was deeply emotional and moved by persuasive power. Although he started off slowly he soon flew into a rage. Shaking his massive fist he blared his words into the microphone, his pudgy frame swaying with emotion.

Van Nosdall basked in the glory of the *Bundesführer* and pacified the tumultuous mob with considerable difficulty. As the strains of the Nazi anthem *Horst Wessel Lied* came from the portable, the audience jumped to its feet, raised its arm in the Hitler salute. On the platform Van Nosdall stood trimly at attention, heels together, paunch pulled in, right arm held out stiffly.

Sickened with mob scenes, I decided to investigate a "super-patriotic" group which met on Fridays at the quiet midtown Hotel Iroquois. The meetings of American Patriots, Inc. were in the form of luncheons which cost $1 and kept away the rabble. The crowd was distinctly Park Avenue, composed mostly of women wearing dresses fashionable a decade ago; bloodless, bitter old dowagers looking for political excitement and willing to pay for it. I recognized Mrs. Schuyler in what seemed to be the same black hat and dress, and nodded to her. We were fast becoming "friends."

Chairman of American Patriots was Allen Zoll, an old hand in the movement. Few of the ladies who contributed to American Patriots, Inc. knew about Zoll's background. An indictment for attempted extortion against New York radio station WMCA hung against him. In August, 1935, Zoll visited Berlin. On his return he took a turn at Japanese propaganda, letting Japanese agent Roy H. Agaki publish an article in his magazine *American Patriot,* which began:

Japan is fighting, not only in her own self-defense, but also in the interest of civilization. . . . Japan's demand upon China is to divorce China from Communism and to induce her to cooperate with Japan in the peaceful economic development of the Far East. . . .

Zoll also wrote his own brand of Japanese propaganda:

The carefully suppressed tales of Chinese cruelty are absolutely beyond description. . . . It is said that they take no Japanese prisoners. Those captured are mutilated in the most terrible fashion.

A tall, harsh-faced man, Zoll was promoting "patriotism" as a racket by appealing to a certain kind of woman. He paid particular attention to fat old ladies with the fat pocketbooks who at the same time were suckers for the "Communist menace" bogey. At one of his meetings Zoll introduced Joseph McWilliams, whom I had already heard at the Nationalist Party meetings. Handsome, suave, carefully groomed, McWilliams made an instant hit with the old dowagers.

"Do you realize what a Communist revolution will mean to your daughters? Do you realize what it will mean to have

13,000,000 Communist niggers turned loose? Need I tell you what happened to Hungarian peasant girls?" He paused, letting the thought sink in. "Do you want the same thing to happen to white, Christian, American womanhood, the pride of the nation?"

The old ladies with imagination sucked in their breath in horror.

"He means the Jews," someone whispered.

"What we need now is an organization . . ." McWilliams said.

"A lot of organizations," a woman shouted.

"No," McWilliams continued, "we need *one* national organization, from which others can branch out. Such an organization is being formed right now. We need your help—every contribution we can get. We're going to make this country a place where white Christian American women can live safely."

He paused at the applause, then followed up his advantage.

"The time for tolerance is past. Let us forget tolerance. Let us banish the word from our daily life. Let us learn to hate from now on. Hate. Meet hate with hate!"

Allen Zoll thanked McWilliams and urged him to speak at a "patriotic rally" to be held at the Great Northern Hotel next week. An old lady had an inspiration. Why not organize a group of uniformed young men to act as ushers? Zoll immediately leaped up to second the idea and ask for money. Thoroughly frightened at McWilliams' dread picture of Communism-around-the-corner, the heavy pocketbooks opened and plump, feminine hands came up with five- and ten-dollar bills. I noticed that a woman who I learned was Mrs. A. Cressy Morrison contributed heavily; as did Mrs. Schuyler.

Holding a sheaf of bills Zoll said beaming: "Some day this patriotic youth movement may become nation-wide and deal Communism its death blow."

Then a committee was appointed to select the boys. Someone suggested that they be recruited from the Boy Scouts. There were shouts of protest.

"The Boy Scouts aren't interested in our kind of patriotism. They're tied up with Jewish internationalism. Ours is a strict nationalist venture," the fat woman next to me said.

Another woman stood up. "We could get boys from the Bund to help us. They have youth groups, you know. They could also give us information about the price of uniforms and tailoring."

A chorus of approval met the suggestion.

"The Bund is both patriotic and nationalist."

"They have had so much experience in fighting Communism."

Zoll appointed a committee to approach the Bund for advice. Everybody agreed that that was the best way to handle it. The meeting broke up and the plump, well-fed men and women passed out into the hall to buy their copies of *Social Justice* and Senator Reynolds' *The American Vindicator*, both for sale in the lobby. I walked out with the crowd.

"Hate! Did you hear what he said? Hate! We must learn to hate!"

Hate was the fascist formula.

Hate was the international cement that held fascism together, and America's fascist leaders built their organizations on a framework of hate. Hate was their handshake and hate their parting word. To join a "one hundred per cent Christian-American-Patriotic" group you didn't have to be Christian or American. Heathens and Mohammedans were welcome. Japanese were eligible. Crooks, thugs, racketeers, step right up. There was just one requirement. Hate! Hate the Niggers, the Jews, the Polacks, the Catholics, the Communists, the Masons, the bankers, the labor unions! Democracy. Hate anything, but hate! And call anything you hated by a common name. Rich man, poor man, art, science, logic, politics—tie them together, stick an odious label on them and hate that label for all you're worth.

I heard hate preached at a meeting which started with a prayer tendered by Father John J. Malone. The audience blessed itself and the meeting started. Then, as the priest looked on, McWilliams roared to a huge overflow crowd at the Great Northern Hotel.

"They are beginning to call me Nazi. You can't speak for Christianity without being called an anti-Semite and you can't talk against Communism without being called a Nazi. Hitler and Mussolini are men of peace. They believed in

peace. They proved it at the Munich conference. Europe was set for a generation of peace when Franklin Delano Roosevelt got them to fighting again. Roosevelt is one of the most vicious men. . . ."

"Don't say that," a woman shouted. "He is our President. He is the symbol of our Government."

The goon squad hauled her out as bony hands were clamped tight against her mouth. Her feet did not touch the floor!

"Some day I'll tell that to the President's face," McWilliams finished.

The ever-present Mrs. Schuyler—sitting on the platform in an official capacity—shook McWilliams' hand. Others leaned over and congratulated the rising young fuehrer of American Fascism. Seated on the platform, the priest looked on, as the crowd roared its approval and a thirty-six-piece band played martial music.

This was the "patriotic" meeting Zoll had announced at the luncheon. Its sponsors were a coalition of a dozen New York "patriotic" societies led by the Christian Front. But the "Pro-American Rally"—so it was advertised—developed into a regular Christian Front meeting. Bernard D'Arcy, wholesale distributor of *Social Justice,* made a plea for increased sales. John Eoghan Kelly, Christian Front organizer and promoter of the Franco cause in America, talked on "Public Enemy Number Two—John L. Lewis" who, according to the inside information obtained exclusively by Kelly, had "100,000 armed Communists rarin' to Sovietize America."

"Who is Public Enemy Number One?" I asked of the man next to me.

"Roosevelt. Who in hell did you think it wuz?"

Kelly was followed by New York State Senator John J. McNaboe, who had also spoken for Allen Zoll's fascist meetings. A youthful speaker with an alert face and aquiline features took the platform next. His gestures were dynamic, his voice resonant. His manner was fiery and intense. He was Jack Cassidy, fuehrer of the Christian Front.

I was beginning to put together the pattern of American Fascism in-the-making. It was unquestionably inspired by Nazi sources, but here in America it was taking many courses moving deep into the fibre of our society, digging at our flesh on many different fronts.

I learned that these are some of the ways fascism can come to a country. It starts with Nazi agents laboring night and day in a hide-out, printing "patriotic" literature based completely on Nazi-manufactured lies and distortions. By these means the comparatively harmless, old-fashioned type of *social* anti-Semitism was converted into a *political spearhead* against Democracy, a dissolvent of national unity and a weapon to serve Nazi aims.

It starts with a group of politically uninformed working men and women who are exposed to fanatic speakers. It starts with a few embittered wealthy old ladies, a gang of thugs, a crew of slick propagandists. It dignifies itself by calling on the support of churchmen and duped public officials. In every level of society it sets up organizations to spread the word of hate. It develops a potential weapon of destruction, mixed fear and hate and blind rage.

Unfortunately, the fascists are not really attacking Communism. They are attacking a self-created image which includes anyone who is even mildly liberal. I hold no brief for Communism, but there is an intelligent and democratic way to meet Communism. The Congress of the United States, the Federal Bureau of Investigation and the United States Army and Navy Intelligence Services are capable of handling the situation without aid from private armies of "patriots." The men who are clever and unscrupulous enough to use that weapon can build a fascist state. That is their sole objective in America under Nazi auspices.

The conviction that fascism was essentially a *mass movement*, parading under the guise of "patriotism," came to me only after I had attended numerous meetings. Everywhere I saw the American mind subjected to a ruthless barrage of hate propaganda. It was dinned into them day and night, in multiple forms, and the American masses were its main victims. One of the speakers at Crusaders for Americanism told me:

"Our idea is to sell nationalism [alias fascism] to the people first. It's easier that way. Once we sell it to the mob, then the big boys will swing around."

CHAPTER IV

COUGHLIN'S "CHRISTIAN CRUSADE"

> "Rest assured we will fight you in Franco's way, if necessary. Call this inflammatory, if you will. It is inflammatory. But rest assured we will fight you and we will win."
>
> REVEREND CHARLES E. COUGHLIN

ON SUMMER EVENINGS in 1939, groups of men used to meet in a basement room beneath the Church of St. Paul the Apostle, at Columbus Circle and 59th Street, New York City. The group numbered about thirty men, ranging in age from eighteen to fifty, wearing small metal crosses in their coat lapels and greeting one another with the Nazi salute. As the local fuehrer stepped up to the table at the front of the room, he raised his arm in a fascist salute and called out, *"Pro patria et Christo!"*

"Pro patria et Christo!" the men answered his salute, rising to their feet. "Members of the Christian Front . . ." the speaker called out.

This was the original unit of the Christian Front. Some of those present were also members of the Bund and the American Nationalist Party. Later they joined the Christian Mobilizers. From street corners, pool-rooms and respectable homes they had come to answer the call printed in *Social Justice* on May 23, 1938:

Let your organization be composed of no more than 25 members. After a few contacts with these 25 persons you will observe that two of them may be capable of organizing 25 more. Invite these capable people to do that very thing.

"Father Coughlin has sent an important message to us," said the platoon leader. "You and your group are directly affiliated with me. When the proper moment arrives and not before that time, Father Coughlin will assemble all organizations whose leaders care to follow him. Remember that, men of the Christian Front. Every move must count. You're to act on secret orders and only on orders. That's the way the Christian Front works."

Meetings like this were common during 1939. Later, as they were ousted from St. Paul's Church, Manhattan units met at Donovan's Hall on 59th Street—just off Columbus Circle. These meetings were the outgrowth of a plan spawned by the priest of a once obscure parish in Royal Oak, Michigan, whose nation-wide publicity campaign had gathered about him a flock estimated at several million, in the fold of which were blind fanatical followers whose every belief and action was molded by the hand of the Royal Oak cleric.

From among the more fanatical Coughlinites sprang the Christian Front. This facet of the American fascist movement known as Coughlin's "Christian Crusade," had as its ultimate aim the establishment of a so-called "Christian" government modelled upon the corporate-clerical state of Franco. The tactics used by the Christian Front were identical with those of Hitler, even to the organized gangs of strong-arm men.

When the low rumble of drums began to sound from the Shrine of the Little Flower, the Christian Front throughout the country fell in step. Jack Cassidy became most widely known because of the publicity he received as fuehrer of the "Sports Club," an ultra-revolutionary gun club founded within the framework of the Christian Front.

It is a matter of record that the first unit of the Front held meetings in the Rectory of the Paulist Fathers, and that ap-

AMERICANS
Keep this a Christian Country!
Join Picket Line

KEEP { AMERICA OUT OF WAR
WAR OUT OF AMERICA

Write to Your Congressman and Tell Him

CHRISTIAN FRONT

Typical Christian Front slogans inspired by Father Coughlin.

plication blanks were printed by the Paulist Press. Mail was received at P. O. Box 69, Station G, registered in the name of the Paulist Fathers. Walter Ogden, a worker at the Rectory, became the first executive secretary. The Fathers probably thought they were encouraging a group dedicated to the propagation of "Christianity." As soon as they learned its true nature they severed all connections and Reverend Edward Burke, C.S.P. who had served as advisor, was transferred to another parish.

Father Coughlin continued to inspire and direct the incipient fascist movement. Its units functioned independently and in secret; only the unit leaders were aware of the plans of the others. By the fall of 1939, there were Front units in Philadelphia, Pittsburgh, Boston, Minneapolis, St. Louis, Detroit and numerous smaller cities. Like Hitler's Brownshirts, the Christian Front was ostensibly organized to combat the "rising tide of Communism." All Jews were called Communists. All liberals, New Dealers and labor organizations were called Communist; and since the Communist Revolution in America was scheduled to take place "any day now," the Christian Front—always under Coughlin's inspiration and guidance—shouted that a private army was the only means to "save America."

The record shows that while Monsignor Fulton J. Sheen, outstanding Catholic spokesman, said: "Hitler . . . would destroy Christianity all over the world, if he could," Father Coughlin filled the pages of *Social Justice* with Hitler's sewer-spawned lies. He made *direct* use of Goebbels' speeches, quoting the Nazi almost word-for-word. He quoted widely from *World Service* and numerous other Nazi organs and their American imitators. He denounced the "poppycock of Democracy" and branded Democracy as a version of Communism and Communism as an invention of the Jews.

"The German hero in America for the moment is the Reverend Charles E. Coughlin," cabled Otto D. Tolischus to *The New York Times*. And Silver Shirter Pelley wrote in *Liberation:* "This past week the aggressive Father Coughlin went on the air . . . and delivered what amounted to the prize Silver Shirt speech of the year." Boasting that his "Sixteen Principles of Social Justice" had all been adopted by the Nazi and Italian fascist parties, the would-be reverend-dictator tried to foist his clerical fascist plans on America by organizing the National Union for Social Justice. One William Lemke was candidate for president.

In the sphere of Christian religion Father Coughlin injected the contemptibly un-American issue of racialism. By his rash and violent utterances he provoked an increasing wave of anti-Catholic sentiment throughout the country, especially among those who unjustly saw in him a mirror of the entire Catholic clergy. His incitements to treason and conspiracy and the revolutionary overthrow of our Democratic order earned him the censure of his superiors. But he defied them repeatedly. He challenged the censure of George Cardinal Mundelein; the Most Reverend Edward Mooney, Archbishop of Detroit, and other members of the Hierarchy.

Coughlin's tactics were denounced by the highest authorities of the Catholic Church. Pope Pius XI declared: "Anti-Semitism is a movement in which we Catholics cannot share. It is not possible for Christians to take part in anti-Semitism. We are Semites spiritually." And in a letter to the American Hierarchy, His Holiness added: "No true Catholic will take part in the persecution of his Jewish compatriots. A blow against the Jews is a blow against our common humanity."

A *New York Times* despatch dated September 3, 1936 reported from Rome: "The Reverend Charles E. Coughlin's political activities and his attack on President Roosevelt . . . were severely criticized today by the *Osservatore Romano*, which usually reflects opinions of the Vatican."

The Reverend Doctor Francis X. Talbot, editor of *America*, an important organ of Catholic opinion published by the Jesuit Order, stated: "If Father Coughlin is a thorn in the side of the Jews, he is also a thorn in the side of the Catholics. If he is arousing anti-Semitism, he is also arousing anti-Catholicism."

Father James M. Gillis, noted editor of *The Catholic World* observed: "God forbid! But unless the Jew-baiters, some of them clerics, change their tune, blood will be upon their souls."

Even Westbrook Pegler, Catholic layman and columnist,

realized the Coughlin "Christian" menace and wrote on January 23, 1940:

Both the government and the newspapers for years have handled Father Coughlin far too gently, but now that he has identified himself with the so-called Christian Front he has called for a showdown. . . . The Dies Committee should have treated Coughlin just as it treated Earl Browder, but tiptoed around him for fear he would cry up a holy war.

In addition, Coughlin was rebuked by the Most Reverend John T. McNicholas, Archbishop of the Cincinnati diocese. He was also rebuked by Monsignor John A. Ryan, professor of moral theology and industrial ethics at Catholic University. And an apology for Coughlin's political utterances was released to the press by Bishop Michael J. Gallagher of Detroit, Coughlin's immediate superior. In true dictator fashion the black sheep priest of a once obscure parish amazingly defied the entire Hierarchy . . . and intensified his Nazi efforts with every criticism.

Disgraced before an overwhelming majority of true Catholics, Coughlin continued to exploit his collar and transfer the prestige of the Roman Catholic Church to his own revolutionary and anti-Democratic ideas. Despite the opposition, he achieved enormous influence and became spearhead of the organized assault on Democracy by his spiritual control of hundreds of groups throughout the country dedicated to substituting authoritarian rule.

On April 24, 1939, while I was at Stahrenberg's, Father Coughlin wrote in *Social Justice:*

For ten years this country has suffered under a depression. It was not an accident. It was deliberately created. . . . That depression robbed you of your bank savings account, then of your jobs, and in many cases, of your homes—and nobody in all America shot a banker! We continue without jobs, 12 million of us; 22 millions subsist on dole rations—and we do not revolt! HOW MUCH WILL WE STAND?

What was the secret of this priest-politician's power over hundreds of thousands of Americans? Why did they follow him in blind, undying loyalty despite the censures of his superiors? That secret is simple when explained. Father Coughlin reached the American *family* with his assorted hate gospels. With the establishment of Christian Front "neighborhood" auxiliaries, his "Christianized" Nazism penetrated deep into the sanctity of the American *home*. ". . . The only unbiased source of truth is Father Coughlin," he said modestly, and the gullible took him at his word. At its peak, the weekly circulation of *Social Justice* passed the million mark and it was estimated to be on sale at 2,000 churches Sunday mornings and at many Catholic social affairs. This was hardly the work of a "crackpot" but on the contrary, of the most sinister mind of its time in America!

At the Tri-Boro Palace in the Bronx in the summer of 1939, I heard John Eoghan Kelly—a promoter of Franco-Nazism in America, address an audience of mothers and children.

"You think I'm talking through my hat about the danger of Communism? No blood has flowed yet, but the Communist revolution is going on just the same. One of these days, maybe

MAY 9, 1938   *Social Justice*   7

MUSSOLINI KNEW...TWELVE YEARS AGO

by George Sylvester Viereck

Author of "The Kaiser on Trial," "Spreading Germs of Hate" and "The Strangest Friendship in History."

THE REUNION of Austria with Germany was no surprise to Mussolini. He knew for years that "Anschluss" was written in the stars—it was "manifest destiny." The Fascist chief did not change his mind under German "pressure." The Duce was not "tricked" by Hitler. Mussolini opposed "Anschluss" for a time, not because he looked upon it as a threat to vital interests; his action was prompted purely by political expediency.

Twelve years ago, when I first bearded the Fascist Lion in his den, he told me that it was "easier" to deal with Berlin than with Innsbruck, the provincial Austrian capital, which had been the center of anti-Italian agitation.

"If," I asked, "Germany accepts a Greater Italy, would you be willing to recognize a Greater Germany, including Austria?"

"The inclusion of Austria in the German federation," Mussolini retorted, "is probably far more important to Germany than to

The Reputed "Capture" of Austria by Germany is Given a New Angle of Revealing Import in This Exclusive Article by Mr. Viereck. Nationally Known Publicist and Editor. Austria. Not Germany has been the Traditional Seeker for Anschluss. This Article Discloses. Since the Days of Bismarck, Berlin has been Cool Toward the Idea of "Reunion in Vienna."

cally forbidden by the Treaty of St. Germain. Some years later Chancellor Curtio attempted to bring about "Anschluss" economically in the form of a "customs union" between mutilated Austria and the German republic. This attempt, too, was frustrated by threats from Paris and London. Forcibly thrust back upon her own slender resources, Austria

by men of those who held power in Germany before the advent of National Socialism.

"Germany," Hitler once remarked to me sadly, "is the only great nation in Europe that has not achieved national unity." The union of Germany and German-Austria is a great forward stride in the direction of national unity. It cannot be the ultimate step. Hitler added 6,500,000 to Germany without shedding a drop of blood. Will he be able to fulfill the rest of his program—the union of all Germans contiguous to Germany with the motherland, without bloodshed? The future of Europe depends on this question.

Hitler may be compelled to sacrifice some of his countrymen to maintain his friendly relations with Italy and Poland (not to speak of Czechoslovakia). Hitler made a 10-year truce with Poland, he surrendered Germany's claim to Alsace Lorraine and, in his letter to

Soon after his series of articles appeared in *Social Justice*, Viereck, a personal friend of Adolf Hitler, registered with our State Department as a Nazi agent.

next month, or the month after, you'll wake up and see blood
in the gutters. And it'll be Christian blood, your blood, the
blood of Christian boys and Christian leaders! If you think
it can't happen here," Kelly shouted, "we'll show you tonight
what happened in Spain."

After Kelly came Father J., a close-shaven, humble little
Spanish priest from Philadelphia, who explained that Franco
was fighting a Christian crusade and that Hitler and Mussolini were unjustly criticized.

"All they want to get out of their intervention in Spain is
the satisfaction of having helped a Christian country. That
is all. The same form of satisfaction which France got when
Lafayette helped in the American Revolution. Only the enemies of Christ are opposing Franco, Hitler and Mussolini in
Spain!"

As the tumult of applause died down, a representative of
the Christian Front held up a small brochure inscribed "Christian Index. Think Christian. Act Christian. Buy Christian."
On the back page were the words: "Christ himself sponsored
this little leaflet for your protection." The idea of this brochure originated with the German-American Business League,
subsidiary of the Bund. "I want every one of you to have one
of these," the Front-er called out. "This is the list of Christian
stores that hire Christians only. They are giving us their support and they deserve to get yours."

During the main event of the evening—a showing of the
propaganda film *Spain in Arms*—the commentator fanned the
passions of the mob by saying that the Jews had inspired a
sinister, Bolshevik horde to wipe Catholicism off the face of
the earth. A shot of Franco giving the fascist salute brought
down the house. John Eoghan Kelly jumped up.

"I want to close this meeting by repeating the words uttered
by Father Coughlin in his radio speech last Sunday. 'We will
fight you in Franco's way if necessary. Call this inflammatory,
if you will. It is inflammatory!' "

It no longer shocked me to see Father Coughlin place a
sword in Christ's hands thereby crucifying him a thousand
times and killing Christianity forever!

"Here y'are. The finest Christian magazine in the country.

Anti-Communist. Pro-American. Father Coughlin's *Social Justice*. Ten cents."

I decided to sell it in order to gain the confidence of Carl R. Pinkston, alias Carl Muller, president of the Social Justice Distributors' Club, one of a thousand such "clubs" maintained to promote sales. I picked the financial district on lower Broadway to peddle Coughlin's poison sheet and my greatest fear was that I would be seen by friends who knew nothing of my investigations.

I moved from corner to corner, keeping a sharp lookout for my respectable friends. Suddenly I met someone I knew. He sneaked up from behind and pinched my arm. Startled, I was relieved to see he was Patrick Finnegan, one of Stahrenberg's closest associates. I was delighted that he heard me selling:

"The magazine for the American home. Send Communists back where they came from. America for the Americans. The family magazine. *Social Justice*. Here y'are. Ten cents."

"Good boy, George," Pat winked, buying a copy.

I sold ten copies in several hours' time. My customers were elderly folk with the exception of a young, apparently Irish girl.

I went out half a dozen times after my initiation as poison-peddler, each time reporting sales to Pinkston of about ten copies. After my first experience, however, I merely destroyed copies of the magazine and made good out of my own pocket. And when after each "trip" I returned to headquarters I boasted how I had insulted the Jews, pointing to a few self-inflicted scratches to show that "the Jews" had tried to beat me up. The ruse worked. I worked my way into Pinkston's confidence.

Behind the scenes I saw how Coughlin worked with clerics who followed him. The Reverend James A. Keeling, participant in the meetings of Crusaders for Social Justice, was one of them. The Reverend Edward Lodge Curran, president of the International Catholic Truth Society, was idolized as the "Father Coughlin of the East." Pinkston, alias Muller, was a Protestant but he was trusted by the Royal Oak priest and claimed to carry on correspondence with him in code. He traveled frequently to Royal Oak for conferences.

Lawrence Gilpatrick, a Christian Front speaker, burst in one afternoon with the announcement, "I have an important message from Father. . . ."

He looked around, saw some strange faces and went into a whispered conversation with Pinkston. Pinkston jumped up and excitedly went to the locked drawer of his desk. From underneath some papers he took out a telegram and placing it in a legal size envelope, handed it to one of his trusted lieutenants of the goon squad. I edged over and saw that it was addressed to the Reverend Peter Baptiste Duffee, of St. Francis of Assisi Church who, incidentally, also kept in close touch with Francis Moran, New England Christian Front leader.

The cause of the secrecy was disclosed in a few days. Father Coughlin was sponsoring a mass "Anti-Communist parade in Manifestation of Christianity." When Pinkston divulged that the goon squads would be on hand to "guard Christians from the Jews," I was convinced that the so-called parade would serve as the pretext for another bloody riot, adding to the already shameful record of Coughlinite hooliganism in New York.

Pinkston was enthusiastic:

"George, we're going to have one hell of a big parade for Father Coughlin. We're getting 25,000 guys to march for us. The Bund boys are going to get all beered up and join us. We're distributing 150,000 leaflets and contacting all the patriotic organizations."

"I'll be there with a thousand of my boys," said a man who had been listening intently. He was Walter J. Bailey Bishop who had once been introduced at a Christian Mobilizer meeting as an organizer of Pelley's Silver Shirts.

"And if they blame Father we can show 'em this telegram," Pinkston shouted triumphantly. The telegram was signed by Bernard D'Arcy who had sent it while at Royal Oak, forbidding the parade to be held under auspices of *Social Justice* magazine. Pinkston was delighted at the strategy worked out by the Royal Oak master-mind.

"We'll show them this telegram," he repeated. "It says Father has nothing to do with the parade." He winked.

"Nothing. He ain't got nothing to do with it. . . . Not much!" and he broke into laughter.

But as the day of the parade drew near and the goon squads went through rehearsals, as the Bundists and Silver Shirt-ers and Christian Front-ers, and members of a dozen other gangs readied themselves for a "Manifestation of Christianity" by the use of brass knuckles and lead pipes wrapped in newspaper, the atmosphere grew tense. It was whispered that Mayor Fiorello H. LaGuardia would refuse to grant a license, and was quietly urging Father Coughlin to call off the parade.

When Father Coughlin finally did call off his goon squads and riot-duty "patriots," they all went back to peddling *Social Justice* and cussing the "Jewish New Deal" they had got. "Roosevelt won't have a chance if Coughlin opens up on him," someone put in. "*Social Justice* is too pussyfooting to suit me."

"That's what you think," Pinkston answered heatedly. "But that don't prevent Pelley and the Bund from riding on the shoulders of Father. The real purpose of *Social Justice* is to hand out mild propaganda and prepare the minds of the people for revolutionary action later on."

I listened attentively, memorizing Pinkston's statements.

Many of about five hundred salesmen of *Social Justice* in the New York area frequented Pinkston's offices. The rest got their papers from Royal Oak. Many young people of both sexes and elderly folk sold the magazine. One of these, Miss Florence Nash, 42, of Brooklyn, was convicted of disorderly conduct and denounced by Magistrate Michael A. Ford, who said:

"There is no place in this free country for any person who entertains the narrow, bigoted, intolerant ideas you have in your head. You remind me of a witch burner. You belong in the Middle Ages. I'm a Roman Catholic myself. I'm ashamed of you. . . . He who instills such ideas in your head, be he a priest or anyone else, does not belong in this country."

Was *Social Justice* an approved Catholic organ of expression even though published by a priest and circulated widely at Catholic Churches? The answer was provided by Monsignor Edward J. Hickey, Chancellor of the Detroit diocese: "*Social Justice* is . . . not a Catholic paper. . . . The archdiocese of Detroit has no responsibility, direct or indirect, for *Social Justice* magazine."

Pinkston's office was a hang-out for subversive individuals and a den of seditious thought. Sober fascist minds mixed in with the many crackpots who achieved self-importance by identifying themselves with a nation-wide revolutionary movement to overthrow Democracy.

From George Agayeff, White Russian crew manager of a gang of salesmen, I got the first inkling that the Brooklyn unit of the Christian Front was maintaining a rifle club under the guise of a game-shooting "sports club." I tried to pry more information but Agayeff was pledged to secrecy. I disbelieved the White Russian at first, but upon further reflection I believed anything possible under Coughlin's "Christian Crusade."

At that time, the Front was picketing radio station WMCA because it had ruled Father Coughlin off the air when he refused to submit advance copies of his speeches. The picket line was organized by Allen Zoll—the same Zoll who had sponsored the American Patriots luncheons and, according to reports which were then current, tried to do business with Japanese agent Roy H. Agaki, for the purpose of "winning public confidence" for the Japanese.

Failing in this, Zoll flew to Royal Oak, as a result of which he teamed up with Merwin K. Hart of the New York State Economic Council, and the Reverend Edward Lodge Curran, *chargé d'affaires* of the Christian Front in the East. The trio set out to evangelize the Atlantic coast with the gospel of clerical fascism.

Having drummed up protests against the "persecution" of Coughlin, Zoll eventually approached WMCA officials with an offer to call off the picket line. His price was $7500. Zoll received $200 in marked bills from Donald Flamm, president of WMCA, and was indicted for extortion.

The picket line Zoll helped organize was a long, straggly mob of six hundred and included many women and children. One of the first persons I met was Mohammed Abed, the Turk whom I had seen buying anti-Semitic stickers at Stahrenberg's. I stepped into line. The WMCA picketing was a family affair. Children tagged along and more than one woman carried a baby in her arms. When she got tired the father took charge and fed it candy to keep it from crying.

"Be a good Christian, baby. Father Coughlin won't like you if you cry."

Some of the "Christian patriots" waved small American flags as they marched slowly up and down the block. Several large framed pictures of Coughlin were dressed in a cluster of American flags. There were signs reading: "We Need More Father Coughlins" . . . "Keep This A Christian Country" . . . "Read The Truth In *Social Justice.*"

As they marched they chanted a curious mumbo-jumbo: "Let Father Coughlin speak . . . God bless Father Coughlin . . . Let Father Coughlin speak . . . Hitler will free America like he freed Germany . . . Let Father Coughlin speak. . . ."

"God bless Hitler, Franco and Father Coughlin," one woman said to her companion. "I pray for them every night."

Several clergymen picketed with the laymen; one of them carrying a sign: "Remember, F.D.R., Communism is Russian Cancer."

"Keep moving," Coughlin's lieutenants advised as they ran up and down the line. "Keep up the noise." "Keep it high." I shouted louder than the others, eager to impress the strong arm boys that my "allegiance" was second to none.

Picketing stopped at five o'clock to permit mothers to feed their children. While the women went home, many of the menfolk retired to taverns to get "all beered up." After this they formed into squads and headed for Times Square "to have some fun." The idea was to provoke rioting to help Coughlin play up the "persecution" angle. Often this sort of thing resulted in curious episodes like the Maynard affair.

Lawrence Maynard, a Christian youth, was standing a block from station WMCA one Sunday afternoon in May, 1939, selling a pamphlet exposing the deadly parallel between articles in *Social Justice* and Goebbels' propaganda. Without warning, a Coughlinite named John Dugan stepped up to Maynard and smashed him on the mouth. Maynard fell, bleeding and unconscious. Taken to Special Sessions Court on a charge of assault, Dugan offered no defense. The judge praised him for the frankness with which he had confessed the unprovoked attack, warned him to count thirty before doing the same thing, then suspended sentence. Such justice could have been dispensed with equal honor in Turkey. I had not expected to see it take place in America.

In addition to picketing the radio station, Coughlinites had organized to picket shops which advertised over WMCA. On a Saturday night I was asked to join a gang picketing Sach's furniture store in the Bronx. It was a comparatively deserted section, a long dark street running under an elevated train. We were ten pickets. The leader carried an American flag, the others carried placards reading: "Refugees Get Jobs in This Country. Why Don't 100% Americans Get Jobs?" . . . "Buy Christian Only."

"We want Mayor Hague. He can handle things," we shouted, marching.

"Wait till Hitler comes over here."

"Heil, Hitler!" one of the pickets yelled every once in a while.

About ten feet away from us a woman was passing out leaflets announcing a Christian Front meeting. A tall, distinguished looking elderly German with a military air joined us. His Irish companions kidded him about "doing the goose step" on the picket line. A few weeks later I saw the same man in the uniform of a Bundist goose-stepping at Bund Camp Siegfried.

Promptly at eight o'clock the picket lieutenant ordered us to stop and take up stations at another store further up— Michaels Brothers. It was located near "Christian Square" in a well-lighted, busy thoroughfare in the Bronx. Here I dreaded the thought of being recognized and made an excuse not to join the line telling Dan Walker who was selling copies of *National American* and *Social Justice*, that I had a sore foot.

"Why don't you give out some leaflets?" he asked. "Go ask Van."

I couldn't refuse. Van Nosdall was on another corner, his pockets bulging with blue mimeographed slips. "Glad you turned up, George," he called out. "Here, take a batch. I gotta go. I'll be right back."

Under the pillars of a roaring elevated train, amid a stream of passers-by I yelled: "Americanism meeting. Tuesday night. All Christians welcome."

When a police officer with a gold shield came up, I repeated what I had been instructed to say: "We're working with Father Coughlin."

"Let me see what you're givin' out," the police captain said. I handed him one of the leaflets and he read:

Attend meetings for Christian Americanism. "NOT TOLERANCE MEETINGS." . . . Edwin Westphal, Rev. Herbert W. Lewis, and other interesting speakers will address you AGAINST embroiling this country in a foreign war. . . . Only one 'ism' in America—AMERICANISM. All ARYAN Christian Men and Women should become Members of Crusaders for Americanism. Only Americans on Guard.

The captain shuffled away and I kept on distributing. Gangs of hoodlums loitered in the darkened entrances of shops ready to pounce on anyone who dared talk back to a dozen poison peddlers.

Our actions followed a well-laid schedule. At exactly ten o'clock the rabble-rousers finished their deliveries on "Christian Square." The mob which had been listening to them joined the pickets and was augmented by others who, in the meanwhile, had been getting beered up. By ten fifteen P.M. we had been organized, lieutenants had been appointed and orders were given for the march on Times Square, the main battlefield for "Christian" social action.

Marching together in formation, heiling Hitler, screaming anti-Jewish slogans, the mob trooped into the subway station and each group pushed its way into a separate car. As soon as the doors closed, the salesmen of *Social Justice* and *National American* started up and down the aisle shouting insults at Jews, ramming their way between the strap hangers, stepping on toes and deliberately kicking out at anyone who appeared to be Jewish. The goon squads were on hand to quell comebacks instantly. Most of the passengers looked on sullenly. A few were amused. No one offered physical resistance—to the distinct disappointment of the hard-knuckled toughs ready to pounce on anyone who protested their "Christian" storm-troop tactics.

"Them Jews is too yella to fight," one of them hissed.

As we approached Times Square I was in mortal fear of being recognized by my respectable friends.

"Here, let me take that from you," I called out. "I gotta do my share for Father Coughlin." I grabbed a large placard from one of the girls and buried my face behind it. It advertised a meeting next Thursday at which William Lemke, candidate for President on the National Union for Social Justice ticket in 1936, was to speak under Coughlinite auspices along with Herbert A. O'Brien and Judge John A. Matthews.

"Read *Social Justice* and loin how to solve the Jewish question."

"How?" I turned to the pimply youth in his early teens.

"Line them up against the wall and give 'em the rat-tat-tat!"

He was typical of the youth whom Coughlin had corrupted by his feedings of a corrupt species of "Christianity." He was typical of the younger set of storm-troopers Coughlin was engaged in developing. He was symbol of the "Christian" youth Coughlin was spawning as America's future citizens.

At Times Square we poured out of the train, still screaming slogans. As we came up into the street Dan Walker grabbed my sleeve. "Let's get a glass of beer first. I got a feeling there's gonna be trouble."

After a second glass, Dan confided that he was a member of the National Guard, Communications Division.

"There's plenty of us in the National Guard. It's a good place to be in because they learn ya how to handle a gun. The captain of my division knows all about me giving out literature, but he don't give a damn. He told me to take it easy, play smart and don't get caught. You ought to join up with the National Guard," Dan advised. "They got guns and they teach you how to use them."

We moved along to Times Square and stopped in front of Nedick's orange drink stand at the corner of 42nd Street to watch five *Social Justice* salesmen in operation. Pete Stahrenberg was there, waiting for Dan and me. After a while Dan displayed the *National American* and began to call out his slogans.

"I'll be watching you if anything happens," Pete told Dan.

Then it suddenly happened . . .

A Jewish youth with thin features and large eyes, goaded by the insults the hawkers were screaming, knocked down the pile of *National American* from Dan's hand. Dan swung with his free right hand and the blow caught the youth on the shoulder. A crowd gathered instantly and I saw the goon squad coming down on the run—eyes blazing, fists ready to pummel the Jewish youth into a bloody pulp. I turned away my face.

"C'mon, c'mon, keep moving you. Break it up."

By the Grace of God the cops got there first, surrounded the Jewish youth, protectively backing him up against a taxicab fender, and pushed Dan away. More police stepped in and dispersed the crowd. Dan and the Jewish youth were then led away, followed by Pete.

When the salesmen for *Social Justice* resumed their hawking, the goon squads glared menacingly at Jewish passersby.

"Those Goddam cops beat us to it," they muttered. "We gotta get there first next time."

"Yeah. It ain't no fun if you don't do nuthin'."

I stood there alone, leaning against a building, stunned by the nightmarish scene. Again I had that curious feeling of unreality. I kept saying to myself: "This is New York. This isn't Berlin. This is the City of New York, in the United States. You are not in Turkey. You are in New York."

I looked up. The clock atop the Paramount Building pointed to midnight.

Chapter V

NATIVE FUEHRER

"I'd run this country like a factory. I would appoint all the key men, and have absolute control. There will be no opinion but the American Destiny Party opinion. This nonsense about Democracy and equality is through when I'm in power."

JOSEPH ELLSWORTH McWILLIAMS

EARLY IN THE summer of 1939, the editors of *Fortune* decided to withhold their proposed series of articles on subversive activity, and I was released from my temporary work as investigator. I now faced the choice of continuing with my magazine work exclusively, or continuing as investigator. I could choose a comfortable income, respectable friends, regular hours and a pleasant social life, or, I could choose the harried existence of an independent under-cover man. It meant a life of self-denial and social ostracism, of late hours and constant personal danger. I could lean on no official agency such as the F.B.I. for help.

I decided to continue with my under-cover work. I had no illusions that as an individual I was of any great importance, but I felt that if I could do it long enough to penetrate to the core of fascist operations, I might prove of some help in preserving for America the Democracy I had been denied in Europe. Most of the persons I knew had no idea of the desperate fight going on to breed hatred and dissension in the United States—and some of those who knew did not care. I decided to do my part in helping to counteract the Nazi and native Nazi ideology seeping into the daily life of unsuspecting America.

I also determined to quit my magazine job as soon as possible in order to devote my full time to under-cover work. I made it a point to become familiar with organizations engaged in combating fascist propaganda, and I turned over to one of them several carbon copies of my reports. They liked my work and after a thorough check-up of my background, I was hired at a modest salary to continue from where I had left off. Excited at the prospect of probing the hidden enemies of my adopted country on a full time basis, I quit my magazine work. As to my parents, I decided to tell them nothing. My former secrecy became even deeper as from that moment on I became a "Nazi," moving mysteriously through the subversive underworld, with my employers the only ones who knew my every move.

Up to now, I had been working around the edges of the fascist movement. How was I to get in on the inside? After some preliminary thought I went to Stahrenberg with a bold plan.

"Pete, I'm thinking of putting out a newspaper of my own."

"Trying to take business away, George?" he asked laughing.

"No, Pete," I said. "Your paper goes to thousands of readers all over the country. I want mine to be a small mimeographed weekly that'll tell patriots what's going on in New York."

"That's a damn good idea," Pete said. "What'll you call it?"

"I want to call it *The Christian Defender*," I said.

Pete agreed to design the masthead and print my name prominently as editor and publisher. Using this ruse of being a "patriotic publisher" I planned to attend secret meetings, establish contact with important fascist leaders and learn at first hand their revolutionary schemings against Democracy. I was encouraged by the fact gathered from my readings, that the F.B.I. had made use of similar devices to gain the confidence of the saboteurs.

"I'll do a good job of printing," Pete said. "Leave it to me."

In a few days Pete had printed the masthead of *The Christian Defender*, using the same type he had used for the *National American*. "George Pagnanelli, Editor and Publisher" was sprawled conspicuously beneath the masthead.

"How does it look, George?" Pete asked.

"Swell, Pete," I said, looking at the bold black lettering.

"Now give the Jews what's coming to 'em," he prompted.

I walked out of his shop and went to my room at Mrs.

Meyer to cut my first stencil on the portable typewriter; I had already arranged to run it off Van Nosdall's mimeographing machine. *The Christian Defender* first appeared on August 8, 1939. It carried the news of a joint meeting of the Bund and the Christian Mobilizers; a story lifted from *Social Justice* praising the Christian Front; another advertising the Coughlin-Pinkston parade "in manifestation of Christianity"; an original parody on "Muddom Eleanora" which went over big with female critics of the First Lady. I also reprinted a poem from the *National American*, adopted the Bund slogan "Free America" and used as fillers the phrase, "A Common Front Against a Common Enemy." The second issue was even more "patriotic" and carried the line, "Free America from Stinkweeds."

The Christian Defender was deliberately designed to be one of the coarsest sheets published in New York. The cruder it got, the more it lied, the more it slandered the Jew and assailed Democracy, the more popular it became. I mimeographed 200 copies of each issue and sold 150 copies at two cents each at "patriotic" meetings and through the Germania Bookstore, using the balance for my correspondence with American fascists. The income covered all expenses. I had no qualms about publishing the hate sheet because it circulated only among those who already were confirmed fanatics. The first three copies of every issue went to the pro-democratic groups with which I was associated. Subsequently, I filed a complete set with the Department of Justice.

The Christian Defender gained for me the respect of countless American Nazis, including Father Coughlin, who thanked me by letter and through Carl Pinkston asked that two copies be sent him every week. Even Seward Collins, the wealthy intellectual fascist, called it "bright" and asked me to leave three copies at his office.

The Christian Defender also became my passport to Nazis abroad. I began to hear regularly from the *Deutscher Fichte-Bund*, named after the German philosopher who taught that Germany was predestined for world domination. Its director, Theodor Kessemeier at Hamburg, addressed me as "Dear Friend" and placed me on his mailing list. He sent me copies of Hitler's speeches, reams of lies about the Jews and told me

DEPARTMENT OF STATE
WASHINGTON

November 28, 1939

In reply refer to
Co 800.Chtl Registration -
Christian Defender

Christian Defender,
Tri-Boro Palace,
2514 Third Avenue,
Bronx, New York.

Attention: Mr. George Pagnanelli, Editor

Sirs:

I refer to the Department's letter of October 5, 1939, enclosing, for your information, a copy of the pamphlet, Agents of Foreign Principals and of Foreign Governments, containing the laws and regulations administered by the Secretary of State governing the registration of agents of foreign principals and the notification of agents of foreign governments.

... assumed from the fact that you have not yet registered ... of law and regulations set ... pamphlet that you ... within the meaning ... if you would in... ...ption in order that ... to this matter may

of State:

[signature]
Division of Controls

The Christian DEFENDER

GEORGE PAGNANELLI, *Editor & Publisher*

VOL. 1 NO. 3   PUBLISHED EVERY MONDAY   PRICE 2 CENTS

JEW YORK WILL HEAR DEATHERAGE, McWILLIAMS

NATIONAL COMMANDER OF THE KNIGHTS OF THE WHITE CAMELIA AND DYNAMIC LEADER OF THE CHRISTIAN MOBILIZERS TO SPEAK AT INISFAIL STADIUM ON WEDNESDAY: 25,000 EXPECTED AT HISTORIC RALLY AGAINST COMMUNISM

REV. CHAS. E. COUGHLIN
ROYAL OAK, MICHIGAN

Mr George Pagnanelli
Tri-Boro Palace
2514 Third Ave.
Bronx, N.Y.

My dear Mr. Pagnanelli;

In this brief note I wish to acknowledge receipt of your recent communication.

Please accept my sincere thanks for your thoughtfulness in forwarding copies of The Christian Defender.

With kindest personal regards, may I remain

Sincerely yours

[signature]
Via Italian Line.

Editor
"The Christian Defender"
Tri-Boro Palace
2514 Third Ave.,
Bronx, N.Y.   U.S.A.

HAMBURG

The Christian Defender. Letter of commendation from Father Coughlin and cover of package of Nazi literature sent to author by *Deutscher Fichte-Bund.* Letter from State Department urged Pagnanelli to fill out the questionnaire required of propagandists in the pay of "Foreign Governments."

of Germany's valiant crusade for world peace and world justice. I was sent pictorial "proof" of Polish "atrocities" and was invited to enter a contest sponsored by the Institute for Aryan Studies:

> Should we succeed in bringing out on these essential questions ten pamphlets that are elaborated in a conscientious, clear and sound manner, then they will (united together in one volume) . . . constitute the 'Bible' of our movement and our best means of enlightenment.

The Nazis were not satisfied with one bible, *Mein Kampf,* they wanted a second one to complement the first. As a Christmas gift, Kessemeier sent me a picture of Adolf Hitler addressing the *Reichstag.* The letter arrived marked "Via Siberia," showing that Soviet Russia during the Hitler-Stalin pact served Germany as an unwitting collaborator.

The mainspring of Nazi strategy was to keep the masses confused, servile and forever ignorant. That is why my *Christian Defender* was so successful. My formula was simple. Everything hostile to Nazi aims was called Jewish or Communist and the two made synonymous. I realized how easy it was to become a merchant of hate. Lies. A typewriter, a mimeograph machine, paper and Lies! Simple as that.

Although I did my utmost to confine its distribution to those who already were chronic hate mongers, *The Christian Defender* found its way to Washington. The State Department sent me a form to ascertain whether I was an agent of a "foreign principal." The Treasury Department demanded to know why George Pagnanelli hadn't filed an income tax. My name was also listed in the *Congressional Record* as a Nazi worker.

For those who are interested in the fate of this provocative sheet I may say that after several months' publication, I gave up *The Christian Defender* which by then had served its purpose. Known and highly respected from coast to coast as a sterling "patriot," my last issue carried the paragraph:

DEFENDER SUSPENDS PUBLICATION

Due to the pressure of work, and ever increasing calls on the energies of your editor to engage in the Cause of Christian

Americanism, *The Christian Defender* will suspend publication for the time being. We hope to resume later on, but for the present duty calls us to other battle fronts in the fight for a Christian America and a Christian Republic.

As Nazis in the summer of 1939 were telling their American henchmen that the collapse of Democracy was but a matter of months, the Christian Mobilizers burst upon the American scene. Its new fuehrer emerged as Joseph Ellsworth Mc-Williams—"handsome Joe McNazi," as he was later known. When I visited Bund Camp Siegfried, a uniformed Bundist thrust a leaflet into my hands announcing the first meeting.

ACTION!   ACTION!   ACTION!

Thursday, July 6, '39, at 8 P.M.

Tri-Boro Palace

2514 Third Avenue, Bronx, N. Y.

Lexington Avenue subway to 138th Street and Third Avenue

A DYNAMIC MEETING

will be held that will be as significant to American History as was the Boston Tea Party

Only CHRISTIAN MEN—18 years of age or over are invited

Speaker: McWILLIAMS

Sponsored by:

The Christian Mobilizers

A Christian Front Organization

As publisher of the newest "patriotic" organ on the fascist horizon, it was my duty to attend. I heard McWilliams say:

"I'm gathering around me the meanest, the toughest, the most ornery bunch of German soldiers, Italian veterans and Irish I.R.A. men in the country. I'm going to have the greatest collection of strong-arm men in the city. And if anybody tries to stop us . . . they'll think lightning hit them."

McWilliams kept his promise. His retinue was a prize collection of cut-throats, convicts, rapists, pimps, burglars and goon squad bruisers. The Christian Front toughs paled into insignificance. One night Christian Mobilizer "patriots" beat up two policemen sending one of them, a captain, to the hospital for treatment.

The first meeting I attended was memorable, for it outstripped anything I had seen before. It had everything: action, slander, terror! Mayor LaGuardia was called a "stinkweed" and the President "the biggest bum of them all." Tri-Boro Palace was jammed with a steaming, sweating, smelly mob of five hundred "patriots" in their shirt sleeves, beered-up and ready to "go to town." In the sickly yellow light and the haze of tobacco smoke I read placards "Buy Christian" . . . "Stop Persecuting Christians" . . . "America for the Americans." Two large tables were piled with Bund and Coughlinite leaflets and the poison literature of Pelley, Edmondson, True and Sanctuary.

Joseph Hartery was speaking as I entered. He was an undersized, pug-faced man with a large metal cross pinned on his shirt. An ex-Christian Front-er, Hartery was known as the "Little Napoleon" and had pled guilty in 1932 to the charge of being a procurer (arrested under the alias Joseph Herman). Two years later he was discharged from work for attempted attack on a fellow worker with an axe. Later, he was sentenced to the workhouse for threatening a man with a clasp knife.

"Not until they stop insulting the name of Fritz Kuhn (applause), not until they learn to respect Adolf Hitler, Benito Mussolini and General Francisco Franco (more applause) will we stop talking against the Jews," he yelled. "Long live our Savior, Father Coughlin."

Hartery was followed by Edwin Westphal, a sadistic youth in his twenties with a crippled arm. As a member of the Bund he had spoken at meetings of the Crusaders for Americanism. In 1929 Westphal had pled guilty to and served time for burglary, was twice convicted for violation of the Copyright Law and also convicted for disorderly conduct. In a rasping voice, dripping with hate, Westphal screamed:

". . . And when we get in power, guys with my type of mind will go to work on them Jews with a vengeance. There won't be enough lamp-posts to hang them on."

And then came McWilliams. His stance was studied to achieve the greatest dramatic effect, and his shock of black hair on a large well-molded head made him an imposing figure. I shall never forget how the electric intensity of his delivery brought the mob to its feet in paroxysms of violent emotion. McWilliams paralyzed and terrorized by the sheer power of oratory:

"This is another revolution," he thundered. "A revolution for a nationalist America. Don't let anyone tell you anything different. It's a revolution against the Jew first, then against Democracy, then against the Republican and Democratic parties. Both are rotten. Both useless. We are going to drive them both out and we are going to run this country with an iron hand, the way Hitler runs Germany . . . We are his fellow-fighters in a great world drama. Fellow-fighters in an immortal cause. We are fighting for a Christian Aryan America and you men here are part of that revolution. We want soldiers. We want strong men. Men to fight for America's destiny and link it with the destiny of Adolf Hitler, the greatest philosopher since the time of Christ."

In the hushed silence, a lone voice called out in the rear of the room. "You're right, Joe. You're Goddam right, my boy."

He had hardly said the words when three of the yeggs pounced on him and were dragging him out, when McWilliams called out: "It's all right boys. Let him go this time. He won't interrupt again."

McWilliams' organization was spawned from the ultra-radical clique within the Christian Front. On the advisory board were ex-Front-ers, Thomas Monaghan, Joseph Mc-Donagh, Joseph Hartery, James Stewart, James Downey, Edmund Burke (arrested for breaking into a jewelry store and stealing a tray of rings). Joe patterned his organization on the fuehrer principle. His word was law! "I'll do the thinking around here. You guys do just as I say," he told his followers.

Joe's goon squad was officially known as the Guard Unit. A dozen pickaxe handles were always kept at headquarters and standard "patriotic" equipment for outside duty were brass knuckles and lead pipes wrapped in newspaper. Commander of the Guard Unit was John Zitter, convicted for burglary in 1934. John Olivo was captain.

"Members of my Guard Unit," McWilliams told me, "will become generals in tomorrow's Christian army. My guard trains secretly in cellars to beat the hell out of the enemy."

"How about fellows who try to investigate you?" I asked.

"We love those guys. We'll knock their heads in as we find out who they are. Remember the guy with the dark glasses and . . . ?" I did not need to be reminded about the absence of several youths on whom suspicion had been cast as investigators. "And I got a special intelligence section that does some very personal investigational work," Joe added.

I became charter member No. 737. My code initials were WGBO.

McWilliams' first major effort at national publicity was in August, 1939. New York was flooded with the announcement of an "historic event . . . under the star-filled summer sky, where with flags flying and bands playing, the new horizons of America's tomorrow will be opened."

Joe and his aides spent a month in preparation for the event at Innisfail Park in the Bronx. A banner sixty feet long was suspended from a scaffold, portraying a large cross in red, surrounded by a field of blue and a circle of stars in white. It was flanked by other banners thirty feet long. Father Peter Duffee's Cadets composed of a hundred youths, blared martial music. Seventy-five uniformed Bundists formed a guard of honor, shoulder to shoulder with thirty members of the Mobilizer Guard Unit. Maintaining watch over the assembled fascists was the Phalanx, an ultra-secret gun club. I was set to watch for "suspicious" characters.

Powerful arc lights flooded the field. Loud-speakers carried the voice of America's Quislings out into the night.

General George Van Horn Moseley was to be our guest of honor, but was unable to attend. Instead, the illustrious champion of Americanism Fritz Kuhn was present with James Wheeler-Hill, Gustave Elmer, and a retinue of Bundists. Seven thousand befuddled Americans composed the audience.

Substituting for Moseley was George E. Deatherage, fuehrer of the American Nationalist Confederation. Its symbol was a red-white-and-blue swastika. Functioning mainly in the South, Deatherage had once announced that the time had arrived "for a practical and constructive plan of government to be offered to the nation . . . the Fascist State." He was in constant touch with Nazi propaganda chiefs at Erfurt, Germany, and relayed instructions to American Nazis.

A sensual-looking man with a fleshy face, Deatherage spoke on "Counter-revolutionary Tactics" and spurred the mob against a "Red revolution" which seemed to be not even as far off as the proverbial corner. Actually, Deatherage's speech was a well-planned incitement to revolution. In it he: 1) established the presence of the hypothetical "enemy"; 2) frightened, then spurred the religious to action; 3) enlisted the family man into action to protect his "loved ones"; 4) established the need for "counter-revolutionary action" under the guise of self-defense; 5) laid the foundation for secret revolutionary cells; 6) provided for the caching of arms and ammunition; 7) declared the need for a "holy war," and added: "I am not content to walk in the footsteps of Christ. I will walk ahead of Him with a club." Deatherage called to the mob with these typical remarks:

. . . It is recommended that each person NOW secure at least 500 to 1000 rounds of ammunition . . . it is recommended that as many as possible join the National Rifle Association. . . . Taking into consideration the present state of affairs . . . your best policy is to organize into ten-man neighborhood posts or secret cells. All these should be trusted citizens who properly and legally armed, can combat Red units who will act in the streets.

Fritz Kuhn rose to speak and started by giving the Nazi salute. The uniformed Bund troopers snapped to attention and lined up in front of the platform in a cordon of honor.

"Free," called out their leader in a ringing voice.

"Amerika," yelled back the storm troopers.

Three times the leader called out "Free." Three times the storm troopers responded "Amerika."

James Stewart, another Mobilizer henchman, was chairman: "We are not fascists nor do we believe in fascism for America. We are Americans and we stand for one hundred per cent Americanism. The salute we give is merely the symbol which defeated Communism in Italy and Germany."

After the meeting, as publisher of *The Christian Defender* I was invited to join Kuhn, Wheeler-Hill, Elmer, Deatherage and McWilliams in a glass of beer. Surrounded by a dozen members of the goon squad watching my every move, I interviewed Deatherage and obtained the original copy of his speech. In the next issue of my hate sheet, I gushed out:

15,000 ATTEND PATRIOTIC RALLY

New York—The Christian Mobilizers, which since its organization a few months ago has virtually terrorized the enemy with the most militant program of Americanism ever attempted here, held a mass patriotic rally at Innisfail Stadium last Wednesday which for size and sheer dramatic color was unprecedented in the annals of New York.

Shortly after this, the Christian Mobilizers, which had been spawned by the Christian Front, achieved maturity in a spiritual merger with the Bund. Witnesses to the marriage held at the Shrine of Ebling's Casino in the Bronx were 1800 assorted *Deutschesvolk*, Coughlinites and representatives of sundry fascist groups. Gerhard Wilhelm Kunze was best man. Fritz Kuhn personally performed the ceremony before a swastika-marked platform.

"This iss a historik meeting. We shall back der Christian Mobilizers in every respect, whenever they are in trouble . . . Der German Amerikan Bunt does nott try to overthrow down Amerikan government. Dat's Joowish propaganta. We fight for nothing else but Amerikanism. Don't stay home any longer but come, join us in our fight for Amerikanism."

Joe McWilliams stood with bowed head while this marriage vow was performed, following which John Olivo, captain of the Mobilizer Guard Unit (arrested on October 11, 1934 for attacking and raping a woman in Central Park then fleeing with her purse; sentenced to the Penitentiary, December 10, 1934) dipped the Colors, as the Bund choir sang *Carry On* (to the tune of *O Deutschland, Hoch in Ehren—O, Germany, High in Honor*).

America, so dear to us,
Whose flag we proudly hail,
One duty stands so clear to us,
Her trust we must not fail. .

CHRISTIAN ✚ MOBILIZER

AN AMERICAN | NATIONALIST WEEKLY

VOL. I. NO. 1   SATURDAY, SEPT. 23, 1939   NEW YORK, N. Y.   PRICE 5 CENTS

Mobilize Against War

**Dynamic Leader Opposes
All Who Advocate War**

The Christian Mobilize
ganized to stop America
decline. That decline has be
about by the disease of inte
ism. An early symptom of
sence of these bugs in the
body was our participation
World War (1916-18) to sav
racy and to end all war. And
symptoms were the silly effo
rehabilitate Europe by loans

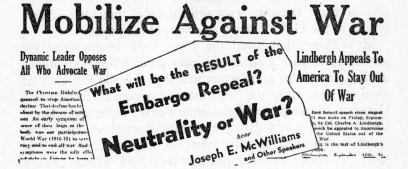

What will be the RESULT of the Embargo Repeal? Neutrality or War?

hear
Joseph E. McWilliams
and Other Speakers

**Lindbergh Appeals To
America To Stay Out
Of War**

first formal speech since August
21 was made on Friday, Septem-
b. by Col. Charles A. Lindbergh.
peech be appealed to Americans
the United States out of the
War
e is the text of Lindbergh's
ech:
Washington, September 15th. In

Joe McWilliams began his obstructionist efforts against national defense more than two years before Pearl Harbor. In another issue of *The Christian Mobilizer* he ranted against the increase of our peace time army to 280,000 men.

Toastmaster Joseph Downey, who next to fuehrer Joe was the most dynamic rabble speaker on the Mobilizers' roster, started by giving the Nazi salute, then said: "I consider it an honor to speak from this platform and salute you German Americans. I can admire a man who beat the British at their game. Hitler had defied the British, and we Irish know what the British are. I respect a man like Adolf Hitler."

A few weeks later I saw Downey again. On the left side of his shirt, just above the heart, was pinned the emblem of the *Wehrmacht*, the Nazi Army, composed of a swastika and German eagle.

Much to my disgust while with the Mobilizers, I met two Dashnags, both of whom took prominent part in Mobilizer affairs. These two Dashnags were the only Armenians I met in the subversive world in my four years as investigator. One of them was a realtor named Richard Koolian; the other a youth who used the alias of Edward C. Adrian, but whose real name was Edward Masgalajian. He contributed under both names to the Dashnag organ, *Hairenik Weekly*. My role as a synthetic Italian was so effective that they never suspected my identity.

Adrian told me of the youth division of the Dashnag, known as the *Tzeghagron*, coined from the Armenian words *tzegh* (race) and *gron* (religion). The program and philosophy of these fascistic "race worshipping" nationalists were similar to the Hitler Youth, Adrian told me proudly.

McWilliams dominated the New York fascist scene for several years with a series of clever publicity-gaining stunts, holding twenty or more street meetings a week. His gang of speakers were truly the "meanest and orneriest" in the city. His goon squads picked fights almost every night and boasted about them the next day. Joe exchanged speakers with other "patriotic" groups. It really mattered little under whose auspices they spoke. For example, the "Reverend" Herbert Lewis started to speak for the American Nationalist Party and the Crusaders for Americanism, then he spoke for the Bund, the Christian Front, the Christian Mobilizers and finally, for the America First Committee.

McWilliams plastered New York with "Buy Christian" stickers and a "Christian Consumers Guide." He galvanized into action many of those who had been mere bystanders and inspired several score of "patriotic" groups into taking more aggressive action. He was in close touch with "patriotic" leaders throughout the country and collaborated closely with Coughlin interests, James True, Reverend Edward J. Brophy, Colonel Sanctuary, Newton Jenkins, the Chicago fascist, referred to as *der führer der dritten partei* (fuehrer of the Third Party). Reverend Edward F. Brophy, another promoter of the Christian Front, not only spoke at a Mobilizer meeting, but also promoted Joe's Nazi group in other ways. Joe bought $30 worth of Brophy's booklet *The Christian Front* for resale to his own "Christian" clients.

McWilliams bragged that on his visits to Washington he conferred with Senators and Congressmen, including Senator Rush D. Holt and Representatives Hamilton Fish and Jacob Thorkelson. At the same time he moved in the sphere of such "respectable" fascists as Lawrence Dennis and Allen Zoll. Mc-Williams had the uncommon gift of being at home with the illiterate as well as with the Park Avenue patriots. As to his oratory, it was matchless in both camps. He campaigned violently against passage of the Lend-Lease Act and clamored against appropriations for defense and the Selective Service Act. Speaking to me with uncommon frankness, he said:

"Between you and me, George, this isn't my class of people. But you've got to have the mob with you in any revolution and this movement of ours is nothing but an American National-Socialist revolution in the first stages. I don't believe half of this anti-Jew stuff I preach, but you can't talk politics to these people unless you make it simple by bringing in the Jew every time. It's the only language they understand— the language of hate. Hitler made it work and that's what I'm trying to do here. I want to give the man in the street a Christian New Deal."

Joe organized the American Destiny Party, the political arm of the Christian Mobilizers and from the same platform at Ebling's Casino from which he and Fritz Kuhn had spoken jointly, announced his candidacy for Congress. In the hushed silence of an audience awaiting momentous news Joe blared:

". . . And our party emblem shall be one hundred per cent American. The covered wagon, symbol of America's greatness, symbol of the days of Washington and Lincoln, symbol of our peerless American heritage. . . . Our emblem shall include forty-eight stars. Through the streets of New York, drawn by two white horses, telling the American people of the great destiny of America under the American Destiny Party . . ."

"Heil, Joe McWilliams!"

"Joe for President!" the mob yelled

All through the spring, summer and early fall of 1940, Joe carried his campaign to the voters of Yorkville from the rear platform of a covered wagon which at night was lighted by kerosene lamps. The publicity given him by individual sensation-mongers in the democratic camp made his name known to thousands outside of New York. Joe did not intend to win. Publicity to the Nazi cause was what he wanted, and instead of burying him in a grave of silence some of our gullible and excitable democratic forces fell into the trap and boosted him with uncommon nation-wide publicity.

"If you were elected President, how would you run this country?" I asked Joe in the privacy of Destiny Party headquarters one day.

"I don't want to be called President, you understand that," he said, sternly. "I'd run this country like a factory. I would appoint all the key men and have absolute control. Once in power there will be no opinion but the American Destiny Party opinion. Labor will do as it's told and it'll be satisfied with what it gets. I'm against violence for Christians, but I would have absolute control regardless of the price."

"What'll the next step be?" I asked.

"As soon as I get in power I'll kick all the Democrat and Republican politicians out on their ears and raze their headquarters clear to the ground. This nonsense about democracy and equality is through when I'm in power." He paused dramatically. "Our next step would be to break the people of the voting habit. I want streamlined, modern government. Efficient as a factory, methodical as a machine. Republicans, Socialists and Democrats represent nineteenth century ideas. A new leadership is needed for a new America . . . the America of tomorrow."

I was with Joe McWilliams day and night and during nearly three years' association I do not recall on his part even one instance of kindness or the expression of gratitude. Unscrupulous, unfeeling, sensual to the extreme, popular idol of the masses and the ladies, Joe had the essentials of a glamor-boy fuehrer to act as the "front" for sinister Nazi politicians. And they used him unsparingly to carry on their schemes of corruption-and-control, divide-and-conquer. Joe was an agitator by nature, a ruthless destroyer who had no sense of constructive politics and was fired solely by insatiable personal ambitions and lust for power.

He was born on the Cheyenne Indian Reservation, Hitchcock, Oklahoma, in 1904. In 1925 he came to New York and during the following years invented a number of mechanical gadgets which he sold successfully. While working on a new razor blade patent in New York, part of his living expenses were met by loans from a Jewish friend, Ray Halpern. From

February 1930 to April 1938, Joe spent nearly all his time in the company of four American Jews: George Howard, Jerome and Wilbur Shapiro and Aaron Cecil Snyder (United States District Attorney in Puerto Rico). For years, before he turned fascist, Joe lived on the bounty of his Jewish friends.

During the winter of 1935, Joe's Jewish friends took him to Sarasota, Florida, to recuperate from a severe attack of rheumatic fever. His only friend there was a Jew named Hirshfeld. While there Joe continued to receive $30 weekly from Alfred H. Bamberger for whom he had worked in New York. His condition did not improve and he was brought back on a stretcher. Eventually Halpern drove McWilliams in his own car to Los Angeles where he recovered completely.

When I interviewed Jerome Shapiro, formerly Joe's personal lawyer and George Howard, a stock broker, both of whom knew the Yorkville fuehrer intimately, they told me that Joe's views from 1928 to 1938 were so violently Communistic that they avoided the subject. McWilliams attended the Communist Workers School in 1933 and later became affiliated with the Trotskyite element of the Communist Party. He attended W.P.A. public speaking classes, and those who heard him said his speeches were strongly Marxist, anti-Hitler, anti-Democracy.

Early in 1939, McWilliams inexplicably switched from the extreme Left to the extreme Right, and began associating with Christian Front interests. From that point on, Joe was suckled by Father Coughlin's own elements in the East, nurtured by the German-American Bund and reached maturity under expert Nazi guidance. Debts of several thousand dollars to his former Jewish and non-Jewish friends remain unpaid.

At the trial of Fritz Kuhn at General Sessions in 1939, Bund chief August Klapprott asked his friend if he were Catholic.

"Hell, no, I'm no Catholic," McWilliams called out disdainfully. "I'm a Protestant. I don't believe in no Pope. The whole damned bunch of them have been racketeers. Don't get the idea I'm a Catholic because my name sounds Irish."

Not long after this, Henry Curtiss, speaker for the American Nationalist Party and star performer for McWilliams, started a paper of his own and asked me to serve as reporter on the *American Bulletin*. Curtiss acted as contact man between "the rabble" and such "respectable" fascists as Seward Collins. Curtiss' real name was John Gaede. Arrogant and self-centered, he was an extremely unpleasant "patriot" to deal with. Back in 1935 he wrote for Mrs. Ann Tellian's *American Bulletin*. Mrs. Tellian was a Nazi agent and correspondent for Julius Streicher's *Der Stürmer*. My prestige as a rising leader of the fascist community was boosted through my association with Curtiss.

One of the oddest fanatics I met outside the Mobilizers, completely insane on the "Jewish question," was a Norwegian-born, gray-haired spinster named Miss Therese Holm. She worked effectively for the Nazi cause by acting as liaison agent between those new in the movement and the veterans. She collared me at Kurt Mertig's meeting one night and, inviting me to her room, told me some of the most fantastic whoppers I had ever heard about the Jews. She wrote for *Social Justice* and the *Deutscher Weckruf*, but was most proud of the editing she had done on the notorious book, *The World Hoax* by Ernest Elmhurst, which Pelley published.

Among her friends, also, was the patron saint of latter-day fascists, former Congressman Louis T. McFadden—who was the first to insert into the *Congressional Record* excerpts from the *Protocols* and Henry Ford's *Dearborn Independent*. McFadden addressed meetings of the Order of '76 whose "Christian" members bore cards marked: "In case of pogrom, please pass the bearer through police lines." Royal Scott Gulden, distant relative of the mustard king, was President of the secret order which met with Pelley, Colonel Sanctuary and Colonel Fritz Duquesne, the Nazi spy.

McWilliams often boasted to me of his friendship with Wall Street brokers and other "influential men." It was not mere vanity, because one day while looking through Joe's files—which were open to me—I saw the application for membership of James Frederick Ryder, who had listed himself as a Lieutenant-Colonel in the United States Army. Joe's income from Irish and German Americans was considerable, as I gathered from a list which fell into my hands. He also received anonymous favors from many well-dressed men and women.

I used to see Joe in the company of numerous women, some youthful, others old dowagers. He paid particular attention to about six girls in their late teens who attended his meetings, for reasons which I suspected were hardly political. His "harem" usually arrived with Joe and left the meeting hall in his company late at night.

Among Joe's guest speakers who referred to Joe as a "staunch American" was Representative Jacob Thorkelson. Anti-Semite and apologist for fascism, this relentless grave digger of Democracy gave up the practice of medicine to turn politician. He stepped into the shoes vacated by fascist Congressman Louis T. McFadden and made the *Congressional Record* the sounding board of totalitarian ideology.

The services to native fascism of this Norwegian-born super-patriot consisted of the insertion in the *Record* of quotations from the *Protocols*, from *World Hoax*, from Blackshirt Sir Oswald Mosley's *Action*, from the *Christian Free Press*, a Nazi organ published by Mrs. Leslie Fry at Glendale, California, in addition to Nazi lies and diatribes against Jewry.

Thorkelson defended himself by saying that the "... words, 'Nazi,' 'fascist,' 'anti-racial,' 'anti-Semitic' ... were created by the anti-Americans as a cloak to shield their own subversive activities." He exonerated the Bund completely by stating that "their principles of organization are not destructive to the Government of the United States."

Thorkelson's Washington offices became the hang-out for Mrs. Fry, Pelley, General Moseley, Colonel Sanctuary, Deatherage, True, Edmondson and McWilliams, as Thorkelson tried to effect a merger of major native fascist groups. He was idol of American Nazis and a particularly close friend of Pelley, for whom he spoke at Silver Shirt meetings.

Pelley "honored" Thorkelson by publishing a collection of his speeches in Congress under the title *Rescue the Republic*. Thorkelson wrote frequently for Pelley's *Liberation* and Winrod's *Defender*. He defended Hitler and Mussolini on the floor of Congress and denounced Democracy: "Democracies are always weak for there is not one Democracy which has survived for any length of time."

On the night of August 13, 1939 at a street meeting of the Mobilizers, the Guard Unit gave a particularly "patriotic" account of itself. Edwin Westphal was haranguing a mob at the corner of Crimmins Avenue and 141st Street. the Bronx. His yelling could be heard a block away.

"When we get into power, we'll get our vengeance. We have special means. I'd like to see a million more Jews come here, then our revenge will be complete. We'll fix the Jews the way Hitler fixed them. What are you waiting for, you people out there? Waiting for tomorrow? Tomorrow never comes. . . . Tonight . . ."

The mob swirled around in anger. At that moment, Captain John T. Collins of the Alexander Street station, mounted the platform:

"This is an unlawful meeting because of the unruliness of the crowd. The meeting is over. Break it up . . ."

Collins acted with scant knowledge of the "patriotic" temper of the Guard Unit.

"Shut up, you Jew," a voice called out thickly. It was the signal.

A dozen hands clawed at Captain Collins and dragged him to the ground. Benjamin Stafford, powerfully built ex-pugilist, lunged at Collins' throat. Louis Popchinsky pounced on Collins' midsection. Sergeant Robert McAllister rushed to the assistance of his captain, and even after being clouted with a lead pipe, which caused a deep gash over the left side of the head, he fought half a dozen members of the Guard Unit until police reinforcements arrived.

Stafford and Popchinsky were finally hauled away in a police wagon. Police, however, found the entrance to the station house blocked by an angry crowd of 2,000 Mobilizers. Unable to force an entrance, the wagon cruised around the block for an hour. Westphal was in command of the milling crowd at the police station and shouting orders at the top of his voice.

"Stand your ground, men. Don't let these lousy Jew cops bring in Stafford and Popchinsky. This is a frame-up. Don't give in. Stick to your Constitutional rights."

Doherty, a pipe fitter and member of the Christian Front, rushed to Westphal's assistance as police emerged from a side door. William O'Connor, member of the Christian Front, the Mobilizers, Social Justice Distributors' Club and the Social

Justice Motion Picture League, took charge while Westphal and Doherty tussled with the police.

Stafford and Popchinsky were found guilty and sent away. Westphal was placed on probation by Judge Masterson. Doherty was fined. O'Connor, because of his age (he was eighteen, he told me and had been ejected from Evander Childs and DeWitt Clinton High Schools because of subversive activity) received a suspended sentence.

In the meanwhile, my taking notes at meetings for *The Christian Defender* and the *American Bulletin* aroused the suspicions of Mobilizer henchmen. One night after a late meeting, Joe called me aside and asked me to meet him in one of the back rooms. His unusually calm voice should have aroused my suspicions, but it didn't.

"I'll be right down, Joe," I said.

The door was locked. As I knocked, it was flung open. Joe and his henchmen were seated at a table. Lining the walls were four of the most sinister gangsters of his goon squad.

"What's up, boys?" I asked, trying to be nonchalant.

"There's a leak of information somewhere. Maybe more than one," Joe said, "and we want to ask you a couple of questions."

"You have nothing to hide, have you?" asked Tom Monaghan.

"Hell, no. I have no secrets. You boys know everything about me. Shoot. What's the first question?"

"Some of the boys here say there's something funny about you. They don't think you're an Italian."

"I'm as Italian as any wop that believes in Mussolini and the Italian Christian State," I burst out heatedly, spilling a few oaths in Italian.

"Now there's these items that appeared in newspapers. How did they get out?" McWilliams showed me four clippings. One of them mentioned the American Destiny Party as the political arm of the Mobilizers. I was guilty of publicizing Joe's plans to run for Congress, but other reports were the work of a clumsy investigator who hadn't bothered to get his facts straight.

"You've been talking about the American Destiny Party for some days now," I said. "You might have said it while you were at a bar or something. Maybe it's one of them girls . . ."

"Leave the gals out of this. They're strictly personal business."

I faced the battery of Joe's henchmen for nearly two hours and was searched by them, but nothing to justify their suspicions was discovered.

Joe finally broke into a smile.

"Okay, boys, George is all right.'

He and the rest of his henchmen apologized for their suspicions. We all went downstairs for several rounds of beers. It was the closest call I had yet had.

CHAPTER VI

DRILLING FOR *DER TAG*

"Not faith, hope and charity, but faith, hope and
terror. Remember that, men. Terror! Terror! Terror!
That is our password from now on."

JAMES BANAHAN

I BEGAN NOW to probe into organized terrorist organizations
operating deep underground. Remembering the cue supplied
by Agayeff the White Russian youth of the existence of
"rifle clubs," I approached James McGee, a fellow Christian
Mobilizer and asked what he knew about them.

"That's going pretty deep, George, but I guess I can tell
you. Here, read what we just printed." He tossed over a
card:

REAL AMERICANISM IN ACTION

MIDTOWN SPORTING CLUB

Objects: Sportsmanship and Self-Defense

Meets at

310 West 59th Street, New York

This Card Admits One on.............1939 at 8 P.M.

"The guy in charge will be here," McGee said. "Hang
around."

"What's his name?" I asked.

"He has so many aliases, I don't know which one he's using
today," McGee said laughing.

A furtive youth in his middle twenties walked in, and after
looking me over sat down. McGee gave me a glowing introduction.

"Here's a good man for you, Herman," he said. "George
is an Italian that's as militant as hell. Ever read his paper,
The Christian Defender? It's hotter than the *Deutscher
Weckruf.*"

"Hell, yes," Herman said. "I've always wanted to meet the guy who put it out. Shake again, George. Glad to meetcha."

I was thus initiated into the terrorist aspects of the fascist movement which took me from the world of McWilliams and Coughlin into a deeper Nazi underworld where terror and revolution were bywords.

The night was hot and I was broiling in sweat as I marched in military maneuvers in a company of twenty-four members of the Midtown Sporting Club. We were being drilled on the third floor of Donovan's Hall while a slim, dark-haired young man in military shirt, black trousers and tie barked commands from a platform. He was Hermann Schmidt, alias Mike Strahinsky, commandant of the secret Iron Guard, known informally as the Midtown Sporting Club. Schmidt's real name was James Banahan but he rarely used it in the revolutionary underworld.

On the platform with Banahan were Carl Muller, alias Carl Pinkston; John Olivo, captain of the Mobilizers Guard Unit and Dan Walker. Dan who acted as an assistant to the drill master, sat stiffly in his chair, an arrogant smirk on his face and watched me closely as I tramped back and forth with the squad. I sensed his chill attitude.

At the end of half an hour Banahan blew sharply on his whistle.

"Companee . . . halt!"

After talking for a moment with Walker he called out: "Pagnanelli, step forward."

My heart sank as I wondered what Walker had told him about me.

"Pagnanelli, you will step outside for a moment."

I stepped out of line and walked to the door. Banahan turned the drill over to Dan and followed me. In the darkness of the staircase he suddenly asked:

"Pagnanelli, what do you do now for a living?"

Taken by surprise, I sputtered: "I work in a stock room . . . in an office."

"Where?"

"Near Wall Street."

"You were seen going into the Time and Life Building twice in one week, and trailed to the offices of *Fortune* magazine."

"I often get sent there on errands."

"What's your religion?"

"I'm a Christian."

"What's the matter, nervous?"

"No, why should I be nervous?"

Banahan looked at me searchingly and then said: "We're not entirely sure of you. You're still on probation. Dan Walker here is not sure. And Stahrenberg says we shouldn't take any chances. You know what'll happen to you if you ain't with us, don't you?"

"Yes, sir," I said.

"That's all," Banahan said, shutting me up.

When we returned to the drill hall, I stepped back into my place and Banahan addressed the budding storm troopers as follows:

"Members of the Iron Guard! What I am about to say you must keep buried in your brain. The penalty for betraying our secrets is death, swift and without warning. We have men watching every one of you, men without mercy. Men who don't give a damn. They are the guardians of the Iron Guard. You are the soldiers of Christ. Men like you fought in Spain. Men like you will fight in America. We are the trained body of Christian citizens who must give aid and defense to all of the Christian groups that, at present or in the future, shall need such support.

"You will train in small units and be taught to take care of any situation which the ordinary means of law enforcement cannot cope with. You are the defenders of the Faith. Your duty is to fight for Christ and Country. From now on you will be trained to serve as shock troops in any internal explosion that may come. But never forget. The penalty for betrayal is death, swift and unmerciful and sudden. You will further be required to swear to this oath before admittance to the Iron Guard." A hushed silence met his measured words. "Read the oath, Lieutenant Walker . . ."

In a thick, harsh voice, Dan read from a green colored document in his hands:

I do hereby solemnly swear to uphold and defend the principles of Christian nationalism and the aims and ideals of this, the Iron Guard. I will carry out this program even if it means the shedding of my blood. On the pain of whatever consequences may be decreed, I shall not at any time divulge information regarding the secrets of the Iron Guard. So help me God.

"Men, we have received orders from General Headquarters. Some of you must join the Christian Mobilizers and march for General Moseley. Further secret instructions will be sent you. We will now pledge allegiance to the American Flag."

Our hands shot out in the Hitler salute.

"Repeat after me . . . I pledge allegiance to the flag of the United States . . . to an Indivisible and Nationalist America."

Walker then stepped forward:

"Tonight is your last military drill. You will next be trained in riot duty—how to break up Communist meetings, how to protect yourself in a riot, how to help your Christian comrades. Come dressed in old clothes. Companee, dismissed!"

I walked downstairs and waited for Walker. In a little while he came down with Banahan, Patrick Finnegan and James McGee. The five of us walked to Columbus Circle and

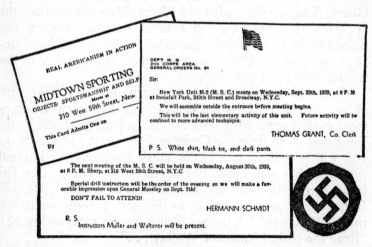

Meeting notices of the Phalanx and imported swastika sticker distributed by Fuehrer James Banahan.

entered Thompson's Cafeteria, where I protested vigorously against the suspicion that had fallen upon me. How dare anyone suspect me? Me of all people! What was I to do when I was sent on an errand by my boss? Could I tell him I did not want to go to the Time and Life Building?

McGee was on my side and won the others over but not Walker. Something had come over him. He just sat and looked at me. In the end he said. "In a movement like ours it's better to be suspicious than to wait till you're betrayed."

Over the next few months, however, I proved my "loyalty" to the Iron Guard and was finally allowed to attend a really secret session. Ten of us met in James Banahan's home, in a room that was little more than a bare cell. Banahan's bed was in one corner. A strip of linoleum on the floor, a half dozen straight-backed chairs, several armchairs and a small round table with an open *Bible* lying on it composed the furniture. Across the pages of the *Bible* lay a bayonet. Several rifles leaned against the wall. I saw an envelope on the bureau written to Banahan and bearing Father Coughlin's return address.

I sat down facing the emblem of the Iron Guard, a large black circle and an inner circle of white. Within the circles was a red arm holding in its fist a flash of lightning. The outer circle of black was rimmed by eight short spokes.

Banahan pointed to the insignia.

"It signifies the power which will be in our hands when *der tag* comes," he said, using the German words. "Each one of the spokes has a special significance. It will all be explained to you later."

Among the ten of us were James McGee and his son Arthur; Zimmerman, a former member of the Bund; Carlos, a Spanish youth who had served in the Guard Unit of the Mobilizers; a man named Henry Dietrich who experimented with homemade bombs, and another young ruffian who belonged to the Bund. There was also a man who introduced himself as Norman Miller and claimed to be a Captain in the United States Army.

Banahan unfolded a large poster-size leaflet entitled "American Defenders Protective Tactics—Plan No. 1," prepared by a Major Frank Peace, a friend of General Moseley. It listed the "strategic points" and "key positions" common to a metropolis. These included radio stations, gas works, water works, police stations, armories, Federal buildings, telegraph offices, etc. Beneath it was the following explanation:

Anti-revolutionary, defending, patriotic minorities must be familiar with what to defend, be trained to defend and armed to defend. To illustrate this is the purpose of these American Defenders Protective Tactics and this Plan.

. . . In Petrograd in 1917 Trotsky had but 1000 armed men in taking over that city. It was done, not by mass attack, but by hurling storming parties and technicians and gangs of armed men led by engineers against Petrograd's industries and public services.

We repeat that . . . armed minorities of patriots can successfully defend their lives and properties, protect their community and its industries. . . . Once this knowledge is familiarized, once your own invisible manoeuvres are perfected by repeated practice, you will then be in possession of permanent, practical, defensive preparedness, without which, both patriots and the nation are in great danger.

Through these tactics you can save yourselves and all America from Communism's elsewise inevitable blood bath.

Banahan explained the Plan.

"We are laying the foundation for the day when we'll be called upon to fight a Communist revolution in this country. It's about time we Christians got up and fought for a Christian government. If there's no Communist revolution soon we'll start one ourselves. We're nationalists and we stand for a nationalist form of government. We are fascists, American Fascists, and the Iron Guard is out to help bring fascism to this country." Banahan stood in the middle of the room, looking around at us, toying with the bayonet. "Democracy is a tool used to do away with Christianity. The time is ripe for something entirely new—fascism! And it will come. It will march triumphant in America. Christian nationalism," he said excitedly, "will march hand in hand with militant fascism everywhere to conquer the world."

"What'll we do in case this country goes into a war?" I asked.

"In time of war we are all saboteurs," Banahan answered. "We'll blow the hell out of this country. We'll blow up docks, power plants, ships, bridges. We'll raise hell. They'll blame the Communists. We'll spread confusion and chaos. War will play everything into our hands!"

"And then?" I put in.

"That's where the Iron Guard comes in," he shot back. "That's where we'll need men with iron guts. Men who can handle a gun, who can use a bayonet. Cold steel and hot lead, that's what'll count. There'll be street fighting. There'll be sniping. There'll be dirty work, plenty of it. Blood will flow like water!"

"What if the F.B.I. finds out about this?" Carlos asked.

Our commandant lowered his voice, speaking confidentially.

"In case of trouble we deny everything. You understand me? . . . deny everything. You know nothing. You have seen nothing. You have done nothing. You don't know each other. You are members of a Sport Club, interested in shooting rabbits, see? If they catch you with guns, we are members of the National Rifle Association, catch on?"

Tall, bespectacled Captain Norman Miller spoke up:

"Every Christian who is dissatisfied economically is a prospect. It is good strategy to recruit him to our cause. He has nothing further to lose, everything to gain. Enlist such dissatisfied Christians in the nationalist army."

We looked at each other, nodding approval.

"Today is the anniversary of Hitler's Beer Hall Putsch," Banahan resumed. "It was on this day sixteen years ago that Hitler started the movement which liberated the German people. We are going to do the same in this country, starting tonight."

He then walked to the door, made sure no one was listening outside and went on with measured words:

"You men are designated as captains—captains in the Army of Christ. Each one of you will be assigned a district in the section of New York, Brooklyn or Bronx where you live. You will be held responsible for whatever action may be ordered in your district."

He took out a map of New York.

"The city will be divided into twenty-one districts. I'm

going to assign each one of you to your post. Get your district straight."

I was assigned to the Grand Central Station district.

"The most important part of the city," Banahan observed.

"Here is what you all do! You are to familiarize yourself thoroughly with the district assigned to you. Know the location of every arsenal, subway station, power house, police and gasoline station, public building and hide-out in your district. Then chart those vital centers on your map. The maps will be forwarded to General Headquarters, where a master map of the entire city will be made."

He paused.

"You will be required to file a report every week. Every Communist headquarters in your district must be reported, and if possible, the floor plans obtained. At first you will report to me, but later you will communicate in code directly with General Headquarters. You will be known by numbers. Every small bit of information which can prove valuable must be turned in. You'll get target practice and complete drilling in the art of street fighting, roof fighting, sniping and the putting up of barricades by men who have already done it once.

"Later on we'll get trans-receivers; they're small compact radios that send and receive messages. When the internal explosion comes you will send and receive orders on them. The sets are so small they can be carried in a brief-case and no one will know what's in it. You are to recruit a platoon of seven men—reliable men, who will help you fill in the map." Banahan went on, amidst hushed silence. "These men will be your lieutenants. They will carry out your orders. You will meet with them once a week, but never allow any of them to meet any one else but you. Each of you captains will have your own cell, your own sabotage machine, your own revolutionary group for a nationalist America."

Captain Norman Miller stood up to say a few words:

"Hitler had to do the same things. We must model ourselves after the same pattern. Up at headquarters they have a complete blueprint of the coming revolution."

Banahan then dismissed the meeting with the Nazi salute.

"You will be notified of our next meeting place. Remember," he said grimly, "ask no questions; answer no questions. Good night."

As we filed out someone asked him: "Who is behind this movement and who will protect us if we get into trouble?"

"I can't tell you exactly," Banahan answered, "but I'll give you a hint. There are twelve of them and seven are army men."

Following one of the meetings at Donovan's Hall, I had asked the same question and Banahan's reply had been: "I can't tell you the details, but I can say that Father Coughlin is our spiritual advisor."

Iron Guard meetings were taking place late in the summer, fall and winter of 1939, at a time when the Christian Front was reaching the peak of its activity. Most Iron Guardists were members of the Front, or had been at some time. The main unit under Jack Cassidy was operating in Brooklyn. The Midtown Sport Club was one of many throughout the country specializing in revolutionary tactics. It differed somewhat from the others in that it was also a co-ordinating unit—men of other nationalist groups were eligible for membership.

The second of our secret meetings was held in the home of Thomas Moore, one of the captains who already had begun to organize his platoon. Of the men who had met at Banahan's house, only McGee and I were present. The others were: Patrick Coyne and John Kennedy, both of whom said they had seen action in the Irish Republican Army; a beefy German, Leon Thieson; a fellow named Thomas Murray who claimed to be a code expert and John O'Connell, working on the W.P.A. As at the Banahan meeting, rifles stood in the corner and the Iron Guard insignia was placed against the wall, beneath a large framed picture of Father Coughlin. A *Bible* with a bayonet lay on the table in the middle of the room.

Suddenly from the door behind me emerged a dark-hooded figure robed completely in black, except for the eye-slits.

"The Supreme Commandant, boys," Moore called out.

We jumped to our feet and gave the Hitler salute. While we remained standing, Moore announced that five candidates had applied for admission.

"Have they been thoroughly investigated?" the hooded figure asked.

"They have, Commandant."

"Ask them to place their hands on the *Bible*."

Each recruit placed his right hand on the *Bible* while the rest of us stood at attention, arms outstretched in fascist salute.

"Repeat after me," the voice called out. . . .

I . . . repeat your name . . . as a Christian American, do solemnly swear, in the presence of my fellowmen and patriots and Almighty God, that I will do my utmost, as directed by the officers of the Iron Guard, to keep the United States of America a Christian nation, and to oppose all those who would make this nation a shambles and destroy those Christian traditions upon which it was founded. I will carry out this purpose even if it means the shedding of my blood. I will fight for Christian Americanism. I will look to my God for guidance, look to my arms for courage, look to my leaders for the hour to strike.

When the candidates had finished their oath the black hooded figure called out: "Your instructions for the present are: 'Ask no questions. Answer no questions.'" After this it disappeared as suddenly as it had come. A half hour later the doorbell rang. "Quick, clean up the place." Moore hissed.

While we did away with the emblem, gun and anti-Semitic stickers McGee had brought, Moore passed around copies of sporting magazines. We sat back and began to talk innocently of baseball and duck shooting.

When the door was opened, James Banahan entered.

"Good evening, men." He gave the Nazi salute, then took off his coat and walked to the center of the room.

"I have surprising news," he announced. "General Headquarters has told me we are changing our name. From now on we'll be known as the American Phalanx and work right in with the Christian Front, the Bund and the Christian Mobilizers. We are the arm of the revolution. We are the police and the soldiers, the terror division of the nationalist revolution."

"When do we get the guns?" Pat Coyne asked. "My fingers are itching."

"I also have orders from General Headquarters to start a gun fund tonight. Each of you will give whatever you can. If you can't pay it all, you'll be given a gun anyway and you can pay as you go along."

While each one of the men dug into his pocket, Banahan appointed me to visit three gun shops and inquire about prices, then file a confidential report with him. Pacing back and forth, talking excitedly he urged:

"Headquarters has passed on orders that you are to train yourselves in smashing up stores—Jewish stores—and beating the brains out of Jews that put up a fight. You men will put the fear of God in the Jew. You'll be known as the Death Legion, and will specialize in terror . . . Not faith, hope and charity, but faith, hope and terror. Remember that, men. Terror! Terror! Terror! That is our password from now on."

His voice mounted as he pronounced the word.

The next meeting of the Phalanx took place in the cellar of Neville's Tavern, 125th Street near Eighth Avenue. We had instructions to file in individually at an appointed time and take a drink at the bar. We were not to greet each other. At exactly nine o'clock as instructed, I asked the barkeeper where the telephone booth was. He directed me to a rear stairway which led to a spacious whitewashed cellar. Banahan and a number of the others were already there.

"We'll hold drills and meetings here," Banahan said. "We can have target practice here too. It'll be sound-proof when covered with monk's cloth. We'll get some sand bags and use them for targets."

Having been appointed by Banahan as his right-hand man I set about fixing the place; putting cardboards and burlap bags against the windows and arranging the large benches in rows. I swept the place as Schmidt unrolled a new, freshly painted emblem of the Phalanx.

After nine-thirty P.M. the other members of the Phalanx began to arrive. First to come down were James McGee and Thomas Moore. Then came Frederick Grimm, another captain of the Mobilizers Guard Unit, who brought three new recruits: Carl H. Otto, James McQueeney, Hermann Sturm (an alien German youth) all of whom were members of the Christian Mobilizers Guard Unit. Coyne and Kennedy also arrived, followed by Leon Thieson, John McGath, A. Hewlett and Harry Nelson, alias Ralph Thompson, a quiet-mannered fascist who had worked with Stahrenberg for many years.

"What do you think of our new home, boys?" Banahan asked.

"Swell!" the assembly answered in chorus.

"From now on we go to town. Our first goal is to blow up the Communist headquarters right around the corner. The next thing for us is to get the guns," Schmidt went on. "The gun fund is growing. We can get new guns, 30/30 caliber, damned near free. General Headquarters is trying to adopt a standard model and it'll take some time before they decide. In the meantime we'll get what we can."

We lined up, swore in the six new recruits in the same ritual as at Moore's apartment, and then went into military drill. James McGee and Thomas Moore—both World War veterans—were drill masters. Back and forth, for a full hour marched the "Army of Christ" drilling for the American *der tag*.

Suddenly Banahan yelled: "Companee . . . halt! at ease." We dragged the hardwood benches out on the floor and took seats. Banahan stood before us.

"The Phalanx is now affiliated with the Ku Klux Klan," he announced. "We are also officially connected with the Bund. Orders from General Headquarters say that we are to expand and consolidate with every nationalist group in town."

"Isn't the Klan anti-Catholic?" I asked.

"Shut up!" Banahan yelled, glaring at me, then explained:

"In the South the Klan is anti-Catholic, but in the North it's only anti-Jewish. We will ride in blood, spreading confusion and terror in the Jew. Not little Ikey Moscowitz who keeps a stationery store, but the big Jews. You don't have to think how it'll be done. We don't want you to think. We'll do your thinking for you."

He glared at me again.

"Forget this Democracy stuff. Obey orders. It's for your benefit. Like a doctor who prescribes medicine and tells you what to do. Same with us. We know what's wrong with this country and we're prescribing the medicine. All you got to do is to take what's given to you. Obey orders. We'll do your thinking for you.

"I'll talk to you later," Banahan turned to me.

"We'll be making bombs soon," he divulged. "At General Headquarters, up in Yonkers, they've already begun to make them. They're laying in supplies—metal, powder, fuses . . ."

Banahan said he'd procure literature on the subject and get someone to give us special instructions in blowing up bridges and vital communication centers.

"Here are a few tricks to remember. You can slip a time bomb into a brief-case, then leave it in the men's room and walk away. Or dump it in a rubbish can right in the building. I'd like to be able to pick up the paper some day and read, 'Grand Central Station Bombed,' 'The White House Blown to Bits,' or '*Queen Mary* Sunk at Her Dock.' You know, men," Banahan went on, "Hitler was holding meetings in a cellar not long ago. He was being persecuted too. You men are making history. You may not know it, but you are. You're fighting to preserve a Christian America and Hitler and Mussolini are fighting with you."

I waited around for Banahan when the meeting was over and together we went to the German-American Athletic Club in the heart of Yorkville. We ordered beer. I expected to be called down for my question about the Ku Klux Klan, but he had evidently forgotten about it.

"It was right in this room," Banahan confided after the third beer, "that I met representatives of the German Government. The Iron Guard was financed with German money, you know," he said proudly.

"How much did you get?" I asked, showing great interest in the fact that the Nazis thought Banahan important enough to give him money.

"All I wanted," Banahan answered. "By the way, I've got your membership card." He fumbled in his pocket and brought out a card with cryptic symbols and numbers. Across the face of the card, printed in colored inks, were three large letters "PAX."

"That PAX stands for Phalanx. In Latin it means peace. So if you ever get caught with the card on you, you can say it's for a peace organization." We sipped our beer in silence

for a while, then Banahan confided: "But you've got to promise not to ask foolish questions in public."

I promised.

"George, you are my confidential secretary, and I'm going
to show you the Plan of Organization of the Phalanx." Glancing around furtively, he handed me a carbon copy of the Plan,
typed on thin paper, probably a fifth or sixth carbon of the
original.

"Where's the original and the other copies?" I asked with
enthusiasm as I studied the plan.

"Other units of the Phalanx have them," he answered.

The fanaticism with which Coughlinite interests impelled
their duped followers is indicated in these brief excerpts from
the four-page document:

Section I—Purpose

. . . We must take a solemn oath never to give up this battle
until either we have won the fight, or until we have drawn the
last breath of life. We must realize that this is a battle to the
death, which once begun cannot be stopped. We shall be judged
by our actions, not by the jurists of our enemies, but in the eyes
of Christ the King.

Below appear the regulations and organizational outline of the
Phalanx. Under no circumstances shall any of these regulations be
altered except through a general order from the General Staff.

Section II—Membership

1. Membership in the Phalanx shall be open to those Christian
Americans of the Aryan race who have been vouched for by one
who is already enlisted. Males only shall be eligible.

2. The age limits are between the years of seventeen (17) and
sixty (60).

3. Every prospective member shall appear before an examina-
tion board appointed by the General Staff, and must be passed on
by this board before membership becomes final.

4. Upon being enlisted every member must take the following
oath, with his right hand upon a Christian *Bible* . . . (The oath
administered by Banahan followed).

5. Upon being enlisted, each new member will be turned over
to the district training center, where his education in military
science and tactics will begin. Here he will also be under close
observation and his movements and actions recorded.

6. The final action before he is accepted by a membership board, will be deferred until a full report is received from the Intelligence Section, which is entrusted with the task of thoroughly investigating each and every application.

7. Each member will be issued a numbered membership card upon which will appear his photograph and his right thumb print. Under no circumstances will anyone be permitted to enter a meeting or drill without this card, no matter how well known.

8. Each member must sign a pledge to respect, to the best of his abilities, the commands of officers of the Phalanx, and to devote as much time as possible to the cause.

The Plan and the purposes of the Phalanx were identical with those of the *Cagoulards*—the Hooded Ones—the French terrorist organization formally known as the Fascist Secret Committee for Revolutionary Action subsidized by Hitler and Mussolini. It was estimated that 100,000 members were trained and heavily armed for "fifth column" work.

A few days before Christmas, 1939, in response to an urgent note from James Banahan, I met him at his home. He had just heard that the "sport club" in Brooklyn was contemplating a merger with Manhattan units. While I sat at his typewriter he dictated a letter to Joseph M. Conlan, Bronx leader of the Christian Front, making an appointment with him.

Several days later, Banahan, Conlan and I met in a parked car in front of the 125th Street Post Office. Four Christian Front bruisers lounged outside the car, keeping a lookout. Conlan told us that the Front in Brooklyn had 200 men, many of them armed, and were in an "advanced" stage.

After outlining the activities of the Phalanx, Banahan exclaimed, "Look, Conlan, why don't we work together? We could help each other plenty."

"Tell you what," Conlan said, "we may be able to swing it together if we don't have to give up our identity. We don't want to be absorbed, see. I can't give you any definite word until I speak to the big boys, but I think it can be arranged."

Banahan clapped Conlan on the shoulder. "That's the way I want to hear you talk. We'll make a real outfit, one that's really tough. . . . Suppose I get in touch with you right after Christmas, then the leaders of the Brooklyn Sports Club and the Midtown Sporting Club can arrange a joint meeting."

"Suits me. What are you fellows doing now? Nothing? Suppose we all drive over to Star O'Munster Hall. There's a Christian Front meeting going on."

I looked at Banahan for an answer.

"Sure, let's go. Anything that'll help the revolution."

I saw myself involved in situations from which I would have great difficulty extricating myself. These men were outlaws who stopped at nothing. Now was the time to call a halt *before* they carried through their threats! I felt it my duty to inform those who could deal with the situation. The next morning I presented myself at the offices of the Federal Bureau of Investigation, arranged a meeting with Special Agent Peter J. Wacks and turned over the evidence I had gathered.

The Phalanx was ready to march. Moore, Coyne, McGee, Kennedy and others had almost paid up for their guns. Dietrich was experimenting with bombs. Banahan was arranging to hold outdoor target practice on a farm near Peekskill in New York State. Arrangements to co-ordinate the Phalanx and Cassidy's Brooklyn Sports Club were proceeding smoothly. New members poured into the Phalanx, every one of them itching to get into action.

On January 13, 1940, the F.B.I. cracked down on Cassidy's Sports Club and hauled into Federal Court seventeen men of varying ages, charging them with conspiracy to overthrow the Government of the United States. Newspaper accounts showed that Cassidy's group was modelled on lines identical with the Phalanx.

The Phalanx disbanded immediately after the arrests.

Banahan and some of the others were questioned by the F.B.I. but were eventually released. The "big boys" behind the scenes were never made public. Back to the street corners and the taverns, and the pool-rooms went the men of the Phalanx, to wait until another fuehrer called. When the case against the Christian Front was heard the jury brought out a verdict of "Not Guilty." More than a verdict, it was an echo! An echo of the words of Berlin police officials who on May 14, 1926, were quoted by foreign correspondents:

Berlin police officials who yesterday discovered a mass of documentary evidence which revealed the existence of a plot to establish a German fascist dictatorship, are now inclined to consider existence of the alleged plot greatly exaggerated.

"Not guilty!"

Borough President George U. Harvey of Queens defended the Christian Front saying, "They're Americans." Father Coughlin praised the Christian Front, saying: "They're Christians," and elaborated:

The Crusaders of old were Christian Fronters. . . . I take my stand beside him [William H. Bushnell, Jr.] and his fellow Christian Front prisoners, be they guilty or be they innocent! . . . not retracting one word which I have said today or on previous occasions. . . . For us there is no white flag of surrender!

Echoes!

When on September 23, 1930, in the German City of Leipzig three young members of the Nazi Party were brought to trial for treason, Hitler had yelled: "These are patriotic Germans." And though the young Nazis were found guilty, they were let off with eighteen months in an army fortress—a special prison for those who committed "Honorable crimes."

The Phalanx and the Christian Front marched the streets of New York—fighting, Jew-baiting, plotting revolution and the sabotage of Democracy. And all this in the name of "anti-Communism" and "patriotism."

On the streets of Berlin during 1929, Hitler's Brownshirts had been playing the same game. On October 19, 1930, Novelist Thomas Mann told reporters: "I regard the National-Socialist Party as a flash in the pan which will soon be over." Three years later Adolf Hitler ruled the Reich, and Thomas Mann came to America as an exile to warn us of the dangers of fascism he had minimized in Germany.

And in America, how many listened to him?

CHAPTER VII

PUPPETS OF ADOLF HITLER

"The German has no right to renounce his Germanism. He was born a German by the will of God. There is no greater sin than voluntarily to renounce German blood. A German remains a German whether he lives in China, Japan, France or elsewhere. Our mentality is not determined by climate or location, but by race and blood."

ERNST WILHELM BOHLE

I PROVED MYSELF such a "loyal" worker and *The Christian Defender* pleased Stahrenberg so much, that he urged me to sell copies of the *National American* at Bund Camp Siegfried. I went there with Carl Halder and Gus Hettler, his associates at the shop. With 1000 Jew-baiting leaflets, 500 copies of Pete's hate sheet and 50 copies of my own poison stored in the trunk, we drove over Route 27 and after passing through a number of sleepy Long Island towns, turned left into Yaphank. We were stopped by storm troopers with gray uniforms and military boots, who jotted down our license number and plied us with questions.

Carl answered them: *"Er ist einer meiner italienischen Freunde. Ich kann für ihn vollauf garantieren."* (He is an Italian friend of mine. I vouch for him.)

Overhead was a sign: *Herzlich Wilkommen* (Hearty Welcome).

Camp Siegfried was one of twenty-four Bund camps in the United States. It consisted of a forty-four-acre tract of flat ground. Hidden from the public were the parade grounds and Hindenburg sport field. Deep within the Camp grounds, snug among the trees, were the O.D. houses (*Ordnungs Dienst Haeuser*) for the storm troopers. The year-round homes had swastikas built into the masonry or painted on the façade. All speech was in German. Camp Siegfried was operated by the German American Settlement League, Inc. and its mission was to found a German-speaking colony—a Sudetenland in New York State.

Our Camp is designed principally to be a place which breathes of the spirit of the new Germany. . . . We want to be helpers and advisers who are ready at all times to do any work; to provide for order and to make propaganda for the ideals of our great German racial community. Hereby we consecrate you as a little piece of German soil in America, as a symbol of our motto, "obligated to America, tied to Germany."

Carl and I set up shop in the picnic grove beneath the pines. While he remained in charge of the tables, I trudged away with the poison sheets and sold them, at the same time taking pictures and talking to residents and visitors. In the parking lot I had seen an unusual number of expensive cars, many with New Jersey and Pennsylvania plates. Who were the owners? I believed it worth finding out and managed to record the license plates of 163 of the better class cars.

German slogans were conspicuously placed throughout the Camp.

"*Deutschtum Erwache*"—one sign read ("Germans awake").

"*Wir Amerikaner Deutschen Blutes Ehren die Heimat*"— ("We Americans of German Blood Cherish the Fatherland") was another sign.

Also: "*Ein Volk, Ein Reich, Ein Führer*" ("One Folk-Race, One Germany, One Leader").

At three o'clock a car drove up and twelve uniformed members of the *Jugendschaft* filed out. The *Jugendschaft* (male Youth Division of the Bund) was modelled directly after the Hitler Youth. They wore swastika buttons and carried their emblem—a short flash of jagged lightning set against a black background. The short daggers they carried were inscribed "*Blut und Ehre*"—Blood and Honor—signifying eternal allegiance to the Fatherland.

At the parade grounds Bundsmen took charge of youths and adults alike.[1] The O.D.'s then appeared with flags, ban-

---

[1] Loyal German Americans are exempted from all my ensuing remarks. Otto Kunze, an exceptionally fine marionette maker who came to America voluntarily before Hitler's advent, symbolizes the loyal American of German descent.

"Germany is hopeless," he told me as I interviewed him in New York. "The people did not make it what it is. It was the militarists—men without

ners, and pennants, massed them at the head of the troops and at the word *marsch* led the procession down Hindenburg Field. Grim and defiant, father, son and daughter obeyed all military commands. Massed American flags fluttered between dozens of Bund banners and Bund emblems. Some of the American flags were on flag-staffs surmounted by swastikas.

Leading the parade was Fritz Kuhn. On his left was Gustave Elmer, followed by other Bund dignitaries. On his right walked fuehrer Joseph McWilliams. I snapped their picture together and also managed to include Richard Koolian, the Dashnag, walking alongside.

Speakers of the day were Herman Max Schwinn, Bund leader of the West coast; the patriotic twins, Kuhn-McWilliams; and William Meyer, speaker of the American Nationalist Party. Meyer spoke in English but sprinkled his talk liberally with German and closed urging: *Opfer, Opfer* [Sacrifice, Sacrifice] in every way you can on behalf of true Amerikanism. *Frei Amerika!*"

"*Heil, Amerika!*" the crowd yelled back.

After considerably more heiling, singing of Germanic songs and the prolonged oratory of Nazi speakers, the ceremonies of *Deutscher Volk Day* (German Folk Day) came to an end and the Hitlerite dream of "a little piece of German soil," a Sudetenland in "Amerika," was planted this side of the ocean.

Camp Siegfried was a symbol of the Bund of yesterday.

At Ebling's Casino I saw crowds of 2000 men, women and children on a hot summer night sing the *Horst Wessel Lied* and *Deutschland, Deutschland Über Alles* until they could sing no more. When the blistering campaign in Poland was shown on the screen and a bomb heaved from an airplane laid waste an area teeming with life, the audience went into hys-

---

character, morality or Christianity. From childhood they trained the people to goose-step to war. I knew the old German culture was going to die . . . and I wanted to live. I came to America. America is still an unfinished country. Everything lies ahead. Everything remains to be done. Next to His coming this American melting pot is the greatest experience in the history of man. It is Christianity really at work."

I believe Otto is a great and humble American, as great as Carl Schurz but not as well known, and I believe America will be enriched by his immigrant talent.

By the same token, the majority of German-Americans are behind the war effort and participating in the fight against Nazi-Fascism.

terics. When a German submarine was shown torpedoing a helpless Allied ship and the ship turned turtle, sinking stern first, the sea dotted with human beings crawling like beetles, the audience roared lustily!

"Wonderful!" *Wunderbar!*

The foundations of the Bund were laid in 1924. It originated with the Chicago unit of the Teutonia Club when that club raised a platoon of storm troopers modelled directly on Hitler's Brownshirts, and adopted the swastika. The Teutonia Clubs were originally founded in Detroit by Fritz Gissibl, a German alien who was with Hitler in the Munich beer hall *Putsch*. Eight years later under Heinz Spanknoebel, a former worker for Henry Ford, the Friends of the Hitler Movement was founded in Detroit and in other cities.

When Hitler became Chancellor on January 30, 1933, Spanknoebel was called to Germany. On his return to America, the Friends of the Hitler Movement changed its name to Friends of the New Germany—(*Freunde des Neuen Deutschlands*) and continued to function under that name. In the meanwhile, Fritz Kuhn, also working as a chemist in Henry Ford's plant, became the fuehrer of the Detroit regional group. In December, 1935, a merger of all the scattered "Friends" was effected and Kuhn was appointed supreme *Bundesführer*. In June, 1936, the "Friends" were Americanized to the German-American Bund (*Amerikadeutscher Volksbund*) and launched on a national campaign of treason under the guise of star-spangled "patriotism."

Controlled by the *Deutsches Ausland Institut*—the Foreign Section of the Nazi Party directed by Ernst Wilhelm Bohle —and backed by Nazi money, the Bund flourished all through the depression years. The United States was divided into three *gaue* (districts) each with its own *führer* or *gauleiter*. The fifty-seven Bund cells were subdivided into *Ordnungs Dienst* (uniformed storm-troopers); *Jungenschaft* and *Mädchenschaft* —the male and female Hitler Youth corps; *Frauenschaft* (women's auxiliary) and *Deutscher Konsum Verband*, or the German-American Business League which was maintained by the Bund and published a business guide boycotting anyone not in sympathy with it.

All these Nazi cells sent their savings to Germany and received propaganda instructions and trained consular agents like Captain Fritz Wiedemann and Colonel Ulrich von Killinger to direct espionage and revolutionary activity.

The influence wielded by the Bund in our political dissensions must not be underestimated. The Bund was the spearhead of the anti-Democratic crusade and set the pattern for the Christian Front and the Silver Shirts and countless others like them. Viewed over the years, the swastika-heiling period was a temporary expediency staged to arrest public opinion and enthrall the admiration of frustrated and simple-minded Americans in the lower classes of our society.

The *Deutsches Ausland Institut* launched a two-pronged pincer attack on our Democracy. Leadership of the first "fifth column" was entrusted to German-Americans, while the second was entrusted to carefully selected candidates of non-German "one hundred per cent American" ancestry—the Edmondsons and Pelleys—whose job it was literally to translate Nazi propaganda into English terms and serve it as "patriotism" to those who would swallow it as such. The American wing of the Nazi psychological fifth column penetrated Park Avenue society, or business and industrial circles and eventually projected itself deep into the halls of Congress.

In the meanwhile tons of propaganda—from the mills of Hamburg, Berlin, Erfurt and Stuttgart—flooded the United States. "National-Socialism would be worth nothing if it restricted itself to Germany alone and did not seal the rule of the superior race [*herrenrasse*] over the whole world for at least 1000 to 2000 years," Hitler said, and lavished an estimated $300,000,000 a year on agencies *im ausland* (overseas) to help promote the world revolution. The *Ausland Institut* stated in its yearbook in 1936 that it maintained 46,000 German organizations abroad, more than 20,000 of which were in the United States. And wishfully prophesied Carl Hubl, Nazi Party leader of the British Kenya Colony:

I am convinced the foreign section of the Nazi party is an instrument on which some day the *Führer* will play a mighty melody. We Germans abroad are the strings of this instrument. We must be certain that in case of necessity it is ready to be used.

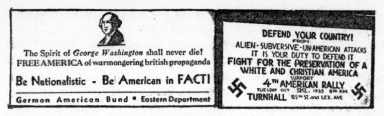

The Bund "honors" George Washington. The poster at right was placed on a truck and driven through Yorkville streets.

A horde of Nazi agents travelled back and forth. Consul Herbert Scholz directed operations from Boston; Gerhard Alois Westrick worked the New York area; from his home overlooking the San Diego naval base, Count von Bülow managed the vital Western coast with wily Fritz Wiedemann, San Francisco consul, who was finally expelled. Hans Borchers. Frederick Draeger. Nazi clergymen like the Rev. S. G. von Bosse furthered Nazism from the pulpit. At Columbia University Professor Friedrich E. Auhagen, and at Wittenberg College in Ohio Frederick K. Krueger propagated the Nazi cause in an extensive Nazi network that permeated every corner of America and made its influence felt in every class of our social, economic and political life.

It was the boom period for espionage in which the boats of the Hamburg-American Line played a prominent role. Dr. Colin Ross, a Nazi of Scot ancestry, toured America photographing our industries, harbors, power plants and rallying Hitlerites in our key cities. "Germans in America, too, have experienced their Versailles," he wrote. "A man will arise and rally them, a German Thomas Paine."

In the meanwhile the Bund had so antagonized most Americans by its swastika-heiling phase that orders came from Berlin to cut out public singing of the *Horst Wessel Lied*, shelve the Sam Browne belts and marching boots and "go American." The party line changed, as a bucket of red-white-and-blue paint was applied to make overnight "patriots" of the Nazis. The *Deutscher Weckruf* became *The Free American*. And no longer professing to convert the United States to National-Socialism, the Bund became nationalist and isola-

tionist, showed great concern for the welfare of the Republic
and adopted the slogan: America First.

When Fritz Kuhn was jailed for misusing party funds,
Kunze took his place and promptly identified himself with
the great Carl Schurz in leaflets titled *Blood Is Honor* and
Germany, America's Great Friend In Need. "The spirit of
George Washington must never die," the Bund screamed.
"To none is his memory dearer than to Americans of German
origin."

Disguising itself as the *Männerchor* (Male Chorus) the
Los Angeles Bund attended a meeting of the League to Save
America First, managed by T. W. Hughes. After the meet-
ing had started the storm-troubadours unfolded packages re-
sembling sheet music and distributed them to the audience.
It was Nazi literature.

The Bund, that is the Nazi arm of the same old Bund, went
underground to plot sabotage and espionage, while its
"American" wing gushed out in patriotism and socialized with
native fascists. Basically anti-Catholic, the Bund went in
heavily for "Christianity," sponsored "giant Christian American" meetings, and frothed at the "persecution of Christians" by a handful of American Jews. Most laughable were
attempts to "prove that Christ was not a Jew." Kuhn said
Christ was an Armenian!

With the change from the Hitler salute to spurious Americanism and Christianity, the Bund spirit penetrated deeper
into native American strata. Taking advantage of the depression years and making expert use of anti-Semitism, Roosevelt-
hate and the pitting of group against group, the Bund began
to radiate and to syphon its influence in the mass "Christian-
American-Patriotic" movement. The promotion of native
American "fronts" as a screen to Bund activity became standard practice, backed by illimitable capital and the extensive
Nazi network of organization. With those native fascists it
could not control, the Bund collaborated.

All this went on so subtly that the average American dismissed their noisy antics as merely crackpot. While most of
America was lulled into sleep, the Bund and its elements went
quietly about their work of injecting the toxin into the American blood stream without hurting the patient. The Bund was

governed by the law laid down by the *Ausland Institut* and enunciated by Fritz Kuhn in the *Deutscher Weckruf* on his return from Germany:

One thing must be considered quite definitely. . . . We must impel American politics with a pure German feeling. . . . We must demand from the candidates that they, above all else, must always use their influence that America, under all circumstances, must keep out of any European war. That is the greatest service that we can show Germany. . . .

Our task is first the consolidation of all German racial groups and second, the acquisition of influence for a subsequent show of power in American politics. This second part is most important. American Germandom must become dynamic, turn against its adversaries. . . . Our battlefield is right here, and here is where we must fight it out.

When the Hitler Youth—"future carrier of German racial ideals in America" was Americanized with its parent, the front cover of its organ, *Junges Volk,* displayed a picture of Abraham Lincoln and of Horst Wessel (a procurer for Berlin brothels until he was killed in a brawl). The caption read: "German blood our pride—a Better America our Goal." And below the pictures of Lincoln and Wessel was the caption: "Both died for the future of their people."

These youths were taught that only German contributions to America, only the German racial strain, only the Germanic ideals mattered. German blood was superior not in the United States alone, but the world over. "We are first of all Germans in race and blood and language" was the slogan dinned into them. I came to know many members of the *Jugendschaft*. Their slavish obedience to authority, their complete absorption in Bundist doctrine made them difficult material for future citizenship. A special prayer was written for them by Baldur von Schirach:

Adolf Hitler, we believe in Thee. Without Thee we would be alone. Through Thee we are a people. Thou hast given us the great experience of our youth, comradeship. Thou hast laid upon us the task, the duty, and the responsibility. Thou hast given us Thy Name [*Hitler Jugend*], the most beloved Name that Germany has ever possessed. We speak it with reverence, we bear it

with faith and loyalty. Thou canst depend upon us, Adolf Hitler,
Leader and Standard-Bearer. The Youth is Thy Name. Thy name
is the Youth. Thou and the young millions can never be sundered.

How *could* these American-born youths healthfully participate in the American way? While among themselves,
speaking in German, they were at ease, but they sputtered
and stammered in the presence of non-Germans. They kept
aloof, either through a false sense of "Aryan" superiority, or
what I suspected as probable, a feeling of inferiority before
other nationalities who mixed as fellow Americans, laughed
freely and thrilled normally.

As Hitler dictated to his Youth groups, Hitler also laid
down the party line for the more respectable German-American groups when he said according to Hermann Rauschning:

It is a good idea to have at least two German societies in every
country. One of them can always call attention to its loyalty to
the country in question, and will have the function of fostering
social and economic connections. The other may be radical and
revolutionary.

The Bund was only one arm of the Nazi octopus—the
"radical and revolutionary" arm of the scheme for America's
conquest. Fantastic as it may sound, Nazi leaders who had
already carved the world for themselves, had actually mapped
out a "German *Lebensraum*" in the midwest which planned
to have its own autonomous laws, press and political representatives, and would some day establish its independence—
the identical tactics which Conrad Henlein was assigned to
follow in the Sudetenland. The final aim was to be the re-
alization of *unser* (our) *Amerika:* a German America!

Questionnaires were actually sent out to midwestern German societies to determine the number of votes controlled
by German racial elements. It was the wild Nazi dream to
convert German-American communities into solid German
racial blocs (*Volksgemeinschaft*) which would vote to elect
pro-Nazi officials to office and thus serve the role of a "constitutional" fifth column. Hence the vigilant attempts of Nazi
agents to establish *Deutsche Volksgruppe* (national groups)
and instill in them racial solidarity and pan-Germanism. Di-

rector Ernst Wilhelm Bohle's dictum to those German-Americans who listened was:

We only know the concept of the complete German who, as a citizen of his country, is always and everywhere a German and nothing else but a German. . . . The German has no right to renounce his Germanism. He was born a German by the will of God. There is no greater sin than voluntarily to renounce German blood. A German remains a German whether he lives in China, Japan, France or elsewhere. Our mentality is not determined by climate or location, but by race and blood.

The German-American National Alliance with headquarters in Chicago served the midwest as a "respectable" front for Hitlerite views. Throughout its 350 units, the Alliance vigorously promoted *Die Einheitsfront*—the "United Front" (of "American Germandom race-conscious, politically unified, and economically secure"). It supported the America First Committee and exhorted members to "assist financially and morally" all isolationist and appeaser causes. In a pamphlet entitled *You are Wanted*, the Alliance argued:

We constitute about 25% of the entire population of the United States, but constitute a part equal to almost nothing of the government of our country. It is for lack of equal political representation on our part that certain groups which are very powerful politically, have been able to ridicule and persecute everything that is German-American in this country for the deliberate purpose of thereby silencing the voice of German-Americans, which they fear otherwise would have been expressed and heard in favor of a free and internationally independent America.

Die Einheitsfront succeeded in inducing the Chicago Censorship Board to refuse the exhibition of the movie *Pastor Hall* showing Nazis in an unfavorable light. But it applauded *Sieg im Westen* (Victory in the West) which advertised Nazi military power. Speaking on July 9, 1940, over a daily "German Hour" maintained by the Alliance, its spokesman Walter H. Silge warned:

I have made it clear, time and again, how urgent it is for every United States citizen of German descent to join the *Einheitsfront*, thus furthering cooperation among America's Germandom. Those who join our *Einheitsfront* in good time may discard all fear. Apprehension of the Future Impends Only For Those Who Stubbornly Remain On the Side Lines.

The Germans knew what this warning meant.

Aristocrat in its class, the Steuben Society hated the Bund because of its difference in tactics, shunned wild Nazi talk and avoided in recent years the public heiling of Hitler, while the Bund continued as before. In the reception room of the Society in New York, I found a large American flag standing in one corner. On the walls were pictures of General Von Steuben and of Washington and Lincoln. The Pledge to the Flag and the Bill of Rights hung neatly framed between them. High up was a bunting in red-white-and-blue. The room oozed patriotism. The Society published *The Steuben News*—a "Newspaper for Patriotic Americans"—and described itself as:

... a patriotic, civic and educational political society endeavoring to awaken in the hearts and minds of American citizens of German extraction the necessity for taking a more active part and interest in the political affairs of our great country.

Its program demanded "strict discipline" on the part of its members, and rejected "persons who are shifters and trimmers, or who are known to possess no race pride." The Steuben Society strongly emphasized Racial (Aryan) consciousness and political objectives. In addition to numerous units throughout the country it also maintained a Junior League Division, a Ladies' Auxiliary, and sponsored numerous German-language schools.

The New York Times and other newspapers stated that a confidential letter was sent to one hundred wealthy members by President Theodore H. Hoffman asking $100 from each "to fight British propaganda." But while Hoffman regarded Anglophilism as unforgivable, neither he nor any other official of the Steuben Society declared themselves against Hitler's regime. When asked to comment on Nazi propaganda here, Hoffman is quoted to have said: "I'm not interested."

This view is understandable in the light of Hoffman's record as director of the Steuben Society.[2] It goes back to his trip to Germany and his reception by Hitler. Hoffman told the story in a by-lined article in the December 20, 1934 issue of the *Deutscher Beobachter* published in New York:

Whoever thinks that National-Socialism rules by oppression, is mistaken. . . . My personal impressions of Hitler were that he is an idealist, an unusual organizer and a man of tremendous energy. It is my conviction that he is honest and sincere in his endeavors not only to unite the German people, but also in his determination to break the chains of slavery. . . . He is the one man who filled the life of the German nation . . . with new hope of the future.

A year later Hoffman returned to Germany, this time with a delegation of Steubenites who were entertained by Hitler on August 7, 1935, and were also received at the *Deutsches Ausland Institut* and by Nazi Party officials.

A few months later—on October 6, 1935—Dr. Hans Grimm of the *Ausland Institut* appeared as guest of honor at *Deutscher Tag* (German Day celebration) sponsored by the Steuben Society in swastika-draped Madison Square Garden. The Steubenites sent Hitler a lengthy telegram which was printed in the *Deutscher Beobachter* on October 10, 1935:

. . . Greetings, bearing our thanks to you, the *Führer*, who, relying only upon your belief in the eternal destination of the German people, has moved unto the light of fulfillment the dream, millenniums old, of our ancestors. Greetings of vowing faith to our nation, a faith which is and will be forever the guide of our doings. We greet you, the reason for our pride, symbol of our love of our nation, you, the *Führer* of New Germany.

Next year, Dr. Karl Stroelin, President of the *Ausland Institut* arrived in person and addressed a wild mob of hyphen-

[2] I am indebted for these startling facts on the Steuben Society leadership to T. H. Tetens who since 1934 has made an exhaustive study of Nazi activity in North and South America, and has accumulated a vast store of documentary proof of the historic development and extension of the pan-Germanic scheme for world domination . . . "Hitler is but the greenest shoot of the great unholy oak of Wotan," he wrote. "Even after Hitler's defeat the world will never find a lasting peace as long as ruthless Prussianism and fanatical pan-Germanism endure."

ated Americans celebrating *Deutscher Tag*. And once again cables of loyalty were sent by American citizens to *der Führer* on foreign soil.

Hoffman's personal attachment with Nazi agents did not end here. The *Deutscher Beobachter*—an organ which reported Bund and Friends of the New Germany activity—told how Hoffman spoke at the Säar-Festival celebration of the purely Nazi *Stahlhelm* (Steel Helmets) in New York, together with Freiherr von Schrotter, *Stahlhelm Landesführer* (District Fuehrer). According to the record, "huge waves of applause" greeted Hoffman.

George Sylvester Viereck was one of the founders of the Steuben Society which was founded in 1919 and immediately adopted the program of the German National Alliance (which upon Congressional investigation had been dissolved during the World War) to aid in the reconstruction of a defeated Germany and form a pro-German bloc in the United States. Viereck wrote in the August, 1921 issue of his *American Monthly* that membership in the Steuben Society was open only to German Americans who had "never betrayed or denied their race."

The Steuben News reprinted articles from the pro-Fascist Italian daily, *Il Progresso Italo-Americano*. It recommended books by the notorious *Ausland Institut* and ran many articles by Nazi agents. *The Steuben News* praised as "extraordinary and valuable" the book *Scarlet Fingers* published by Flanders Hall, the propaganda mill financed by Nazi agent George Sylvester Viereck, and urged that orders be sent direct to Steuben Society headquarters.

Steuben News columnist Herman C. Kudlich lavishly praised Conrad Henlein—the Fritz Kuhn of Czechoslovakia—and urged readers to send gifts to *Bund der Sudetendeutschen* (Sudeten-German Bund) in New York for forwarding to the Sudeten Nazi as a token of moral support.

The Steuben News took offense because George Cardinal Mundelein of Chicago "had the extremely bad taste to speak of the present German chancellor as a former paper-hanger, intending thereby to belittle him." In an article on "The Innitzer Case" *The Steuben News* justified the treatment given Cardinal Innitzer by Austrian Nazi hoodlums:

The press here grows indignant at this "brutal" attack on the Catholic religion. It is nothing of the kind. It is an attempt to compel the priesthood to keep out of affairs of the State.

The Steuben News followed the accepted party line of pro-Nazi isolationists. It headlined the speeches of Lindbergh. It championed the late Senator Ernest Lundeen—some of whose speeches were written by Nazi agent Viereck—and on one occasion devoted eleven columns to one of his defeatist speeches. It reprinted from *Social Justice* and *The Herald*, American Fascist weekly. It ran large advertisements for the America First Committee, reprinted its bulletins and urged its members to support it financially. The Steuben Society fought desperately all measures to arm those European Democracies which resisted Hitler's brutality. And *Steuben News* also quoted liberally from the *New York Enquirer*, published by William Griffin, who was later shown to have associated with Viereck.

When Nye ran for re-election in 1936 three branches of the Society assisted him financially according to published accounts. In return, Nye inserted the propaganda of the Society in the *Congressional Record* and sanctioned the mailing of thousands of copies, free. "Come and greet our friend," read the appeal of the Society announcing Nye's appearance at the Steuben Day banquet. "He has fought your battle. This is a call to arms to show your appreciation . . ."

Another darling was Representative Hamilton Fish who

The Steuben News

REGISTERED U. S. PATENT OFFICE 1929

A NEWSPAPER FOR PATRIOTIC AMERICANS

Germans of Czechoslovakia
(November, 1936)

These Germans are oppressed by the Czech government, and every possible means is employed to suppress their cultural and economic activities and to reduce them to the position of helots.

They are fighting for their very existence and have united under the leadership of a man who has won their hearts and whose name will go down in history as their savior

This man, Konrad Henlein, some years ago conceived the idea of uniting his people, to convince them that their only salvation lay in this very unity. With indefatigable zeal he has convinced them that only by standing together in one and only one party, disavowing and discontinuing all factionalism could they hope to preserve themselves.

There are resident in this city a number of these Sudeten-Deutsche. They have formed a federation or Bund for the declared purpose of coming to the assistance of their German brothers in Czechoslovakia, to give them moral and material support, to foster attachment to the land of their birth among those hailing from Sudetenland and to participate in the mutual

This is a very commendable undertaking and should receive the support of everyone hailing from that section and also of all Germans who were formerly of the old Austrian monarchy and Hungary. The address of the Bund der Sudetendeutschen is Austrian Hall, 245 East 82 Street, N. Y City.

HERMAN C. KUDLICH.

also was a close friend of Viereck. The Steuben Society promoted the founding of the National Committee to Keep America Out of Foreign Wars, collected enormous sums from its memberships and turned the leadership over to Ham Fish.

The Steuben News also expressed uncommon affection for Senator Rush D. Holt and it quoted liberally from and concurred in the sentiments of the following officials: Senator D. Worth Clark; Representatives Jacob Thorkelson, Martin L. Sweeney, Clare E. Hoffman, Roy O. Woodruff, Lewis D. Thill, Harry Sauthoff, Bernard J. Gehrmann, H. Carl Andersen, Robert F. Rich, Jeanette Rankin, Harold Knutson, William B. Barry, James O'Connor, Louis Ludlow, George H. Tinkham.

In the summer of 1940, I came upon a copy of *Today's Challenge* in the Germania Bookstore. It contained a series of articles by Lawrence Dennis, William R. Castle, Senator Ernest Lundeen and Representative Hamilton Fish. It was inspired by George Sylvester Viereck, registered as a Nazi agent with the German Library of Information and managed by Nazi agent, Friedrich E. Auhagen. To the uninitiated who knew nothing about Viereck's guile *Today's Challenge*—organ of the American Fellowship Forum—was an innocent magazine and had a lofty purpose:

Only through cooperation among men and women of all walks of life, bound together by an enlightened self-interest in the welfare of our country, is it possible to make progress in the right direction. . . . And it is to the creation of such a spirit that the American Fellowship Forum has been dedicated. . . . As a nonpartisan, educational institution, it is dedicated to a more enlightened, a more united and more prosperous America.

Lieutenant Commander of the United States Navy C. Bailey, and Rear Admiral of the United States Navy D. E. Dismukes (retired) both sent in long letters "as a slight corrective for the propaganda that is dragging the people of this country into war." In his letter Commander Bailey quoted from a "noted English military authority" also recommended by Father Coughlin and Pelley.

Meetings of the American Fellowship Forum naturally

avoided Bund elements. Members paid $5 to join and were promised the "satisfaction of working for a truly constructive and patriotic cause, unmarred by any selfish or ulterior motives." It held meetings in exclusive hotels and sponsored high-class social affairs in order to attract American prototypes of the British Cliveden set. Its role corresponded to that of the Anglo-German Fellowship of London whose members were linked with Nazi cartels and were the respectable Quislings.

The Forum coveted the friendship of army and navy men. At one of Allen Zoll's luncheons I met its field scout, Miss Ima Gotthelf and saw her speaking with Major William Lathrop Rich who had long associated with super-patriots. I saw them go off to one side and talk earnestly together, whereupon I saw the Major write down an address and phone number for her. Under Viereck's guidance the Fellowship advocated a strict nationalist policy—America for the Americans, Europe for the Europeans.

Congressman Thorkelson was advertised to speak for the Forum, as he had spoken for the Mobilizers. Lawrence Dennis, a champion of American National-Socialism, was a regular contributor to *Today's Challenge*. He was Viereck's close friend and an ardent promoter of the Forum. John A. Zellers, president of the New York Board of Trade spoke before the Fellowship Forum, as did Otto A. Stiefel, of the German American Conference. But Viereck's prize catch was William R. Castle, our former Ambassador to Japan and under-secretary of state under President Hoover. Castle swallowed Viereck's cunning propaganda at one gulp. He wrote several articles for *Today's Challenge* and in one issue wrote vacuously on "Wanted—International Courtesy":

Fascism is essentially nationalistic. It has no desire to create other fascist states except in so far as the spread of fascism seems to create a more sympathetic world in which to try to get the space and the raw materials which it needs. Let us at least be wholly honest with ourselves. . . . We must recognize also that he [Hitler] has kept the movement purely German, that his seizures of territory have been of territory inhabited by Germans. . . . That is why Hitler is so popular in Germany.

For weeks, as I weaved in and out of "patriotic" meetings,

I had been seeing quantities of pro-Nazi literature bearing the imprint of Flanders Hall. I was on the verge of writing them when a mimeographed card from Mrs. Elizabeth Dilling of the so-called Chicago Patriotic Bureau, announced that she was sending me a Flanders Hall book, entitled *Lord Lothian vs. Lord Lothian*. What surprised me was that she made *optional* a payment of $1, which to me suggested that she had either received the book gratis or at an extremely low price. It also showed that Flanders Hall was anxious to have its stuff get around. What axe had they to grind?

I wrote them, inclosing a copy of my *Christian Defender*. In a few days I received a cordial letter from Siegfried H. Hauck and a quantity of catalogues for distribution. A few weeks later, I received a book *The 100 Families that Rule the Empire*, by Giselher Wirsing, editor-in-chief of *Münchner Neueste Nachrichten*, a Nazi publication, whose American correspondent was Viereck. The introduction was written by Viereck, the great American patriot in Hitler's pay.

Flanders Hall published a list which included twenty books urging strict isolationism and seeking to prejudice opinion against aid to the Allies. As a German agent during the World War, Viereck had played an almost *identical* role. He published *The Fatherland* and later *Viereck's American Monthly*, on whose masthead was the motto: "America First and America Only." In his book *Spreading Germs of Hate* which he wrote after the war, Viereck indicated:

Every propagandist drapes himself in the flag. The objective of German propaganda was three-fold; to strengthen and replenish Germany; to weaken and harass Germany's foes; and to keep America out of war.

Among Flanders Hall authors was Shaemas O'Sheel who served as the Kaiser's propagandist during the World War and tried to embroil us with Mexico. Another Flanders Hall book, *The Hapless Boers* by Eugen Vroom, one of Viereck's many aliases, was dedicated to "Colonel Fritz Duquesne, Undaunted Warrior and Avenger of His Stricken Motherland." A year later Duquesne was convicted as the master-mind in a Nazi spy ring. Viereck's other aliases were George F. Corners,

James Burr Hamilton, Donald Furtherman Wicketts, and Dr. Claudius Murchison.

Through devious means I ascertained that some of the Flanders Hall books were translated directly from the Nazi propaganda of the *Deutsche Informationsstelle* (German Information Center) operating from Berlin. Its books, however, were promoted under the following appeal:

Flanders Hall has embarked upon a campaign of education. Ours is a patriotic task, for which we freely ask the support of all those who believe with us in America First and America Only.

I paid a visit to Flanders Hall at Scotch Plains, New Jersey, which I found to be a pretty, sleepy little town an hour's ride from New York. Siegfried Hauck was seated in an office cluttered with files and stacks of books. Hauck was in his late twenties, a former small-town newspaperman, and had cordial manners. He did not talk like a Nazi. He was not anti-Semitic. He was not openly anti-British. He described himself merely as "pro-American." Time and again he emphasized that Flanders Hall was an American publishing enterprise and he wanted Americans, rather than "German-Americans," to distribute its books.

"I'd like to see Father Coughlin get behind our books and push them the way he pushed *Lord Lothian* and *100 Families*," he said, referring to the lavish reviews in *Social Justice*. Hauck was particularly eager to obtain the co-operation of various "patriotic organizations." Any non-German organization would do he added, as long as it was "old-established." When I asked if he intended to publish any anti-Semitic books his denial was prompt.

"We won't touch that stuff here," he said winking. "You understand why. We'll let others do what they want to do. Furthermore," he continued, "we are an American house. We are not engaged in any propaganda."

Casually I asked Hauck if any of his books were translations from the German. He answered curtly:

"We don't talk of that here."

When he told me that *Publicity*, an American fascist weekly published in Kansas, had ordered a hundred copies of the *100 Families*, I observed that *Publicity* was anti-Semitic.

"We can overlook that," Hauck said. "He is an American publisher. As a matter of fact, I don't care who orders our books as long as they are not Germans. We are an American house. We would like to have more people like Mrs. Dilling work with us. She did us a lot of good by sending our books all over the country."

Hauck was about to issue *We Must Save the Republic* by Representative Stephen A. Day—a leading spokesman for the America First Committee. "The Committee," Siegfried added, "has agreed to buy a considerable number of copies of Day's book." When I asked how he had had the advance sale arranged, Hauck answered: "General Hammond of the America First Committee took care of it. And that isn't all. We're going to come out with a whole series of America First books by other Congressmen and Senators."

Hauck chatted amiably as he drove me back to the station. He was impressed by the abilities I professed as "book salesman." As a result of that visit Hauck authorized me to represent Flanders Hall in the New York area, and gave me a list of old American groups to contact—advising me to get orders from college and public libraries. "Eventually," he said, "we might get you to travel for us all over the country. We can use a man of your abilities."

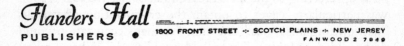

Flanders Hall

PUBLISHERS   ●   1800 FRONT STREET ∴ SCOTCH PLAINS ∴ NEW JERSEY
FANWOOD 2 7949

June 23, 1941

To whom it may concern:

    The bearer of this letter, Mr. George Pagnanelli of New York City, is a special sales representative of this firm, and is authorized to sell Flanders Hall publications and to solicit orders for them.

S. H. Hauck, President
FLANDERS HALL

In due time our Department of Justice trailed George Sylvester Viereck to the inconspicuous offices in Scotch Plains and soon established the fact that he "financed, controlled, and directed" the "American" publishing enterprise.[3] When finally arrested by the F.B.I. Viereck said blandly: "I have tried hard to help the President keep his pledge to which he owes his re-election."

A week after visiting Hauck I heard from him again:

You mention that you may go to Washington; coincidentally, I have just returned from a four day visit there. I spent much time with our fine patriotic congressional leaders and other prominent American citizens, making final arrangements for the publication of our new series, AMERICA FIRST BOOKS.

The first of these books by Congressman Stephen A. Day will be followed by two books by the fighting young Senator, Rush D. Holt. These are the books that we have long been waiting for. I dare say, they are books that all America has been waiting for. Please plan to help us push them as much as possible. . . .

I determined to go to Washington to interview Day and Prescott Dennett, director of the Columbia Press Service and Washington representative of Flanders Hall. I was not hopeful of being received by Day. None the less I wrote him a cordial letter, inclosing a copy of my *Christian Defender* to see how he would react to the vile hate-sheet. Immediately on my arrival in Washington I phoned Day's office, expecting a rebuff by his secretary. On the contrary, after a minute's wait I was switched to Day's wire and spoke to him personally. He had received my letter and was eager to see me. We made an appointment for three-thirty P.M. the next day.

I was on time, and as I surveyed the high-ceilinged room speculating on how to act, Day emerged from his office—a squat, bald-headed man with bushy brows and a taciturn way about him. He shook my hand cordially. I started off by saying that Mrs. Dilling had sent me a copy of his speech against Union Now. Day acknowledged knowing Mrs. Dilling well and commented favorably on her various "patriotic" stunts.

[3] In 1915 Adolf Hauck, Sr., now a teacher of German at Plainfield (New Jersey) High School, was associated with George Sylvester Viereck and they had served together on a committee. Twenty-five years later his son carried on in his father's footsteps with considerably greater success.

When Day told me that his book would be issued in a few days, I asked what he thought of his publishers.

"Flanders Hall is the only American publishing house daring to put out pro-American books," he said earnestly.

"How did you happen to learn of Flanders Hall?" I asked.

"Through Prescott Dennett," Day answered.

"That's the man I came to Washington to see," I said. "I didn't think you knew him."

"Of course I know him. Here, I'll phone right now and you can make an appointment," Day volunteered to my astonishment.

He went to the phone and as soon as he had contacted Dennett he motioned to me. I arranged to meet Dennett at five o'clock. Then I thanked the Illinois Congressman for his co-operation.

"Perfectly all right. Glad to do it," he said, smiling. "I appreciate your efforts to promote my book in New York. And by the way, give my regards to Prescott when you see him."

In the lobby of the Old House Building at five o'clock I faced a tall, beefy man, in his thirties, with a fat body and flabby hand shake.

Dennett proved to be shrewd and tight-lipped, but after a while he began to talk cautiously, first by boasting that he had once toured Europe on a Pulitzer travelling fellowship. He told me of his associations with the War Debts Defense Committee, on which Representative Martin Sweeney and former Senator Ernest Lundeen were members. Dennett had also promoted through his Columbia Press Service propaganda for the Make Europe Pay War Debts Committee, and Islands for War Debts Committee all of which were publicized in *The Steuben News*. These were created under the magic and Midas touch of George Sylvester Viereck and used as dummy organizations to further his schemes. Dennett made clear that his role was that of "contact man" between his clients (Viereck and Flanders Hall) and susceptible Congressmen. He added that Senator Nye was working on a book which Flanders Hall would publish right after Holt's two books, *Who's Who Among the War Mongers* and *The British Propaganda Network*.

"Holt has a mailing list of 250,000 names," Dennett said. "The America First Committee is getting behind many of the

Flanders Hall books. You can understand why. It's just what they've needed. And Flanders Hall is the only pro-American concern that will publish patriotic books of this kind."

Dennett knew many Congressmen personally and spoke in highly complimentary terms of Martin Sweeney, Paul Shafer, Usher Burdick, Roy Woodruff, Burton K. Wheeler, James O'Connor, John Coffee and Jacob Thorkelson. Throughout our interview in a restaurant off Capitol Hill, I had the feeling that Dennett was hiding a great deal from me. His silence at my key questions, his repeated use of the phrase "pro-American" and the general atmosphere of plotting he conveyed, convinced me that there was a great deal more to Dennett than I had yet dug out. I suggested dropping in at his home the next day for some literature to take back "to the boys back home."

"Sure, come right over. I've got lots of stuff."

His home at 1430 Rhode Island Avenue, N.W. also served as office for the Columbia Press Service.

"I'll get the literature right away," Dennett said. It was apparent he did not want me to hang around the premises. But while he went into an inner room I took the opportunity of looking over his desk. I could see nothing to interest me. It was clean, suspiciously clean.

"There's so much stuff back here that I can't find what I want," Dennett called out from inside. "Wait in the hall. I'll be right out." After a while he emerged with a stack of envelopes containing Congressional speeches.

"They're all ready for mailing," he said. "All you do is address them to the right people, put them in the mailbox and off they go free."

"That's mighty convenient, isn't it?" I observed.

"Very much so. We send thousands of them out from here."

The literature he handed me included some of his own press releases in defense of Lindbergh, the Islands for War Debts and the War Debts Defense Committee. The franked envelopes bore the signatures of Congressmen Clare E. Hoffman, Henry C. Dworshak, Bartel J. Jonkman, Harold Knutson, John G. Alexander, Hamilton Fish, James C. Oliver, Gerald B. Nye, D. Worth Clark and Robert R. Reynolds.

Reynolds had become involved in Viereck's sly schemes by

inserting into the *Congressional Record* propaganda letters, news releases written by Dennett and other publicity in support of Viereck's projects. Written under Viereck's tutelage this publicity received wide, free distribution under the Congressional franking privilege.

Congressman Sweeney had helped Viereck by inserting an article by Linn E. A. Gale, secretary of Make Europe Pay War Debts Committee, while Congressman Day had fitted into Viereck's plans by speaking on "War Debt Sunday" under the auspices of War Debts Defense Committee.

According to the evidence Dennett turned over to me, Senator Nye had inserted in the *Congressional Record* editorials from the *Gaelic American* in praise of Viereck's pet projects.

The other Congressmen and Senators had served the cause of Viereck-approved appeasement, defeatism and national disunity in various capacities of innocence or spite against the Administration.

That wasn't all I learned. Dennett had also penetrated the American Coalition of Patriotic Societies, a high-brow superpatriotic Washington group and was a friend of Walter S. Steele, another super-patriotic leader in Washington.

"Both the Coalition and Steele have accepted complete sets of Flanders Hall books," Dennett said.

I asked if he knew Lawrence Dennis, Viereck's associate.

"Oh, yes, I've talked with Dennis. I think he has a brilliant mind."

But Dennett would not elaborate and I thought it best not to arouse his suspicions further. Just before I left Dennett pressed in my hand several sheets of stamps, red-white-and-blue in color. They depicted Uncle Sam holding an IOU and the slogans: "No Foreign Wars. Make Europe Pay War Debts. No War Loans." They were inspired by Viereck.

"Ask your patriotic friends in New York to order some," Dennett advised. "I'll sell them out cheap. And when you get back," he urged, "be sure you see William Griffin, editor of the *New York Enquirer*. He is a swell fellow. I've worked with him."

My talks with Dennett showed how Viereck had improved his propaganda technique since World War days. His tireless efforts to make Nazi poison acceptable to leaders of the America First Committee, his attempts to reach the halls of Congress via sympathetic Representatives and Senators, and his efforts to feed the American people blatant Nazi propaganda in the name of "patriotism" were crowned with success. I realized that the enemy we faced on the home front was infinitely more cunning and deceptive than the military enemy. And while we could arm ourselves for battlefronts abroad, against the guiles of the enemy at home we were still defenseless and pitifully weak.

CHAPTER VIII

THE PIED PIPERS OF "PATRIOTISM"

> "The great masses' ability to absorb is very
> limited, their understanding small, and their forget-
> fulness is great. For these reasons any effective
> propaganda must be confined to a very few points,
> and must utilize these slogans until the very last
> man cannot but know what is meant. . . . The masses
> are so stupid that . . . the less its scientific ballast,
> [of propaganda] and the more exclusively it consid-
> ers the emotions of the masses the most complete its
> success."
>
> ADOLF HITLER

THE NAZI EDUCATION for ignorance continued to be propagated by American-born "patriots" serving as Hitler's hatchet
men, and to function as the native arm of the psychological
fifth column against Democracy. Prominent among them was
George E. Deatherage who had coined the phrase "Constitutional Fascism." He explained it in the *News Bulletin* of the
American Nationalist Confederation, "Official Organ of the
Fascist party in America" . . .

Constitutional Fascism, briefly, is nothing more or less than an
exalted patriotism (alias nationalism). . . . Fascism is based on the
principle of America for Americans. . . .

Thousands of otherwise rational Americans were led to believe that fascism could be reconciled with the Bill of Rights
and were told in the same breath that they must never ask
questions. If you asked, you were either a Jew, a Communist,
or a "liberal."

World Service was the *Bible* of pro-Nazis the world over
and Deatherage was one of its chief American correspondents.
It was published in more than a dozen languages under the
charge of the notorious Lieutenant-Colonel Ulrich Fleischhauer, and circulated in every country Hitler wanted to

soften up. The March 1, 1938 issue was thoughtfully dedicated to "saving" America. Here's how:

You can help save America, yourself and your family from the folly of other nations. . . . Inform yourself and inform others. Then join a fighting organization and become active in spreading the truth. . . . The publications and organizations listed below are fighting the battle with all they have—Help them!

Some of the organizations listed on the Nazi roll of honor were:

Industrial Control Reports, Washington, D. C. [James True]
Christian Free Press, Glendale, Calif. [Mrs. Leslie Fry]
The Defender Publishers, Wichita, Kansas [Gerald B. Winrod]
Mrs. A. W. Dilling, Kenilworth, Ill. [Patriotic Research Bureau]
Robert Edmondson, New York [*American Vigilante Bulletins*]
The Pelley Publishers, Asheville, North Carolina, W. D. Pelley
Charles B. Hudson, Omaha, Nebraska [*America in Danger*]
Industrial Defense Association, Boston [Edward Hunter]
American Nationalist Confederation, St. Albans, W. Va.

And the publications recommended by *World Service:*

Waters Flowing Eastward, by Mrs. Leslie Fry
The Secret World Government, by Major-General Count Cherep Spiridovich
The Socialist Network, by Mrs. Nesta Webster
Join the C.I.O. and Help Build a Soviet America [by Joseph P. Kamp]
Fools Gold, by Fred R. Marvin
Aryan Americanism, by Olov E. Tietzow

While these were the more illustrious members of what we, in our ignorance called crackpots, I could not dismiss them as such. My experience convinced me that under the slogans of "patriotism" they were inoculating innocent Americans with the virus of hate, undermining confidence in our leaders, promoting doubt and suspicion. Under the guise of "Americanism" they were sowing the seeds of social discontent which Hitler hoped, would eventually break out in revolt. And their pleas of "Christianity" were nothing more than a ruse to attract those who could only be attracted to the term "revolution" on a "Christian" basis.

Eleven pied pipers of "patriotism" deserve mention.

The "World-Service", which is issued in (Il-Informed Gentiles, irreproachab…

PATRIOTIC RESEARCH BUREAU
For the Defense of Christianity and Americanism
DIRECTOR, ELIZABETH DILLING
Room 708 - 8 S. Dearborn
Chicago

Support the War Chest
ATTEND
3rd American Rally
of the
Combined - Mobilized
Bronx - New York - Brooklyn Groups
at the
TURN HALL, Tuesday, October 8, 8:30 P.M.
Speakers:
Col. E. N. SANCTUARY
"The New Deal and Its Communist Program"
National Leader ANTON HAEGELE
"An Appeal to American National Socialists"

Deutscher Fichte-Bund e.V.

(The Fichte-Association was founded in January 1914 in memory of the great German philosopher Fichte)

Union for World Veracity

Serves the cause of better understanding by giving free information about
the New Germany, direct from the source

To protect human culture and civilization
by disseminating facts about
the subversive powers in the world

COLONEL EUGENE NELSON SANCTUARY

It was in the luxurious home of Mrs. Schuyler that I first met Colonel Eugene Nelson Sanctuary, a sombre man in his sixties with a long face, austere, frozen in its gray pallor. Dressed completely in black and slumped in a stuffed chair, the Colonel reminded me of a heap of ashes. He had been evicted from the office building at 156 Fifth Avenue because of alleged "pro-American" activity and begged me to air his grievance in *The Christian Defender*. I obliged in order to gain his confidence. I learned that this retired reserve officer had addressed meetings of the American National-Socialist League in New York and had also unwittingly spoken at gatherings directed by Nazi spy, Colonel Fritz Duquesne, Viereck's friend.

After our initial meeting I visited Sanctuary at his home

and found that his friends ranged from General Moseley and Senator Wheeler to the Imperial Wizard of the Klan. Sanctuary's home was a Germania Bookstore in miniature, with nearly every scrap of fascist literature circulated in America available. I gathered so much evidence against the Colonel, all of which I wrote down in carefully prepared notes, that I can best illustrate with a few notes in diary form.

May 2, 1940: The Colonel had finished reading *The Eighth Crusade,* a book distributed by the Nazi *Fichte-Bund* and said he had enjoyed it immensely. I learned that Stahrenberg was now doing his printing.

September 24: Again in high spirits, the Colonel had spent three hours with General Moseley, in New York on a mysterious errand, and described him as "a prince of a fellow." Sanctuary was trying to sell Republican Party leaders his song on Willkie and also copies of his new opus, *The Roosevelt Saga.* He boasted that his speeches written for Jacob Thorkelson had been inserted in the *Congressional Record.* Together we mailed another speech of 5,000 words and an article to Winrod's *Defender* for which Sanctuary wrote regularly.

September 30: It made me happy to see him droopy and glum, his face the color of a mummy. Republican Party leaders had turned down his song and also his article, *Roosevelt and the Real Fifth Column.* He was stuck with ten thousand copies of *The Roosevelt Saga* and I found him wailing at the lack of "patriotism."

December 10: Claiming to be working with his friend, Joseph P. Kamp of the Constitutional Educational League, the Colonel observed that a wealthy Southerner had put up $5,000 for Kamp's printing of *The Fifth Column in the South.* I asked him about Seward Collins, one of the brain trusters of the American fascist movement whom he knew personally.

"Do Collins and Kamp know anything about the Jewish question?" I asked, to provoke an answer.

"Of course they do!"

"Then why don't they come out with it like you do?"

"They won't stick out their necks now because the time isn't ripe. They're helping the nationalist cause without taking such a risk. Only men like Joe McWilliams and James

True can talk anti-Jew and get away with it. We've got to save our big guns for later."

February 6, 1941: The Colonel showed me a stack of copies of the *Nationalist Newsletter* issued by the notorious American Nazi front known as The National Workers League of Detroit. He delegated me to induce McWilliams to buy quantity lots of *Planned Economy* by Mrs. Leslie Fry at a bargain price. Sanctuary told me that Senator Rush D. Holt had ordered fifty copies of *The Hidden Hand,* a typical bit of Naziesque propaganda printed on Stahrenberg's presses. He also confided that he received *World Service* regularly in addition to *News From Germany* and *Views From Germany.* The Nazi literature was addressed to "Mr. A. J. Sanktuary." At my request he gave me sample copies of the magazines and I also managed to obtain for the record one of the envelopes.

February 25, 1941: I found the Colonel in high spirits, just returned from Washington. "It was Sunday but Senator Wheeler was waiting for me in his offices," he said, "and we talked for forty-five minutes. The Senator certainly knows what is going on!" Sanctuary claimed to have visited *eleven* Congressmen and Senators, prominent among them he named Senator Nye and Ham Fish. He had called on Miss Cathrine Curtis, of Women Investors in America who was lobbying with Mrs. Dilling and Charles Hudson against the Lend-Lease Bill. The Colonel offered for sale fresh stocks of Japanese agent Ralph Townsend's *The High Cost of Hate,* as well as the *Protocols* and *The Octopus,* but I told him I had already bought my copies from the Christian Mobilizers.

Several months later I visited the Colonel again and he showed me a stack of the inflammatory leaflets *Your Crucifixion* which Stahrenberg had printed. He placed a quantity in my hands for distribution. Sanctuary had also just organized The Tocsin Publishers and its first book was a history of the Klan on which he had collaborated with a fellow colonel, Winfield Jones of Atlanta. I expressed surprise at Sanctuary's friendship with the Klan.

"They are one hundred per cent American," he explained. "They have been misunderstood, that's all." And when I asked how he had met Colonel Jones, Sanctuary replied: "General Moseley put me in touch with him."

MRS. LESLIE FRY

Major General George Van Horn Moseley, retired with a distinguished record, became involved in the first Nazi *putsch* ever attempted in America. Among those who victimized the politically innocent General was Mrs. Leslie Fry, twice listed on the *World Service* honor roll. I had found her friends wherever there was talk of the New Order. She even penetrated the D.A.R., for it was Mrs. Schuyler who loaned me the book endorsed by *World Service* titled *Waters Flowing Eastward*.

Mrs. Fry, alias Paquita Shishmarova, alias De Shishmareff, was the wife of a Czarist officer. After a sojourn in Germany, she went to London and served as a companion to Lady Queensborough. When her ladyship died, the British Secret Service expedited her departure to other shores. She came to America about 1936.

Here she established herself in Glendale, California and organized a nation-wide network of intrigue and propaganda. As liaison agent she used Henry D. Allen, an ex-convict. But she herself was under the orders of tall and taciturn Conrad Chapman who only rarely made public appearances. Supplied with plenty of cash, she founded the American League of Christian Women, the Militant Christian Patriots, the American Anti-Communist Federation and through the Nazi *Christian Free Press* honeycombed the country with Shishmareff Americanism.

She helped promote the fantastic Nazi revolutionary plot. The plot was the brain child of Baron Manfred Freiherr von Killinger, Consul General of San Francisco. Involved in the *putsch* were Deatherage, Chapman, Allen, Ulrich Fleischhauer of *World Service*, assorted Nazi emissaries who remained in the background and numerous American-born dupes. The threads ran through the German-American Bund, the Ku Klux Klan, Silver Shirts, Christian Front, Irish nationalist elements and many smaller groups. New York broker Dudley Pierrepont Gilbert (his family had been here since 1634) contributed $8,000 to start the ball rolling.

A general staff of thirteen men under a district leader was to be set up in the United States. "The quotas I have set," von Killinger wrote "are: three Germans (Nazi sympathy), three white Russians (anti-Soviet sympathy), three Italians (fascist sympathy), four Americans (Republican sympathy). All native-born or naturalized." To insure victory, von Killinger advocated the cultivation of sectional prejudices as a means of fomenting national disunity. "In each area we must study the composition of the population about us and agitate accordingly." A master board of strategy composed of five men including two of von Killinger's selection and 'three prominent Americans' was to direct the entire program. The plan further provided that . . .

. . . as each district is organized, the district's highest leaders should tie up with the high leaders of adjacent districts, and so on until national leaders are contacted by sectional leaders of Pacific, Rocky Mountain, North Central, South Central, North Atlantic, Mid-Atlantic and South-Atlantic areas. . . . It is a complicated web which the enemy [the United States Government] will find impossible to re-trace and stamp out.

The plot needed a "Man on Horseback." Killinger, Fry and Deatherage decided that General Moseley was their man. Personally I am convinced that Moseley knew nothing of the sinister plot and had no designs to committing treason, but like many other innocent Americans he was "taken in" by wily fascist propagandists. His sympathies, however, had endeared him to the "patriotic" gangsters, particularly his quoted remarks about sterilizing refugees from Europe, and his interview in the *Atlanta Journal* on February 25, 1940:

Democracy, hell! It's nothing but Communism. My motto is "Restore the Republic." A democracy pulls everything and everyone down to the level of an average and that makes it Communistic. . . . We don't want the mob rule of democracy.

Deatherage in the East and Mrs. Fry on the Coast helped popularize the General. Prompted by the network of Nazi strings the "patriotic" press from New York to Glendale saluted Moseley as the long awaited White Knight in Shining Armour. He was received throughout the country by an adoring multitude of Bundists, Klansmen, Silver Shirts and

Coughlinites. "Hail Moseley!" Edmondson headlined one of his *American Vigilante Bulletins:*

Millions of fighting Americans now informed as to The Cause of their suppression and suffering, impatiently await fearless, selfless able leadership to coalescence into a mighty liberation army. . . . Vigilant legions have been crying for "The Leader." Hail Moseley!

In New York the General spoke under the auspices of the *Patriot Digest.* The cream of New York's Park Avenue "patriots" served on the Committee of Honor: John B. Snow, Joseph P. Kamp, Allen Zoll, Mrs. A. Cressy Morrison, Fred R. Marvin, John Eoghan Kelly, John Cecil and Major William Lathrop Rich. The General was invited to speak before the New York Board of Trade and entertained at the home of Mrs. Rudyard Uzzell. Somewhat bewildered by the publicity and the motive behind it, he attended these functions wholly unaware that he was being groomed as the messiah of an American *der tag.* The befuddled General—who on September 7, 1939 wrote Joe McWilliams: "I am deeply impressed with you, your character, your energy and your ability. I want to be in the same camp . . ."—thought he was just being patriotic.

Suddenly hailed before the Dies Committee to answer for his "patriotism," Moseley made a pathetic spectacle of himself as he tried to portray the principles of the *Protocols* and the Nazi lies of Deatherage and Fry as "truth." Von Killinger's abortive *putsch* failed dismally and Mrs. Shishmarova, alias Fry, slipped back into Germany when the F.B.I. began looking for her. Deatherage and the other von Killinger tools also crawled back into their holes to await *der tag* under different leadership.

GEORGE E. DEATHERAGE

Mrs. Fry's friend, George E. Deatherage, was an engineer by profession and lived with the C. R. Barton family in a spacious country home high on College Hill, St. Albans, West Virginia. From here he directed his two organizations,

Knights of the White Camellia, and the American Nationalist
Confederation which, Deatherage claimed, in its heyday was
composed of a coalition of seventy-two fascist groups.

In 1938, the Confederation's *News Bulletin* carried the
notice: "This issue carries at the masthead our newly selected
emblem—the swastika, a real Christian Cross." Deatherage
was invited to attend the convention of *World Service* Quislings at Erfurt, but he could not forsake his "patriotic" preparations here so he wrote a lengthy article which was published in full in Fleischhauer's Nazi organ:

The American Nationalist Confederation has prepared and in-
forced constructive program of Nationalism which we hope all
decent Americans will accept in a nation-wide unified attempt to
solve our troubles. . . . As it [the swastika] brought Germany out
of the depths of despair, so it will bring us. . . . The issues will
be fought out in the streets.

Deatherage distributed Julius Streicher's *Der Stürmer*,
Hitler's speeches and vast quantities of propaganda sent him
from *World Service*. Not neglecting the American "patriots"
he recommended as "books which penetrate the fog," Mrs.
Dilling's and Mrs. Webster's works; the *Protocols;* James
True's and Joseph P. Kamp's leaflets. *The Truth About Spain*
by Dr. Paul Joseph Goebbels was mailed out in the same
envelope with *Battalions of Death* by Representative Clare E.
Hoffman, the literature of the super-patriotic American Coalition, and *Spain and the Christian Front* by Arnold Lunn.
Senator Robert R. Reynolds turned over to Deatherage a
mailbag containing more than one thousand of his speeches
for distribution among "patriots."

Adopting tactics of the Klan of which he was a member,
Deatherage decided to strike "terror and fear into the hearts
of many" by burning a swastika. He gave instructions in a
confidential leaflet to "Christian Leaders" urging the hours
between nine and eleven o'clock.

A high spot, overlooking the town or city should be chosen,
where it can be easily seen. Only a few men are needed to handle
it as the swastika should be built in sections, bolted in such a way
that it can be easily transported in a touring car.

Deatherage worked hard to integrate Canadian, American and Mexican Nazi cells. He formed the North and South American Fascist Union, helped unite six Canadian Nazi groups, including the largest among them, the Canadian National Christian Party, and was a close collaborator of Pelley, Kuhn and Reverend Winrod. Deatherage proved himself a tireless worker for the American Nazi cause.

CHARLES B. HUDSON

Hudson's historic statement at a Fry-Deatherage sponsored "Christian" Conference had been: "Most of the literature put out by the Christian Churches today is Communistic." I had already met the Omaha native fascist and *World Service* patriot at the June 7, 1939 meeting of the American Nationalist Party in New York. A short, fanatic, plump man with a bald pate, Hudson told the mob that he was proud to be "water boy to a man of the calibre of the General."

The episode he recounted went back to the time of General Moseley's appearance before the Dies Committee. Serving as major-domo and keeper-away-of-the-evil-spirits, Hudson hung onto the General like a shadow. When Moseley reached out for a glass of water Hudson suddenly snatched at the glass, dumped the contents with a shudder, filled a paper cup with fresh water and told mystified newspapermen: "The water might have been poisoned by the HIDDEN HAND."

From then on Charles B. Hudson became known as "Poison Cup Charlie." He was always the kind of a "patriot" who always saw poison plots and the HIDDEN HAND everywhere. Copies of his bulletin, *America in Danger* were filled with references to the HIDDEN HAND. The HIDDEN HAND (always capitalized) gave him the jitters. Not so humorous was the fact that he tutored a considerable following in the Midwest in the fundamentals of fascist Americanism.

Hudson's home-office became one of the major outposts for defeatist and appeasement propaganda in the Midwest. He promoted the obstructionist poisons of John B. Snow, James True, Sanctuary, Congressmen Thorkelson and Hoffman,

Father Coughlin, Joseph P. Kamp. Mrs. Fry, Mrs. Dilling, George E. Sullivan, a Washington Coughlinite attorney. Hudson was chief distributor of a scurrilous anti-Semitic volume, *The Octopus* by Reverend Frank Woodruff Johnson.

He was one of the first to distribute the infamous leaflet entitled *Your Crucifixion,* depicting "Uncle Sam," "Liberty" and "Justice" being crucified by Wendell Willkie, the President and members of the Cabinet while the "swelling tide of nationalism" (fascism) threatened to engulf the "internationalists." It was an extremely potent leaflet which suited Nazi aims perfectly.

Hudson ascribed to the Jews every calamity in American history—from the assassination of Lincoln to the Johnstown flood. His pet phrase, "Judeo-Socialistic-Communistic NU-DEAL Organized-Jewry-Finance World-War I" was later shortened to the "Synagogue of Satan." As Hitler's soldiers succumbed to ravages of the Russian Army and to typhus, Hudson once again saw work of the HIDDEN HAND and he warned the nation:

If preventative measures [are] not taken, our large cities too will be laid low by Typhus Epidemics, for we have absorbed "refugees" who carry the seeds of that Plague.

This was not so funny when judged by the number of impressionable and uninformed Americans who were impressed by the profound "truth" of his lies—the course prescribed by Hitler in his education for mass ignorance.

MRS. ELIZABETH DILLING

One of Hudson's closest workers and one particularly admired by Deatherage, was Mrs. Elizabeth Dilling who was also listed on the Nazi honor roll of "loyal Americans." She stands as a painfully acute symptom of the jittery decade since 1930. In her book, *The Red Network* she branded as "Communist" such institutions as the Y.M.C.A., the Federal Council of the Churches of Christ and the Civil Liberties Union. Reverend Harry Emerson Fosdick, John Dewey and Sinclair

Lewis were all Reds in her eyes. Even Monsignor John A. Ryan, professor of moral theology at Catholic University, did not escape her branding irons, while the Catholic Association for Internal Peace and the American Federation of Teachers were placed in the same category as the Communist Party.

Addressing a group of students at the University of Chicago, she cried out: "You're all guinea pigs of Stalin. The University of Chicago is a Red school." Anyone who does not see eye to eye with Mrs. Dilling, from the President down, is a Red. That's her formula.

As consultants for her book, Mrs. Dilling had the advice of super-expert-patriots (her own phrase), fascistic Mrs. Nesta Webster, who was held in high esteem by *World Service;* Walter S. Steel, "manager of the 100-percenters' *National Republic* magazine," a friend of Prescott Dennett, and Harry A. Jung, a wholesale distributor of the *Protocols* in Chicago. It is little wonder that with such super-patriotic help her views should take on a distinct fascist hue. Speaking of fascism, she wrote in her *Red Network:*

It seeks a harmony between all classes and concedes to industrialists, white collar, professional, as well as laboring workers, a place in the social order as necessary parts, not "class enemies" of the whole, but under State control. It defends some property rights and religion. . . . Fascism in Italy is not anti-Semitic.

Because of her indiscriminate and wild-eyed Red-baiting and her listing of true Liberals and scientists as "Communists," *The Red Network* became a top vehicle for fascist propaganda, along with *Social Justice* and Pelley's *Liberation.* Mrs. Dilling made several trips to Germany, each shrouded in mystery. When she returned in 1938 she established the Patriotic Research Bureau, dedicating it to "the defense of Christianity and Americanism." Then she set to evangelizing America, travelling from coast-to-coast to falsify and defame Democracy. She spoke for Allen Zoll's American Patriots, and mailed me copies of *Your Crucifixion* and other vicious anti-Jewish stickers. One of her main devices of promoting fascism was to split hairs on definitions:

Our U.S.A. form of government is a Republic, not a democracy, the difference being between government by checked and balanced Constitutional law and representatives, or government by direct "mobocracy."

Her crackpot Red-baiting and slurs on Democracy by no means found praise in the *Deutscher Weckruf* alone. Unfortunately, her brand of "patriotism" had many adherents among Park Avenue "patriots" and also among Congressmen. Writing of a trip she made to New York, Mrs. Dilling betrayed her wealthy friends:

I enjoyed a data-collecting, gabfesting expedition with my friend, Joseph P. Kamp. . . . The A. Cressy Morrisons, one of the dearest and finest couples I know live in a beautiful Park Avenue apartment, where I visited them, keep drained of funds trying to support every phase of the patriotic movement; . . . I briefly addressed an assembly at a tea as the guest of my patriotic friends, Reverend Hunt and Mrs. Roberta Tubman. In a beautiful drawing room . . . a crowd of society folk were assembled. . . .

My "Red-baiter" friend, John Snow, brought an interesting lawyer to see me. . . . I have new proof that [N. Y. District Attorney] Dewey was in constant communication with the notorious Red American Civil Liberties Union. . . . From a group including Merwin K. Hart, head of the New York State Economic Council, and Roscoe Peacock, foe of Red Educators, I rushed to the home of Miss Cathrine Curtis, who heads Women Investors in America. I had lunch with her and her big burly assistant, Mike Ahearn, a brilliant writer with whom, formerly, Albert [Mr. Dilling] and I visited the office of a Congressman.

Congressmen, Senators, wealthy Park Avenue fascists—these were Mrs. Dilling's real friends and backers, and not the "crackpots" she was accused of harboring. I have learned never to minimize the role of any so-called crackpot. Each has a role to play, each a niche to fill in Hitler's blueprint for America. In Mrs. Dilling's bulletins there was hardly a line of censure against Nazism. She absolved it of all guilt—and heaped abuse on the President, the Jews, the British, the Communists, Democracy. Hitler was an angel.

JAMES TRUE

No "patriot" who visited Washington would think of passing up James True, friend of Mrs. Dilling. Like his friend, Sanctuary, there was not a fascist worth his salt with whom True hadn't worked. When I visited him I found a white-haired septuagenarian who looked like a minister. But in the upper right-hand corner of his desk lay an automatic pistol ready for action and on the wall hanging by a leather strap, was the "kike-killer." It resembled a policeman's nightstick, but it was shorter and more rounded. It came in two sizes— one for the ladies. True had actually obtained a patent for it— Number 2,026,077.

Joe McWilliams and I visited True together. I had accompanied Joe and his gang of about fifty select "patriots" in September, 1939, to protest against "war mongering" by Congress. The two super-patriots were mutually attracted and talked intimately while I listened. Both looked upon Moseley and Lindbergh as presidential timber on a third party ticket and both thought highly of the Bund.

"God bless you, my boy," True told McWilliams as we left. I, too, came in for a share of the honors. "I like to see fine young men like you take an interest in their country. I wish we had many more like you," True said, patting my shoulder.

True was editor of the *Industrial Control Reports*, a bulletin serving the American Fascist cause since July 10, 1933. The *Reports* served as fascist guideposts because True often got the party line first, even scooping the *Deutscher Weckruf*. True was the eyes and ears of patrioteers, serving as lookout-man for Pelley, Winrod, Jung, Joseph P. Kamp, Deatherage and countless others with all of whom he exchanged information. No major plan was carried through without True's advice. "All honest and informed Americans are with the German-American Bund heart and soul in their educational program," he wrote. And he distributed not only German propaganda, but also that of the British Union of Fascists. And he was not averse to putting in a good word for the Japanese: "Japan should not be condemned for cleaning out Communism in China," he asserted.

James True told me that he had "three or four guns around the house." He tried to do business in the trafficking of firearms by taking Henry D. Allen, Mrs. Fry's contact man and runner between the Gold Shirts of Mexico and American Nazis into his confidence. True wrote Allen:

If your friends want some pea shooters, I have connections now for any quantity and at the right price. They are United States standard plus.

True was the first to apply the fascist-nationalist phrase America First when in August, 1934 he organized America First, Inc. "for the protection of the Constitution, American Industry, and individual enterprise." Shortly after, however, he bared his truer sentiments: ". . . Fascism is the answer . . . it is the last defense of Christian capitalism."

True defended fascism—the *arch enemy* of capitalism! and his duped followers took him at his word.

ROBERT EDWARD EDMONDSON

With his friend James True, Robert Edward Edmondson held a ranking place on the *World Service* scroll of honor. He hung out his shingle the year Hitler came to power. His base of operations was first in New York, then later a hide-out in the Pocono Mountains of Pennsylvania. His output as Nazi pamphleteer was terrific. "Patriots" were snowed under by a series of *Vigilante Bulletins* with more than 400 different titles. One of them was directed against J. Edgar Hoover who had dared say ". . . vigilantes, no matter in what manner they act or what ideals they proclaim, are un-American, un-patriotic and subversive." Edmondson bristled back at Mr. Hoover's "dogma," called it "repugnant to fundamentals of the nation. . . ."

In the interest of Nazi patriotism, Edmondson undertook to "prove" the President's "Jewish Ancestry," and that Secretary of Labor Frances Perkins' real name was Wutzki or Lazanski. He wasn't sure which. Eventually Miss Perkins wrote Edmondson that she was descended from the revolutionary James Otis, with nary a Wutzki or Lazanski in her ancestry.

When he was unable to accept the invitation to attend the *World Service* Congress in Germany in 1937, thoughtfully Colonel Ulrich Fleischhauer sent him a glowing letter bearing the signatures of the Quisling delegates present:

We are sending you this letter to show you that we are thinking of you and admire you for your tenacity and great moral courage in fighting this greatest of all fights against Jew domination of all that we hold noble and sacred.

To which Edmondson replied:

I have received your fraternal greetings containing signatures of the Representatives of twenty-two Nations in successful convention assembled, endorsing my crusade in behalf of Free Speech and National Patriotism. . . . This unqualifiedly generous testimonial of commendation from the highest assembly of our noble Cause of Liberation has overwhelmed me, who am but a humble instrument. On with the self-preservation fight. . . . Pro Deo, Pro Patria!

In 1938 Edmondson was hailed to court for slandering American Jewry. Judge James Garrett Wallace, who had no sympathy for the defendant, declared: "We must suffer the demagogue and charlatan in order to make certain that we do not limit or restrain the honest commentator on public affairs." He held that charges of libel or slander were valid only when committed against a specific organization or individual, but not against a religious or racial group, whereupon Edmondson redubled his efforts.

In one of his letters, Edmondson wrote me:

All my time is given free to this great movement for God, Home and Country. . . . Shall be glad to co-operate pro-patria in any way possible. Tell that to Mr. McWilliams. . . . Command me in this great fight.

Edmondson was that kind of a man—used to being commanded!

WILLIAM KULLGREN

Linked to Edmondson in the bonds of "patriotic" friendship was William Kullgren—who trafficked in "astrological prophecy" by publishing a monthly super-patriotic magazine known as *The Beacon Light*. In Kullgren America had a pea-size reproduction of Goebbels, who we are told is Hitler's astrological prophet. But the prophecies of the Seer of Atascadero, California, were in strict keeping with fascist propaganda tradition.

Kullgren let it be known to the faithful that Hitler "in the role of an avenging angel would make a lightning strike at Russia and reach Moscow"—during 1940! Kullgren followed the rather unique expedient among American Nazis by placing the blame for defeatist, anti-democratic, anti-Semitic, violently Nazi and appeasement propaganda on the heavens.

In the same vein, Kullgren let it be known that "Willkie is going to be elected by a very close margin," because he was "as independent as a hog on ice," also "the cage or net is yet to be made that will trap him." But the real reason that Willkie would win was (now we go into profound trade secrets):

Uranus conjoined to Moon and Trine to Sun would make him very quick on the upgrade, but he [Willkie] also has Mars in good aspect to Mercury, and Mars is the fiery independent sign of Sagittarius.

Kullgren maintained one of the largest subversive outlets on the West coast. He peddled the *Protocols* and offered for sale, at bargain prices, nearly 250 Nazi party-line titles ranging from Congressmen Hoffman's and McFadden's speeches in the *Congressional Record*, selling for a few cents to Nesta H. Webster's *Secret Societies and Subversive Movements* which retailed for $7. Kullgren rendered glowing tribute to Congressman Stephen A. Day's book and promoted the projects of Flanders Hall; those of the Constitutional Educational League; those by Arnold S. Leese, notorious British fascist author of *Jewish Ritual Murder*. The un-American mouthings of Mrs. Dilling, Winrod and Japanese agent Ralph Townsend, were best sellers.

Kullgren started his wishful prophecies in 1933 and since then his acquaintances among Nazis have become worldwide. He entertained Captain Henry H. Beamish, the "Henlein of South Africa" at his home, and said of Edmondson:

"He has done more to awaken America to the diabolical Jew control than any other man in America, and I honor him for it." Kullgren named as his "co-workers" Sanctuary, Mrs. Dilling, Hudson, Deatherage, Charles W. Phillips, editor of *The Individualist* and "scores of others," including John B. Trevor, President of the American Coalition. Kullgren frequently reprinted Trevor's bulletins.

Resorting to the art of ancient soothsayers, Kullgren gave out health advice, sold fruit-juice extractors, doled out investment counsel and printed "preparation articles" in which he urged disciples to prepare for *der tag!*

Friends, we have all got to discipline ourselves very severely if we are going to fit into the New Order; and that applies just as much to me as it does to you. The point is, I want you to start weaning yourself away from the habits of a debauched civilization such as we have today. . . . Don't you think it's time we got religion?

Kullgren, who called himself "an educator, not a butcher" also insisted on his honesty. "I love the truth more than all the property and possessions in the world, so I do not regret sacrifices. . . . I still have my self-respect, and that to me is priceless, and cannot be bought." His followers believed implicitly in his "patriotism," his Naziesque "prophecies" and his native fascism and supported him year after year.

GEORGE W. CHRISTIANS

A collaborator with Deatherage, a friend of Harry A. Jung and Oscar Pfaus, an espionage agent, George W. Christians of Chattanooga, Tennessee, was an odd combination of comedian and sinister revolutionist. Secret Service men kept him under surveillance when he threatened to cut off electric power in Chattanooga the night the President was to arrive. "Lots of things can happen in the dark," he said. He minced no words:

The Crusader White Shirts, known as the American Fascists, is a military auxiliary of the Crusaders for Economic Liberty and is organized to fight for the same objectives. It embraces the

Fascist idea of personal leadership, unity, force, drama and nationalism. It is opposed to dictatorship.

With a toothbrush mustache that resembled Hitler's, George
W. Christians walked about in an elaborately decorated white
shirt and a sprawling Crusaders' cross running down the
length of the buttons. Letterheads of Christians' multiple organizations were decorated with the Statue of Liberty,
crossed American flags, a torch spouting red, white, blue
flame. And he often used green and brown colored typewriter ribbons for his letters. With characteristic frankness,
Christians once issued orders, to whom it may concern, to
seize control of the Government:

The first objective should be to take control of the local government in the following manner: March in military formation
to and surround the government buildings. Then, by sheer numbers and a patriotic appeal, force the officials to accept and act
under the direction of an economic adviser appointed by the
President of the C.F.E.L. [Crusaders for Economic Liberty].
This adviser's first duty will be to repudiate the public debt.

In *The Strategy of Terror* Edmond Taylor tells how the
systematic cultivation of a spirit of rebellion and disrespect
for authority were integral to Nazi propaganda. And Christians exemplified it well. Owner of the American Asphalt
Grouting Company, Christians did not depend on the racket
for a living. He was not anti-Semitic, but was strongly anti-
Catholic and circulated tracts which read "Kick the Roman
Catholic Political Corruption out of Our Halls of Government."

WILLIAM DUDLEY PELLEY

Once called "the most dangerous man in America," William Dudley Pelley organized his Silver Shirt storm troopers
the day after Hitler seized power. He then founded a spurious
Galahad College in Asheville, North Carolina, for which he
sold unregistered stock. He was convicted for felony and lost
his citizenship for four years.

It did not disturb Pelley. In 1936 he moved to Seattle to
run for President on the Christian Party ticket, backed mainly

by Nazi funds. For campaign manager he appointed one
W. W. McDonald, better known in Seattle as "Twitcher
McDonald" because of a nervous disorder which caused him
to tremble and shake, especially when frightened. McDonald
had one arm. His appearance was slovenly and he earned a
precarious living peddling newspapers. As campaign manager
of the Christian Party his most profound—and only recorded
remark—was:

"Jews gotta be wiped out!"

Pelley's campaign cry was: "Christ or Chaos!" Another
variation was: "For Christ and Constitution." His appeal: "I
am calling on every Gentile in these prostrate United States
to form with me an overwhelming juggernaut . . . for Christian government."

Speaking before the German-American Folk Union in Seattle, he asserted: "The time has come for an American Hitler
and a pogrom." He then confided: "When I'm President I'll
incorporate the Silver Shirts into a combination of Federal
army and police force. I'm going to do away with the Department of Justice entirely."

Pelley's Fellowship Press at Asheville was equipped to turn
out 30,000 propaganda bullets a day. He published an extensive list of seditious booklets and plastered the country with
them. His *Liberation* became notorious and was *must* reading
for every American Nazi who could afford ten cents. Its sales
ranked next to *Social Justice* and Winrod's *Defender*. Early
in 1941 Pelley ended the ignoble career of *Liberation* and
started *Roll Call*, "The Voice of the Loyal Opposition." It
was a roll call to appeasers who were flocking to the America
First Committee. "Keep America Out of War" became
Pelley's slogan and the sabotaging of defense legislation his
aim. Senators Wheeler and Nye, Congressmen Fish, Day,
Thorkelson and the America First Committee were showered
with praise and Lindbergh was worshipped as the up-and-
coming fuehrer.

No nickel-and-dime revolutionary, Pelley rarely complained of a shortage of funds. From September, 1937 to July,
1939 the Dies Committee estimated that he received at least
$166,000. A wealthy woman in Massachusetts sent him $3,000
while George B. Fisher of Darien, Connecticut remitted at

least $4,800 in checks. Complacent Americans would not have
dismissed Pelley as crackpot if they had paused to look at the
corrosive effect of his revolutionary literature and Nazi lies
on the minds of impressionable Americans.

EDWARD JAMES SMYTHE

Flames from the wooden cross, forty feet high crackled
into the night throwing lurid shadows on the participants below, some of whom were dressed in hooded white robes,
others in the gray uniforms of the German-American Bund.
The scene took place at Bund Camp Nordland in New Jersey
on August 18, 1940 when the Klan staged a "monster anti-
war, pro-American mass meeting" jointly with the Bund.

Members of the Christian Mobilizers and the Christian
Front who came with me restrained themselves with difficulty
as Klansmen berated "Romanism," called Catholics "dumb
ring-kissers" and linked nuns and priests with the time-worn
canards. I was not surprised at the parallel between the Bund
attack on the Jews and the Klan attack on Catholics:

"Whatever power or money the Jews had, has been con-
fiscated. But a world-wide militant Catholic organization
directed from Rome remains a sinister threat to our Americanism."

By mid-afternoon 3,500 Klansmen and Bundists had assembled at Camp Nordland. The Reverend Edward J. Young, a
flabby man in his fifties, declared himself to be for "American
Americanism and no other brand." Edward James Smythe
appeared on the platform dressed in a khaki shirt and black
necktie and gushed:

"Fritz Kuhn and I have tried for three long years to bring
about a meeting like this, but it never worked out till this
year. I'm not asking any credit for it. It's just my patriotic
duty on behalf of my country. Dear Fritz is not in our midst
today; God bless him. His only crime was in trying to bring
friendship between the United States and the German
dominion. The heart of every Christian is with you, Fritz, my
friend, I shall always remember our pleasant associations.
They go back to the days of the Friends of the New Germany."

I had seen Smythe at many Bund, Mobilizer and Christian Front meetings. I had heard him on street corners. I had smelled his whiskey breath. A rowdy sort, with thick leather neck and florid face, I had watched him write his weekly column for *Publicity*, the fascist sheet published at Wichita, Kansas. Smythe had committed every political vice permitted under the slogan "Christian-American-Patriotism." As head of the Protestant War Veterans, he had lauded Father Coughlin on one hand and denounced the Roman Catholic Church on the other. Smythe was a standard fixture in the Nazi underworld in which I moved.

Smythe was followed on the platform by August Klapprott. Speaking with a thick German accent, the vice-president of the Bund shouted:

"When Arthur Bell, your Grand Giant, and Mr. Smythe asked us about using Camp Nordland for this patriotic meeting, we decided to let them have it because of the common bond between us. The principles of the Bund and the principles of the Klan are the same."

The Grand Giant extended his hand to the *Bundesführer*, and symbolized the merging of international fascism with the nationalist, or American brand of fascism.

Fantastic, isn't it?

CHAPTER IX

HITLER AND HIROHITO IN HARLEM

> "If the United States is to include subject and
> ruler peoples, then let us be honest about it and
> change the Constitution and make it plain that Ne-
> groes cannot share the privileges of the white peo-
> ple. . . . If it [Democracy] is right, then let us dare
> to make it true."
>
> PEARL BUCK

FANTASTIC AS IT SEEMS, Hitler's agents invaded Harlem—New York's Negro section. Despite its garishly lighted avenues and multitudinous taverns which are the scenes of noisy revelry until dawn, more than 350,000 Negroes live in tenements foul beyond description, and I regard Harlem as one of the most tragic "cities" in the United States; a blot on our Democracy.

Harlem Negroes had little to look forward to. Jobs for the men were few. Discrimination was rife. Streets teemed with young girls willing to sell themselves to passers-by.

New York newspapers periodically sensationalized a Harlem "crime wave." Mugging and robbery were committed in daylight—let alone at night. Negro youths started on their crime careers while still in their teens, giving Harlemites—the majority of whom were law-abiding—a black eye.

For want of anything better, vigorous young Negroes lounged around taverns, pool-rooms and hallways. Their days began at midnight. Discontented, frustrated, resentful, idle men were ideal material for fascism—and fascist agents knew it. And the Negro, oppressed, clannish, emotional, himself a victim of racialism, was easily brutalized by exhortations to violence.

It was on September 23, 1940, that I first heard "Heil Hitler" shouted out in Harlem. There were a dozen street speakers with their dark groups of listeners stretched from 114th Street to 135th Street on Lenox Avenue. They were fanatic speakers, some of them illiterate, others intelligent and persuasive—all of them angrily denouncing Democracy and white man rule. Each was mounted on a stand and displayed an American flag, as required by law.

Arthur Reid, director of the African Progressive Business League shouted. "I like Hitler . . . yeah, I like Hitler for what he is doin'. He is doin' all right. Let the white man kill his brother white man. It'll leave fewer whites to bother with later—when the black man can step in and get justice for himself."

His face distorted by hate, Ras de Killer yelled: "I was happy to see Hitler declare war on the white man. I'm mighty happy to see him winning." Lashing against miscegenation, he ended his speech with: "When I sleep I want to sleep with a woman of my own blood. I don't want no white woman to sleep with."

At 131st Street and Lenox Avenue I was attracted by a large crowd gathered around a woman speaker: "Do as Japan does. Copy like she does. She don't preach no social equality stuff. There ain't no such thing. She just walks in and takes what she wants. Be like her. Step up and take your freedom. Don't you believe all them things about brotherhood. There ain't no brotherhood for the colored man, except in his own kind. The white man can never do you no good."

The mob applauded her, glared at me—the only white man in their midst—and compelled me to applaud loudly with the rest.

I joined one of the groups that formed after she had come down from the platform at eleven P.M., as the law compelled. One of the Negroes exclaimed:

"Hitler's doing things because he has to. Somebody has gotta do the job and he is doin' it."

"There'll be a change. And it's coming now," said a second Negro. "I'll fight for it with all I got. There'll be mighty few white folks left after it's over. Maybe I won't see the day but my children will."

"Yes, you will too," put in the first. "Inside of five years you'll see the fighting goin' on in this country. Man, I'll fight like I never fought befo'. There'll be race riots like they never was."

"We'll have to start all over again. Africa belongs to us and that's where we want to go. America for the Americans, Asia for the Asiatics and Africa for us Africans. Them is my principles," another put in.

Other nights I listened to speakers at the corner of 117th Street and Lenox Avenue—which at the time was perhaps the most congested red light district in New York. Anyone who looked as though he had a dollar on his person was accosted at least a dozen times from the corner of 116th to 119th Street. The district was fertile ground for Nazi propagandists.

Carlos Cooks, a forceful youth haranguing a large crowd, shouted in the half light of a street corner lamp:

"Jews are all Communist, and Communism wants to exploit the Negro just like the white man. I wouldn't lift my finger to save a Jew. . . . We came here against our will. They brought us here as slaves and they've treated us as slaves. We owe nothing to America. America owes everything to us. This isn't my culture. Cooks isn't my name. This isn't my home. My home and my culture and my name are in Africa. I'm a foreigner here.

"I'm a persecuted man here. I'm hated here. But I tell you what I am right now—I am a black nationalist: and I want the colored people to live like colored people. I want colored people to have their own civilization, their own government, their own cities, their own officials. I want the black man to go back to Africa, and I'll back up anybody that says 'Africa for the Africans.'"

Cooks operated the African Pioneering Syndicate, Inc. Its purpose was to initiate commercial relations with Africa and devote the proceeds to the welfare of the black man and the resettlement of the Negro. One of the more intelligent fascist leaders in Harlem, he published *The Street Speaker*—violently fascist, anti-British, anti-White. Cooks also maintained a Department for Racial Enlightenment, with headquarters in a large basement hall on St. Nicholas Avenue. He made no secret of his Axis leanings:

I reject completely the theory that the Negro must give unquestioning obedience to the State and its leaders. We feel no enmity with people of the totalitarian powers, especially Japan. The Japanese have never lynched or exploited the Negro. . . .

Between Nazism and Democracy, the two evils, I would choose Nazism, for the Blacks can sink no lower than they have today in America.

Of the many Negro fascists Samuel W. Daniels was the most frightening at close range. I didn't know this when I wrote Daniels, inclosing copies of *The Christian Defender* and asking for back numbers of his magazine *Negro Youth*. Daniels sent me an urgent letter saying that he wanted to see me. I had never met him before and his plea made me somewhat suspicious.

None the less, I went up to his room at 2286 Seventh Avenue. It was a big room, with a bed, desk, chair and newspapers scattered on the floor. Daniels, a fierce powerfully built Negro, subjected me to a wild oratorical barrage, during which he paced back and forth in the room and gesticulated with massive fists not more than six inches from my nose.

"The injustices of the British against Negroes are crying out to be avenged," he roared and lashed himself with a passionate defense of the Negro as he cried out:

"The blacker the Negro the finer the Negro. The blacker the Negro, the greater credit he is to his race. Mulattoes are bastards. They will side with the white man. They are enemies of the black Negro. We want an empire of Blacks in Africa. We want nationhood based exclusively on black men. The salvation of my race is a religion with me. What Hitler said about the nobility of the Aryans, also applies about the nobility of the Negro."

As he was getting more and more heated by the persuasiveness of his own oratory and his huge fist edged nearer to my nose and denture, I asked him bluntly why he had asked me to come up.

"I'll tell you why," he said, toning down. "I want you to go to your wealthy white friends, those who feel as we do about nationalism and get their financial help so I can carry on with my work. I want to liberate the Negroes of the world. I want them to have the liberty and the nationhood they deserve! I want the white man to help me."

I promised to visit my wealthy white friends on behalf of Samuel W. Daniels. After leaving him I wandered through the streets of Harlem listening to the voice of Nazism among this oppressed and tragic people, trying to trace the propaganda source, trying to trail the master propagandists who were encouraging political fascism in the minds of the Negro leaders. I wanted to know who was pulling the strings.

I did not find the answer until I met Robert Jordan the night of September 27, 1940. Listening to a volatile speaker on the outer fringe of the mob was a short, powerfully built Negro, with flat nose and sharp, fierce features. After Cooks had closed his meeting and the usual huddled groups had formed, I joined them and wiggled myself into the conversation. A few anti-Semitic phrases and the fascist slogans I had heard from Harlem's own black fuehrers were enough to draw out the opinions of the man I learned later was Robert Jordan.

The magic of *The Christian Defender* and my association with Joe McWilliams whom Jordan admired, soon established a friendly basis. Before long Jordan was sitting beside me in a neighborhood café and was telling me his personal history. A West Indian by birth, forty-one years of age, he had served as sailor with the Nippon Yusen Kaisha, Japan's largest steamship company. In 1935 he had visited Germany. That same year he had organized the Ethiopian Pacific Movement, Inc., and proudly wired Hitler that the Negro people of the world were with him in his fight against injustice.

"Why should I be one," Jordan grunted, when I asked if he was a citizen.

Before going to Germany he had stopped in London, where he was arrested for anti-British agitation. He boasted of his personal friendship with Jawaharlal Nehru, former president of the All-India Congress who, Jordan claimed, had received him with open arms. Jordan was violently anti-British and anti-Semitic and repeated the Nazi mouthings that the British Empire was ruled by "International Jews."

I met Jordan frequently after our initial meeting and listened to his plans for an African Empire. He told me of his contempt for Democracy, and there was not the slightest doubt in his mind that the Axis would defeat the Democracies. He prophesied that Japan would eventually declare war on the

United States and asserted that Japan was far more powerful than Americans realized.

"They'll find that Japan is no push-over. I ought to know."

"What side will Negroes take in such an event?" I asked.

"Japan's," Jordan declared, "Japan is the black man's friend. Racially, Japan is the same as the Negroes. At one time all Japanese were black people."

He advanced the fantastic explanation that the inhabitants of India, Burma, Malaya and the Pacific Islands belonged to the "dark races" of the world and constituted a vast Negro Empire linked by common blood ties. Jordan explained that Japan constituted the "master race" of the Far East.

"Japan is destined to rule all of the Far East," he said mystically. "It is her divine mission. If American Negroes looked ahead they would fight for the interest of Japan, the leading dark nation. Japan's mission is to save the darker races of the world from Communism, just as Hitler's job is to save the White races in the west from Communism."

Jordan's historical and anthropological data were based on instructions by representatives of the Black Dragon Society here. But he believed in it. Tens of thousands of other Negroes believed in it and thousands propagated it. And like them, Jordan also believed in Hitler's and Hirohito's other lies that the Axis would "liberate" and give complete independence to the Negro.

I decided to write to the Reverend John Cole McKim, a former resident of Japan for many years, chairman of an America First Committee chapter and columnist for the Japanese organ, *The Japanese American Review*, to ask whether Japan intended to "liberate" Negroes if she were in a position to do so. This Japanese sympathizer wrote back:

I am sorry to disappoint your coloured friends: but I am sure that the case is as I have stated it. The Japanese do not regard themselves as a particularly coloured race. They consider themselves as at least equal to all others and superior to most. They are not, in fact, darker than Europeans taken as a whole. . . .

Certainly they would be astounded at the suggestion that they had any sort of racial community with Africans; or are racially nearer to them than Europeans are. As a matter of fact, they are not. Being now at war with us they might be glad to encourage and to take advantage of any discord that Afro-Americans might create: but they would only be making tools of them. I am quite certain that Afro-Americans have nothing to gain from a Japanese victory and everything to lose. . . . That is a very detached opinion: I have no sentiments either way concerning Negroes: but I should be sorry to see them get into trouble.

None the less, Jordan spoke nightly on Lenox Avenue and 116th Street, spreading Hirohito's blatant propaganda. And because of the violence and brutal directness of his language, the lavish promises he made of "revenge" on the hour of "Japanese liberation of the black man," the crowds he drew were larger than those of any other Negro speaker. I did not see Jordan for a while after this, and one day received a note from him which read:

I would suggest that you call to see me Thursday evening at eight o'clock. I have a lot of information for you. I have already started to work for the New Order. Please let me know when I will see you, if for any reason you cannot make it Thursday.

The Wednesday before our meeting, I met him unexpectedly at the campaign headquarters of William T. Goodwin, the "Christian Front candidate" for New York Mayor. Asked what he was doing there, Jordan explained that he wanted to rally the Ethiopian Pacific Movement behind Goodwin's nomination. Jordan also informed me that he had met and been highly commended for his work by John Eoghan Kelly, the Christian Front organizer.

Joe Hartery, "the little Napoleon" on Joe McWilliams' speakers bureau, addressed one of Jordan's outdoor meetings, quoted extensively from the literature of the America First Committee and distributed it to the crowd. Hartery also spoke regularly at Jordan's indoor meetings using the alias Ashley.

Shortly afterwards he and Jordan addressed a Christian Front meeting in the Italian section of New York, not far from Stahrenberg's former office on 116th Street. That collaboration between white and black fascists was being promoted by the fascist hierarchy was proved again when a certain Dr. Mills, a speaker for the Christian Mobilizers, addressed one of Jordan's meetings. From that time on Jordan climbed socially and politically. He visited the American Review Bookshop operated by fascist Seward Collins.

"How did you learn about the bookshop?" I demanded.

"I was asked to come down," Jordan answered. "Conrad Grieb, the office manager, sent for me. He heard me speak the other night and liked the way I talked."

"What else did Grieb say when you saw him?" I asked.

"We talked about Negro nationalism," Jordan answered. "He knew all about Marcus Garvey and had the Negro nationalist movement down pat. It was a pleasure to talk to him. He knew everything."

"Did you see Collins?" I asked.

"Collins was away," Jordan answered. "But Grieb took down my name and address and will write me as soon as Collins comes back."

On his second visit to the American Review Bookshop, Jordan told me he had talked with Seward Collins about publishing a leaflet, to be financed by Collins but to bear Jordan's name. Collins had expressed great interest in the promotion of a dynamic Negro fascist movement and Jordan had answered that American Negroes could be aroused easily "with enough money and some brains." Collins had sounded out Jordan on his South American contacts, particularly in Puerto Rico and the West Indies. Jordan had boasted of an extensive network of friends in the West Indies and told Collins he could easily establish contact with South American nationalists on short notice.

"Collins asked me to see him again after he got a chance to think over the whole thing," Jordan said proudly.

One day Jordan informed me with glee that the Japanese Christian Association had given him a fine letter of recommendation to the Japan Institute, the central Japanese propaganda agency maintaining the Japanese Library of Information in luxurious offices in Rockefeller Center. When Jordan returned from that visit he reported that he had been received cordially by its director, given the "run of the place" and sent home with a stack of Japanese propaganda. Among the books he had got were: *Manchukuo Today; Japan's Diplomacy, Its Aims and Principles;* and *Japan—Her Cultural Development.*

After this initial meeting Jordan visited the Japan Institute frequently, to read and study and engage the director in quiet conversation.

From Jordan I learned of Japan's "B" and "BB" plans. "B" stood for Buddhist. He explained that it was Japan's strategy in the event of war to use the Buddhist priests throughout India, Burma and Malaya to act as a native "fifth column."

"If war comes Japan is ready. The Buddhist priests are already under orders. They don't want white rule any more than the Africans. They will let the Japanese soldiers infiltrate secretly, will hide them in temples, dress them up like natives and give them all the guns they need. We Negroes are a part of the Black Brotherhood," Jordan went on. "This is a racial war—the Whites against the Blacks. Japan will protect us. Japan will fight for us. We will fight for Japan, because Japan is our only friend."

"What is the 'BB' plan?" I asked this "Black Aryan."

"The Black Brotherhood plan," he explained, "applies to the United States. It is Japan's plan to use the Negro. . . ."

He paused, looked at me sharply and said: "I've said enough." He would talk no more that day. But he did talk the next day. After a drink he needed little prodding to brag about the "confidence" the Japs had in him to lead an American Negro fifth column to revolt.

After his visits to the Japan Institute Jordan inaugurated a series of indoor meetings. I was handed an application for membership in the Ethiopian Pacific Movement the first night I attended. Under "Aims" I read:

To disseminate truth based upon historical knowledge; to study with an open mind the struggle between the New Order and Old and to secure for our selves and posterity the rights and privileges guaranteed under the U. S. Constitution.

I was one of the few white men among 250 Negroes allowed to attend the meeting. The night was hot. The passions of the Negroes around me mounted as the night wore on. I sat next to a fat burly Negro who sneered at me. I thought of the night I was beaten up at the Mobilizer meeting. I was completely encircled by zealot Negroes, their passions rising by the minute. I thought of expressing some particularly vicious and loud anti-Semitic remarks during the frequent periods of applause. From then on I became "pals" with the burly Negro next to me. "It's those sonovabitch Jews," he kept repeating for the rest of the night.

Time and again Jordan evoked loud cheering at the mention of Hitler's name, but the loudest noise was reserved when he mentioned the "Japanese brothers."

"Japan wants to liberate the black man, and give Africa to the Africans. . . . We black people are with Hitler. . . . Hitler loves us; the Axis powers are fighting our battle for us. They will take Africa from the British and give it to the Africans who deserve to have it."

Despite the assurance of friendship by the anti-Semitic Negro next to me, I became uneasy when Jordan went into violent tirades against all white people and American Democracy in particular. Purely in self-defense I applauded wildly and conspicuously as Jordan yelled:

"Every white man is your enemy. No white man is ever a Negro's friend. Don't let 'em get next to you. Kill them before they do that. Give him his medicine. . . . The only hope for the black man is to collaborate with the Japanese."

After that meeting I noticed that Jordan regretted having talked too freely to me. His Japanese friends on the Black Dragon Society had no doubt warned him against all whites, without exception. Several incidents, such as the time I became violently ill after a cup of coffee, caused me to suspect foul work. I took it as a warning to keep away. I did not want to be mugged and my body hung in a dark alley. I made sure that Federal authorities were aware of the explosive situation in Harlem, and trusting them to do an infinitely better job of watching Jordan and his colleagues than I ever could, I stayed away from Harlem for a while.

The Ethiopian Pacific Mov., Inc.

AIMS :   To dissiminate truth based upon historical knowledge; to study with an open mind the struggle between the New Order and Old and to secure for our selves and posterity the rights and privileges guaranteed under the U. S. Constitution.

CHAPTER X

POISON IN THE PULPIT

"In this way I believe I am acting in the spirit of
the Almighty Creator; by opposing the Jew I am
fighting for the Lord's work."

ADOLF HITLER

ONE NIGHT IN November, 1940, my constant ringing of the
doorbell of an apartment on the New York West Side brought
out a man in his late sixties, with benign white hair and whisk-
ers. When I had told him my name he grabbed my hand and
walked me to his study—one of the most unkempt tenement
rooms I had ever seen.

My host—the Reverend John Jefferson Davis Hall—pointed
to the "chair of state," an antique thing, while he sat down on
another equally decrepit. A profusion of Biblical quotations,
printed and hand-painted were stuck into mirror corners,
nailed to the wall, placed against the desk, the window and
the door. A battered old typewriter nestled in a foliage of papers, magazines and newspapers.

The telephone was off the hook and when I called the Reverend Hall's attention to it, he smiled. "The minute I put it
on it begins to ring," he said. "Begin to count," he laughed
as he put it back on the hook. I had counted up to twenty-six
when the phone rang. Hall picked up the receiver, listened for
a moment, then spoke. "Yes, brother, I will give you a message. A message from heaven. I want you to pray to God.
He'll hear you. Europe is in a mess today because it has forgotten how to pray. Prayer is our salvation. Pray for your sins,
brother."

He had hardly placed back the receiver when the phone
bell rang again. Hall recited another message to the stranger
over the wire, then disconnected the phone. "See!" he explained. "They give me no peace. I spread the gospel of Jesus
Christ everywhere. I speak in the streets, in subways, in terminals—everywhere, but I have to have some rest."

A moment later, he raised his eyes to the unpainted ceiling and recited a prayer for my benefit and asked the good Lord's forgiveness for my sins. I had told him that occasionally I drank beer with the boys. The prayer over, the Reverend Hall turned to me suddenly:

"The *Bible* says nothing about purgatory, nothing about saints, nothing about special prayers for the dead, nothing about Mass. It's all a racket. A business racket. The Catholic Church is a business. It's in the game for money." He, however, approved of Father Coughlin. "I don't like his going into politics, but his spiritual message against the Jews is very good and very timely."

Reverend Hall puzzled me. At first I thought he was another Young, the Klansman, but when I noticed a copy of Winrod's *The Defender*, I reasoned that his sympathies were with the anti-Catholic sect of Fundamentalists with which Colonel Sanctuary associated. Hall accompanied me to the door when I left. There he recited another prayer for my benefit and conferred upon me the religious title, V.S.

"What does it stand for?" I asked.

"It stands for Volumes of Sunshine, brother."

The Fundamentalist wing of the Protestant religion has its stronger adherents in the Bible Belt. It lists seventy-five different denominations, including the Church of God, Assembly of God (subdivided into fifteen brands), Holiness Church, the Holy Rollers, and estimates of their strength run as high as 10,000,000. That the Jew must ultimately be converted they all agree. But they disagree on the method. Some believe that personal salvation should be achieved by converting the Jews through non-violent missionary methods. The majority of Fundamentalists subscribe to this doctrine.

But a small, extremely powerful and well-knit group of fanatic religionists among them insist that missionary efforts have proven a waste of time and that the salvation of the Jew can be achieved only through the persecution of the Jew; by slander, violence and denunciation. This group has headed straight for the Nazi camp. The leaders of this sect, located principally in many sections of the midwest, regarded Hitler as the savior destined to give battle to the anti-Christ, overcome him at Armageddon and fulfill a so-called *Bible* prophecy for a peace to last one thousand years. The Reverend Gerald B. Winrod was the religious fuehrer of this revolutionary minority and had been fully endorsed by *World Service* as qualified for the job.

Fascist Fundamentalist leaders have told me that the present period of world turmoil is the pre-millennial period of "tribulations," following which "Armageddon will be fought, Christ will return as the King of Kings and Lord of Lords, the nations will be judged, Satan will be bound and the Golden Age will be inaugurated. Peace will then fill the earth, as the waters cover the sea, men will know war no more and human nature will be regenerated."

As to Hitler's defamation of Christ, Christianity, organized religion and his substitution of pagan gods, fascist Fundamentalists said these were Satan's lies about him. I saw plainly that while the rest of America slept, the Nazis had crept quietly into the fold and gained the ears and minds of a gullible religious following. The main apostle of the hate creed was this same Reverend Gerald B. Winrod, with a large and militant following in the midwest.

In Wichita, Kansas, Winrod directed a quasi-religious propaganda group known as the Defenders of the Christian Faith and was pastor of the Defender Tabernacle. He published *The Defender* with a peak circulation of 125,000 ("A prophetic voice crying in the wilderness"), *The Constitutionalist*, *The Revealer* and was one of the most prolific publishers of Nazi party-line literature in the country. One of Winrod's closest collaborators was Colonel Sanctuary. Others included Joseph P. Kamp, Jung, True, Pelley, Edmondson, Mrs. Dilling, Henry D. Allen, Mrs. Fry, several Nazi consuls, and Herman Max Schwinn, notorious Bund leader of the West coast. Winrod sold the *Protocols*. The columns of *The Defender* promoted practically every major anti-Semitic, anti-Democracy, anti-British book published in the past eight years.

In the summer of 1934 Winrod, then still a poor, struggling revivalist minister buying his clothes and furniture on the installment plan and making one-dollar payments, wrote in *The Defender:*

The richest and most distinguished Protestant congregation in Berlin has Dr. Martin Niemoeller for its pastor today. . . . He dares to resist the power and threats of Reich Bishop Ludwig Mueller . . . defiantly refuses to preach about the pagan gods which Hitlerism has injected into Christian interpretation. Worshippers in his church hear only the old Gospel. It remains to be seen how long he will be able to continue.

But along about the fall of 1934, Winrod changed completely. His preachments suddenly became anti-Catholic and anti-Jew. Somehow and from somewhere, he obtained enough money to finance a trip to Germany and remain there for several months. When he returned in February, 1935, he cleaned up all his outstanding debts in lump sums, by check, boasting to his satisfied creditors that while in Germany he had met many important Nazi officials. While in Germany, too, Winrod learned that it was the Jew who had spawned Communism. He evangelized in *The Defender:*

. . . Nazism and Fascism are patriotic and nationalistic; Communism is not. . . . Hence of the three forms of government, Nazism and Fascism are as far in advance of Bolshevism as the twentieth century is from the Dark Ages. One stands for life, happiness and prosperity; the other, death, misery and starvation.

Winrod founded a second magazine, *The Revealer*, to reveal the "World Jewish Conspiracy" and began to print and distribute the *Protocols*. Tens of thousands of Fundamentalists in the Bible Belt were deluged with hate-inciting pamphlets that echoed all the lies of the Nazi propaganda mills. The Catholics fared no better. *The Defender* referred to the Pope as "Mr. Pius of Vatican City" and called the Roman Catholic Church "the harlot woman" of the *Bible*.

The circulation of *The Defender* boomed in the Klan and Silver Shirt-infested midwestern states.

Just before the national elections in 1936 Winrod made another trip to Germany. On his return he visited Washington, conferred with James True, spent hours at the German Embassy and held consultations with Hans von Reitenkranz, at that time Hitler's personal representative here. Invigorated by his new "Christian" contacts, Winrod published a series of

(July, 1937)   *Defender*

Catholicism and Fascism

By W. J. Grandoschek, Bakersfield, Calif.

Commentators have long since established a connection between the Roman Church of history, and the Woman who rides the Scarlet Colored Beast of Revelation seventeen.

While the Harlot Woman of this passage refers to Catholicism, the Scarlet Beast depicts the ten puppet dictators and the one master Dictator, who will come forth from the chaos of Europe, within the territory of the old Roman Empire.

History confirms this passage. The Church has always sought to hold sway over governments. And this policy is prophesied to continue right down to the end.

Fascism is the spirit of ancient Rome. If it can be shown that the Catholic Church is really cooperating with Mussolini's program for restoring the Roman Empire to its ancient power and grandeur, another link will be

forged in the chain of prophetic events. This fact would serve to definitely establish the "Mother Church" as the "Mother of Harlots" mentioned in Revelation 17:5.

THAT SUCH AN INTIMACY EXISTS BETWEEN CATHOLICISM AND FASCISM IS WELL KNOWN TO ALL WHO ARE TRULY CONVERSANT WITH RELIGIOUS AND POLITICAL AFFAIRS IN EUROPE TODAY.

A sample of anti-Catholicism which Winrod promoted. *Commonweal*, a Catholic weekly, evaluated anti-Semitism as "one side of a coin on whose reverse is inscribed 'No Popery.'" Winrod's premise that Catholicism is fascist parallels Coughlin's equally vicious lie that "Communism is Jewish."

wild Nazi lies charging that the Lindbergh baby was killed as a part of a Jewish-Communist plot, that President Roosevelt was a Jew and that both the Spanish and Sino-Japanese wars were Jew-inspired.

When in 1938 Winrod decided to run for the Senate the Reverend L. M. Birkhead stepped into the picture. A Unitarian minister from Kansas City, Missouri, the Reverend Birkhead in 1935 visited Germany while on a vacation tour. Quite by accident he discovered the existence of a clearing house for international Nazi propaganda under the direction of the world's leading professional Jew-baiter, Julius Streicher. Masquerading as a fencing academy, Streicher's institution kept a catalogued index of those *im ausland* (abroad) who were favorable to the Nazi cause. Winrod was rated highly by the Nazis.

Alarmed at the inroads which Nazi propaganda had made in America even as early as 1935, the Reverend L. M. Birkhead left the ministry soon after his return from Germany and founded the Friends of Democracy. Its object was to combat impartially both Communist and Nazi activity in the United States. When Birkhead learned that Winrod was running for Senator, he carefully analyzed Winrod's publications from 1934 on.

In a searing and historic booklet titled *Keep Fascism Out of Kansas*, he exposed Winrod's fascist sympathies and Winrod lost the race. But in obtaining 54,000 votes, which in Kansas was substantial strength in a four-way race, Winrod showed how deeply his Nazified "Christianity" had already seeped into Kansas.

Winrod's influence extended far beyond the borders of his state. A tall, heavy-set man, a powerful speaker and astute politician, he won the confidence of simple people who knew nothing of his checkered political career which was akin to that of the Royal Oak priest-politician. Religious and simple folk are trusting and do not doubt what a preacher tells them; especially one who like Winrod spoke of God as an older brother of his.

Though Martin Dies investigated other fascists, he never probed Winrod because of an odd series of circumstances. The story is best told in the words of N. J. Roccaforte, director of the Messengers Tract Club, Houston, Texas and a true Christian Fundamentalist who has testified as witness before grand juries. Roccaforte's signed statements to me read (I abbreviate):

In Houston, Texas, during the year of 1934 . . . [I] organized what was then known as the Defenders Tract Club. . . . At this time, Winrod having been impressed by our aggressive activity in Christian circles and the fact we established a record for getting subscriptions to his magazine *The Defender*, he offered us a position with his firm in Wichita, Kansas. . . .

We agreed on a salary of $25.00 a week to start, but if the Tract Club took any of my time other than my own time, he would deduct my salary accordingly. We agreed to this plan. Mrs. Roccaforte who went into Winrod's office as a typist was promised a salary too. . . .

We arrived in Wichita May 2, 1935 and went to work and soon were shocked to learn Winrod's employees were being paid from $6.00 to $10.00 per week. At the end of the first week my check of $25.00 came through all right but Mrs. Roccaforte did not receive her salary. When we asked about it Winrod evaded the question; thinking we were in Christian service, we went about our tasks anyway. . . .

Disillusioned, we continued to work. Mrs. Roccaforte continued for nearly two years for which she never received her salary. We have estimated that Winrod owes the two of us nearly $5,000.00 for printing and back salaries. After this incident, we developed our tract work rapidly. We purchased printing equipment which was placed in the basement of my private home. . . .

Life went on uneventfully except that we pushed Winrod's work. We conducted great subscription drives, advertising campaigns, improved the efficiency of his office generally until we had expanded his magazine's circulation to well over 120,000.

The senatorial campaign of 1938 came along and it was then that we were finally convinced Winrod's work was neither Christian nor patriotic. . . . We severed our associations with Winrod October 17, 1938; a few days after we asked Winrod to pay us what he owed us. This he refused and instead suggested that we move our printing plant and all our tract work to his premises. . . .

When we left his office, we borrowed money to pay a few of our creditors and returned home with our printing equipment and home furnishings. . . . In April, 1941, we re-established our tract work. . . . Since that time, the Tract Club has been rebuilding gradually . . . is concentrating on Gospel literature for service men and calling America to prayer as well as publishing religious literature of a general nature. . . .

Roccaforte had this to say relative to the Winrod-Dies episode which he learned at first hand:

The call was from Newton, Kansas, and Mr. C. H. Willms, manager of the Herald Publishing Company, the printers of *The Defender* Magazine, was on the wire, Mr. Willms said in substance that a government investigator who was sent by the Dies Committee from Washington was in his office demanding to see their books and records of Winrod's account.

Immediately, Winrod conferred with an attorney who advised against showing the investigator anything. Meanwhile, Winrod placed a long distance call to Rev. Harry H. Hodge in Beaumont, Texas, who is the pastor of the church frequently attended by

Mr. Dies when at home. It developed that Mr. Dies had heard Winrod on several occasions when in Beaumont on speaking engagements.

Mr. Winrod suggested to Mr. Hodge to immediately wire Martin Dies and advise him that he was making a mistake, and to recall at once his agent who was in Newton, Kansas, trying to investigate his business affairs. Accordingly, Mr. Hodge wired Martin Dies in Washington. In turn Mr. Dies recalled his representative who immediately left the city. The next day Winrod placed a long distance call to Congressman Dies in Washington and thanked him for his favor.

Winrod's contacts extended from Senator Reynolds and others high in public service to the lowest Nazi propagandists. Here is a letter he sent the notorious Edward James Smythe, Bundist and Klansman, on December 27, 1940:

Acknowledging receipt of your letter dated December 23, 1940 ... will say that we share your attitude with regard to the magazine to which you refer. This subject was given attention in the article beginning on Page 12 of the enclosed Magazine. Wishing you the choicest Christian blessings for the New Year, I remain, faithfully yours. . . .

Like Edward James Smythe, Winrod fought the Lend-Lease Bill, urged strict isolationism and opposed all defense measures. He was a bulwark of the America First Committee in the midwest. Spreading his black wings into South America, Winrod's Puerto Rican branch issued *El Defensor Hispano* (*The Spanish Defender*), a twenty-page monthly magazine carrying translated articles which disseminated typical Winrod doctrines. Who paid for *El Defensor Hispano?*

Fundamentalist ministers like Winrod have been riding the midwestern plains to lay the groundwork for the rise of a dynamic fascist leader. Fascist-Fundamentalists were the backbone of the Ku Klux Klan in the midwest; many members of the Silver Shirts were Fundamentalists; and Mrs. Dilling, the noisiest super-patriot in the country, collaborated with these preachers of hate.

Among Winrod's disciples was the Reverend W. D. Riley of Minneapolis, founder of World's Christian Fundamentals

Association, and a frequent contributor to *The Defender*. He directed the Northwestern Bible Seminary where he gave "sound training to some fifteen hundred or more scholars a year," according to Mrs. Dilling.

When *The Minneapolis Journal* charged Riley with membership in Pelley's Silver Shirts, he made no protest. An ardent propagator of the *Protocols*, Riley believed that the "Russian who discovered them and brought them to light" was a "good and godly man . . . and a real patriot." He was convinced that "no money expended is so effectually lost as money on Jewish missions"—a conviction that cleared the way for him to follow the Nazi pattern of persecution. Although basically anti-Catholic (which they called Romanism), many among Winrod's klan of Fundamentalists were mysteriously reconciled to Father Coughlin's brand of "Catholicism," and Riley even gave a series of four sermons commending "the philosophies of Father Coughlin." And in the March, 1940, issue of his organ, *The Pilot* he whitewashed the Royal Oak fascist and the cleric's co-revolutionists:

> . . . I have found more intelligence in this Priest's deliverances, and more evidence of loyalty to true democracy and to constitutional government . . . than I have received from any other orator of the hour. . . . Instead of being a revolutionary club, these 17 young men were members of a rifle club. . . . A Christian Front we need! Nothing less will save our land!

Elizabeth Dilling referred to Riley as "that staunch lion of Christianity and patriotic Americanism." The "lion" countered: "I thank God for Elizabeth Dilling." And when Winrod was accused of being a Hitlerite, Riley explained to a correspondent that this was not so at all:

> I do not believe that Winrod has the slightest connection with Hitler. I find many men who have been over to Germany—in fact, most of those that I have talked with—complimentary to German conditions at the present time . . . I will gladly send you a copy of the *Protocols* if you have not read them.

This was the Fascist-Fundamentalists' way of saying that all's well with National-Socialism "at the present time."

Hate, which knows no boundary, flourished in the Kingdom Temple, Los Angeles under Pastor Joseph Jeffers, who like Winrod, had taken a post-graduate course on applied "Christianity" in Germany and Italy in 1938. On his return Jeffers boasted to reporters that he had spoken with Mussolini and Goebbels personally.

In the spring and summer of 1939 Los Angeles newspapers buzzed with scandalous stories involving Jeffers and his pretty wife of nine months on charges of holding "orgies," and with allegations of "unconventional practices while naked for the entertainment of house guests." A red-haired beauty-shop operator figured prominently. The matter was investigated by the District Attorney's office and Jeffers was brought to trial on a morals charge, but he managed to secure an acquittal.

Despite the incident, "Joe" as he is affectionately known to his cult, had many thousands of followers who filled Kingdom Temple and were treated to a combination of politics, religion, anti-Catholicism and shrieking "Americanism."

Jeffers was notorious for his association with the Silver Shirts. In 1939 he permitted the showing at Kingdom Temple of a four-reel recruiting film which depicted "Silver Shirt activities in the Northwest." Pelley-organizer, Roy Zachary, who at a Bund gathering had threatened to assassinate President Roosevelt "if nobody else will," was narrator. Mrs. Fry's agent, Henry D. Allen, was on hand to speak on *The Cause of Communism*. The Kingdom Temple congregation was treated to the spectacle of hearing a would-be assassin, a former convict and a so-called minister of the gospel who had been tried for sexual perversion, talk on "Christian morality" and "Americanism."

Jeffers was also addicted to a strange new cult initiated by William J. Cameron, Henry Ford's public relations counsel, known as the Anglo-Saxon Federation. Its "teachings" were a combination of bigotry and superstition based on a wishful and distorted interpretation of the *Bible*. Like Winrod, who was somewhat of a co-cultist to the Federation's teachings, Jeffers spoke mystically of the "Kingdom Message" and its promise of reward to such peerless "Christians" as Jeffers and his followers. But The Kingdom of God would not be delivered unto the Catholics. No sir, because——

. . . The Black Pope has had his hands in the political affairs here, and in Tammany Hall with its Rum, Romanism and Rebellion. But that is going to be changed. And we shall see it come. We shall see a religious revival and a revolution come in America at the same time.

I followed the train of poison preachers to Michigan. On a Labor Day week end I posed as a "pilgrim" and with thousands of Coughlinites visited the Shrine of the Little Flower at Royal Oak. I found there a Coney Island built around the dignity of the Church, and Father Coughlin in the role of chief barker. I made six attempts to interview Father Coughlin. But on each occasion I was told that he was playing golf, or else riding around in a magnificent Cadillac car in his shirtsleeves late at night.

The Reverend Charles E. Coughlin was neither liked personally, nor respected for his business shrewdness by those in the neighborhood who had had dealings with him. And those who turned against him were largely Catholic. They told me that Coughlin neglected his parish and turned over his clerical duties to a corps of assistants. He was disliked by many of the clergy.

He was not only censured by George Cardinal Mundelein who said that Coughlin "is not authorized to speak for the Catholic Church, nor does he represent the doctrine or sentiments of the Church," but the Most Reverend Bernard J. Sheil, Senior Auxiliary Bishop of Chicago, in a nation-wide radio address hinted directly at Coughlin by denouncing "*emotional charlatans* who have become statesmen overnight and whose unctuous voices betray a first urge to hear themselves no matter whose thought they convey."

The Shrine was located on Detroit's super-highway, Woodward Boulevard, which made it convenient for tourists. Father Coughlin operated the Shrine Inn, a restaurant, several souvenir shops teeming with customers, hot dog stands and the Shrine Garage. Coughlin had wanted to buy off all adjoining property and build a super-garage-and-restaurant but the owners would not sell. As a result, Paul's Pup Tent (its hot "pups" were bigger than "Shrine" hot dogs) and Fred's Garage adjoined Coughlin's concessions.

Father Coughlin maintained a large parish school and also owned a thirty-acre plot with a fine building which he leased to the Social Justice Publishing Company. He collected rent from that, too. His parents lived in a magnificent home which I estimated cost about $25,000. As a community booster, Father Coughlin impressed me as a matchless asset to any local Chamber of Commerce.

Delegates of "Pilgrim's Clubs," devout believers in the Coughlin "Christian Crusade," curio-seekers and suckers were as thick as on the Coney Island boardwalk in summer. Only the Hawaiian dancers and the freak shows were missing. Otherwise there were plenty of sideshows. Women walked into the Church in gay-colored robes some of which were anything but modest. Youths hawked *Social Justices* and souvenirs. Children bawled, mothers screamed, fathers yelled as offspring ran into a street more crowded than Times Square. There were no policemen, and traffic snarls were as common as popcorn. Trains, buses and autos dumped their human content every few minutes in a bedlam of noise and confusion.

This was the Shrine of the Little Flower when I visited it on Labor Day, 1940.

The interior of the Shrine was designed magnificently, but I counted at least thirty-three repositories for coin. I had no sooner entered with 3,000 others than twenty-four ushers began from the front rows and worked back, exacting a seat tax of twenty-five cents from each person—aside from several other collections which followed. They handled the coin to see if it were good. They made change on the spot, then vanished—having collected $750 in four minutes at one Mass alone. I was amazed at their machine-like efficiency.

I have attended many Catholic Church services and I've been deeply moved by them, but I saw nothing but commercialism and heard nothing but revolutionary politics here. Coughlin spent ten minutes in the ritual at the altar after which he disappeared, to reappear a few minutes later in the pulpit. He impressed me as a man of considerable ego, love for power and wealth—distinctly a man of the flesh and not of the spirit. He spoke on politics for an hour with the heaving passion and flaying gestures of Joe McWilliams. And like Joe he berated labor and Democracy. He praised Hitler and clerical fascism. "Watch America degenerate from now on," was his theme because it had denounced his preachments.

Then he came down from the pulpit, hurried through another fifteen minutes of ritual, and as he disappeared into the narthex the thought swept through me that such a man could prove so great a thorn in the side of the Church that even with its venerable store of experience, it could hardly dare silence "Silver Charlie" (as he was dubbed for speculating in silver while he preached against it) without painfully pricking its fingers.

The Winrods, Jefferses and Coughlins were on the rampage. Where one would least expect to find Nazi propaganda at work—in the Church—I found it organized as effectively as outside the Church. Down the broad stretches of the Mississippi Valley, through the corn belt of Indiana, Iowa and Nebraska, through the valleys of Ohio and Missouri, a host of pseudo-Christian ministers were engaged in undermining the foundations of Democracy.

"Nazism and fascism stand for both home and church," counselled Winrod.

"In this way I believe I am acting in the spirit of the Almighty Creator; by opposing the Jew I am fighting for the Lord's work," said Adolf Hitler.

CHAPTER XI

SPIES!

"Always push the people more and more for the revolution. America must and will feel the hammer-blows of the Nazi-Fascist might. We must work now, so the *Führer* can come to the White House. . . . He will make men of America's weak children."

HUBERT SCHMUEDERRICH

COUNT ANASTASE ANDREIVITCH VONSIATSKOY-VONSIATSKY was a legendary figure in the Nazi underworld in which I moved. His name was spoken in awe and his deeds whispered in secrecy. But he was no myth—he was very much alive! With considerable foresight, the penniless ex-Czarist officer fell in love with Mrs. Marion Stephens, divorced wife of a wealthy Chicago attorney, daughter of Norman Bruce Ream, multi-millionaire. The Count was twenty-two and she forty-four. After they were married he worked for a while in the Baldwin Locomotive Works. Trilled the Countess:

"My dear Anastase is going through all the various departments, so that if the Czar's government is restored, which Anastase believes will happen, he will be equipped to become the company's representative."

But the Count soon dropped his work and began to plot a revolution to restore Czarist rule. His wife's palatial estate in Thompson, Connecticut, became the base for intrigues which girdled the globe. As fuehrer of the All-Russian National-Socialist Labor Party, Vonsiatsky in 1934 went to Berlin to scheme against the Soviet and establish the basis for a network of espionage agents.

From Berlin he hopped to Tokyo, and in league with Japanese officials organized an espionage network from that end of the world. From Tokyo Vonsiatsky went to Harbin and Shanghai, both of which already were centers of Russian White Guard activity. Reporting to Berlin for further instructions, he was sent to Budapest, Belgrade, Sofia and Paris.

In each city the Count established White Guard cells serving the Nazi espionage ring.

When Count Anastase Vonsiatsky finally returned to Thompson with a feeling of work well done, he set to manipulating the strings which he hoped would restore his wealth of Czarist days. He founded *The Fascist*—an all-Russian magazine, and in America his group of Quislings became known as the Russian National Fascist Revolutionary Party. His most intimate friends became Fritz Kuhn, and others of that type whom he lavishly entertained at his home or at the Russian Bear, a night club adjoining the estate and operated by a relative.

During the Spanish Civil War Vonsiatsky ran arms to Franco and established contact with the Mexican Gold Shirts, who were also interested in the traffic of arms. The Count militarized his revolutionary party. One section of his Thompson estate became an arsenal, lined with rifles and machine guns. Drills were held regularly on its cloistered recesses. Sleepy, colonial Thompson village far off the main arteries of travel, became the center of intrigue, espionage and revolutionary plotting. And Countess Vonsiatsky could do little about the "patriotism" of "my dear Anastase."

Armed with this background of the legendary Count, I visited him in the summer of 1941. Rather than direct his spies to the license of my car I parked it on a side street, and walked the distance to his estate which I found to be even more magnificent that I had imagined. I knocked, and after a minute's silence in the course of which I sensed myself watched, a growling police dog threw itself against the heavily screened door. Then from the inside came a deep-throated roar. I wasn't sure whether it was another dog or a human being until, seemingly out of nowhere, emerged a huge man. He was a heavily-muscled giant, weighing well over 260 pounds, with a large blunt nose, full coarse lips and an enormous head— bald and shiny. He was dressed in khaki shirt and trousers. Behind him was another police dog.

"You are George Pagnanelli, yes?" he asked in a bass voice.

I walked in while the Count held back the growling hounds and locked them in an inner room. I was disappointed when he led me not to the arsenal—but to his office. It was filled with maps, numerous ship models of the Czarist Navy, photographs of the Czar and other dead heroes of a dead order. This was the time (in 1941) when Hitler was digging deep into Russia and a Hitler victory was uppermost in Vonsiatskoy-Vonsiatsky's mind.

"By November 7 the German line will be Leningrad-Moscow-Rostov. The Christmas issue of *The Fascist* will be published in Berlin and the New Year issue from Moscow. I am already packing for the trip. In America I am now through."

I looked on in silence as he edited copy for what he thought would be the final issue of *The Fascist* in America. He resumed in his thickly accented English: "I don't belong in this country. Of my countrymen here 300,000 want to go back with me to Russia. I am not American. I don't want to be American. In *The Fascist* there is not one line in English. In America I don't care what happens. I am here only to do my work."

Vonsiatsky was uncommonly frank, thanks to the groundwork laid through copies of *The Christian Defender* and our circle of acquaintances which over-lapped. We both knew Boris Brasol, the notorious White Russian agent and we both knew "the boys" at the Bund. He received the *Deutscher Weckruf* and was also a subscriber to *Social Justice*. But his interest in American affairs seemingly did not extend beyond that, for his heart was in Europe and he marked time until he could go back.

I asked Vonsiatsky about the work of the America First Committee, mentioning Nye and Lindbergh by name in order to get the reaction of this Russian Nazi.

"That America First Committee does good work. It has sympathizers many times more than the membership. It is all very, very good education for nationalism. In America you will have it. It is must when Hitler wins. Your Wheeler, Nye and your D. Worth Clark, will save your America for you Americans."

His emphasis on "your America" and "you Americans" struck me as odd. But it was natural for a man who had no respect for the United States.

"And Lindbergh—what do you think of Lindbergh?" I repeated.

"Lindbergh, ahhh, Lindbergh he is great person. You will yet hear from Lindbergh. He will save your America with your Wheeler, your Nye, Clark and your Father Coughlin."

In parting, Vonsiatsky grabbed my hand in his massive fist. "I shall send you *The Fascist* from Moscow," he said.

But Count Anastase Vonsiatsky never got there. First, because of the heroic Russian fighters; and second, because of our own F.B.I. J. Edgar Hoover nabbed the Count, linked him on charges of espionage—*in America*—with Gerhard Wilhelm Kunze. And instead of Moscow, a jury of "you Americans" sent the Count to an American Federal penitentiary.

And there was Hubert Schmuederrich, a short, powerfully built, barrel-chested super-Nordic, with beady blue-gray eyes who lived in a world of his own making. Hubert had such odd and "patriotic" friends that the Department of Justice took a permanent interest in them. As for Hubert, he was an odd egg himself. He was seldom steadily employed but worked occasionally in grocery and butcher shops. Hubert was always getting kicked out of a job for proselyting Nazism, and he boasted that he lived on the proceeds of unemployment insurance. "This dumb Democracy pays you for doing nothing," he sneered. Every cent he could afford went to pay Stahrenberg for the printing of his own inflammatory leaflets.

Schmuederrich had participated in the early Nazi agitations and had joined in the Nazi rioting and street fighting. He came to the United States in 1926. His friendships were multitudinous. He had worked with Anton Haegele, former fuehrer of the National-Socialist League, with Gissibl, Spanknoebel, Mrs. Fry and Sanctuary. He had helped finance *The American Bulletin* published by Mrs. Anne Tellian, the Nazi agent.

He was eager to make a leader out of me for the Grey Shirts a storm troop outfit he was then reorganizing. "I will give you training. You must believe in my person and I'll show you what I can do for you," he would say in his thickly-coated English. He urged me constantly to better myself in

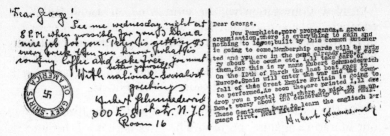

Prophesying a lightning Nazi victory, these cards were mailed to Pagnanelli in February, 1941. "Don't worry about the courts," Schmuederrich wrote: "I'll take care of them." He is now in Federal prison.

preparation for *der tag*. His favorite expression was, "It will all come by a rebellion."

Hubert tried to induce me to write a leaflet on *Refugees in North America* of which he would assume the cost of publication. "Write what I tell you, George, and we will send copies to Herr Goebbels. I make sure he sees it. When the British Empire crashes and Hitler comes to the White House, Goebbels will want to know those who worked with me for National-Socialism. You will be fixed with a good job. You tell me what you want and you'll get it."

To know Hubert was to understand the utterly fanatic and unbending Nazi spirit; the one-track, uncompromising drive toward a single goal, that mental state which believed in the "invincibility" of the "master race" and plunged its believers, seemingly mesmerized, into the jaws of death. To know Hubert was to understand how a German agent need not be on the Nazi pay roll to work for Nazi aims. Sometimes Hubert went hungry and without clothes, but he always managed to scrape up money for a new line of seditious literature. In his *Bill 1776—or the Last Pillar of Democracy*, he wrote:

This New Order of time will erect new temples and shrines with a spirit that comes from these holy places, Munich and Rome. A defeated England and a defeated America will bury this devilish spirit which comes from the free-masonic lodges of a now defeated France.

A New Constitution will be written which stands for obedience, credence and combat and which will last not merely another 150 years, but for time eternal. I urge my followers wherever they are, to do their duty in regard to our belief and the idol of us all, Adolf Hitler. . . . Our World Revolution is Victorious! Long Live Our Leader! Adolf Hitler!

"In the meanwhile, George," he advised, "organize and give out literature against the Jew. The laws here mean little to us who are in the revolution. There is too much Democracy here, forty-eight kinds, and the people are weak. They need the protection of the National-Socialist might."

"You don't think men like McWilliams can lead the revolution, do you?" I asked.

"Men like him we use to make the ground ready for the real leaders. For us there is no going back. Like Hitler I'll live to see the end of the Catholic Church not only in Germany but in America. It has already begun to fall to pieces in Germany. Half the Catholic Churches are empty. Education of German youth does that. Only the old people go to Church in Germany."

"How about Father Coughlin here?" I asked.

"It is necessary to work with him because he has a big following and we don't want to go against him now. We'll settle with him later."

Bending over the table at which we were seated in a Yorkville café, Hubert exhorted: "Always push the people more and more for the revolution. America must and will feel the hammer-blows of the Nazi-Fascist might. We must work now, so the *Führer* can come to the White House. *Der Führer der Teutonen wird gewinnen. Er wird starke Maenner aus Amerikas schwachen Kindern machen,*" he ended in a burst of Prussian arrogance.

"The Teutonic *Führer* will win. He will make strong men of America's weak children."

In the spring of 1941 Hubert insisted that I become acquainted with the prospective members of his underground storm-troopers. Among those he asked me to visit was one Josef August Klein. The house was in a shabby neighborhood in the lower Bronx, next to a row of condemned tenements. The streets were dark. I climbed cautiously to the top floor and nervously knocked on Apartment 18. I got no immediate response, but in a few minutes I became aware of an inner door being opened. The next instant the door on which I had knocked opened noiselessly. A short man, followed by a huge dog, stood in the doorway. Seeing the dog made me think of my visit to Vonsiatsky.

"Who are you?" the man asked.

"Hubert Schmuederrich sent me up," I said. "I am Pagnanelli."

I followed Klein in as two doors closed silently behind me.

"Lie down, Pal," Klein yelled to the growling mastiff. "George here is a friend." But the dog had keener instincts and kept growling. "He doesn't seem to like you," Klein observed. "Pal usually has a good reason when he dislikes anyone. What is your work, Pagnanelli?"

I told Klein I worked in the stock room of a business concern downtown.

The transformation as the doors were closed behind me was like a screen play. A large precision clock, the kind seen at railway terminals, was on the wall. Looking through the open door at my left I saw a large studio camera, an enlarging machine on an easel, several developing tanks, photographic paper and chemicals. Outside the door was a curtain of monk's cloth. On the floor were various pieces of electric apparatus with a maze of wire leading to another room to which Klein led me by the arm. This room, larger than the others and filled with radio equipment, transmission and receiving apparatus of many kinds, resembled the control room of a broadcasting station. The entire apartment was a maze of multiple wires, extending through the walls. I estimated that the equipment was easily worth $2000.

Not a sound came from the outside. The floors were thickly carpeted and the walls were lined with monk's cloth. An eerie violet ray light came from overhead. Half the room was set off from the other half with a wide stretch of monk's cloth.... The huge dog followed, constantly growling and sniffing at me.

"He is a suspicious animal, isn't he?" I said.

"He is my best pal and smells trouble a mile away," Klein said.

"By the way, Arthur McGee was talking of you. Said you were okay. You gotta be careful these days who you talk to."

"Schmuederrich talked to me about you and what he says goes a long way with me," I said, returning the compliment.

As we talked I heard transcriptions of Hitler's speeches which Klein had made. There were also recordings of McWilliams' voice. Klein had been a member of the Christian Front, but now spent most of his evenings with his radio set and his girl, Virginia—an extremely pretty brunette, according to her photograph—of Italian parentage. Klein was not yet a citizen, but expected to get his final papers shortly. "As soon as I get my American citizenship, I'll work for the Grey Shirts. In the meanwhile, I have to lay low."

As Klein talked, I wondered at Schmuederrich's choice of a recruit for the Grey Shirts. Klein impressed me as being too mousy and timid to be of any use in a revolutionary organization! I thought, of course, of his photographic laboratory and radio apparatus—but had no idea that the colorless Josef August Klein could be anything but a timid sympathizer of Nazi Germany.

Just off Fifth Avenue, facing Rockefeller Center was B. Westermann, a bookshop whose showcases were filled with innocuous imported lithographs, American etchings, magazines and collectors' items. Its interior was spacious and respectable. Max Albrecht Blank was office manager of the bookshop, one of the oldest in the country. Blank was average in size and weight, with a ruddy complexion and blue eyes. Soft-spoken and quiet, the only conspicuous mark about him was an ear lobe which was split in two. "He is a good man for you to know," Schmuederrich had said.

When I met Max Blank the first time, he asked if I had read that week's issue of the *Deutscher Weckruf.* I shook my head. He then went to a drawer and brought me one and also brought back issues of *In Retrospect,* a magazine distributed from the offices of the Nazi German-American Vocational League. It featured reprints of articles by Lawrence Dennis and Charles Lindbergh.

I had no trouble in convincing Blank that I was "all right."

My *Christian Defender* and our common friendship with "patriots" were enough to gain his confidence. Like Klein he had also heard of me as a "good man." Blank next tried to sell me a copy of *The Talmud Unmasked*, by Colonel Sanctuary and *War, War, War*, by "Cincinnatus," pseudonym for a pronounced American Nazi whose identity no one seemed to know. While I was talking with Blank, Kurt Mertig of the Citizens Protective League came in.

"I knew I'd find myself in good patriotic company," he said, laughing.

After greeting me, he withdrew and began talking earnestly in German with Blank. When Mertig had left, Blank called me over. On the shelves, arranged so that they were recognizable only when a few feet away, was an array of Nazi best sellers: *Seeking Foreign Trouble* by Ralph Townsend; *The Truth About England* published by the League to Save America First; a large assortment of Flanders Hall books, and back copies of Viereck's *Today's Challenge*.

"Of course you belong to the Bund?" I asked. "Why haven't I seen you at any of the meetings?"

"No," he answered. "I never belonged to it. They are all thickheads. I used to be a member of the Friends of the New Germany long ago. I gave the Bund advice but they did not take it. I told them that they were too blunt with their approach and were taking in people without investigating them. I now work alone and I'm very careful who I talk to."

"I use the right technique," Max Albrecht Blank resumed. "I study people. If it's a new customer, I break him in gradually. First I give him a book like *European Jungle* by Major F. Yeats Brown. Then I suggest he read *Smokescreen* by Samuel Pettengill, [a book violently hostile to the New Deal]. If he likes these I suggest *The Truth About England* by T. W. Hughes. Then come the Flanders Hall books. I use the right strategy and not only make a customer for the store but also a friend who can help the cause either now or later on."

I was becoming increasingly disappointed in Hubert's selection of storm-troop fodder. I had expected to meet tough Aryan sluggers. I told Hubert my reactions. "Never mind what you think now," he said, "you'll think different later. Now you go and talk to Paul Scholz."

Paul Al W. Scholz was plump, with a well-padded girth
and soft hands; seemingly a genial, easy-going German-American who earned a livelihood—so I thought—as salesman at
Germania Bookstore. Paul and I became friendly, and as I
brought in copies of my *Christian Defender*, we used to talk
at length.

Though heartily sympathetic to the Bund and the Christian
Mobilizers, he kept away from the meetings. He did his part
for Hitler by distributing vast quantities of Hubert's and
Sanctuary's pamphlets. He sold the *National American* and
all of Pete's publications. When Pete went underground,
Scholz continued to distribute his stuff surreptitiously. Scholz
was not a loud-mouthed fanatic and he was not a joiner. "I
don't join nothing," he said.

Then, one day, while reading my newspaper, I saw his
name in the lineup of Nazi spy suspects rounded up by the
F.B.I. Later, I visited the courtroom to assure myself that
Scholz was actually the Scholz I had known at the Germania
Bookstore. It was indeed the same, grown fatter and somewhat paler. I also recognized my other "friends" Max Blank
and Josef Klein.

Scholz was convicted with Colonel (Frederick Joubert)
Fritz Duquesne, the "master spy." The record showed that
the amiable, plump-faced German had a more sinister record
as a spy than even Blank or Klein. Paul Al W. Scholz is now
serving *sixteen years* in Federal prison! Blank pleaded guilty
and was let off with six years. Klein got five years. And I
have been wondering what Virginia has been doing since
the incarceration of her mousy Josef. Was she a "plant" to
distract the attention of the F.B.I. from his sinister activities?

As to Hubert Schmuederrich, I have often thought of him.
He may have been a spy himself, and his bluff manner a mere
blind. The ways of the Nazis are so deceptive that the most
harmless looking German may prove to be a spy and the
loudest defamer of Democracy a mere windbag. Anyway,
whether spy or windbag, Hubert boasted that he never filed
an income tax report and was also "proud" of being a draft
dodger. The F.B.I. eventually sent him to join his friends in
jail after which denaturalization proceedings were filed against
him and he was deprived of his citizenship.

CHAPTER XII

PARK AVENUE "PATRIOTS"

"What is the reason for the hatred stirred up against Japan? . . . I have been in both countries and during the week spent in China I saw cruelty such as I shall never forget all my life; during two months in Japan I saw nothing but kindness, love of nature and of children."

MRS. NESTA H. WEBSTER

My TRANSFORMATION from a rabble Christian Mobilizer to a Park Avenue "patriot" was easy! A change in my necktie, the pressing of my "Pagnanelli suit" and slightly better diction accomplished the change. The language spoken was much the same, and whatever difference there was in social caste went by the board in the grand upsurge of "patriotism."

My Park Avenue "friends" read *The Christian Defender* and *Social Justice* and loved it. They thought *World Service*-endorsed Mrs. Dilling was "simply grand." The stuff peddled by Nazi agencies became palatable when translated into acceptable English by Americans of colonial stock, with no swastika embroidery and no mention of Hitler as the "liberator." Instead of talking revolution and founding "sport clubs,"

ADOLF HITLER: HUMANITARIAN, PEACEMAKER
Will We Let Europe's Strong Man Bring America Greater Prosperity?

Regardless of the subversive mis-information handed us by many daily newspapers, Adolf Hitler actually has accomplished for the people of Germany the employment and prosperity which has been only promised by our American bureau-cracy (or dictatorship)—in promises not fulfilled except by more prom-ises; and Germany today is enjoy-ing the prosperity and respect and world leadership which is making her and her great Leader the admira-tion of all Nations.

There is no unemployment in Ger-many — there are fifteen per cent more "jobs" than there are workers "Heil Hitler"—and no wonder their great Fuehrer is regarded by them as a living personification of the ideals of CHRIST And as Christ was maligned and persecuted, so is Hitler hated and lied about by the same vicious world haters and de-spoilers of mankind. The people of

Hitler is ridding Germany of crime and subversive activities and he is freeing the German people from "racketeering" oppression. By in-vitation, he united Austria with Germany and freed the Austrian people from their former oppressors.

With such great advantages al-ready in their favor, Hitler will not tolerate war anywhere if he possibly can avert it—although he and his allies now are strong enough to win any conflict

Even were Hitler to die or retire, his successors are ready and his policies will be continued. Adolf Hitler is the George Washington of Germany (and, maybe, of all Europe)

We need more Americanism in America. When real Americans ex-pose the un-American activities of radicals and stand up for the

Hitler-worshipper James Sheppard Potts boasts that his ancestors came to America in 1619—which was supposed to have made him a good American.

Park Avenue demanded a "new leadership" and founded groups to propagate a refined brand of dissension and defamation of Democracy among members who had better table manners than the goon squad.

Justification for Hitler's methods became subtle, hushed down, and was whispered *sotto voce* only behind locked doors. I know, because I was often behind those locked doors. It wasn't quite Emily Post to say "Jew"; so "alien" and "minority" became substitute words, just as "new leadership" became synonymous with "revolution." Park Avenue insisted that all *isms* bear the label "Made in America." It insisted that "Heil Hitler" become "Save America First."

Take the case of James Sheppard Potts, editor of *Southern Progress* of Richmond, Virginia. In his own words, his ancestors were "of the purest British stock, Captain Francis Potts having been a successor to Captain John Smith in the very earliest days of the Colony . . . twelfth generation Americans." And yet in one of his editorials Potts looked upon Hitler as "the great world humanitarian and peacemaker," then he added solemnly: "Adolf Hitler is the George Washington of Germany (and, maybe, of all Europe)."

Nazi propaganda became so refined through the years that when it reached Park Avenue parlors, the Harvard Club or the Lotos Club where Lawrence Dennis and Seward Collins respectively entertained, it was almost unrecognizable as such. Only those who had studied its coarser manifestations among the "know nothing" rabble recognized Hitler's voice in the cocktail lounge. Nazi henchmen succeeded in influencing certain Park Avenue circles to believe that the New Deal was "Communist" and was out to suck them dry of their property and bank accounts. The influence of Nazi agents upon the Park Avenue "patriots" I met rested mainly on this cooked-up tenet. Here is an instance:

The late city edition of the *New York Times* for May 16, 1941, carried the following news item:

WIFE LINKS EX-HEAD OF LEGION TO NAZIS
Spafford, Suing for Divorce, Is Accused of Conspiracy

Edward E. Spafford, former national commander of the American Legion, was accused yesterday before Supreme Court Justice

William T. Collins and a jury of conspiring with Nazi agents in this country to "fabricate" divorce charges against his wife, Mrs. Lillyan Mercier Pierce Spafford, because of her "anti-Nazi attitude."

. . . Both attorneys mentioned Ernest Schmitz, manager of the German Tourist Information Office, which has been under investigation by the Dies Committee as one of the "Nazi agents." Mr. Gottlieb declared further that Mr. Spafford and the Nazis wanted "Mrs. Spafford out of the way" because she objected to having Nazi agents as guests in her home and made statements to the F.B.I.

Who's Who listed Edward Elwell Spafford as Lieutenant Commander of the Navy during the World War and later chairman of Naval Affairs of the American Legion. Spafford was national commander of the American Legion in 1927 and was awarded the Distinguished Service Medal, also receiving medals from the Italian, French and Greek Governments. The Nazi Dr. Schmitz was registered with the State Department as director of the German Railways Information Office.

I sensed that there was more to the *Times* story than was printed. I visited Mrs. Spafford at her home in New York City and gained her confidence through my connections with democratic organizations. A spirited woman and intensely anti-Nazi, she explained that her husband had once been as "much of an American as the President." Then, about six years ago. . . .

"We were happily married until we met the Schmitzes; Dr. Schmitz, his wife and their son, Frank. They began to come regularly for week ends at our farm. They talked to my husband. They went together on long hikes. They continued their conversation at dinner. It was always about Nazi Germany, how great and powerful and righteous she was. They talked about the Jews—how bad they were. And they talked about the coming revolution—how it would liberate America. My husband began to change. He began to think and to talk like the Schmitzes."

"How did they influence him?" I interrupted.

"They worked it so cleverly that he didn't realize he was being pulled into the Nazi net. Our house became flooded with propaganda literature from Germany and from the United States. A lot of it came from the Schmitz office."

Mrs. Spafford went on, excited at the scenes she recalled: "I could not stand those Nazis making a fool of my husband. In the first place, a man in his position had no business to associate with them so intimately. And he had no business entertaining them at our home almost every week end. It was disloyal of him to knock our Democracy and praise Nazi Germany. It became impossible for us to live together any longer. I sued for divorce. But to serve him with divorce papers I had to go to the Schmitz home to find him.

"On the wall above Schmitz's desk was a large framed picture of Hitler. My husband was sitting right under it. I spat on Hitler's picture, then looked at the large Nazi flag and said, 'Why do you hang that rag here? This is America. A Nazi flag has no place in this country.' And then I told the Schmitzes they had no business breaking up the homes of Americans."

I was determined to hear Commander Spafford's side of the story. I wrote him and curious for his reaction, inclosed a particularly vicious copy of *The Christian Defender*. The *next day* I received a warm invitation to visit him.

The Spafford "farm" proved to be a sumptuous country home located two miles from Brewster, New York. A colored servant opened the door and ushered me into the living room; a stately, rectangular affair with oak beams, a fireplace and all the comforts one would expect at a country lodge. I looked out onto the magnificent grounds—on the tennis courts, stables, dairies and the acres of beautiful rolling meadows. I heard Commander Spafford come down the stairs and turned to face him.

A large, fleshy man with pudgy head and sandy complexion, he greeted me cordially and sat down opposite me on the sofa. He impressed me as a simple-minded man politically; and somewhat like General Moseley, easily flattered. He readily admitted entertaining Schmitz on many occasions. Not only *Herr* Schmitz, but . . .

"I also had Franz Ritter von Epp [1] and Dr. Dortmueller

[1] General von Epp was one of Hitler's most trusted underlings; he was among Hitler's earliest supporters and headed the German Colonial Society.

up to my house several times when they were here in 1936. Von Epp is now a high German official in occupied France. Dortmueller," Spafford went on, "is director of the entire German Railway Combine."

"And what do you think of Von Epp, Dortmueller and Schmitz?" I asked.

"They are all fine gentlemen. I regard them all as my personal friends, otherwise I would not have invited them to the farm. People have told me," Spafford reflected, "that Mr. Schmitz is a Nazi agent. He is nothing of the sort. He is just telling the truth about Germany. He is breaking no laws. The Constitution gives every man the right of free speech. That man wouldn't do anything to hurt this country. At least," Commander Spafford added in afterthought, "not while we are at peace with Germany."

This was the time of Rudolf Hess' flight to England and I asked Spafford if he thought Hitler was suing for peace.

"Mr. Hitler does not have to sue. He is already the victor. He has always been for peace and has never wanted war. You know damned well it was the international bankers who started this war. Mr. Hitler had nothing to do with it."

He felt safe with Pagnanelli. *The Christian Defender* assured him that I was one hundred per cent for Hitler. Commander Spafford boasted that Mussolini had personally decorated him with the Order of the Crown of Italy. He was so well known as a friend of Italians, he said, that "Lucky" Luciano (a convicted pimp, gangster and head of a vice syndicate in Brooklyn) had once made an appointment to see him.

"Why should a man like that want to see you?" I wondered.

"He wanted me to help him file his income tax return. He had heard Italians speaking well of me," Spafford replied. "I referred Mr. Luciano to a lawyer."

I asked the opinion of this former Commander of the American Legion as to whether Nazi agents here were stirring discontent with the ultimate aim of overthrowing our government.

"Bunk!" Commander Spafford exploded. "That is a lot of propaganda. Those Germans are no more interested in the overthrow of our government than are the Eskimos."

Just before leaving, the Commander carefully pointed out that all his forbears had come to this country before 1657, had fought in every war and gloriously served their country. He basked in the glory of his forbears. "I'm American to my finger tips. No one can raise a finger against me on that. I stand for one hundred per cent patriotism for my country. My record shows that."

MAUDE S. DE LAND, M.D.

I was urged to visit Dr. Maude S. DeLand by Kurt Mertig chairman of the Citizens Protective League, whose meetings she attended. A woman past seventy, she had been a medical psychiatrist at the Topeka State Hospital in Kansas and was retired from practice. Her room in the Dixie Hotel in New York was cluttered with a large selection of "patriotic" books, many of them in German.

Before going to see her I familiarized myself with her background by reading a lengthy, six-page letter she had written the Reverend L. M. Birkhead on October 2, 1935, in which she. professed her friendship with Reverend Winrod; with Arnold S. Leese, London editor of *The Fascist*, and completely justified Hitler and Hitlerism. She also added:

Germany is a much more religious nation than U.S.A. . . . I happen to belong to the "Friends of the New Germany" and it also happens that my ancestors came to this country from *England* before the Revolutionary War and some of my ancestors fought in that war and my father fought in the Civil War. . . .

As I faced her in the hotel room, I asked Dr. DeLand how she had become interested in the "patriotic" movement; she answered:

"While working at the State Hospital, I read a medical book translated from the German. 'I wish I knew German,' I said to myself and when I tried to get someone to teach me the language, I found a German exchange student who offered to teach me. Wasn't I lucky?" [These students were sent by the Nazi overseas bureau as carriers of "cultural propaganda."]

Under his tutelage Dr. DeLand apparently learned more than German grammar. In 1933 she travelled to Germany.

"I was treated very kindly," she said. "Whenever I forgot anything on street cars it was always returned to me. I lost only a pair of rubbers in Germany and that was in an American church in Berlin." Upon her return to America Dr. DeLand joined the Friends of the New Germany determined to give her time to "patriotic activity."

"I dread to see German soldiers die," she asserted. "I look upon those fine young men as sacred human beings dedicated to their mission of carrying the torch of Aryan civilization to all corners of the world. I don't see what wrong Hitler has done," she continued. "He saved Germany from the Communists. He made it a world power. Hitler wanted nothing but peace and now he's been trapped by the international bankers into fighting for it. Can you tell me just *one* thing Hitler has done that I should disapprove?" she questioned.

As George Pagnanelli, editor of the "patriotic" *Christian Defender* I didn't know one thing of which she could disapprove.

Dr. DeLand had acquired a considerable number of friends since her decision to turn "patriot." She got to know Colonel Sanctuary and liked Seward Collins. She knew Mrs. Leslie Fry. She sent items to Father Coughlin. Dr. DeLand also showed me her correspondence with True and Edmondson. She knew Deatherage personally and regarded him as a "great man." She had worked with Joseph P. Kamp and John B. Snow. She knew Mrs. Schuyler intimately and was a friend of Miss Cathrine Curtis. She had spent many hours with "my good friend Elizabeth Dilling."

She knew Pete Stahrenberg well and also knew H. D. Kissenger, a Kansas City attorney who contributed to Pete's *National American*. She told me she had met Thorkelson and turned over to him "evidence" of an American Communist "plot" which had promptly found its way into the *Congressional Record*. For mysterious reasons of her own, Dr. DeLand spoke of Fritz Kuhn with uncommon enthusiasm.

Dr. DeLand loaded me down with an enormous quantity of literature, including booklets from the German Library of Information, Pelley, Winrod and others. Unfortunately her supply of tracts from the Imperial Fascist League and British Fascists, Ltd. was exhausted, she said.

Dr. Maude S. DeLand acted the role of a "co-ordinator" and "scout." She was on the alert for fascist leanings among professional people and those in the upper crust of society. To every likely prospect she instantly dispatched an assortment of "patriotic" literature. She was a lone wolf operator, but her background gained her *entrée* into the homes of many Park Avenue fascists. And her admiration for National-Socialism was matched only by her fanatic hatred for the British. Just before I left, Dr. DeLand confided that she was leaving soon for Washington to carry on liaison work among susceptible members of Congress.

JOHN B. SNOW

John B. Snow lived at 45 Park Avenue and did not object to being called a "gentleman fascist." As director of the League for Constitutional Government, he deserved the major share of the "credit" for propagating the myth that the Administration was "Communist." Snow was familiar with *The Christian Defender* and my own "patriotic" background. Once, as we chatted pleasantly in his office about Joe McWilliams, Snow reached over and handed me a book which *World Service* had recommended for reading—*Fools Gold* by Fred R. Marvin.

"I think you'll enjoy reading it," Snow said to me. "I sell a great many of them."

A short, pink-faced man in his forties, he had a way of raising his eyebrows and cocking his head to one side as he talked. He talked softly, and his hatreds were discernible more in the overtones of his voice rather than his words. He was very, very refined and seemingly detached from fascist politics. Suave and slick, Snow would not commit himself except to his most intimate friends. But he did not hesitate to sell the *Protocols* and to peddle the fascistic books of Mrs. Nesta H. Webster. One of them, *Germany and England*—printed by the Boswell Publishing Company of London, who issued *The Patriot* and printed the *Protocols*—carried these typical passages:

Bolshevism is destructive of all that constitutes civilization, while Fascism sets out to correct those parts of a civilization which, in common with all sincere social reformers, it regards as defective. . . .

What is the reason for the hatred stirred up against Japan? It is now the fashion to speak of the cruelty of the Japanese character. . . . I have been in both countries long ago, and during the week I spent in China I saw cruelty such as I shall never forget all my life; during two months in Japan I saw nothing but kindness, love of nature and of children.

To supplement Mrs. Webster's efforts Snow sold *The High Cost of Hate* by Japanese agent, Ralph Townsend; *Is Your Town Red?* by Franco worker, Merwin K. Hart; *Wolves in Sheep's Clothing* by Coughlinite George E. Sullivan of Washington. These books among many others were the items of diet with which Snow nourished his Park Avenue clientele. As an adjunct to the League, Snow founded Madison & Marshall, Inc. to specialize in the distribution of super-patriotic books, ranging from Mrs. Dilling's $1 books to Nesta H. Webster's $7.50 volumes. Under the pretense of exposing "un-American activities" John B. Snow served as clearing house for fascist literature molded to Park Avenue taste.

He copied Mrs. Dilling by splitting hairs between "Democracy" and "Republic" and decided that Democracy was a "mobocracy." Therefore, Snow's perverted reasoning ran, Democracy was "Communist" and gave rise to "chaos and anarchy." Thus he planted the seeds of doubt and disrespect for Democracy among America's prototypes of the Cliveden set through a brochure, *Democracy, a Misnomer* which left the way open for the acceptance of Snow's fascistic beliefs.

One of his warmest friends who maintained a personal interest in the League for Constitutional Government was H. W. Prentis, Jr., chairman of the Board of the National Association of Manufacturers, and Snow's stanch purveyor of misinformation. Prentis denounced the direct election of Senators, the primary, the initiative, the referendum and recall, all of which were bringing us closer to what he termed "the pitfalls of Democracy." Said he: "Hope for the future of our Republic does not lie in more and more Democracy."

Supreme Court Justice Robert H. Jackson took exception to Prentis' slurs while speaking before the Law Society of Massachusetts on October 16, 1940:

. . . The complaint of these gentlemen, who now seek to discredit government by the people, is not new and is not against something new. They are spiritually and intellectually one with the group that opposed freedom and independence of the colonies from the king. . . . They are the same type as those who fought the income tax and who now want wealth to escape its share of the burden of national defense, who think of defense in terms of opportunity for profits not in terms of burdens.

. . . the blunt fact is that many of the men who are agitating for a differentiation between these words are against popular government under either word or either form. . . . These new bottles are filled with the old wine of caste, of economic exploitation, and of privilege. That is why the reversion to the old arguments against Democracy is important today.

Personally I regarded Snow as one of the most calculating fascist minds in America serving the interests of old guard, reactionary business men. His closest collaborators were Joseph P. Kamp, Merwin K. Hart, Cathrine Curtis, Walter S. Steele (editor of *National Republic*) and John B. Trevor of the super-super "patriotic" American Coalition. All served the same masters and all shared in Snow's views.

Snow championed Charles Lindbergh and promoted the No Foreign War and America First Committees. A relentless baiter of the Administration, Snow's hand was visible in every move initiated among Park Avenue circles to discredit the New Deal and foment obstructionism and dissent. In the summer, Snow retired to his summer home near Suffern, New York, and there lived the life of a country gentleman, remaining a foreigner in spirit to the Democracy of his native land.

MRS. A. CRESSY MORRISON

Mrs. A. Cressy Morrison was president of American Women Against Communism, Inc., dedicated to "outlaw Communism in America" with little said about fighting Nazism, or the native fascist columns of Coughlin or Pelley. "We have not considered the fascist movement of sufficient hazard to warrant dividing our efforts," she wrote once.

Mrs. Morrison was a member of the Society of Mayflower Descendants, the Daughters of the American Revolution, an intimate co-worker with Mrs. Schuyler, Mrs. Dilling, Miss

Curtis, Dr. DeLand, John B. Snow and also Allen Zoll. Her
officers included Miss Charlotte C. Aycrigg and Mrs. Clarence
G. Meeks, of the Daughters of the Revolution (not to be
confused with the D.A.R.), both of whom had served on
Zoll's American Patriots. She helped sponsor General Moseley's testimonial dinner.

I first met Mrs. Morrison at Allen Zoll's meeting. A tall,
gaunt woman, wearing pince-nez glasses, Mrs. Morrison reflected an air of authority and precision. Her offices were at
52 Vanderbilt Avenue, New York City, but they were not
listed on the directory. "They're in room 814," the elevator
man said. A large American flag was splashed against the
wall and the office crowded with the literature of Mrs. Dilling,
Joseph P. Kamp and a wide variety of their own.

Mrs. Morrison was dreadfully afraid of Communism and
always spoke of our "glorious Republic." But she did not
hesitate to print and distribute the speech of John Cecil,
Christian Front and American Nationalist Party speaker. In
common with the fascist practice of labeling as "Communist"
all liberal movements, Mrs. Morrison fell in step and pro-
claimed:

. . . The Red Marxism of Moscow is often disguised as "lib-
eralism," "socialism" and other "isms" opposed to fundamental
Americanism, so that we have come to refer to these subversive
"isms" by the term "radicalism."

Soon after Joe McWilliams had horrified her at the Zoll
meeting with the query about "13,000,000 Communist niggers
turned loose," Mrs. Morrison issued the printed warning:
"Communists Incite Racial Uprising and Bloody Revolution
Among Negroes of Dixie: Seek to Establish Negro Republic
in Black Belt." Mrs. Morrison also became agitated when
"Communists" threatened to grab all the farm lands and
flooded the midwest with a flurry of leaflets: "Do you want
to lose your farm? Do you want to suffer the same fate as
the Russian farmers did. . . . The danger is here."

At another time Mrs. Morrison discovered that atheism
was rampant in the Federal Council of the Churches of Christ
in America, and in league with Joseph P. Kamp and his asso-

ciate Alexander Cloyd Gill, produced "proof" in the form of an elaborate chart entitled: "Termites in the Temple Gates."

In her office there worked an anti-Semite and Bund collaborator, Edwin Perry Banta, who insisted on proof of my membership in the Christian Mobilizers before he would talk to me. Banta had testified before the Dies Committee on his investigations of Communist Party activity. Concurrent with his testimony he had also "exposed Communism" at meetings of the Bund and the American Nationalist Party. He had worked with Anton Haegele, fuehrer of the American National-Socialist League.

Banta told me he was a member of the Christian Front. "I admire Father Coughlin and his Americanism," he said. "And because I am a great despiser of the Jews, I've done a lot of good work for the Christian Front.

"Banta used to be Bonte, a German name," he went on. "I've received lots of letters from Germany. They know me in Berlin all right. I used to turn over a lot of the information I got on the Commies. I corresponded with a fellow named Orville Wood in Germany and they used to send my stuff all over the world. The Bund paper also used my information on the Communists that I turned over." He went on: "I once collaborated with a German writer on some articles for *Liberty* magazine."

"Who was that?" I asked, intensely curious.

"Viereck. George Sylvester Viereck. I gave him the information on the Communists and he put it in writing. We were supposed to split the profits, but Viereck got most of the money."

There is more to Banta's "Americanism," but his story is typical of many Americans who serve as Nazi dupes because of their blinding hatred of Communism.

SEWARD COLLINS

When in the summer of 1938 the F.B.I. first cracked down on a Nazi spy ring, Dr. Ignatz T. Griebl made such a hasty exit that he left Mrs. Griebl behind. When she was held as a material witness by the F.B.I. to forestall her taking "French leave," the *Deutscher Weckruf* wrote indignantly:

What followed is proof that traditional American chivalry and fair play have not become obsolete in the United States. Mr. Seward Collins put up the $5000.00 bail in five $1000.00 bills and Mrs. Griebl was released. But the accounts of the case had aroused his interest and spurred his indignation against what he regarded as injustices and a reflection on American civilization.

Seward Collins also bailed out Allen Zoll who was being held on extortion charges. Collins had command of money and was listed in *Who's Who* as former editor of *The Bookman* and *The American Review*. His wife was Dorothea Brande, author of *Wake Up and Live*. Seward Collins was strictly Park Avenue, but my *Christian Defender* scored with him and proved the medium through which I gained his confidence.

Many wild tales were told about the American Review Bookshop at 231 West 58th Street, New York, but I can only state what I saw with my own eyes. The building was of red brick, three stories high. A large hall in the rear of the ground floor was filled with stacks of newspapers, while the front office housed a considerable quantity of fascist propaganda. At a desk sat a man in his thirties, with a bristling mustache and prematurely gray hair.

I had first met Conrad K. Grieb at Allen Zoll's meeting and bought my first copy of Senator Reynolds' *The American Vindicator*. At the time he gave me a leaflet which described the function of Collins' bookshop:

New York's only "right wing" bookshop, specializing in nationalist books, pamphlets and periodicals, published in this country and abroad. Anti-Communist material, sympathetic presentation of anti-Communist countries—Italy, Germany, Spain, Portugal, Japan, and nationalist movements in other countries. Rental library. Books rented by mail.

Grieb proudly told me that he was "pure German on both sides," was friendly with Joe McWilliams and Pete Stahrenberg, but being too busy to attend "patriotic" meetings, he asked me to keep him informed of what went on. I welcomed these attentions which *The Christian Defender* earned for me and was particularly pleased when, upon leaving, Grieb asked

No. 203 (REGISTERED AT THE G.P.O. AS A NEWSPAPER)   "BRITAIN FIRST"   January 25, 1940

Sample of British Fascist propaganda sold by Seward Collins. Note the slogan "Britain First," paralleling Stahrenberg's "America First."

me to find a buyer for a set of *The International Jew* reprinted from Henry Ford's *Dearborn Independent*.

"Six dollars for the set is a very good buy," Grieb said.

I frequented the bookshop and bought five types of Axis propaganda. I bought Sir Oswald Mosley's British fascist sheet, *Action;* Japanese agent Ralph Townsend's *Seeking Foreign Trouble; Spain*, by the Spanish Library of Information, an issue of *Fair Play*, an Italian propaganda organ, published by Louis Caroselli, which contained articles by George Deatherage, Dr. Friedrich E. Auhagen, and one by Congressman George A. Dondero titled, *U. S. Never Was a Democracy*. Samples of Joseph P. Kamp's many booklets and *Patriot Digest* by the blustering "patriot," Robert Caldwell Patton were also on sale, in addition to other fascist items from France, Germany, England.

One day, as I had called to leave three copies of *The Christian Defender*, Grieb reached for the phone and said: "Wait a minute, Pagnanelli, Mr. Collins wants to see you."

I was both alarmed and pleased; if Collins suspected me I knew I'd be kicked out. But I was also pleased at prospects of finally interviewing this strategist of American Fascist policy. Waiting impatiently, I finally heard him coming down the stairs.

"So you're Pagnanelli," Collins said sizing me up. "You've got a bright little sheet there. I enjoy reading it."

"I'm trying to improve it, sir," I said. "I've been reading some of your nationalist books."

"That's fine, that's fine. Come, let's go up."

His desk was on the third floor, buried amid a pile of books and papers. Sitting directly under the skylight, Collins' face was oval, blond, with light gray hair parted in the middle. His manner was brisk to the point of being nervous. He acted like a man who had a lot on his mind but could not rid himself of it. After he ascertained my contacts with Stahrenberg and McWilliams, he spoke with unusual frankness.

Collins had seen McWilliams "three or four times in the past few months" and was friendly with Henry Curtiss. "I call him up and we go out together," he said. He had worked closely with John Cecil. Collins also knew Stanley Smith chairman of the American Nationalist Party, then made this startling confession:

"The first meetings of the American Nationalist Party were held in this building—in the hall downstairs. Henry Curtiss used to be one of the speakers."

Collins' views on anti-Semitic propaganda were unorthodox from the Nazi viewpoint. The *Protocols* were outright forgeries, he declared; so was Benjamin Franklin's "prophecy" regarding the Jews; and the "quotations from the Talmud" as propagated by Stahrenberg were utter fakes.

"How about the Jewish plot to rule the world?" I asked in my best Nazi manner.

"What plot? Bunk! There's as much truth to that as the charge that Communism is Jewish."

"Isn't it?" I asked. I wasn't sure of Collins, and suspected that he might be leading me into a trap. I intensified my anti-Semitism in proportion to Collins' "defense" of Jewry.

"Take that *Key to the Mystery* which comes from Adrian Arcand's office in Canada, it's utter fabrication. Roosevelt is no more Jewish than I am. We all have some Jewish blood in us if you go back far enough. I'm tired of arguing with those who tell me of Jewish 'conspiracies' and the *Protocols*. I hope you won't turn out to be that sort. If you want to talk against the Jew there are other ways you can do it."

On leaving, Collins urged me to read *The Jews* by Hilaire Belloc.

At Collins' suggestion on my next visit I brought along John Geis, Christian Front-er, editor of *The American Way* and a strong clerical fascist. Collins greeted us cordially and explained that his political philosophy was that of a "distributist." He defined it by saying that capitalism was "anti-Christian and coercive" and gave birth to Communism.

"A return to the Middle Ages is what I'd like to see," he said.

"Do you think the world was a better place to live in then?"

"No," he answered, then changed his mind and said: "Yes, I believe it was. There was no capitalism then, no Communism, no anarchy, none of this internationalism and no Jewish issue. I suppose I will be called anti-Semitic," Collins went on, "but I don't particularly care so long as I am not mixed in with the crackpots and the bums. I want to be interpreted honestly and not washed in the same water with the rabble. I have a definite political-social-economic program to further and I intend to spend my lifetime and resources toward that end."

"How did you get started in this trend of thinking?" I asked.

"By reading Belloc's book: it influenced me greatly," Collins answered. "But I'm not Catholic at all. I just want to see the end of Communism and capitalism and a return to the life of the Middle Ages. It is a distributionist philosophy."

"It is a very odd philosophy," I observed, eager to have him talk further. "I wish I could place my finger on it."

"I am a fascist, of course I am. I'm also a pagan. I believe in a devil because I see his work all around me. If some day I should lose my pagan beliefs it will be because I first believed in a devil."

On September 8, 1939, Conrad K. Grieb addressed a meeting of the Founders Club of the Christian Front at Donovan's Hall, at which Zimmerman and Harry Nelson of the Phalanx were both present. I also was present and heard Grieb speak for forty-five minutes. Shortly after this, as the crackpots multiplied at his shop and a few clumsy snoopers put him on his guard, Collins issued orders to let no one hang around. He hired Burns detectives to trail those he suspected. Whether they trailed me or not I don't know, but I continued my visits to borrow books and read Lawrence Dennis, Count E. zu

Reventlow, Sir Oswald Mosley and a number of clerical fascist authors who hated everything but clerical fascism.

After a while both Collins and Grieb cooled off toward McWilliams. Grieb called him a "rah-rah rabble-rouser" who had refused to be coached and insisted on wild anti-Semitism. Like Stahrenberg, Collins went underground and it became extremely hard to see him. Just before he dissociated himself from the "rabble" fascists Collins, a violent British-hater, told me that he attended meetings of the Irish Republican Army.

Collins had a horror of America's entry into the war on the side of the Allies and promoted every appeasement drive of importance. Eventually he moved out to Lake Geneva, Wisconsin, to work closely with *Scribner's Commentator*, unofficial organ of the America First Committee backed mainly by the wealthy Charles S. Payson. Both he and Payson were called to testify before a Washington grand jury. The jury wanted to clear the mystery of a powerful short-wave receiving set atop the magazine office. It also wanted to verify reports that Collins' garage at Lake Geneva housed a considerable quantity of short-wave equipment and large crates ready for shipment. Where?

BORIS BRASOL

Boris Brasol was not a native born Park Avenue "patriot," but he moved so intimately within the orbit and impressed them so profoundly, that his imprint was indelible. In political cunning and craft, Brasol towered above the average American Fascist. To understand Brasol we must go back to the murder of Andrey Yuchinsky, illegitimate child of a woman of the streets of Kiev, Russia, in 1911.

The evidence showed that the youth had been killed by one of many gangs that flourished in Kiev, but the "Black Hundred"—corresponding to our own Black Legion—sent word to Schleglovitoff, Minister of Justice, under whom Brasol worked as assistant that Andrey had been killed by a Jew and drained of his blood for ritual purposes. With Brasol's help, the prosecution required nearly two years to prepare the "evidence" against a poor, blameless Jew named Mendel Beylis. The jury returned an odd verdict. It decreed that Andrey

had been killed in a ritual murder, but that Beylis was innocent. Fourteen newspapers were suppressed and twenty-two
fined for airing the scandal. The attempted frame-up showed
the depths of corruption to which the Czarist courts had sunk.

Brasol came to America in 1916, followed by Major-General Count Cherep-Spiridovich. The passion of these two
frustrated Czarists was the restoration of the Romanoff Czar,
using American dollars and American suckers as their medium. Hatred of the Jew in Russia was transferred to a dynamic hatred of the Jew in America. An old world cancer
was transplanted to the new world. It gained as its chief promoter America's wealthiest but politically most naïve personality—Henry Ford.

Ford was induced to publish the *Dearborn Independent*,
and placed William J. Cameron in charge as editor. It became
such an organ of anti-Semitism that E. G. Pipp, editor-in-chief
of the *Detroit News* who had been hired to run Ford's paper
soon resigned in disgust. But Ford's secretary, E. G. Lie-
bold, insisted that Brasol be added to the writing staff. And
Brasol boasted in a letter to Spiridovich in 1921:

Within the last year I have written three books, two of which
have done the Jews more injury than would have been done to
them by ten pogroms.

This was the beginning of the political black magic which
Brasol-Spiridovich thrust upon Henry Ford and America. Detroit became the Mecca to which disgruntled White Russian
Czarists—and later, Bundists—flocked. They wanted Ford gold;
they wanted to revive the Black Hundred; they wanted to
sabotage Democracy in the land of its greatest attainment.

As soon as Natalie De Bogory, daughter of a Czarist Russian
General made the first translation of the *Protocols* in America,
Brasol turned it over to the *Dearborn Independent*. He also
introduced them as "truth" to the United States Secret Service
and was appointed to a position in our Department of Justice
during the regime of Henry L. Doherty. Vouching for the
veracity of the scandalous forgeries Brasol then induced the
staid American Defense Society to distribute them to its members. In a brilliant and revealing series of articles, *Henry*

Ford's Jew-Mania, Norman Hapgood the famous journalist and Minister to Denmark wrote:

Politically it meant that history was repeating itself. As Brasol was chief in this country of the expatriate Russians trying to put the Romanoffs back on the throne, it meant that Ford's persecution [of the Jews] had, with the logic of events, joined with that crusade, centuries old, that the despots of Europe stirred up repeatedly, in order to inflame, for their own purposes, the ignorant religious passions of the dark masses.

The *Dearborn Independent* articles defaming the Jews were published in book form and are still making the rounds among Park Avenue and rabble "patriots." They were peddled and promoted by all those who had earned a place of honor on the *World Service* list: True, Winrod, Pelley, Hudson, Deatherage, Edmondson, Mrs. Fry—and countless others, including

U. Bodung-Verlag

World-
Service

Erfurt, Daberstedterstrasse 4
December 7-th 1937

Mr.
Baltimore Ave.
K a n s a s   C i t y, (Mo.)
USA

Dear Mr.

     Thank you for your letter of July 12, which we were not able to answer earlier owing to the International Conference of World Service in September this year. The Conference has been a great success; more than 20 nations have been represented;

     Nevertheless we sent you the pamphlets ordered. We can tell you to-day that you can have a copy of *Ford' International Jew* from us, however printed in German! If that suits you, please let us know. In English it is hard to get, owing to the "Chosen people". You may try it with the *Imperial Fascist League*, 30 Craven Street, London, W C 2, England. Anyway they will be able to tell you where you can get, if at all.

        Yours very truly,

This letter is signed by the director of *World Service*, Lieutenant-Colonel Ulrich Fleischhauer.

Sanctuary and Kullgren. Mrs. Schuyler loaned me a copy. The Klan made capital of it in vitally important Detroit. Every Nazi from Mrs. Fry down to McWilliams used it as a reference source. Translated into more than sixteen languages they spread to many corners of the world and served as an invaluable supplement to the *Protocols* from which they were inspired. And all of it was due to the trusting nature of a wealthy old man, a genius in his business but unskilled in politics—and to the energies of such alien minds as Boris Brasol.

I interviewed this man in the offices of the Russian-American National Committee in New York. But I had to go there five times, and write frequently before I finally cornered him. I found the shades of Brasol's office drawn and the room merged in semi-darkness.

"Do you always work in this kind of a light?" I asked.

"Yes," Brasol answered. "I can see better this way."

As my eyes became accustomed to the semi-gloom, I noticed that the room was thickly carpeted and the walls were lined with bookshelves. Brasol's own desk was cluttered with papers, among which I saw three checks. Brasol was a short man, with sharp features, keen eyes and the closest resemblance to Goebbels of any man I have ever seen. He had the same aquiline nose, receding forehead, same shape of mouth, the same look of cunning and ruthlessness. He lacked a club foot.

I felt at a loss on how to begin the interview. There was so much I wanted to ask, yet feared to ask on our first meeting. I began by asking what he thought of McWilliams. "Oh, I've met him," Brasol said. "I know them all in the movement except Lindbergh. I've never met him. I'd like to have a long talk with him some day."

I asked his opinion of Lindbergh.

"Lindbergh is a leader, one of the very few who can lead America out of her difficulties."

Seeing a reprint of one of Senator Nye's speeches on his desk, I asked if he knew Nye. "I've corresponded with him extensively," he said. "I've also corresponded with Congressman Day."

Brasol knew John Eoghan Kelly, the Franco operator. "He

came to my office and we had a very long conversation," he said. Brasol had visited Seward Collins at his office. He was close to Colonel Sanctuary, Mrs. Schuyler, and had coached Russell Dunn, Bund and Christian Front speaker. "Yes, I know her very well," he said when I mentioned Mrs. Dilling and on my query about Merwin K. Hart, he nodded his head vigorously. Brasol was also in touch with Carl H. Mote, president of the Northern Indiana Telephone Company.

"Yes, I've met Adrian Arcand," Brasol asserted, referring to the Canadian Nazi leader. "I'm sorry to see him in jail. What we should do from now on is to train leaders secretly, keep them in the background so that when they put us in concentration camp these leaders can keep up the movement.

"A great man," was his comment on Father Coughlin. But when I asked if he had written for *Social Justice* as had been reported, he hesitated, then unconvincingly shook his head. I had already picked up many of Brasol's leaflets at America First Committee headquarters, and when I asked whether he had written anything new, he handed me a dozen copies of his latest article in *Scribner's Commentator*, entitled *Aid to Stalin? Incredible?*

Author of a number of books, Brasol lectured at many American universities, and injected his old-world poison into the blood of those who had money and influence—and little knowledge of world politics. Brasol worked loyally with clerical fascists in America and the world over. He made frequent trips to Germany, the last in 1939, to confer with high Nazi authorities—and to give, rather than receive advice. He collaborated in Nazi intrigue on three continents and helped in the training of a psychological American fifth column.

Brasol escaped public censure because of his tactics. He refused to give interviews to those he did not know. He worked unobtrusively, year by year boring into our democratic foundations in order that his frustrated dream—the restoration of a Romanoff Czar—might come true.

Before leaving, Brasol urged me to see Baron Charles Wrangel and to write to Carl Mote, the Indianapolis utility magnate. The most remarkable note of my interview was that during the hour I was with him, Brasol did not utter one anti-Semitic remark.

I found Baron Charles Wrangel—a Czarist officer related to General Wrangel—lounging in his apartment; unwashed breakfast dishes and a stack of cards littered the table. His wife, a beautician, was at work, while the Baron complained that he could find no work. He had been a liquor salesman, but had given it up to promote America First appeasement.

"I didn't know you were with the America First Committee," I said candidly.

"I worked my head off for ten months," he said, "speaking for them, training their speakers and arranging programs."

He was a close friend of Hamilton Fish. But otherwise the Baron would not answer my questions. He did not want to be bothered. He seemed to want to go to sleep and he was dressed for it—undressed, I should say, as he met me in a practically nude state. The next I heard of the Baron was when he was brought up for questioning about the fire which sank the giant S.S. *Normandie* while she was nearing completion as a converted troop carrier in New York Harbor.

When in 1927 Ford suspended the *Dearborn Independent* after seven years of relentless anti-Semitism and apologized with the lame remark that he was "deeply mortified" for "resurrecting exploded fictions" its editor, known to millions of Americans as "the voice of the Ford Sunday Evening Hour," by no means recanted. In 1928 William J. Cameron gave an interview to Hitler's first emissary to America, Kurt G. W. Luedecke.

That same year, 1928, there appeared an organization known as the Anglo-Saxon Federation, with offices in Detroit. Howard B. Rand was secretary and Cameron was president. It published an expensive magazine called *Destiny* and propagated the astounding thesis that Anglo-Saxons, not the Jews, were the true sons of Israel. Invoking "historical fact" nowhere found in standard history books, *Destiny* held that the ten lost tribes of Israel were not lost at all, but had wandered all over Europe and finally settled in the so-called Anglo-Saxon countries—chiefly in the British Isles. The Federation promoted anti-Semitism by distributing wholesale editions of the *Protocols*.

Cameron wrote a tract denying that Christ was a Jew (he

was Anglo-Saxon-Celtic-Israel); *Destiny* reprinted one of General Moseley's anti-Semitic speeches, while S. A. Ackley, commissioner of the Chicago area, wrote Edmondson: "I am in entire sympathy with what you are trying to do, and appreciate the thoroughness and reliability of your publications." Ackley's letter was reprinted in Stahrenberg's *National American* in whose offices the petitions "Ford for President" had first given me a hint of the famed industrialist's sympathies.

I interviewed Ackley in Chicago and found him to be friendly with Jung, Sanctuary, Kullgren and Hudson. Ackley was filled with a mystic interpretation of the Pyramids, and with a belief in the arrival of the millennium during the next decade, in the course of which there would be no more disease. No hunger. No death. No thieves. No cigarettes. No intoxicating liquors. No naughty women, nor men who wanted such women.

I became a member of the Anglo-Saxon Federation. Interviewing Howard B. Rand at his sumptuous headquarters at

Anglo-Saxon Federation of America

Affiliated with the British-Israel World Federation. London. England

NATIONAL HEADQUARTERS. HAVERHILL. MASSACHUSETTS, U. S. A.

September 16

1 9 4 1

Mr. George Pagnanelli
100 West 86th Street
New York, New York

Dear Mr. Pagnanelli:

Naturally it is impossible for me to be very enthusiastic over any all out aid to Britain when I happen to know, as you probably do, that one of the objects of those in power today is to use this for the purpose of t aking over America and regimenting our people according to a plan that they hope will continue to be in effect after the war is over.

Kindest regards.

Yours sincerely,

Howard B. Rand

Howard B. Rand
National Commissioner

DESTINY
*The Magazine
of the Federation
Published Monthly*

In addition to being anti-Semitic, Howard B. Rand aided the fascist cause by expressing anti-British views.

Haverhill, Massachusetts, whither they had moved from Detroit, I found him to be venomously anti-Jewish.

Mein Kampf refers favorably to only one American—Henry Ford. The original program of the Nazi Party cited "the finest and most universally known example of this kind of manufacturer"—Henry Ford. The first American to be honored with the Grand Cross of the German Eagle was Henry Ford. For years a large picture hung beside Hitler's desk in the Brown House—that of Henry Ford. In his biography of Hitler, Konrad Heiden asserted: "That Henry Ford gave money to the National-Socialists, directly or indirectly, has never been disputed." These reports were so rife that the *Berlin Tageblatt* appealed to our ambassador. And when in 1923 Hitler learned that Ford might run for President, he said according to a *Chicago Tribune* despatch:

I wish that I could send some of my shock troops to Chicago and other big American cities to help in the elections. . . . We look to Heinrich Ford as the leader of the growing Fascist movement in America. . . . We have just had his anti-Jewish articles translated and published. The book is being circulated to millions throughout Germany.

Chapter XIII

THE HAND THAT ROCKS
THE CRADLE

"This is my thundering herd. How do you like it?"
MRS. ELIZABETH DILLING

IN FEBRUARY, 1941 through "chain" recommendations from one American Fascist to another, I was urged to go as a delegate with the Paul Revere Sentinels leaving for Washington to sabotage passage of the Lend-Lease Bill. When I phoned Sanctuary he urged me to come and pick up a "package of patriotic literature."

He loaded me down with a huge bundle containing a variety of anti-war, anti-Semitic leaflets, with instructions to give it to Charles Hudson. "If he's not there Mrs. Dilling will do," he said. About twenty-five of us from the Paul Revere Sentinels and the Christian Front arrived in Washington on the morning of February 26, 1941. Mrs. Dilling was in charge of the Mothers' Movement and the lobby of the Plaza Hotel was crowded with a wild, milling mob of women and some men.

"This is my thundering herd," Mrs. Dilling told me. "How do you like it?"

She was perfect in the role of a herd leader.

"Come on, mothers," she yelled. "Let's picket the Senate Building."

Sixty or more women rushed to the exits and took their places in line, carrying American flags. Round and round the Senate Building they went singing *The Star-Spangled Banner* and *Battle Hymn of the Republic.* Watching from the opposite sidewalk with other men, the demonstration struck me as pointless. Getting no attention from reporters Mrs. Dilling decided to storm the Capitol steps, hoping for publicity by violating Capitol ordinances. The cops promptly stopped the mob, which was just what Mrs. Dilling wanted. It broke into a howl.

"Don't you dare tell us we can't parade with our sacred American flags."

"These are the flags of our Republic, but you wouldn't know that, you Jew stooges," one woman yelled.

"I'll bet it was the internationalists who made the laws."

"Is this America? Who runs this country, the Americans or the internationalist Jews?"

The cops laughed good-naturedly and gently pushed them back. I was amazed at their patience in the face of the abuse and clawing. There was a sentimental side to the scene. Some of the mothers began to cry over sons or husbands killed in the World War. I could sympathize with that and my heart went out to these sincere mothers, for I knew the tragedies that war can bring. But prominent among the mothers was a tall gawky woman who reminded me of the professional weepers the Nazis sent into France to weep in public places and lower morale. When this woman began to cry again, I asked who she was.

"Her name is Miss Rooney," I was told in confidence. "She always cries."

And whenever she cried the short, roly-poly Polish woman from South Bend, Indiana invariably followed. Both began to bawl in sight of reporters, several others began to take out handkerchiefs, and the thing gave signs of spreading through the mob when some of the more farsighted ones put a stop to the crying jag.

"Don't start that now," one of the women whispered to Miss Rooney. "Wait till Mrs. Dilling gets back."

Mrs. Dilling who had quietly gone off, came back panting with the announcement that Congressman Clare E. Hoffman had agreed to see them.

"There, now, there is a Christian man for you," came in a chorus.

The pack instantly fell into line to follow Mrs. Dilling. On the way over they knelt on the dirty sidewalk and committed the sacrilege of reciting the *Lord's Prayer*—for the benefit of newspaper reporters and photographers. Anything which publicized their shameful conduct was deemed "patriotic." A man of fanatic leanings, Representative Hoffman received the herd, commended their "patriotism" and said:

"Apparently the Red flag of Communists and the flag of every other organization and country is today more welcome here in Washington than is the flag which carries the Stars and Stripes."

Led by Hoffman, the pack milled its way down to Roy O. Woodruff, Hoffman's colleague from Michigan. Here the Congressmen posed for photographers, while Mrs. Dilling held a placard "Kill Bill 1776—Not Our Boys" and Hoffman held the flag. So Mrs. Dilling finally got the publicity she craved.

The Mothers had had enough excitement for one day and they retired to their rooms to rest and soak their feet in hot water. Most of them had come a long distance and lived in shabby rooms, making ends meet on limited funds. I had no heart to investigate them or take down their names. Individually some were quite innocent and motherly, even though in a pack they were a nightmare to watch. But it was not all their fault. It was the Dillings and the Coughlins who were churning them into noisy "fishwives."

The so-called "Mothers Movement" and "Mothers March on Washington" stunts were part of the Coughlin "Christian Crusade." Father Coughlin started the ball rolling when on December 11—almost exactly two years before Pearl Harbor—he announced the formation of the Social Justice Unit of the National Legion of Mothers, saying that if his readers wrote "either to Father Coughlin or to *Social Justice*, they will be put in touch with responsible leaders and regional organizers, as well as honestly and wisely counselled on their problems by the beloved Radio Priest of Royal Oak." The result was a flood of letters from Coughlinite women—married, old maids and neurotics—resulting in a nation-wide epidemic of appeasement, defeatism and organized dissension which delighted Nazi strategists. The first unit of the Coughlin Legion of Mothers was founded by Mrs. Mary A. Decker of Detroit, who organized the Mothers of the United States of America and was later replaced in leadership by Mrs. Rosa M. Farber.

Publicity became the mania of their leaders in order to create the impression that their stunts represented the majority of American mothers. This was far from true. "News crazy" reporters, however, provided wide publicity to such stunts as the hanging in effigy of Senator Claude "Benedict Arnold" Pepper and the "death watch" in which mothers dressed completely in black and sat in Senate and House galleries. They badgered officials hostile to appeasement, but were received with open arms by those who thought in like terms. And these Coughlinite Mothers' groups, noisy and discordant, later became another gear within the multiple-geared America First Committee of organized appeasement and defeatism.

The Chicago group—We, the Mothers, Mobilize for America, Inc.—reached the lowest ebb of unmotherly infamy when over the signature of Mrs. Grace Keefe, it sent a letter to a Louisiana mother mourning the death of her son on the high seas:

Legal experts advise that if any soldier, draftee, or otherwise, loses his life while executing orders which his superiors have no constitutional authority to give, then those officials can be sued as private citizens. We owe it to our loved dead, to the country for which they died, to call to account those who violated our Constitution and heartlessly placed our men in the danger zone between two warring nations while we are at peace. . . .

We, the mothers of American boys, beg you to place the blame for the death of your son where it belongs, and not be deceived by propaganda into blaming a foreign power. In the name of justice, we ask you to call to justice the real murderers of your loved one.

"Impeach Roosevelt" became the cry, with Margaret Norton and Norman Wilson, America First Committee operators from Yonkers, New York, among the first to raise it. "4,000,-000 Mothers to Ask Impeachment," blared *Publicity*, a Kansas fascist sheet. Andrae Nordskog, one of the first native Americans to work with Bund and Nazi agents in Los Angeles, organized the United Party Movement and camped in Washington to represent various "Against War" groups of the West coast. A horde of Mothers groups mushroomed all over the country: Mothers of Sons Forum, Mothers of America, United Mothers, Crusading Mothers, etc.

During the four days I was in Washington, I met a be-

wildering array of "patriots"—crackpot and Park Avenue—
which proved to me once more that the Nazis had penetrated
far deeper into the strata of American life than most Americans were willing to concede. The American fascist world
paraded in the lobby of the Plaza Hotel. All I had to do was
sit on the sofa and introduce myself to anyone who interested
me.

One of the figures I met was J. T. Ward, a "labor organizer"
who talked in hushed tones with the more important mothers.
I followed him one day to the office of Congressman Usher
Burdick and found him talking with Mrs. M. I. Tumy, a
woman of mannish dress and appearance. I was welcomed into
the circle. Pulling Ward to one side I engaged him in conversation. Instead of resorting to hysteria, it was Ward's idea
that American women should organize in small groups of six
or seven and devote themselves to the "Christian cause" as
occasion arose.

"What do you mean by that?" I asked.

"I mean that when Communism rears its head here, these
women can take counter measures. Women can do that as
well as men."

"What would you call such an organization?" I asked.

"Defenders of the Constitution," Ward answered.

Ward indicated that his female platoons in key American
cities were to fulfill the function of a vigilante corps and serve
as auxiliary to male vigilantes. He was working on the by-laws
and was on the lookout for capable female leaders.

Another visitor was Donald Shea, a wild-eyed "patriot" who
regarded Hitler as "one of the world's greatest and most merci-
ful leaders." A veteran of the Nazi crusade, Shea had mailed
out *Fichte-Bund* literature and spoken for the Klan, the Mobilizers, the America First Committee and Italian Fascists.
He directed the National Gentile League. Shea came to the
Plaza Hotel with a bagful of Senator Wheeler's speeches, sealed
in franked envelopes ready for mailing, and distributed them
freely. Privately he spoke to me of "necktie parties"—lynch-
ings—involving Congressmen who voted for Lend-Lease.

Oscar Brumback, who advertised in Winrod's *Defender*,
peddled a large quantity of *A Manual of the Citizens No Foreign War Coalition*. Buying a copy I read some of the chap-

ter headings: "The Great Conspiracy to Destroy Christen-
dom" and "The Plot to Destroy the United States." You
guessed by who. The book was packed with lies rivalling
those of the *Protocols*. The assertions were so wild that even
Mrs. Dilling said to Brumback:

"I'd like to see your documentation for some of these
things."

"I have it all home," Brumback answered.

As I was studying Mrs. Dilling in the lobby, amazed at her
tremendous energy and brazen display of "nerve," she called
me over. "The Reverend Frank Woodruff Johnson got a
letter from you recently, Mr. Pagnanelli," she said laughing.

Reverend Johnson's name appeared as the author of *The
Octopus,* a scurrilously anti-Semitic book sold by Hudson.
"How do you know I wrote him?" I asked puzzled.

"I am the Reverend Frank Woodruff Johnson," Mrs. Dilling laughed. "Hudson forwarded me your letter." Then she
bent over and cautioned: "Please don't tell anyone. You see, I
never sign my name to anything anti-Jewish. The Jews can
never prove that I'm anti-Semitic. I'm too clever for them."

One day while we were seated at dinner at the Plaza Hotel
with a gathering of Coughlinite Mothers and Francis P. Moran,
fuehrer of the New England Christian Front, Mrs. Dilling
suddenly started to sing a mildly ribald song about a young
lady and her fiance. Later she crossed her eyes to illustrate
some point in her conversation. A moment later she stuck her
left thumb into the air, "snatched" at the thumb with her
right hand and made it "disappear." She laughed hysterically
while she pinched her left arm to illustrate how policemen had
allegedly mishandled her on the Capitol steps.

Moran was accompanied by a pretty, blond woman in her
thirties attractively dressed in a gabardine suit. She aroused
my curiosity and I made it a point to sit next to her, but she
refused to tell me who she was or whom she had come down
to see. She went only far enough to tell me that she was writing a book, *But One Defender.* Turning her face away she
talked with Mrs. Dilling in such hushed tones that I could
overhear nothing. I ascertained that she was from Boston, the
mother of two children. She and Mrs. Dilling had an ap-

pointment to see Senator Wheeler the next day. Dinner finished, Moran paid the mysterious lady's check.

"Say what's her name, Francis?" I asked, after I managed to get him in a corner.

"She is Mrs. Robinson," Moran said, "but keep that to yourself. She'll use another name on her book and I'll plug it when it comes out."

Mrs. A. D. Risdon was third in command of the Mothers during Mrs. Dilling's frequent absences. A large and impressive woman, member of the America First Committee and Citizens Keep America Out of War Committee of Chicago, she urged me to write to the chairman of the latter group, Captain William J. Grace. When I told her of Joe McWilliams and his relations with Newton Jenkins fronting for the Bund in Chicago, Mrs. Risdon said:

"You'd better tell him to keep away from Jenkins. He is an opportunist and will turn to anything that promises money. Mr. McWilliams had better get in touch with Harry Jung. He is one million per cent okay."

I could not easily forget her phrase—one million per cent okay!

Mrs. Risdon added that Jung was in the Chicago Tribune Building and that Colonel Robert R. McCormick, publisher of the *Tribune* not only aided Jung financially but allegedly provided free office space for Jung. When I asked her about the German-American Alliance of Chicago, she spoke well of it and said it could be counted on to carry on a "Buy Christian" campaign.

I made several attempts to see Mrs. Rosa M. Farber of the Mothers of the United States who, with Mrs. Beatrice Knowles of American Mothers, led a Park Avenue wing of the "Mothers" Crusade. Headquarters were at the Carroll Arms Hotel. But she was so busy with her mailing and visits to Senators and Congressmen that we did not meet.

Having laid a groundwork by interviewing lesser "patriots" I now had my suit pressed, put on a clean shirt, a red-white-and-blue tie and went off to visit the Park Avenue "patriots" sabotaging Democracy and the Lend-Lease Bill. As an infallible barometer of "patriotism" I had written John B. Trevor, president of the American Coalition of Patriotic Societies, the following letter on stationery of *The Christian Defender:*

I inclose copies of *The Christian Defender.* You may or may not agree with the contents right now. . . . I intend to come to Washington sometime in the next two weeks, and wonder if I may stop in to see you at your convenience?

Somewhat curious at the reaction I gave my name to the receptionist. She returned almost immediately.

"Mr. Trevor is away, but our office manager Mrs. Walker will see you."

While waiting for her I reviewed the data I had gathered about their organization. It maintained a powerful and well-financed lobby and its influence reached high up on Capitol Hill. It was composed of about 115 affiliated groups and included the Daughters of the Defenders of the Republic, Disabled American Veterans of the World War, Daughters of the Revolution and the R.O.T.C. Association.

But the Coalition also had under its wing such groups as Harry Jung's American Vigilant Intelligence Federation, Mrs. Morrison's American Women Against Communism; the American Indian Federation, approved by James True; Christian American Crusade, an anti-Semitic, semi-religious group in Los Angeles; Allied Patriotic Societies, Inc., led in New York by Mrs. Schuyler; the Associated Farmers of California —composed not of farmers, but mostly of bruisers who resorted to terrorism and were financed mainly by oil companies and railroads to beat down organized labor which they called "Communist." It was investigated by the LaFollette Senatorial Civil Liberties Committee.

"Mrs. Walker will see you now," the receptionist said, smiling.

I walked into a trim little office. On the wall was a large poster, "I Am the Constitution." Next to it was a wallpiece in shrieking red-white-and-blue, "I Love You, America." Beneath it sat a prim, attractively dressed woman.

"I read your letter to Mr. Trevor," Mrs. Flora Walker said.

I told Mrs. Walker point-blank that I was a member of the Christian Mobilizers. She had read about us, but made no remark against Joe McWilliams and the flow of our conversacion was uninterrupted. Mrs. Walker was a sharp-witted woman, an unwilling talker and given to asking rather than answering questions. She preferred not to talk about the work of the Coalition except to admit that they were engaged "quietly and tirelessly" against Lend-Lease. "We have our own methods," she answered when I asked how they were going about it.

After attempts to parry my questions, Mrs. Walker admitted knowing personally James True, Colonel Sanctuary, John B. Snow and A. Cloyd Gill, Kamp's chief aide-de-camp. It might have embarrassed her to know that Trevor had published an article in Allen Zoll's magazine in the same issue with the Japanese agent, Roy H. Agaki. Mrs. Walker declared with considerable satisfaction that she was glad to see that Hitler had 750,000 troops in the Balkans (just before the Battle of Greece).

"England cannot back out without suffering badly in prestige, and yet she cannot possibly hope to win against Hitler's superior army," Mrs. Walker observed highly pleased.

Before leaving I asked for literature "for my Mobilizer friends back home." Mrs. Walker agreed willingly and I accompanied her to the stock room. Here she gave me a batch which included a bulletin by a collaborator of the Coalition, Walter S. Steele, against the Lend-Lease Bill; John Cecil's propaganda against "alien" immigration; Senator Wheeler's and Senator Reynolds' speeches and those of Congressmen Fred L. Crawford and Jacob Thorkelson, all in franked envelopes ready for mailing. Only two months ago, I had received Thorkelson's speeches from the hand of August Klapprott, vice-president of the Bund.

I looked upon the Coalition as an extremely potent factor in shaping the minds of Park Avenue "patriots" to the eventual acceptance of a species of nativist fascism with a "Made in America" tag. And I could not easily forget that the names of John B. Trevor and Walter S. Steele appeared as American co-sponsors of an anti-Communist book engineered in 1933 in Berlin, with an opening quotation by "Chancellor Adolf Hitler."

Though maintaining separate organizations and offices, Trevor and Steele collaborated so intimately that they may virtually be regarded as one. Steele published the *National Republic*, "a magazine of fundamental Americanism" and managed a "weekly service to hundreds of editors, to defend American institutions against subversive radicalism; a national information service on subversive organizations and activities; an Americanization bureau serving schools, colleges and patriotic groups." It was all sponsored, said Walter S. Steele, "for the public good."

I wrote him as follows:

I am enclosing a copy of *The Christian Defender*. . . . Of course it does not compare with the *National Republic*. . . . I know Mr. Snow and many of the boys engaged in the fight for Americanism. Next week a lot of us are coming down to fight against America's entry into the war. . . .

Steele, a man with keen eyes and a long scar down the left side of his chin, received me cordially and we became quite friendly, for I knew quite a few of the boys—Joseph P. Kamp, for instance, with whom Steele had worked closely. And James True and Elizabeth Dilling and John Snow. And when I asked him what he thought of Senator Reynolds, he answered, nodding, "A fine man."

A self-styled expert on anti-democratic forces, Steele testified before the Dies Committee. His definition of un-Americanism and how it worked may be gathered from his preliminary statement.

It will be demonstrated to you that there are six major un-American menaces in the United States today; that these can be classified as chiefly alien in design, guidance, and following, and that these six menaces can be further classified as communism, socialism, nazism, anarchism, ultra-pacifism, and atheism. It will be shown that with the exception of one of these, nazi-ism, that there is a grave danger that they may find a common ground on which to complete a "united front.". . . The Communists have made considerable progress in this direction as will be shown.

Steele's testimony filled 402 pages, but less than seven pages were devoted to Nazism and fascism. Of 393 pages devoted to "Communism," about 20 were set aside to "prove" that the American Civil Liberties Union was a "Moscow Front."

About 200 pages were devoted to showing how the "Communists" had undermined our cultural institutions, schools and colleges, while the rest of the volume was devoted to "proving" that our entire labor movement was under "Communist" control.

The *National Republic* suggested in an advertisement that its readers "help the man who helped the nation"—Edwin Perry Banta, "patriotic" collaborator of the Bund, who was selling a razor blade sharpener. As another "expert on Communism" it listed Father Coughlin's eastern agent, Reverend Edward Lodge Curran. The *National Republic* also defended Father Coughlin and his revolutionaries in these terms:

Efforts are being made by the enemies of the Detroit radio priest, Father Charles Coughlin, including certain rabbis, clergymen, left wing educators and Communists, to connect him with the Christian Front. The priest, however, disclaims any direct connection with the organization represented by those arrested. . . .

Throughout my interview with him Steele emphasized his hostility to "European isms" and said: "I believe in promoting Americanism and nothing else." Like the Coalition, his group was lavish with money. Trevor, for instance, lived in a fashionable New York home and travelled to and from Washington. The expense of supporting his lobbying activities were considerable, as were those of Steele's own efforts in sabotaging Lend-Lease. It was apparent that both were in close touch with reactionary business interests who looked upon Communism as the only enemy, and winked at native fascist saboteurs of our Democracy.

I was thrilled at the prospects of interviewing Miss Cathrine Curtis, "the most dangerous woman in America," even though Colonel Sanctuary had discouraged me by saying: "She's very busy and I doubt if she'll see you."

I determined to visit her without previous appointment and without writing or sending her *The Christian Defender*. It was past nine o'clock at night and a bitter February wind accompanied by a chill drizzle beat down as I walked to 1825 Jefferson Place, N.W. where Miss Curtis had rented an entire building to carry on a relentless campaign against H.R.-

Directors of America First! Inc., Activities

James True, president, has been a writer and analyst in the business field for more than twenty years. Since July 10th, 1933, he has edited and published Industrial Control Reports. He was the first Washington correspondent to brand the new deal communistic.

Michael Ahearne, secretary and treasurer, has been a soldier, newspaper man, author, lecturer and organizer. He is co-author of "Handout," published by Putnam's, the first book exposing the propaganda system operated in Washington to prevent the public from learning the truth regarding the new deal. Since the World War, he has investigated subversive activities throughout the world.

Michael Ahearne, Cathrine Curtis' associate, was once a political partner of the notorious James True, as shown in the "Confidential Statement" of America First, Inc.

1776. I had spent several days in studying her background and was alarmed at the influence she wielded. She was a combination of Walter S. Steele and John B. Trevor, adapting the features of their groups to the many organizations she headed. The most active were Women Investors in America, Inc. and Women's National Committee to Keep the United States Out of War, which listed Miss Charlotte C. Aycrigg (associated with Allen Zoll) and Mrs. Rosa M. Farber as sponsors. In addition, Miss Curtis listed seven distinguished groups among her collaborators, including the National Society of New England Women and the National Society of Daughters of 1812.

Into her circle of wealthy and cultured women Miss Curtis injected the same virus which was circulated among the Bund and the Christian Mobilizers. She defamed our system with the venom of George Deatherage and the contempt of Fritz Kuhn and she spoke of Democracy as "that Great Misconception."

Democracy is the stepping stone from Liberty, Freedom and Individual Opportunity to Dictatorship, Regimentation and Slavery. . . . Will we continue to travel the low road of Democracy to national suicide—or will we regain the High Road of the Republic. . . .

Pelley praised "Catherine Alert" for her "masterly memorandum." Hudson and James True endorsed her "patriotism" as fit for their own class of "rabble" readers and the *Deutscher Weckruf* reproduced in its entirety, with accompanying paeans of praise, one of Cathrine Curtis' masterpieces of dissensionist propaganda entitled *Do Coming Events Forecast Their Shadows?* She went even further to earn their acclaim:

> Therefore—to every red-blooded American woman I say—this war is NOT a war for civilization—for Democracy—for Freedom —or for any of the high-sounding phrases put forward to appeal to YOUR emotions and sentiments. Stripped to realities—this war is a Trade War.

Miss Curtis moved in high Republican National Committee circles and had many influential friends on Capitol Hill among whom were Senator Reynolds, Representatives Hoffman and bearded George Holden Tinkham who vied with each other in getting her work published in the *Congressional Record*. Miss Curtis used her influence to appear before the Senate Foreign Relations Committee and air her defeatist views against the Lend-Lease Bill. Miss Curtis claimed that Women Investors was organized "to protect (women's) investments in America, by means of educational, factual and protective activities." Her role actually was to channelize the thinking of female Park Avenue "patriots" into her own interpretation of "patriotism." According to a news story in *The New York Times* she was the first to sponsor Laura Ingalls when that flier—later convicted of being an unregistered Nazi agent —flew over the White House in September, 1939 distributing anti-war leaflets. Later, Miss Ingalls outlined a more ambitious

WOMEN INVESTORS IN AMERICA, INC.

A Non-Profit, Membership, Educational Organization

535 FIFTH AVENUE
NEW YORK, N. Y.

CATHRINE CURTIS
National Director

"Here is a GLEAM OF TRUTH penetrating the darkness and confusion engendered by years of false propaganda! 'The March of Democracy' plainly shows the results of the world promotion of that Great Misconception - Democracy - that now threatens the very life of our Republic.

Sincerely yours,

Cathrine Curtis

NATIONAL DIRECTOR

publicity stunt before a Curtis-sponsored meeting of Mothers in Los Angeles by declaring:

The plan is that I shall fly the petitions you are now filling, to Washington, where Cathrine Curtis will present them to the President; and if she does not, I will take them in the back way myself. I have always been able to reach anyone I really wanted to. . . . I will also call upon Mrs. Rosa Farber to join us in this. We will be able to get publicity because airplanes are news. . . .

What manner of woman was this Miss Curtis who had threatened at a Senate hearing that "the repeal of this bill (Lend-Lease, if passed) will be effected only through the blood of civil strife!" As I knocked on the door of her three-story lobbying headquarters, my hands numb from cold, I wondered at the reception I'd receive. I was met by a man with a thin hair-lip mustache, dressed in gray sport pants and reddish house sweater. I observed immediately that his face was familiar and asked if we hadn't met before.

"It might have been at Verne Marshall's No Foreign War Committee," he said, "I helped him organize it. Or it might have been at the Willkie Philadelphia convention. They packed it you know, the people from the Bronx. My name is Ahearne."

"Aren't you the Ahearne that I heard Joe McWilliams mention?"

"It's me all right. I met Joe and promised to do something for him. When you go back apologize for me, won't you? I've been too busy."

My identity having been established and spurred on by the quiet hush of the late hour, Ahearne talked freely. He knew James True intimately and together with him in 1934 had first organized America First, Inc. Ahearne had advised True to lay low for a while and work under cover. He had passed the same advice to his other friends, Edmondson and Deatherage. Ahearne was closely associated with Miss Curtis as writer and adviser and I was amazed at the frankness with which he talked. I listened while he outlined the technique used by Women Investors in "educating" their clients "progressively."

"One day they wake up and tell *us* that we're the dumb ones and don't know what's going on," he smiled complacently. "And all the while it was *us* who were educating these people. That's how we work, quietly and under the surface. They can't pin anything on us." He laughed, immensely pleased with himself. "Don't worry about the leadership. Just keep working and keep on going. It's foolish to stick out your neck now. Draw it in and work quietly."

That was the Park Avenue formula.

"I'd like very much to see Miss Curtis," I said. "I've come all the way from New York and I'll be disappointed if I don't say just hello to her."

"You're a right guy," Ahearne said. "I'll see what I can do."

He went upstairs, and in a few minutes he motioned me to come up. As I entered, Miss Curtis stood up. She towered over her desk, was nearly six feet tall and I guessed that she weighed at least 200 pounds. Her brown hair was bobbed and brushed back. Ahearne seemed dwarfed beside this political Amazon. Miss Curtis insisted on calling me "Mr. Pagliacci."

"How is Joe McWilliams?" she asked me after the preliminaries of introduction.

"He's very well, thank you," I said. "Do you know him personally?"

"Oh, yes," she answered. "I met him at a dinner given by the American Defense Society in New York sometime ago."

"How is the fight against Lend-Lease coming along?" I asked.

"Very well," Miss Curtis said. "Our women and the Detroit Mothers are visiting all the Senators, particularly Mr. Wheeler. We approach the Congressmen in groups of two and three, show credentials and talk quietly, gaining—we believe—their respect and confidence. Mrs. Morrison was down last week. Mrs. Farber's Mothers have done a particularly good job."

"That is a very constructive way of meeting the problem," I observed, politely. "It is very dignified and effective."

"Why yes. Not at all like Mrs. Dilling. She's giving the movement a black eye. We follow up the personal visits," she resumed, "with a tremendous follow-up mailing campaign to our members urging them to write their Senators to vote against the dictatorship bill. In this way the Senators get the impression that the women of the country are really against the Bill."

"Yes," Ahearne put in, "we work with the America First Committee who also send their men and women to visit Senators and Congressmen."

"We still have a lot of work to do tonight, Mr. Pagliacci," Miss Curtis said, rising. I shook her hand. Ahearne accompanied me to the door. "Lay low and work quietly," he said.

I walked out into the night. It was nearly midnight and a blizzard was raging. It struck me as symbolic of the buzzards hovering around Capitol Hill, seeking to devour Democracy —"that Great Misconception" as Miss Curtis put it.

On my return to the Hotel Plaza after several days' absence, I learned that the thundering herd had been in one jam after another. They had tried to pack Senator Guffey's chambers, and when the Senator insisted on interviewing a delegation instead of the entire howling pack, they broke into cries of "coward," "traitor," "afraid of women."

They had rioted in Senator Claude Pepper's chambers.

They staged a sit-down strike in the Senate Office Building in protest against the venerable Carter Glass of Virginia. One of the women fainted during the melee. Mrs. Dilling was arrested, with an accomplice, Mrs. Clara Henryetta Nibberich and both charged with disorderly conduct. Senator Glass observed: "I believe it would be pertinent to inquire whether they are mothers. For the sake of the race, I devoutly hope not."

I tried to see some of the appeaser Congressmen, but it was virtually impossible because of the Mothers. As I took leave of the thundering herd, intending to return soon, I looked for a last time on the decent, kindly mothers transformed into screaming fish wives and trying desperately to remain respectable under the wild leadership of their herd leader. At this juncture Mrs. Dilling burst in from the outside, her hat askew, hair dishevelled. She had been arrested a second time and had just returned from the police station. She was hysterical and flopped onto a sofa, while the Mothers gathered around her and literally worshipped what I regarded as a shabby imitation of a "Joan of Arc" that they had set up as a wooden idol and which thrived on cheap publicity.

CHAPTER XIV

BEHOLD OUR LIBERATORS!

"It will always remain the best joke made by the democratic system that it provided its deadly enemies with the means of destroying it."

DR. PAUL JOSEPH GOEBBELS

IN JULY, 1941, I returned to Washington, a visit made almost imperative by the cordial exchange of letters with Senator Reynolds. The Senator knew all about my scandalous *Christian Defender,* and I was distributor of his less blatant *American Vindicator.* The Senator's letters to me ended typically: "With assurances of my highest respect, and thanking you for your fine, patriotic, American cooperation, I beg to be, Most Sincerely yours. . . ." And on July 11, 1941, the chairman of the Committee on Military Affairs wrote me:

My dear Mr. Pagnanelli:

Acknowledging receipt of your letter of July 10, I note that you expect to be in Washington next week with the America First delegation, and I assure you that I shall look forward to seeing you at that time. As far as I know I will be in the city all of next week, and I would suggest that you come to the Senate Reception Room and make inquiry.

With all good wishes, and assuring you that I am appreciative of the fine work you are doing in behalf of Americanism, I am, Sincerely yours. . . .

Anticipating a lengthy interview, I came down with a delegation of America First-ers and headed straight for the Senator's offices. But he was so busy that I found it impossible to see him and I spoke, instead, with his tight-lipped associate, Wesley E. McDonald. Later, I met Reynolds in the hallway bowing graciously to two ladies after which he shook my hand, bowed deeply and said, "Yes, I'll see you tomorrow," but he never did.

A politician to his finger tips, the Senator would be a potent spearhead in a native fascist drive. A former barker at a side show, patent medicine salesman, the only Senator to kiss the late Jean Harlow on the mouth in public, to be married four times (once to a Ziegfeld Follies beauty), he was called everything from a mountebank to a demagogue. On May 6, 1939 Reynolds addressed the American Defense Society in New York. After the meeting reporters asked Fritz Kuhn, who was present, for a comment and Kuhn said: "I liked his speech very well. I would underline everything." What probably pleased Kuhn most was Reynolds' remark: "I sometimes think, my friends, that it would be well if the American masses could be provided with sleeping powders in order . . . that they would not hear so much about war in Europe."

The word "alien" was to Reynolds what "Jew" was to McWilliams. He blamed the depression, the war and all our material ills on "alien influence." With considerable backing in April, 1939, the Senator launched *The American Vindicator*, organ of his vigilante-patterned Vindicators and "hammered home Americanism—America for Americans—as the only *ism* this country has time to be interested in." Number one objective on its platform was "Keep America out of war." John B. Trevor contributed a long editorial, *Let Us Have Peace*. Steuben Society Senator Lundeen was quoted and his photograph printed. Bund members were urged to subscribe to and promote the Senator's sheet.

Reynolds' friendship with George Deatherage, the American Nazi (who received a mailbag full of the Senator's speeches for free mailing) received further documentation in a letter Wesley E. McDonald wrote on April 20, 1939 on Vindicator stationery:

While I do not know Mr. George Deatherage personally, we have had some correspondence with him and it appears that he is thoroughly acquainted with just what Senator Reynolds is trying to accomplish. . . . There are absolutely no Jews attached to the membership of this organization.

Reynolds organized a posse for catching "alien crooks" (non-aliens not wanted). It was called the Border Patrol and membership was open to any boy between ten and eighteen. The youth received a badge studded with stars and stripes to show membership in the budding American storm-troop

movement. In addition, he had a chance to win $25 for catch-
ing "alien crooks." America produced no other kind.

For a time the versatile Senator entertained the idea of organizing "The Circle of Seven" to meet in homes secretly. It
was based somewhat on Father Coughlin's "platoon" idea.
"This is merely a movement to get together groups of patriotic Americans, citizens in every single station," Reynolds
explained. "Those who want to destroy our American form
of government are not losing any time."

A close friend of Winrod and many other native fascists,
the Senator inserted his speeches in the *Congressional Record*
and on July 7, 1939 he telegraphed Winrod as follows:

Your most excellent address entitled *Keep America Out of War*
delivered by you over Del Rio Radio Station was inserted in
Appendix Congressional Record yesterday by me and I am now
mailing you copy thereof. Consider it high privilege and honor
to be provided opportunity of bringing to attention of American
public such a marvelous address. Thanks for your patriotic co-
operation. Regards.

Reynolds also used Congress as a sounding board for Franco
propaganda from the Falangist organ, *Spain;* and Italian "patriotism" from the Italian Fascist organ, *Il Grido Della Stirpe*
—whose editor, Domenico Trombetta, was later denatural-
ized and his sheet banned. Reynolds was a leader of the anti-
Lend Lease bloc of so-called "isolationists" and a darling of
America First, anti-British, nativist interests. He fought
against the fortification of Guam, declaring: "It would be
better to give Guam away to anybody who would take it,
along with the Philippines."

Upon his return from Germany Reynolds inserted in the
Congressional Record:

The dictators are doing what is best for their people. I say it is
high time we found out how they are doing it, and why they
are progressing so rapidly. . . . Hitler has solved the unemployment problem. There is no unemployment in Italy. . . . Hitler and
Mussolini have a date with Destiny. It's foolish to oppose them,
so why not play ball with them?

Held in high esteem by American Nazis, Reynolds also observed: "America is going through a very trying period. What is the answer? Nationalism is the answer. The other great nations are realizing it. . . . Germany is going places and we've gotta realize it." Reynolds was idolized by and frequently quoted in the official Nazi Party organ, *Volkischer Beobachter*, and when Hitler invaded Czechoslovakia Reynolds justified it by saying:

Hitler went over and took land in the way that sometimes the boys in Texas and North Carolina used to move a fence with the aid of a shotgun, instead of doing it legally by the way of a surveyor—that's all that Hitler did.

Nor did the Senator who later became chairman of the vitally important Committee on Military Affairs become alarmed over the Japanese. "I think the people of the United States are somewhat fortunate," he said, "in that between us and Soviet Russia there lie the islands of Japan with their ninety-seven million people."

Those bad "alien" Russians! And those dear, friendly Japanese!

While in Washington I made my headquarters at the America First Committee office and met diminutive Miss Isobel French who was in charge. Her summation of the America First position was succinctly expressed in these terms:

"All this agitation is predicated on two schools of thought. We of the America First believe you can come to an understanding and do business with Hitler. The interventionists think you can't. One believes in 'appeasement' as the way out and the other believes in more vigorous measures. Only one of us can be right."

A frequent visitor to the offices was Miss Katrina McCormick, niece of the publisher of the *Chicago Tribune*. She called her uncle a "goofy old man who has a lot of eccentricities" and added that he was one of the "angels" of the A.F.C.

I was excited when I was told that Senator Gerald B. Nye would speak to an intimate group of the A.F.C. Saturday night, July 19th. Perhaps the most vigorous of the America

First promoters in Congress, Nye's record in the Senate had been one of unremitting opposition to all major defense measures for the last three years. He helped lead the fight against Lend-Lease and collaborated intimately with many appeaser-minded groups, regardless of their political leanings.

Nye's record flashed before me. He charged on the Senate floor that the British and not German submarines had sunk the *Robin Moor* and later withdrew the baseless charge. Darling of the Steuben Society, he was quoted in the June, 1938 issue of *The Steuben News* as having said:

Why should we be surprised over what the German leadership and the German people are doing today, when we know that Germany is only striving to win her way out of the injustices heaped upon her by a mad world at the end of the war.

Nye initiated a probe of the movie industry, but the investigation flopped, mainly because he had not seen the movies he charged were "war propaganda." He arranged for Andrae Nordskog, a Los Angeles worker with the Bund, to air his defeatist views before a Senatorial Committee and later distributed Nordskog's speech, free, under his Congressional frank. Tens of thousands of copies of Nye's speeches on behalf of appeasement, defeatism, obstructionism and the Steuben Society were sent out under his frank at the cost of American taxpayers.

Nye was esteemed by the "vermin press." *Social Justice* praised him to the skies: "If a man can be judged by his enemies, Gerald Nye has certainly become one of the foremost Americans of the present day."

The *Deutscher Weckruf* spoke of "the indefatigable efforts of . . . Nye to keep the Ship of State on an even keel," and Pelley's *Roll Call* lauded him: "He [Stephen A. Day] takes his place on the patriotic honor roll along with Charles A. Lindbergh, Senators Gerald Nye and Burton K. Wheeler. Dr. Jacob Thorkelson and more."

This was the man I was to meet.

At about ten o'clock Senator Nye arrived. He was dressed in a deep green striped suit and was a medium, strongly built man, with a deeply lined face and throaty voice. I made it a point to sit only a few feet away from him. He impressed me as an extremely determined man, intense, shrewd and as keen as a blade. His face, tough-textured, reminded me of Kemal Ataturk of Turkey, with its fierce, penetrating look and the same resolute grimness and hard-bitten quality. Wiry and in the prime of physical health and intellectual vigor, Nye showed that he was a dynamic and relentless fighter. The Senator had brought his wife, a beautiful Nordic type, devoted to her husband's cause.

I found myself automatically comparing him with his closest political partner, Senator Burton Kendall Wheeler. Bald-headed and paunchy, Wheeler seemed soft when compared to the armor-plate Nye. While Wheeler, a grizzled veteran of the Washington merry-go-round, could work effectively in the caucus room with back-patting, cigar-chewing politicians of his own mold, he had hardly impressed me as the colorful leader that native fascists could turn to. In that respect, Nye also towered above Senator Reynolds and would easily outlast the average run of politicians.

I remained in the background studying Nye, while others of the A.F.C. crowded around him. There were about thirty of us present, including a man who gave me his name as Clarence Hewes and told me he had formerly been with the Department of State; a Mrs. Merrill, chairman of the St. Petersburg, Florida, chapter of A.F.C.; Brant D. Allison, with the Liberal Arts College of Northwestern University. The room in which we gathered was cozy, with a fireplace on one side and a comfortable sofa at one end, on which the Senator and Mrs. Nye sat, while we sat around them in an assortment of chairs.

"I hope there aren't any government employees present," Nye began. "I don't care personally but it might mean their jobs if found out." We all denied "working for the government" and Senator Nye resumed his talk. It was thoroughly defeatist, the Senator complaining that the morale of our armed forces was "terrible" and even worse among new draftees. He said flatly: "If England were to make peace with Germany the terms won't be half as bad as the terms a victorious England would give Germany."

When he had finished his speech I asked the Senator to

pose for a flashlight picture which he did obligingly, but first insisted that I include the American flag as background.

I was also eager to interview Congressman John E. Rankin because of a tragic event which took place in the House on June 4, 1941. On that day Rankin delivered one of several blistering condemnations of American Jews as "war mongers." Rising to protest against the slander, Representative M. Michael Edelstein pointed out that the meeting of so-called "international bankers" which "took place yesterday on the steps of the Sub-Treasury [Building] was entirely controlled by persons other than Jewish bankers."

As Congressman Edelstein's closing words: "All men are created equal, regardless of race, creed or color" rang to the applause of his colleagues, he strode from the House to go to his chambers. Just outside the entrance he collapsed. He was carried, limp, to a couch in the adjacent House reading room. Congressman Edelstein was dead.

His tragic death was greeted by American Nazis with all the fanfare of a Nazi military victory. Fascist speakers turned down other topics to apostrophize the "patriotism" of the Congressman from Mississippi. Rankin's name became indelibly inscribed on the international fascist roll of honor and was lauded in the January 15, 1940, issue of *World Service*.

This was the man I arranged to see.

A sharp-eyed, shrewd, callous little man, with volatile and fanatic energy, Rankin asked me to leave my camera behind as we walked into his room. My first thought was that he was a Klansman. Peculiarly enough, during the ensuing conversation he brought up the subject and said that he had been charged with being a Klansman. He had answered: "I don't have to belong to any organization to be pro-American."

He had received my letter, he said, and read the inclosures, but could not find it at the moment. He asked for my name again and when I repeated it, he demanded:

"First tell me why you wanted to see me."

I told him that we had read about Congressman Edelstein and I was eager to shake the hand of an "American." This obviously pleased Rankin because he burst into a smile. "Yeah, he keeled over," he said. Crossing his little legs, Rankin turned his face, cross-patched with wrinkles and advised:

"When you go back to New York, you tell them this. There is only one way to win this fight and that is to expose the international Jewish bankers as the war mongers. Tell the people that it is the Jews who want war. Do that and you've got half the battle won." Rankin then boasted that Senator Hiram W. Johnson had said of him: "This man has done more in one minute than any other man in the past six months."

After leaving Rankin I visited George Edward Sullivan. He was a willing talker, but at the same time it was an ordeal for me to be with him for an hour. An utter fanatic in the cause he propagated, Sullivan impressed me as potentially very dangerous to the democratic cause.

As I sat down beside his desk, Sullivan took out my letter and the copy of *The Christian Defender*, read them both carefully and smiled. Before turning to me he cleared away a copy of Pelley's *Liberation*.

"I agree with your paper," he said, then uncorked a blistering and prolonged attack on the Jews. Like Ahearne, he condemned the frontal tactics of the crackpots. His "secret weapon" was to attack Jews through their religion: Jews had no religion, he said, but a hoax posing as religion. And Christ was not a Jew: He was a Hebrew.

Thus he went on until his presence became unbearable to me but I stayed on, at least long enough to learn that he knew John B. Snow and Joseph P. Kamp; that Seward Collins had visited him twice at his office. He also conceded knowing and hinted at having helped the mysterious "Cincinnatus," the author of *War, War, War* but would not divulge his name other than to say: "I know him. He is in the vicinity. He is a pretty old man and has a brilliant mind."

Thorkelson inserted in the *Congressional Record* an article by Sullivan, and Sullivan was quoted enthusiastically in *Social Justice*, James True's *Industrial Control Reports* and his articles were reprinted in Winrod's *Defender*. He served as Coughlin's representative in Washington and also functioned as a one-man information bureau for the dissemination of his brand of "truth." Sullivan told me he had helped Mrs. Dilling with data for *The Octopus* providing her with the same documents which appeared in *War, War, War*.

He was author of a book *Wolves in Sheep's Clothing* which

had been subsidized by the Sodality Union in Washington and was distributed by John B. Snow in New York. Sullivan was planning to write another book—against the Jews, of course. "It'll be a hot one," he said. "I'm going to spend my vacation this summer writing it."

Access to most Congressmen was easy, but engaging them in lengthy interviews was out of the question. The kind I wanted to see were busy with America First Committee officials day and night. Hearing that John C. Schafer, former Republican Congressman and Steuben Society member was in town, I rushed over to interview him.

Schafer had fought *every* measure which tried to bolster American defense and had proved himself an obstinate obstructionist to national defense. Like his colleague, Clare Hoffman, Schafer had voted down all relief and social measures. His speeches appeared in *Social Justice,* and Coughlin's articles found their way into the *Congressional Record.* Washington newspapermen often referred to Schafer as "bullneck." When angered which was often, his neck became red and "glowed like a stop-light," newspapermen said. *The Steuben News* claimed him as an "old time Steubenite affiliated with the Muehlenberg Unit 36 of Milwaukee, Wisconsin."

I met Schafer at his home and my impressions of him are indelible. He had once weighed 300 pounds, but was now a mere skeleton of 250 pounds—a huge, ferocious-looking fellow, with layers of fat bulging around his chin and neck, a shock of blond hair falling over his face. He had the appearance of a zealot about him. He was easily emotionalized by the power of his own oratory and as we talked, he got into the habit of swinging an enormous, club-like fist only a few inches from my face.

I found Schafer no different from the "patriots" back home in his prophecy of a Hitler victory and its natural consequences of a revolution here against Democracy.

"What kind of a revolution?" I asked.

"The BLOODY kind," he roared. "There will be purges and Roosevelt will be cleaned right off the earth along with the Jews. We'll have a military dictatorship to save the country." He leaned toward me and his fist swung like a pendulum grazing my face.

"How about the Constitution?" I asked.

"Oh that? That'll be set aside temporarily until they get some law and order in this country. A revolution is no picnic."

Schafer was getting ready to tour the country: "That's the thing to do from now on. Get the masses all boiled up. Get the mob and the rabble aroused. Get them going. We've got to protect the Constitution and the only way to do it is to get the people behind you."

It was his studied opinion that our generals "can't even fight Indians." He told me that he had served twenty-two months in the World War, never rising above the rank of private. Like Rankin, he claimed to have a large following among World War veterans and huge mailing lists of Legionnaires. He was friendly with Commander Edward Elwell Spafford, friend of Nazi agent Ernest Schmitz.

"Germany cannot be beaten today. If we go on antagonizing her, do you think she'll forget it? She'll jump on us as soon as she is finished in Europe, sure as I'm talking to you now. Hell!" he boomed, "Hitler can cross the ocean in eight hours, drop his pineapples and go back for another load. I wouldn't antagonize any of the fascist nations but try to work with them." That was the extent of Private Schafer's fighting spirit on behalf of America!

Curious to know what she was doing, I called on Dr. Maude S. DeLand who now lived in Washington, and found her typing propaganda. When I told her I had visited Congressman Rankin, she said: "I've met him, too, and I also know Congressman Day."

Dr. DeLand was spending the hot summer days visiting members of the House and the Senate, and making copies of pertinent "patriotic" passages from typically Nazi sources. With these homemade paper bullets she was carrying on her "educational" campaign. Her prize "pupil," according to what she told me, was Rufus C. Holman, Senator from Oregon. A quiet, plodding public servant, Holman suddenly inserted in the March 8, 1941, *Congressional Record* the entire text of *Money, Politics and the Future*, a pro-Nazi propaganda tract defending the German financial system. It was printed in England by the Boswell Publishing Company, printers of British fascist literature.

THE **VINDICATOR**

Number One Second Street, N.E.
WASHINGTON, D. C.

ROBERT E. REYNOLDS
President

WESLEY E. McDONALD
National Sec'y-Treas.

August 2, 1941

Mr. George Pagnanelli,
100 W. 86th Street,
New York City.

My dear Mr. Pagnanelli:

Thank you very much for your letter under date of July 21, 1941, addressed to Group Director, American Vindicator, No. 1 Second Street, N. E. Washington, D. C., contents of which I have read with much interest.

I have just sent to the printer copy for a little booklet entitled "The Circle of Seven" and this should be off the press during the forepart of the coming week and when the first copies are delivered I am asking the secretary who is taking this letter to mail to you a copy, and I shall be glad to hear from you after you have read the contents thereof. Of course we are greatly interested in getting these groups established throughout the country and shall be appreciative of any suggestions that you might be in a position to provide us with.

With assurances of my highest respect, and thanking you for your fine, patriotic, American cooperation, I beg to be,

Most sincerely yours,

Robert R. Reynolds, Editor.

RRR/mob

America For Americans ... Our Citizens, Our Country First

Senator Wheeler of Montana named the Rothchilds, the Sassoons and the Warburgs, as the International Bankers who are trying to push thru the H.R. 1776 Lend Lease Bill and get us into WAR!

Senator Holman of Oregon said: Jewish Political Influence and money interests are exerting great pressure to get the H. R. 1776 Lend Lease Bill approved and passed.

Joseph E. McWilliams, as far back as two years ago, named the Rothchilds, Sassoons, Warburgs and Jewish Political Influence as being opposed to the best interests of the People of the United States of America.

JOSEPH E. McWILLIAMS

American Destiny Party

CANDIDATE for CONGRESS
18th New York Congressional District

The Yorkville Fuehrer finds himself in agreement with certain so-called "isolationist" Senators. In Reynolds' letter note the fascist slogan, "America for Americans."

"I gave that book to Senator Holman," Dr. DeLand boasted, "and asked him to read it. Isn't it wonderful what he did with it?"

Similarly, Holman advertised in the *Congressional Record* a book by Father Coughlin's economic adviser, Gertrude M. Coogan. Her book, *Money Creators* made some startling revelations unknown to reputable historians. According to Miss Coogan, the Revolution was financed on *both* sides by the Rothschilds and Alexander Hamilton's real name was Levine. She grieved: "It is a sorry commentary that so few Americans have ever had an opportunity to learn by their own research the true history of the United States."

A prize follower of America First principles who voted against *every* major defense measure, Holman spoke before the American Coalition of Patriotic Societies, inserted his speech in the *Congressional Record* and had it mailed free of charge to members of the Coalition. And on March 4, 1941, as the Senate and gallery sat tense, the Oregon Senator bluntly praised Hitler and suggested that England and America might advantageously emulate him:

I doubt if the right is all on one side among the present belligerents. At least Hitler . . . has broken the control of the international bankers and traders over the rewards for the labor of the common people of Germany.

In my opinion it would be advantageous if the control of the international bankers and traders over the wages and savings and manner of living of the people of England could be broken by the English people, and if the control of the international bankers and traders over the wages and savings and manner of living of the people of the United States could be broken by the people of the United States.

This speech by one of Senator Nye's close collaborators was received with acclaim by American Nazis everywhere. Joe McWilliams issued a special leaflet telling the world that he had been saying the same thing for years, but nobody listened. And from the Berlin short wave came praise which delighted the Senator's Nazi idolaters. I wish I could say that the case of Senator Holman was the only one of its kind which existed on Capitol Hill.

CHAPTER XV

AMERICA'S DOOM SQUAD

"Let's mind our own business—and keep our powder dry—avoid all the ideologies which are contrary to our own good system. Let us so live our own lives in a world of neighbors that we shall be a power for good because we have the respect of all."

WILLIAM R. CASTLE

ON THE NIGHT OF April 23, 1941, the Manhattan Center Opera House was packed with 8,000 men, women and children each carrying an American flag. The walls were draped with flags. The platform was festooned with flags. At a given signal the crowd began to wave flags, the band burst into patriotic music and the mob howled "patriotism" in a screaming crescendo of Nürnberg super-nationalism.

My old "friends" led the tumult. There was August Klapprott and Gustav Elmer of the Bund hierarchy, surrounded by members of the *Ordnungs Dienst*. Hiding under a big hat, John B. Snow came in the back way because the front entrance was mobbed. George Van Nosdall waved his flag like a child. Edward James Smythe worked his way in and one of the officials scurried about to find him a reserved seat. Lawrence Dennis, the apostle of American National-Socialism, sat quietly on the balcony avoiding publicity until an alert camera man spotted him.

Edwin P. Banta was there and so was Max Kalcher, Bundist salesman of the *Deutscher Weckruf* I had met at Camp Siegfried. In an official capacity, Mrs. Schuyler sat on the platform with the same smugness as at Allen Zoll's meetings. A wide assortment of thugs and sundry hooligans from the goon squads were scattered throughout the crowd. Not to be overlooked was the august presence of George F. A. Boian, self-professed member of the Nazi Rumanian Iron Guard.

"Who wants war?" the speaker asked, waiting for a reply.

"The Jews are the war mongers," the mob yelled back waving flags.

Was this a Christian Mobilizer meeting? A Bund, Christian Front meeting? Or a coalition meeting of all three? The last comes near being the truth. It was a meeting of the America First Committee and Charles Augustus Lindbergh was the featured speaker. Reverend Edward A. Hunt delivered the invocation. When I interviewed him the next day I found that he was not only a friend of Mrs. Dilling, but also of Colonel Sanctuary and Mrs. Schuyler.

A few nights later I went to Carnegie Hall. As George Pagnanelli, the "patriotic" editor, I was invited to grace the platform, but I sat there only long enough to ascertain that the corpulent fellow occupying a platform seat was John Cecil, speaker for the American Nationalist Party and the Christian Front. I saw a lot of ladies dressed in fine clothes, and I saw my rabble pals hobnobbing with Park Avenue. Thomas Malone, salesman for *National American* was distributing free copies of *The American Vindicator*, next to a salesman selling *Social Justice*.

I recognized Bund speaker, Russell Dunn, and Edwin Westphal who had helped in the rioting during which two Bronx policemen were beaten up. Dr. DeLand drove up in a taxi. Dr. Mills, a speaker for Jordan the "Black Fuehrer" was on hand, while "Uncle" Charles V. Miller—a supporter of the Mobilizers and the Christian Front—scanned the audience with a pair of binoculars.

Was this, too, a "coalition" meeting of America First? Not quite. It was a meeting of Women United, an America First Committee subsidiary, and Senator Reynolds was the guest of honor. Deatherage took it upon himself to instruct Mrs. Geraldine Buchanan Parker, executive secretary, on the "respectable" way of disseminating anti-Semitism:

Your literature does not need to state the word—Jew. All you have to do in order to place the blame where the people can understand it is to accuse the international bankers. The masses have now been educated to understand what is meant. . . . Senator Holt can give you the information, you can quote from the *Congressional Record*—it is there.

And on the platform of Ebling's Casino—rich in memories of Kuhn, Kunze, McWilliams, Thorkelson, Cassidy—a short woman in a long bob kept her right hand firmly on her hip, jutted her jaw forward, waved her arms and launched into what seemed to be a cheap imitation of Hitler-Mussolini oratory. She was Cathrine Curtis' friend, Laura Ingalls.

Laura Ingalls quoted from articles in Ford's *Dearborn Independent*, then screamed: "I want a spiritual anger to run through the entire country. I want you all to be fired with emotion and I want you all to be angered by conditions in this country. Americans, have we that light in our eye?"

"Y'Goddam right we have," yelled the mob, whistling and stomping.

"The measure of patriotism is the measure of freedom," she shouted. She mouthed a half dozen of these demagogic phrases that emotionalized the mob to a froth, then ended with the revolutionary cry: "If they mean to have a war, let it begin here."

"We're ready. Let 'er come."

Miss Ingalls had been warned against repeating her favorite stunt of rendering the Nazi salute even though she explained it this way: "We need an American symbol of unity. We ought to adopt the American salute—the outstretched *left arm*. This is purely American and no one can accuse us of being Nazis, for the Nazis use the *right* arm."

When the meeting was over, I filed out with the rest of the mob. From a dark sector of the street I watched for faces I knew, then walked over to Pop Eibach selling the *Deutscher Weckruf*. Chief New Moon (he was Thomas N. M. Dixon, Kuhn's Cherokee Indian collaborator) was distributing anti-war booklets. The Christian Mobilizers were passing out leaflets urging all "pro-Americans" who believed in "America for Americans" to attend their next meeting; while Jack Cassidy's henchmen urged in the name of "Christ and Country, Law and Order" the election of Christian Front leader John H. Henihan for City Council and William Goodwin, "Dove of Peace" candidate for mayor on the Coughlin-inspired American Rock Party. Only a few days ago Goodwin had told me in confidence at his campaign headquarters:

"There's nothing wrong with fascism. Hitler has done a good job in Germany."

"Would you recommend a Hitler for America?" I asked.

"I wouldn't go so far as to say that," he answered. "A man like Hitler won't go over with the American people. We need something else. The Corporate State of Franco would be a perfect system for our country."

These were typical of America First Committee meetings I attended. This was the "new leadership" which Lindbergh demanded in his speeches; and this the "leadership" for which my Nazi associates had been waiting in seething ferment since General Moseley's bubble blew up; this was the "leadership" which fully met Bund and Steuben Society approval and earned the plaudits of the Berlin short wave. It did not come in the form of a "man on a white horse" as the rabble elements had romanticized. It came much more subtly, without the fanfare of swastika or wild revolutionary talk. The America First Committee was not an overnight phenomenon, for it had been in the making for eight years. Nor was the word "committee" the proper term for a nation-wide political mass movement expertly organized, backed by illimitable capital and the shrewdest organizational, but politically uninformed, minds in the country. Indeed it was so gilded with an air of respectability and so carefully guarded—for a time at least—from the taint of the rabble Bund and the Christian Front that some of our most distinguished national figures became its unwitting sponsors, among whom were the Reverend John Haynes Holmes and Captain Edward Rickenbacker, a close friend of Henry Ford's. The Committee claimed a membership of 15,000,000.

True, its leadership at first was as American as Plymouth Rock. But the rank and file following—at first sincere and respectable—was later polluted by the Pelleys, Coughlins, McWilliamses; the Vierecks, Kuhns and Deatherages; by Klansmen; by Japanese and Nazi agents. And its weak-kneed leadership, cowed and bullied by stories of Nazi might, swayed by Chamberlain sentimentality and Pollyanna smugness, took craven comfort in the delusion that they were "defending America." The surrender of a mighty nation in appeasement to Hitler might easily have been the outcome if the designs of its two most publicized spokesmen had been carried through.

Its national chairman, General Robert E. Wood, told Kenneth Crawford a reporter for *PM*, a New York newspaper, that in the event of an invasion of South America by a Nazi armada, he would defend our Latin Allies "only the part as far south as the bulge of Brazil." Without firing a shot in self-defense, the General indicated his willingness to let Hitler seize more than half of South America, plant his legions firmly on the Western Hemisphere and place the Panama Canal at the mercy of his *Luftwaffe*.

William R. Castle, another founder of the America First Committee, expressed amazing shortsightedness for a former official of the State Department. Apparently dominated by Viereck's syrupy assurances that Hitler was the friend of all and the enemy of none, Castle wrote in the Nazi organ *Today's Challenge:*

Let's mind our own business—and keep our powder dry— avoid all the ideologies which are contrary to our own good system. Let us so live our own lives in a world of neighbors that we shall be a power for good because we have the respect of all.

This sample of infantile trust after years of relentless Nazi aggression during which Democracies crumbled one by one because they, too, believed in Hitler's promises, remained dominant with the "new leadership." Faith in Hitler but an unreasoning lack of faith in the Administration—these were the cornerstones of the Committee's policy of appeasement and defeatism which corroded our democratic fibre. It delighted Nazi commentators, who crooned from Berlin: "The America First Committee is known as true Americanism and true patriotism, as opposed to the synthetic brand."

"Patriotic" meetings of the Mobilizers and the Bund fell down in attendance, while most of the other fascistic groups were suspended altogether as their members flocked to America First rallies. Whenever I wanted information from my "friends" I had to go either to America First meetings or the A.F.C. headquarters to find them.

The Committee's backers for the most part were sincere

and well-meaning prototypes of those who had backed Hitler in Germany—a small clique of industrialists, business men and army officers. Ernest T. Weir of Republic Steel Corporation contributed heavily. Thomas N. McCarter, former chairman of the Public Service Corporation of New Jersey, was another heavy donor. H. L. Stuart, president of a leading investment house in the Midwest, was a financial supporter, and so was Sterling Morton, President of the Illinois Manufacturers Association.

The wealthy meat-packer, Jay C. Hormel, gave liberally, as did Mrs. Janet Ayer Fairbanks; Max Wellington Babb, president of Allis-Chalmers; General Wood and General Thomas Hammond. Colonel Robert R. McCormick of the *Chicago Tribune* and Joseph M. Patterson, publisher of the New York *Daily News* supported the America First Committee, and there were reports that Henry Ford contributed $300,000 to initiate the work.

The idea for the Committee was conceived in the spring of 1940—in the mind of a blond, wealthy twenty-four-year-old Yale student, R. Douglas Stuart, Jr., son of the first vice-president of the Quaker Oats Co. Stuart got twenty of his classmates to join. The romantic story released by the Committee went on to say that young Douglas attracted the attention of Chester Bowles, of Benton and Bowles, Inc., well-known New York advertising agents.

From nowhere staid William R. Castle joined the blond youth. Then to Stuart's growing circle of influential friends came Philip LaFollette, former Progressive Party governor of Wisconsin, and was quickly followed by Senator Burton K. Wheeler, General Wood (who was board chairman of Sears, Roebuck and Co.), Henry Ford and Robert Bliss of J. Walter Thompson, advertising agents. Experts in promotion, organization and public relations gathered around young Stuart.

With Douglas and his Yale friends serving as front, Charles Lindbergh addressed a meeting at Woolsey Hall. This made the headlines even though Lindbergh, like Neville Chamberlain, propagated Hitler's ideas by saying: "In order to dominate the Far Eastern situation we must make our peace with the new powers in Europe." After the Lindbergh speech,

General Wood took charge and set to organizing the Committee on a broad, nation-wide basis.

At this stage the Committee was regarded by the rabble fascists as both highbrow and "Jewish" because of the presence of wealthy Lessing J. Rosenwald on the board. Mrs. Dilling denounced the Committee and went on with her own Mothers' group. The rabble fascist element maintained a safe distance, entertaining itself with feverish and hysterical "crusades" and "marches"; with the impeachment of a "Jewish" President and the adulation of Hitler, the misunderstood messiah who loved "peace."

During this period of the Stalin-Hitler pact, Nazi and Communist party liners, in addition to Norman Thomas' Socialist wing, composed a united front to sabotage national defense. Though motives differed, tactics of the Communist front, American Peace Mobilization, paralleled those of the fascist partisans. The "vermin press" and *The Daily Worker* found themselves in mutually embarrassing agreement.

Social Justice, Aug. 12, 1940: "The Burke-Wadsworth Conscription bill is more than a conscription bill. It is a bill to abolish the Constitution of the United States. That is why the Burke-Wadsworth communistic bill must be fought—now, or never.

The Daily Worker, Aug. 16, 1940: "The Burke-Wadsworth Conscription Bill must be defeated. It includes within its confusing and misleading verbiage the basis for American fascism."

Deutscher Weckruf, Aug. 8, 1940: "Compulsory military service is a European institution. . . . Why should we adopt European fashions just to relieve the President of his unemployment problem."

Herman Schwinn, West coast Nazi agent, adopted in a speech the Communist slogan "The Yanks Are Not Coming," while the fellow-traveling Almanac Singers contributed to the cause of obstructionism against national defense by parodying war. For instance:

Don't you want a silver medal, Billy boy, Billy boy?
Don't you want a silver medal, charming Billy?
No desire do I feel to defend Republic Steel;
He's a young boy and cannot leave his mother.

Every "patriot" cell automatically turned into a "peace" cell, and the Reverend Edward Lodge Curran suspended his duties as president of the International Catholic Truth Society long enough to establish the Anti-War Crusaders and needle audiences on extensive lecture tours. Occasionally the rabble elements met under such "respectable" auspices as the National Keep America Out of War Committee, sister organization to the anti-war group promoted by Ham Fish and financed mainly by the Steuben Society.

The New York branch of the Committee was directed by L. M. Bailey, a friend of Allen Zoll. On the committee were Ham Fish, several Park Avenue ladies who had served Zoll, and Arthur Goadby who frequented Seward Collins' bookshop.

William Griffin, publisher of the *New York Enquirer*, was chairman of one meeting of the Keep America Out of War Committee which I attended at Carnegie Hall, and at which Senators Nye and Holt spoke. Griffin's technique was familiar. "Who are the war mongers?" he asked, followed by: "Who are the people who own the radio stations and the newspapers?" Waiting for the answer, he smiled smugly as the mob howled "The Jews." Seward Collins, Van Nosdall and a coterie of other American fascists were present.

When Griffin called for a march on Washington the mob began to yell, "McWilliams, McWilliams!" Griffin then turned to someone on the platform, but the man shook his head as if to say, "No, don't bring him on the platform." But the Coughlinite mob kept calling for Joe to make an appearance, while Joe smiled indulgently in a box seat.

At another meeting I heard Ham Fish speak with Congressman Karl E. Mundt and Mrs. J. Sergeant Cram, a wealthy old lady whose sincere pacifist sentiments were exploited by the fascists. Fish roused the crowd to anti-Semitic outbursts and the frantic renditions of the Nazi salute. Anti-Semitic cries became so violent that a *New York Times* reporter left his seat to spot the callers. Dan Cleason, a confirmed Coughlinite, jumped from his seat and waved a copy of *Social Justice*, while Edwin Westphal moved from a front seat to a section in the rear where the Christian Front-ers were concentrated. As he passed me he whispered: "Ham Fish is all right. Look at him grin up there."

"Germany's claims are just," Fish had told newspapermen while in Berlin, where he was officially honored. If Hitler were given Danzig, the Polish corridor and "anything else" he wanted, Fish was sure that peace would come to Europe. A close friend of the Nazi agent, Viereck, he earned the plaudits of the *Deutscher Weckruf* and received glowing endorsement in Hitler's own party organ, the *Volkischer Beobachter*.

For a time the America First Committee seemed too respectable to get anywhere with the mob. To appease them and to concentrate their energy under one leadership, the hierarchy offered the mob the No Foreign War Committee, headed by Verne Marshall, editor of *The Cedar Rapids Gazette*. Arrangements were made at a dinner tendered at the University Club in New York by Merwin K. Hart, friend of Falangist Fascism. Present were O. K. Armstrong, Charles S. Payson, co-owner and George T. Eggleston, editor of *Scribner's Commentator*, the "American Nazi *Bible*"; several unnamed writers and editors and Charles Lindbergh. As spokesman for the "new leadership" Lindbergh induced Marshall to accept the chairmanship of the Committee. John B. Snow operated behind the scenes with Marshall.

Essentially a showman and somewhat of an eccentric, Marshall was well fitted for his mission. With unlimited financial backing and through a series of clever publicity stunts, Marshall energized the appeasement crusade from coast to coast. He rallied the rabble around him and obtained a tremendous mailing list. He helped to whitewash obstructionism and cleared defeatism and organized sabotage of morale of its Germanic taint.

But after a wild, three-month barnstorming tour through the country, Marshall threatened to place the entire appeasement machine in jeopardy by consorting with anti-Semites and American Nazis. After being denounced publicly by Lindbergh, Marshall was urged by his backers to resign. Just as the No Foreign War Committee was closing shop I visited its New York headquarters and asked for some of the literature being thrown away. I was given a stack and was not surprised to find:

Lord Lothian vs. Lord Lothian, published by Flanders Hall.
Seeking Foreign Trouble, by Ralph Townsend, Japanese propagandist.
Radio Speeches on War and Peace, by Reverend Gerald B. Winrod.
The Beacon Light, published by William Kullgren.
Anti-War Crusade, by Reverend Edward Lodge Curran.
The Guildsman, a magazine published by Edward A. Koch, and "devoted to the cause of a corporative order."

When by March 1, 1941, Marshall's trial balloon had burst, the America First Committee was poised to take over the management. Along with the office personnel, the new sponsors accepted the voluminous mailing lists of Coughlinites and Bundists who had rallied to the side of the eccentric Pied Piper of the new "patriotism." Thus, before it swung into saddle, the backbone of the American fascist movement became the backbone of its "respectable" new sponsors.

As Pagnanelli, the ever-helpful "patriot" in all such causes, I filed my application as volunteer worker. Opposite the line "membership in other organizations," I boldly put down "Christian Mobilizers" wondering whether I would be challenged. I recall that it was a Mrs. I. Pearce who interviewed me. I asked her point-blank whether she knew of "our work." She nodded, smiling. I was accepted as volunteer on the same basis as with the No Foreign War Committee.

From this point on, my role as investigator required attending a bewildering array of meetings that dinned into the minds of the masses—by an hourly diet of street speaking, radio broadcasts and an avalanche of literature—those doctrines I had already learned in the Nazi underworld. Into the America First offices poured a daily stream of my "friends" I knew personally or recognized seeing at subversive meetings. There was no partiality. Anyone who asked for literature got it—free of charge.

The office at 515 Madison Avenue, where I worked as volunteer was a bedlam. Volunteers stayed till the early morning hours, energized by a hot revivalist fever. Mothers stayed away from their homes and family life was disrupted in a crusade for peace at any sell-out price. Sitting at the volunteers' table, I heard a great deal of intimate talk. This sort of thing:

"I haven't cooked supper in three weeks and my husband is sore."

"Well, we've all got to sacrifice to save our country. After all, it's Roosevelt who wants war, not Hitler."

"Roosevelt and the internationalists."

"You mean the Jews. Don't be afraid to say it, sister."

"They ain't all bad. There's a Rabbi Charles Fleischer who speaks for the Committee, and that fellow doing the publicity for us. . . ."

"Sydney Hertzberg, that's his name."

"Yeah, and Mrs. Paul Palmer on the Committee. She's wealthy and she's Jewish, you know."

"These are good Jews, but most of them are bad."

I had been watching a small, kindly-faced grandmother with white hair and a wrinkled face. She worked quietly and rarely spoke. Once or twice we had exchanged smiles and I had taken a fancy to her. I felt she had something on her mind and had noticed her leave the table several times when the discussion was hottest. Suddenly she froze the volunteers by saying in a thin, clear voice:

"I don't think it's fair of you to talk that way about the Jews. We're not fighting this war against the Jews and I can't understand why you are always talking against them. I'm here because I don't want to see my grandchildren go to war, but I'm not going to speak against any race of people. I don't think you ladies are being Christian at all."

I felt like rushing over and hugging grandma, but it would have been my suicide as investigator.

There were many in the America First Committee who were sincere and devout, like grandma, but I observed that the overwhelming majority were fascist party-liners. This was graphically illustrated at the Lindbergh rally at Madison Square Garden. I went early, passing through a cordon of police, hawkers for *Social Justice* and distributors of Boris Brasol's leaflets in order to study Lindbergh at the ringside. Mrs. Schuyler was seated with her sister, Mrs. Barbour Walker and she motioned to me. I had sent her a booklet reprinted by the Ku Klux Klan from the *Dearborn Independent* and was curious to know what she thought of it.

"That . . . that booklet was excellent," she said, without disclosing the name in public. "Get me ten more."

In the audience, too, I recognized Dr. Ulrich D. Marquard, a Wall Street broker, and a Prussian with emphatic Nazi views whom I had interviewed with a Christian Front-er. And I also saw Joe McWilliams in the act of posing for a flock of photographers. The auditorium was packed as the master of ceremonies asked the audience to sing *God Bless America*. An angry howl of boos greeted the request and was an index to what followed later. Irving Berlin's song was always booed and *never* sung at "patriotic" meetings because Berlin happened to be an American Jew. We did not sing *God Bless America* that night.

Norman Thomas, a zealot, leader of the Socialist Labor Party and ardent orator, plunged into his topic without preliminaries and delivered a repugnant defeatist speech: "Have you no more regard for mankind, Mr. President, than to bring total destruction? The worst that could happen would be a negotiated peace. We'll have it eventually. Why not now?" John T. Flynn, chairman, then read congratulatory messages from Cardinal O'Connell of Boston and Bishop Gerald Shaughnessy of Seattle, after which he introduced Lindbergh.

The wildest demonstration I have ever heard met Lindbergh. It was unlike anything else I had known. A deep-throated, unearthly, savage roar, chilling, frightening, sinister and awesome. It was a frenzied mob-cheer adulating the hero of the hour in reckless hysteria.

And what of the blond god who for six full minutes smiled like an adolescent as the mob stood to its feet, waved flags, threw kisses and frenziedly rendered the Nazi salute? Lindbergh impressed me as the most naïve of men politically. He did not impress me either as an organizer or a leader—but as a man who, while himself being led by the nose, had a tremendous capacity to lead the masses by serving as their idol owing to his gift of personal magnetism for a certain class of men and women. Lindbergh—who had turned his back to

America to live first in England, then France, then was reported to be considering the buying of a home in Germany—seemed confused with and uncertain of himself, but a hero with the mob. He fitted the description of the ideal American fuehrer as given by Joe McWilliams:

In a few years we will need a leader who will be like a knight of old. A man in shining armor. A champion of the people. A man who is a mystic. A man that the mob can look up to—but not touch. A man who has come from the people, but has reached so high that they dare not call him their own, but one appointed by God to speak for them! That's what this country needs. That's what we'll need to bring together our forces for a nationalist America.

And McWilliams was present this night also, and shared the spotlight with Lindbergh through a peculiar stroke of circumstances. Joe had made himself conspicuous to camera men, and some of the respectable America First-ers fearing that the meeting might be given a black eye because of his presence, told John T. Flynn. Hot tempered and courageous, Flynn pounced on McWilliams with the fury of a panther and clawed him through the microphone:

"I repudiate the support of the Bund, the Communist and the fascist parties. One of their leaders is in this hall tonight.

CHRISTIAN FRONT NEWS

Bulletin.   May 24, 1940

TO ALL AMERICANS WHO THINK:

COLONEL LINDBERGH IS A PATRIOT !

In the words of Captain Eddie Rickenbacker, America's ace pilot in the World War, the words spoken over the radio last Sunday night by Colonel Charles A. Lindbergh on adequate national defense were "sound and fundamental". Most Americans agree with Capt. Rickenbacker, with the exception of the warmongers, the political parasites, the financial shylocks, the munition moguls, and the people who paraded in the streets of New York last summer to the tune of "Stop-Hitler".

THE CHRISTIAN FRONT
Brooklyn Unit
Prospect Hall, Brooklyn

Lindbergh was the hero or countless American Fascist groups, including the Christian Front

His name is Joseph McWilliams. I don't know whose stooge he is, but newspapermen can always find him where they want him."

But instead of booing, *the Coughlinite mob burst into applause for Joe!!!*

Flynn was taken aback as the fascist pack threatened to get out of control. With the instinct of bloodhounds newsmen, photographers and policemen ran to cover points where riots might break out. With magnificent presence of mind, Flynn jammed his mouth against the microphone and desperately for the next two minutes tried to stem the rising tide of cheering. In the meanwhile, ushers and cops surrounded the spot about ten rows from the ringside, where Joe sat smiling and nonchalant, waving his American flag and enormously pleased at the show. I stole a glance at Lindbergh. He was looking at Joe. He, too, was beaming. . . .

Flynn continued to vilify McWilliams with a sincerity that was unmistakable. After several anxious moments, he finally succeeded in drowning out the applause. A weak, unconvincing round of boos swept up from the respectables, while the bigger Nazi mob withheld its fire. Flynn's heroic endeavors saved the face of the America First Committee. But it showed, even at that early date on May 23, 1941, only a few months after it had taken the reins from Marshall, that the revolutionary following of which Joe was a symbol was already a powerful factor.

Flynn's courageous stand earned him the abuse and wrath of fascist "patriots" and threatened to split the A.F.C. in two. Overnight Flynn became a Communist. Mrs. Dilling screamed that she had always said so in her *Red Network*. Father Coughlin denounced him because he "went out of his way to assail a Mr. McWilliams seated in the audience," and falsely charged him with bigotry.

Coughlin was a force to be reckoned with, and the Coughlin ire had to be placated at his threat of alienating his Christian Front following. Mrs. Lulu Wheeler, wife of the Senator, and extremely active in Committee circles, "explained" in *Social Justice:*

. . . I am afraid that you are a victim of newspaper propaganda, because there never has been any discrimination against Father Coughlin's followers or against any other religious body as far as America First is concerned.

It was not enough. The appeaser-minded leadership had to apologize officially. Even as the Emperor Henry IV did penance at the command of Pope Gregory VII, so General Wood humbled himself before the reverend-dictator of Royal Oak by writing in *Social Justice:*

. . . I have not rejected the Christian Social Justice movement. I welcome their support in our common objective—preventing this country from getting into the war.

To the "new leadership" appeasement—whether to a foreign Hitler or a domestic would-be Hitler—was second nature! This craven attitude was an indication of the extent to which the A.F.C. was enslaved by fascist mentality. After these letters were published, approval of the Christian Front became open and blatant and Front-ers came and went as they pleased. William Gerald Bishop, co-fuehrer with Jack Cassidy and Macklin Boettger, lieutenant in the Sports Club, frequented the A.F.C. offices where I worked as volunteer. Mrs. I. Pearce told me: "The Christian Front is perfectly all right. It is working with us and we think they are fine." Coughlin took advantage of his favored position by writing:

We predict an attempt to establish a National-Socialist Party in America with the emphasis on the word "nationalist.". . . The Marxist democrats, turned militaristic, will obstruct the formation of this party. . . . We predict that if such happens, the National-Socialists in America—organized under that or some other name—eventually will take control of government on this continent. . . . We predict, lastly, the end of democracy in America.

The Mobilizers got a black eye and as a follower of the Yorkville fuehrer I, too, was held in disfavor for a while. In charge of volunteers, Mrs. Jane Lewis asked me to make up my mind between America First and Joe McWilliams, whom she regarded as a hireling paid to "discredit" the Committee.

"He has appeared twice at our meetings and created a sensation," Mrs. Lewis complained. "Can you tell me why he does it?"

Of course I knew, but I could not tell her. At any rate, she asked me to make up my mind and when I said I would take America First, she wasn't convinced, and asked me to please stay away. Joe did not show up at any A.F.C. meetings, but he sent lieutenants with instructions to yell "Jew" whenever A.F.C. speakers referred to "internationalists" or innocuously to "the enemy."

One night, before Joe had started his meeting at the Astoria Casino where he had gone after finally being kicked out of Yorkville halls, I approached him. He was reading Lawrence Dennis' *Weekly Foreign Letter*.

"Joe," I began, "some woman wants to know why you go to A.F.C. meetings and raise hell."

"Tell her this. I want to put it up to those America First guys that they are no different from us nationalists here. Their fine clothes and respectability don't fool me. I've met them up on Park Avenue and down in Wall Street. I want them to wake up to themselves and get up the guts to call a spade a spade. I want them to come right out in the open and work for our nationalism *now* instead of beating the bush and coming out with it later. We can't get anywhere with our people alone. We got to have the America First crowd with us. They got money and they got influence."

"You aren't giving up the fight, are you, Joe?" I asked.

"My mission is done, George," McWilliams answered thoughtfully. "I'm finished for the time being."

I expressed surprise.

"I was brought into this movement for one purpose: to make America Jew-conscious. I've done that. Lindbergh, Nye, Wheeler, Reynolds and the rest of 'em can carry on now. They can reach people I could never reach. Let these big shots take the stage for a while. I did my part and now it's their round. I'll swing back into the saddle when the time is ripe. I'm going to travel—to start little fires all over the country so that they can burst spontaneously into a national flame that'll raze Democracy clear to the ground."

I asked Joe if he had ever met Charles Lindbergh. Joe paused, looked around sharply, hesitated momentarily and said "No."

Then I asked if Lindbergh knew how to handle the "Jewish question" in view of his anti-Semitic speech before a Des Moines audience.

"Not exactly, but he is learning and I happen to know he wants to learn. I'll tell you how Lindbergh is getting his education. He is getting it from the men I've been talking to for months."

"Who have you been talking to, Joe?" I asked.

"Lawrence Dennis is one. I can't tell you who the others are. For months I've been talking to intellectuals on the 'Jewish question,' coaching them and giving them our literature. I've been a regular teacher to them. Lindbergh talked to these men after I had educated them. Indirectly, Lindbergh got his education from me."

I admitted the parallel in thought between Joe's speeches and Lindbergh's.

"You're damned tootin' our speeches are alike. Lindbergh's are more polished. That's the only difference."

"Joe," I asked bluntly, "do you think we'll ever have National-Socialism here?"

"Hell, yes," he shouted in my face. "Can't you see the way the A.F.C. is gradually coming our way? Just wait six months."

From this point on the A.F.C. dedicated its efforts to what it had consistently denied: the formation of a Third Party movement. The first hint came from Father Coughlin. The second was voiced loudly by Philip LaFollette: "There are still two parties in the country," he said, "the War Party and the American Party." His comment was followed by an editorial in the New York *Daily News* which urged the founding of an America First Party. And finally on December 2, just five days before Pearl Harbor, the "new leadership" announced that the A.F.C. was being reorganized "along political lines." It hinted that those who did not fall in line would be "unyieldingly opposed."

In preparation for an American *der tag,* the "new leadership" sought to consolidate its position. With the subtle coaching of the Steuben Society it started off with an ill-timed attempt to "gather evidence" against the "war mongering" motion picture industry. F. Guy Juenemann, an informant for McWilliams, True, Deatherage and the Bund, was engaged to collect "evidence" and turn it over to Senator Nye and the Committee. The move proved a boomerang.

Next the Committee expanded to take within its fold every "patriotic" organization in the country. The Klan easily qualified and *The Fiery Cross* exulted: "The Klan's attitude toward the present world situation was aptly expressed by General Robert E. Wood." The Klan then launched an "Americanization program" with $1,000,000 as its goal. Senator C. Wayland Brooks, prize America First-er, participated at a gigantic rally at Rockford, Illinois, attended by 50,000 Klansmen. The resurgence of the Klan was symbolic of the riffraff which now began to flow unchecked into the America First fold.

All pretense to respectability dropped from this point on. Merging forces with Farmer-Laborites in the midwest, it courted the support of the Reverend John Cole McKim, propagandist for the *Japanese American Review*, who became chairman of the Peekskill, New York chapter; of William J. Baxter, author of many pro-Japanese tracts, who headed the New Rochelle, New York chapter; of Ralph Townsend, the Japanese agent, who slanted his "patriotism" from the pages of *Scribner's Commentator*. The Edward James Smythes addressed their meetings to lunatic fringers while the Snows and Mrs. Schuylers worked behind Park Avenue doors.

Concurrently the Winrods and Coughlins exhorted their congregations to join the "holy crusade for Americanism," while the William R. Castles and Burton K. Wheelers engaged in missionary work among Washington officials. At the same time the German-American elements—many of whom had been "educated" by the *Ausland Institut*, the Bund, the Steuben Society—and thousands of neighborhood groups were urged to redouble their efforts and contributions, attend meetings and flood Congress with letters.

Eager to know how deeply the revolutionary taint had penetrated in the far West, I wrote to the Americanism Committee of the Los Angeles American Legion. From Chairman Ben S. Beery I received an excellent document which showed that the vultures there hovered over Democracy in a pattern identical to that in the East. Nearly 100,000 "patriots" had packed Hollywood Bowl to hear Lindbergh and Wheeler speak. The following is part of the Legion's listing of American fascists who had transferred their allegiance to America First Committee work:

F. K. Ferenz: "Distributor of subversive books, exhibitor of Nazi films, publisher of a swastika-decorated volume of essays entitled *Hitler,* attended twenty-one America First meetings between March 6 and August 23, 1941." He helped prepare posters and banners and participated in the motor parades of the A.F.C.

John L. Riemer: who testified that "a German consulate had paid $215 for printing part of the literature he had been sending from Los Angeles," has extensively advertised America First in connection with his mailings of Nazi propaganda.

Benjamin Franklin Ballard: "Organizer of the American Guards, sponsoring Hitler-style abolition of labor unions, distributor of Nazi propaganda, regular attendant at meetings of the League to Save America First . . . chairman of the downtown chapter of the A.F.C. His talks to America First meetings are outspokenly anti-Semitic."

T. W. Hughes: "who founded the Bund-reinforced League to Save America First, conducts meetings largely directed to inciting intolerance and class dissensions." He wrote *The Truth About England,* distributed at the Aryan Bookstore and also sold at America First meetings. Many America First speakers originally spoke for Hughes' League. Verne Marshall also spoke for it.

Mrs. Faith McCullough: alias Mrs. Frances Maxey, former secretary of the German agent, Mrs. Leslie Fry, is active in the Pasadena and Glendale chapters. Her close associate and fellow traveller, William Hunt, is chairman of the Glendale Chapter.

Bruce Tarkington Dowden: "cooperates with F. K. Ferenz, and advocates 'whispering campaigns' to slur the morals of teachers who support defense programs. He has spoken at least four times at America First meetings."

The American Legion report concluded that "In meetings of America First, processes are at work whereby a person attending merely to seek information may unwittingly be transformed into a Nazi sympathizer, and even into a potential traitor to his country." Chairman Beery submitted his findings to General Wood, who ignored them completely.

As the call went out for more "build-up" for Lindbergh, the American Nazi press responded gallantly. *Publicity* stated that "Lindbergh and Wheeler would prove a 'Moses' in 1944 to lead this nation out of a political wilderness." Laura Ingalls told her audiences: "America must be thankful for its two great heroes—Lindbergh and Father Coughlin." And Pelley, after characterizing him as "The nation's man on a white horse," observed in glaring headlines: "LINDBERGH, FORD, MOSELEY, WHEELER, NEW U. S. LEADERS." Lindbergh helped along with some pointed anti-Semitic remarks, while the *America First Bulletin* also took an anti-Semitic turn by insisting that "A powerful group—the most powerful of all—the refugee Germans and their fellow racial and religious brethren" stood in the way of peace.

Those who knew the Committee only from their contacts with the respectable and sincere elements in it and did not step behind the outer shell to see the cesspools of hate and deceit in which it wallowed, naturally had a superficial impression of America First and its plans for the future.

Only one final step remained to make the old pattern complete—a plan in black and white—such as the one Banahan had given me for the Phalanx. I did not have long to wait for it.

"The Voice of the Loyal Opposition"   WEEKLY ROLL-CALL

Is Lindbergh Becoming the Nation's Man on a White Horse? . .

A STRANGE thing is happening amid the nation's turmoil. At a time when demagogues, war-mongers, termites and stalwarts are striving to sabotage the nation for the cohorts of foreign rancors, a straight, tall, clear-eyed young Cloud-Man has suddenly paused in his goodwill tours of earth

stinctive heroism that kept him the intrepid flyer above the Atlantic wastes, would not let him stay in sanctuary and security

Today "Lindy" is the spokesman for all that is decent and inspiring in Americanism. He is saying things that the Forgotten Man cannot say for himself. He will take no job

Vol. XIV No. 1   INDIANAPOLIS, IND., JANUARY, 1941   Monthly: $1 Year

These Are the Times We Have Awaited for Seven Years

AFTER HITLER TAKES MOSCOW

WEEKLY ROLL-CALL   Page 5

Lindbergh, Ford, Moseley, Wheeler, New U. S. Leaders

Nine Thousand Wildly Cheering Americans Hail Anti-Roosevelt Senator in Cleveland

Pelley names his heroes. All were America First-ers, with the exception of Hitler who was for "Germany First."

I was at the Women's Division one day, when I saw it lying on the desk. It was a secret document and sent to Chapter chairmen only. The plan was doubtless the work of a military mind, possibly that of General Wood or General Hammond, for it commissioned key workers as "generals, captains, lieutenants."

Each general's assignment is to get ten "colonels" who, in turn, will get ten "captains" who, in turn, will get ten "lieutenants." Under this plan of action, you or the mail marshal appointed by you, should be able to phone each general, each general in turn her ten colonels, each colonel her ten captains, and each captain her ten lieutenants, all in one day's time.

Present plans were to apply only to the writing of pressure letters against Congressmen who voted aid for European Democracies and for national defense, but I knew that once a neighborhood was organized on such a thorough plan, other instructions could be handed down from a hierarchy which more and more turned to politics and became the repository for every species of Nazi and native fascist revolutionary doctrine.

The franking privilege which had been designed for Congressmen to correspond, free, with their constituents in their *home* state, became the pawn of fascist interests. A university professor in *Texas* received an envelope franked by James C. Oliver of *Maine* and bearing an address sticker obviously made from an address plate in the *Scribner's Commentator* office at Lake Geneva, *Wisconsin*. From *Omaha* Charles Hudson mailed me *Missouri* Phil A. Bennett's speeches, and the same speech was mailed to me two days later on the stencil of Elizabeth Dilling from *Chicago*. And Representative Hoffman went overboard in his abuse of the franking privilege by sending me his speeches *printed privately* at Cathrine Curtis' expense.

The singers of America's doom whined for a "negotiated peace." The chorus was led by Wheeler, Nye, Fish, bulwarks of America First-ism, and was followed by Senator Robert A. Taft: "I believe in the end we could have a negotiated peace; better than England could now secure, but probably with a Hitler dominant on the continent. . . . War is even worse than a German victory."

The America First Committee had become the voice of American Fascism and the spearhead aimed at the heart of Democracy, carrying to their doom many who were innocent and would have resigned in disgust had they known what went on behind the scenes. An official of the Committee, Judge Mildred Dugan confirmed my convictions by saying candidly:

"Eighty per cent of the membership is Coughlinite, and there isn't the least doubt in my mind that at the present rate the anti-Semites and Coughlinites will come out on top eventually."

The Monday after Pearl Harbor I received the December 6 issue of the *America First Bulletin* and read the headline: "Blame for Rift with Japan Rests on Administration." It was the same old cry of denouncing our own family of Americans and, by implication, exonerating the Axis of all evil. And by an irony of fate, a typical letter from William R. Castle appeared in the New York Sunday *Herald Tribune* on the morning of Pearl Harbor, and it read:

Why should we go to war with Japan? To that question I have never received a reasonable answer, except the answer always made by those who feel we should interfere anywhere in the world. People like our bellicose Secretary of the Navy announce that trouble is inevitable. . . .

America First BULLETIN

Exp. A 11-21-41   Sec. 562 P.L.&R.
U. S. Postage
PAID
NEW YORK, N. Y.
Permit 3046

Official Publication, America First Committee, New York Chapter, Inc.

VOL. I.   NO. 28   NEW YORK CITY, DECEMBER 6, 1941   Published each Saturday by The A.F.C. Bulletin, 515 Madison Ave., New York City, N. Y. By subscription, Three Months for 50 Cents   Five Cents Per Copy

PEACE

The thing that makes Hitler abhorrent to Americans is the system of government and economics which he has introduced into Germany. It is that system which has come to be known as National Socialism. There are powerful and wealthy groups in America who are spending a great deal of money and energy to keep Hitler in person with his early from coming to America. But they do not seem to be alarmed in the least about the far more imminent peril of National Socialism coming here.

Probably there is nothing in this world which the United

Reisner Warns Of War's Costs

All Ablebodied Youth Involved, He Says

American foreign policy today should change its course toward a formula of "peace in the Atlantic and in the Pacific so that the resources of our civilization may be supplied to the good of mankind instead of to its destruction," Dr. Edward H. Reisner, professor of education at Columbia University, declared this week.

Speaking before 1,000 student representatives of fifty-one New York City high schools, Dr. Reisner cited the enormous

Blame For Rift With Japan Rests On Administration

Committee To Fight At Polls For Anti-War Congressmen

Announces It Will Actively Support Senators And Representatives Who Keep People's Trust

The America First Committee will make an energetic effort throughout the country to re-

sions for the people. In the face of this same trend toward fascism in America, the immedi-

President Talks War Without Authorization From People, Congress

A rupture in diplomatic relations between Japan and the United States appeared imminent this week, as a result of either the inability or unwillingness of the President and State Department to adjust questions arising out of Japanese activity in the Far East.

The last issue of the *America First Bulletin* exonerated Tojo and Hirohito of all blame, and announced the formation of a political wing of the A.F.C. "to fight at the polls."

BOOK TWO

AFTER PEARL HARBOR

THE AXIS WAY

Stockholm, Sweden, October 9, 1942—A big clean-up took place in Berlin three weeks ago in which more than 1,000 persons, including many women, were arrested on charges of grumbling and spreading doubts of ultimate German victory . . .

Reported in The New York Times

April 7, 1943—The administration of Premier Hideki Tojo has won for itself sweeping powers to decree death to virtually anyone openly critical of the government's wartime politics . . . The Diet passed a law specifying the death penalty for anyone who "disturbed the smooth operation of the government in wartime . . ."

Reported by the Office of War Information

THE DEMOCRATIC WAY

Attorney-General Francis Biddle: December 21, 1941—"Free speech as such ought not to be restricted . . . at this time every reasonable attempt should be made to maintain both free speech and public safety, and that freedom of speech should be curtailed only when public safety is directly imperiled."

Washington, D.C. March 1, 1943—The Supreme Court reversed the conviction of George Sylvester Viereck, Nazi propagandist, on the *technical* ground that he was not compelled to report to the State Department any of his activities except as "agent of a foreign principal . . ."

CHAPTER 1

UNDERGROUND

"For the time being, we are in a state of quiescence, waiting for events to shape themselves. The trend of things is already becoming less obscure. . . . You can be sure that very few of those who were with us before have changed their minds—although they may have become more cautious for the present."

NORMAN H. WILSON

LIKE MOST AMERICANS, I thought that with Pearl Harbor we had become a united nation. I believed that my "friends" would now become true patriots, stop their disruptive propaganda and back up the Congress and the nation in the prosecution of the war. Feeling sure that my work as investigator was over, I thought of enlisting in order to continue my fight against Axis aggression.

And then I received a mimeographed tract from Boston, postmarked December 8, 1941. It was from Francis P. Moran, fuehrer of the New England Christian Front. Accompanying it was another inflammatory leaflet which read in part:

Mr. Roosevelt has sent our citizens to their death. He is guilty of murder. . . . We advocate the refusal of all sincere and courageous American citizens to pay such taxes on the basis that they are unconstitutional, un-American, and morally unjust, and on the further premise that our first duty is to our own needy and unemployed citizens.

I realized with a shock that my work was far from finished. Instead of burying their past agitations and joining the rest of America in a united stand against Nazi aggression, my "patriotic pals" were going to continue their role as transmission-belters of Nazi propaganda!

Determined to get the new party line, I burst in upon Bund headquarters and told the receptionist, who I knew was a member of the *Maedchenschaft*, that I wanted to see August Klapprott immediately. She led me through a series of doors to the office of the vice-president of the Bund. Like Kuhn, Klapprott's face was scarred by hate. His nose had apparently been broken during brawls for it rose in a high un-Aryan hump at the bridge. His ears stood out. Seated at his desk, Klapprott broke into a smile as I entered.

"What are we going to do now?" I asked.

"Don't worry, George," he answered. "Everything is going to come out all right for us. What the America First Committee should be doing now," he said, "is to be working for a negotiated peace."

His thick, guttural English was difficult to understand.

"Peace is impossible," I said. "What should we do and say from now on?"

Klapprott reached over and picked up the current copy of *Deutscher Weckruf*. I had already read the glaring headlines: "OUR COUNTRY, RIGHT OR WRONG, WHEN INVADED."

"Patriotism," is the answer, he said smiling. I tested his "patriotism" by asking how he would have averted war with Japan.

"Very simple. I would have told Japan, a nation civilized down to the last minute, I would tell Japan that she could take the Philippines, but no more than that. Japan would see that we were a gentleman nation and take the Philippines only."

The *Bundesführer* had ample faith in Lindbergh: "Lindbergh is a fine leader for the country. Ahh . . . if he would only come out in the open and say something that will make the people keep the faith. . . ."

He was telling me about the inevitability of National-Socialism here after the overthrow of Democracy, when the door knob turned and we automatically stopped talking. It was Gustav J. Elmer, treasurer of the Bund. Nodding to me in recognition, he and Klapprott carried on a lengthy conversation in German which was spoken exclusively in the Bund office. Even I had been addressed in German on my first visit.

While the two talked I looked at the neatly framed picture of Adolf Hitler on Klapprott's desk. The same picture

Top: Closeup of *Bundesfuhrer* Fritz Kuhn. See Chapter VII, Book I.

Middle: Unusual candid photo of native fuehrer Joseph McWilliams. See Chapter V.

Below: Symbolic merger of native and alien fascism. Photo taken on August 18, 1940 at Bund Camp Nordland, showing Arthur H. Bell, Grand Giant, shaking hands with August Klapprott, vice-president of the Bund. Behind them (in dark hood) is the Reverend E. H. Young who urged "American Americanism" and (in khaki) Edward James Smythe, anti-Semite and anti-Catholic who engineered the joint Bund-Klan meeting. See Chapter VIII. [*All photos (except top) by "George Pagnanelli"*]

Above: The thundering herd led by "herd leader" Mrs. Elizabeth Dilling (middle) is warmly received by Representative Clare E. Hoffman of Michigan (left, holding flag) and colleague, Roy Orchard Woodruff. Appeasement, not national defense, was their battle cry. See Chapter XIII.

(All photos by "George Pagnanelli")

Top: *Der Jugendschaft* parades at Bund Camp Siegfried, summer, 1940. See Chapter VII, Book I.

Below: The thundering herd of Coughlinite Mothers parade on the Capitol grounds in the summer before Pearl Harbor in protest against Lend-Lease aid to our allies. See Chapter XIII.

FRIENDS: (*Top*): The Reverend Edward Lodge Curran (middle) one of Coughlin's closest collaborators in "patriotism," with his arms around Martin Dies (right) and George U. Harvey, once an ardent Coughlinite and former Borough President of Queens, New York. The trio spoke in 1938 on "patriotism" at a meeting tendered by Brooklyn veterans. See Chapter XIII. Book II. (*Photo courtesy Irving Haberman*)

(*Below*): Gerald L. K. Smith (middle, with sweat-stained shirt) with his arms around (left) Francis E. Townsend, author of an original ham-and-egg movement; and Father Coughlin, promoter of clerical fascism. These three musketeers of unorthodox politics spoke on July 16, 1936 at Cleveland and announced the merger of the forces comprising the Townsend Plan, Share-the-Wealth Plan and Coughlin's Union for Social Justice. See Chapter IV. Book II. (*International News Photo*)

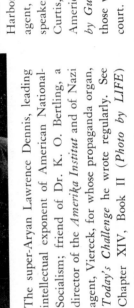

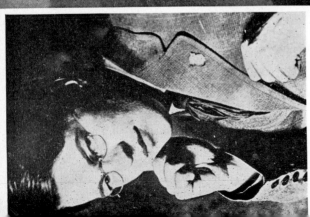

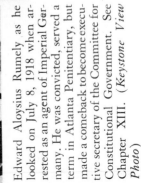

Laura Ingalls, convicted shortly after Pearl Harbor for neglecting to register as a Nazi agent, was a prominent America First speaker and friend of super-patriot Cathrine Curtis, president of Women Investors in America. See Chapter X. (*CLICK Photo by Gus Gale*). "I am a truer patriot than those who convicted me," she cried out in court.

The super-Aryan Lawrence Dennis, leading intellectual exponent of American National-Socialism; friend of Dr. K. O. Bertling, a director of the *Amerika Institut* and of Nazi agent, Viereck, for whose propaganda organ, *Today's Challenge* he wrote regularly. See Chapter XIV, Book II (*Photo by LIFE*)

Edward Aloysius Rumely as he looked on July 8, 1918 when arrested as an agent of Imperial German-many. He was convicted, served a term in Atlanta Penitentiary, but made a comeback to become executive secretary of the Committee for Constitutional Government. See Chapter XIII. (*Keystone View Photo*)

Now I was perfectly at home—for I had never attended a Christian Front or Mobilizer meeting without encountering at least one drunk. I recognized my inebriated neighbor as Edward James Smythe and I nudged his arm. Smythe merely stared at me with glassy eyes—then went back to listening to Mrs. Schuyler.

She had thrown off her coat and was bombarding the hall with a violent attack on our war effort. "We have made mistake after mistake," she said, "but Japan has not made a single mistake so far." She had begun by referring to a "certain island nation" with a "progressive and dynamic people" who had a perfect right to "expand normally," and now Mrs. Schuyler identified it.

"Japan is the only civilized nation in the Orient. The Chinese are not civilized; they have no culture; they do not know what Democracy is. If Japan had been given control of China, she would have made China a powerful nation and made a garden paradise out of her. Wherever the Japanese go they transform even barren ground into a garden."

She tossed back her head and resumed her "patriotic" speech in a high, screaming, piping voice, waving her arms wildly. Kurt Mertig asked me in a whisper whether I'd care to speak. I declined graciously, saying that I'd be in the army soon and there might be some "investigators" in the audience.

JANUARY 5, 1942   SOCIAL JUSTICE

Any honest person will concede that Hitler and Hitlerism were protests against the old order dominated by Britain and the United States; were spearheads of a "new order" to overthrow imperialism. Because the Axis new order is diametrically opposed to imperial Britain's and America's most cherished political, commercial, industrial and financial ideals, the British and Americans (through their governments) oppose it.

the victors. This means that the signatories of the *"Atlantic Charter"* abhor Hitler's Aryan blood superiority but support the British and American imperial superiority.

It is illogical for us, as world reformers, to seek the restoration of the *status quo* in Europe or elsewhere View our enemy, Japan, if you care to see how illogical and impractical it is✔ In Japan there live 75-million persons. Japan is smaller than California. It is one-twentieth the size of Australia. Japan is almost barren of natural resources. Her people are prolific.

Is there not another law, mightier than the *"Atlantic Charter,"* which permits a people to expand to unused territories? Is it not true that *"the earth is the Lord's and the fullness thereof?"*

The Royal Oak American Fascist set the pace for post Pearl Harbor "patriotism." He denounced our war aims, while he condoned Tojo's. He denounced our traditional Democracy while he approved Hitler's New Order.

"I hope not," Mertig said and went over to Horace Haase, formerly in charge of the Speakers Bureau of the Brooklyn America First Committee.

Haase agreed to speak. A cold-blooded propagandist, Haase knew exactly how to pull the propaganda cords. At the end of a carefully-worded delivery, he concluded: "I justify completely the protests of the Axis nations. The next question is, if one accepts as just these protests, may we not also consider as equally just methods the Axis nations have been compelled to follow to rectify the injury done to them? ...My answer is, Yes!"

"Heil!" a woman in front of me yelled.

After the meeting I introduced myself to Haase and was invited to visit his headquarters. He was organizing Americans for Peace and solicited my help.

Mertig approached me as I was talking to Haase.

"So you are going into the army, well, well, well!" he started. "You'd better take some patriotic literature." He urged me to help myself from the table, and refused to accept money, but I pressed a few coins into his hand.

I bought copies of *Social Justice*, *The X-Ray* and a reprint from *Action*, organ of the British Union of Fascists. Edward James Smythe's virulent *Our Common Cause*, and leaflets by California fascist David Baxter regarding the statements of Nazi worker, Kurt Bernhard von und zur Lippe, were also pressed in my hands. Mertig ran to the door after me and handed me a batch of Representative Clare Hoffman's "Judas" speech, seductively titled *Don't Haul Down the Stars and Stripes*.

"These are very good," he said. "Very patriotic. Pass them around to your buddies. You can't get in any trouble."

I went home loaded down with post-Pearl Harbor propaganda.

I decided to look up the Nordic front of my "Aryan" pro-Japanese "friend," Robert Jordan, to see if he was continuing meetings in Harlem. I found that Jordan had taken on an assistant, an alien from the West Indies named Lester Holness and was rooming with him. In addition to Holness the Harlem firebrand speaker, Robert Friedrichs, was present.

"Still holding any meetings, Jordan?" I asked.

"You're damned right we are. There's one tonight."

Jordan was in a jubilant mood. Japan had been scoring initial successes all along: "The war is over in the Pacific," he said. "Japan has all the territory she wants."

Friedrichs broke in passionately:

"We all know Japan is fighting for an ideal. That is why she keeps winning. Japan has the courage of her convictions. This war is just getting to be good now and it's going to get better for Japan and for us. As a matter of fact, the whole of European civilization is going to crumble. White will kill white, cities will be blackened to the ground. Japan will come strong from the East and with Japan the Negro will rise triumphant in Africa. We are blood brothers with the Japanese. When white kills white, then we, with the Japanese, become rulers of the world."

His eyes shone with a glazed, fanatic ferocity.

"What you say interests me, Friedrichs," I said calmly.

"The Negro soldier will kill, but he will not kill a white man for the benefit of another white man. He will kill a white man only if it does him some good as a Negro. But he will kill no Japanese soldier."

And this only a few weeks after Pearl Harbor—in New York City, at 14 West 119th Street, Apartment 5!

As we walked down to the meeting hall, I asked Holness: "Will the nationalist Negroes in America join up with white nationalists and help along?"

"Of course," he replied: "That is what we are working for. We have all got to work together when the time comes for a revolution."

I asked if the Japanese agents who had collaborated with Jordan were still about.

"They have all been apprehended," Holness answered. "But the groundwork has been laid. We are going ahead. Already in St. Louis and other cities the movement is starting up. We hope it will sweep the nation. The groundwork has been laid!"

Friedrichs, Jordan, Holness and Reverend Ralph Green Best all spoke at the meeting. The surprise of the evening was the presence of Joe Hartery as speaker. The same Hartery—with the criminal record who had been a henchman for Joe Mc-

Williams—was introduced as "Mr. Ashley." He was in top form and I wished there were a dictaphone machine to record his seditious speech:

"We think the cause of the Axis nations is just. I don't have to tell you Negroes what to do in so many words. I'd be pinched if I did. But you are not dumb. You know what's going on. Go out and do it and gain your freedom. You deserve it. We white nationalists are with you one hundred per cent."

He and I were the only white men in a hall crowded with about one hundred Negroes. In the half-light of the room, gaudily decorated in deep green and purple coloring, their features seemed to become progressively more fierce as the "Little Napoleon" craftily inflamed their racial feelings: "Get after them stinking white Christians who are persecuting you. Show them you are men. Show them which side you are on. Show them you are with the Japanese and the other Axis powers."

I walked out into the night. After making sure I wasn't being trailed, I took the subway home.

A few days later I went to see Louis Helmond, secretary of the Christian Mobilizers, and heard him paint an ugly and defeatist picture of the national scene. The Mobilizers had just had a meeting to which I hadn't been invited, and Helmond minimized it purposely:

"It was just a social gathering run by the women. I was there. I'm an honorary member of the women's group."

I asked Helmond if the Mobilizers would be revived later on.

"Of course. When the people ask for us we'll be there to organize them. We've got to lay low now, but the minute things look good for us we'll be in there again with our Americanism."

At Kurt Mertig's meeting, I had seen Mrs. Schuyler sell a copy of George E. Sullivan's book, *The Road to Victory*. I obtained a copy and I found it to be a sly and vicious attack on national unity. Sullivan had contrived to revive many of the anti-Semitic canards popularized by the Nazis and applied the poison of the infamous *Protocols* to a current issue.

I also received the literature of David Baxter, the Cali-

fornia fascist, whose poison-pen writings I had first seen at
Mertig's meeting. In writing me Baxter used military terms
to apply to psychological warfare, showing the close relation
between the two forms of war. His letter read:

Yes, I've heard of you from various sources and I understand
you have been quite a fighter in the Nationalist movement.

My opinion of things as they are? Very optimistic. It is merely
that stage of the operation when the patient suffers most. . . . All
that is necessary is to retreat temporarily to our "winter line,"
ride out the storm as best we can (though some of us are bound
to be wounded) and carry on a sort of guerilla warfare to harass
the enemy, meanwhile getting our forces organized for a grand
offensive. What you can do is to be prepared for the time when
public sentiment will swing around. If you know Norman Wilson
he might be a good man to cooperate with.

I was amazed at the tolerance shown in a Democracy toward Baxter's inflammatory bulletins which now began to
arrive. I established the fact that he was associated with the
ring of Los Angeles Nazis which had its center in the local
Bund. As friend of the Nazi agent, Prince Kurt Bernhard
von und zur Lippe und Weissenfeld, Baxter seemed to be a
mouthpiece of official Nazi propaganda. It became apparent
that with Bund cells closed down, native American talent was
being used to do Hitler's dirty work.

Baxter issued a series of tracts called *Study Course of the
Social Republic Society*. The society was a secret organization with headquarters at Colton, California. One of the
"study courses" devoted to "The Corporate State—A Practical Plan for American Nationalists," was decorated with a
masked figure and the emblem of the Society, the fasces, accompanied by the Latin words *Semper Paratus* (Always
Ready). It concluded with:

Once the Corporate State is pushed through and all enemies
of the people and saboteurs crushed, the way is open to put into
effect the whole New Order, including a more satisfactory basis
for our foreign trade.

Tactics was another "study course" which laid out the
tactics for the American Nazi revolution. The tactics ad-

vanced were identical with those Hitler's Brownshirts used. Here are excerpts from Baxter's "patriotic" literature distributed only a few months after Pearl Harbor.

In America the revolution will no doubt be staged by the American Fascistic forces (patriotic American Nationalists). . . . A revolution cannot be *made*. It can be directed, though, when it does come. It can even be hurried up. . . . The actual revolution itself may come through the ballot or it may break out in a violent rash, but the revolutionary must be prepared.

Baxter held reforms in contempt:

A reform is merely an attempt to put a blow-out patch here and there in the old system to hold it together and make it run a little easier. A revolution means complete destruction of an old house and the erection of a brand new one. . . . REVOLUTION ALONE can accomplish the necessary rebirth.

Who will LEAD the revolution? . . . Those who are prepared for it. All of the various nationalist groups hope to lead it. . . . In Germany the National Socialists were only one small minority party out of some fifteen parties. The Nazis had Hitler for leader, just an ex-corporal who had been thrown in jail for trying to start a revolution before the Germans were ready for one. All of the German nationalist parties were reformers except the Nazis, who were revolutionaries. Prepared for revolution, the Nazis, while a small minority, had *secret* members in vital key spots all over Germany. . . . The Nazis simply TOOK leadership, forced the other confused groups to either come in with them or get out of the way, and placed themselves in the saddle.

The Patriotic Nationalists are still thinking and talking about REFORMS. Only one nationalist group, a Social Republic Society, with headquarters in California, Chicago and New York, is preparing for REVOLUTION. They are not concerned with patching up and reforming the old system or with reforming schemes and fantastic plans. They are concerned with the coming REVOLUTION, for which they are trying to prepare. . . .

Baxter urged his revolutionary friends to "engage in a wide circle of correspondence" to "keep alive agitation for nationalism when the flames of liberty burn low." He published a select list of "nationalists" among whom "George Pagnanelli, editor, *Christian Defender*," shared honors with the

Klan, Hudson, Haase and Smythe. I was alarmed at the virulence of Baxter's other "study courses" in revolutionary doctrine.

Making a revolution is one thing—what to do with it when it breaks is another.... A secret society is the best means of organizing leadership to take the revolution into American hands when it breaks. To make an open target of oneself while preparing for a revolution is disastrous.

Baxter closed with the warning:

WARNING—To District Memberships. Do not neglect your arsenals. Buy arms and keep them in a place where they are readily accessible. No immediate emergency foreseen but there is no time to prepare like NOW. Also keep a plentiful supply of ammunition and do not let it become over a year old or it will deteriorate.

While Baxter was engaged in instructing potential Quislings by mail, I also received *personal* instructions on how to be a "patriotic Quisling." And I was aware that the thousands who were being similarly instructed throughout the country, after the attack on Pearl Harbor, were not all investigators. My mentor was Hubert Schmuederrich whom I hadn't met since the America First Rally at Madison Square Garden.

Hubert was in a voluble mood as we sat in his room on East 79th Street. He was working as a butcher earning $40 a week, and boasted that since seeing me last he had mailed 800 copies of the booklet, *National Socialism—and Its Justification* to United States Army men, each stamped with the swastika imprint of the Grey Shirts.

"Did you get replies?" I asked.

"You bet I did," he answered.

From under the bed he pulled out a padlocked leather brief case, but before opening the lock, he went to the window and pulled down the shade. He then rummaged through the interior and pulled out a half dozen appreciative letters—including one from a corporal in Louisiana and another from a sergeant in the air corps.

"As soon as the war is over," Hubert said, "I'm going to

send their names to Goebbels. I want him to know these fine nationalist Americans."

Prompted by a newspaper clipping he dug out from the brief case, Hubert suddenly decided to tell me his personal story.

"That's my former wife, the trash," he exclaimed, showing me the clipping. Her maiden name was Heddy T . . . , a full-blooded Aryan of Hubert's own picking. Together they had come to America in 1926. Eight years after that their child was born.

"I became suspicious of her when she named the child George."

"What's wrong with that?" I asked. "My name's George."

"You don't understand. I am a good German. She should have named the child after Adolf Hitler. Instead, she goes and names him after George Washington!"

I sat back, trying to keep from laughing out loud.

But Hubert had not neglected little George's education. He was beside himself with glee as he recounted how he had taught him to sing the *Horst Wessel Lied* and say "Heil Hitler." When I asked if a child three years old could say "Heil Hitler," Hubert answered:

"Why, of course, that's the first thing I taught him."

"When comes The Day (a favorite phrase of his), I will send the child back to Germany. I will make a good National-Socialist out of him."

Hubert recounted the episode while in his underwear, his bare, unwashed feet dangling over a dirty rug.

"Let's get something to eat," he said suddenly.

He dressed and we walked over to a one-arm joint in upper Lexington Avenue. As customers came in, Hubert lowered his voice and told me in confidence that he had never filed an income tax return, or registered for the Selective Service Act. I asked if he wasn't afraid of being caught.

"They'll never catch me," he boasted.

The proprietor, a close friend of Hubert's, bent over the counter and boasted how he, too, had cheated the tax collectors. With an income of $3900 he had gotten away without paying a cent.

"That is the way to do it," Hubert commended. "I don't

want to do anything with this thing they call the 'defense effort.' I'm waiting to see the swastika fly from the White House . . ."

"What were you saying?" I asked absently.

"I was telling you about Quisling. Look at him. At one time, George, he was like you and me, putting out leaflets. He was the editor of a small paper just like you were. No one paid any attention to him. But look at him today. Like us, he worked his way up from the bottom."

"Honestly, now, what do you think of Quisling?" I ventured to ask, finding it odd to ask someone what he thought of a traitor to his country.

"Quisling is a great man. He looked ahead and saw what was coming. I'd like you to be a patriot like him, George. You are young. We need smart men for the leadership of the New Order in America. How about it. . . ."

And now, answers began to come to my letters from all over the country. From Edmondson who had "retired" to the quiet of a cabin at Grass Valley, California, came this call to arms:

. . . Patriots should not forget to keep the home fires burning on the Altar of Truth, as far as may be possible legally. . . . During the process of correction and reconstruction (after the war) in the scapegoat-hunt the real culprits will be exposed with the assistance of patriots in the know; and let us hope that punishment of the guilty will then fit the terrible crime. The patriotism now awakening, to defend America against outside attack, should become broadly resurgent—and Patriotism is Nationalism. . . . Those who know the answer, must acquire patience and deepen resolution.

And from Norman H. Wilson, one of the first in New York to promote the impeachment of the President as a Nazi device of stirring up discontent, came this broad policy:

For the time being, we are in a state of quiescence, waiting for events to shape themselves. The trend of things is already becoming less obscure. . . . You can be sure that very few of those who were with us before have changed their minds—although they may have become more cautious for the present.

Wilson merely confirmed reports which had been reaching me from all over the nation. Just two days after Pearl Harbor Herman D. Kissenger, a Kansas City, Missouri, attorney who in 1938 provided *World Service* with an American mailing list, circularized Congressmen and newspapers with a letter: "I think it is the Congress and the President that ought to be court-martialed—that is, impeached. . . . The main responsibility for the attack by Japan rests on the shoulders of 'Grandpa Knox.' "

At the Embassy Auditorium in Los Angeles, about 200 people were present when Ellis O. Jones, fuehrer of the National Copperheads supporting Lindbergh, made a speech. "The Japanese have a right to Hawaii," he shouted. "There are more of them there than there are Americans . . . I would rather be in the war on the side of Germany than on the British side."

The main address came from a slick-haired, ranting orator named Robert Noble. "Japan has done a good job in the Pacific," he screamed. "I believe this war is going to destroy America. . . . We are for Germany and for Hitler." Noble and Jones even passed out handbills which began: "Young Man, your lowest aim in life is to be a good soldier."

"Germany and Mr. Quisling," declared Noble, "are doing a fine job of liberating Norwegians from the aggressions of England. I am for the Axis powers because they are the liberators of the world."

A remark made by Mrs. Lyrl Clark Van Hyning, president of the Chicago We, the Mothers Mobilize for America, flashed through my mind: "Our battle really began with Pearl Harbor."

And *our* battle on the home front, I realized, was just beginning also. What I had seen so far was child's play in comparison. The real test of Democracy's fibre lay ahead. Now that the "patriots" had been sent scurrying to underground activity, they would be more vicious than ever before. These were the thoughts which obsessed me as I pushed my way through the milling crowds in Yorkville where until so recently Hitler had been openly heiled and the President cursed. I wondered what was being said right now in Yorkville bars and in those back rooms that were so familiar to me. I was afraid I knew.

CHAPTER II

THE BILL OF RIGHTS—HEIL!

> "Little things . . . every day and every hour,
> coming from somewhere, the finding of fault with
> something that is immaterial . . . are injuring our
> cause, and making it more difficult for our brave
> men to achieve on the battlefield the victory which
> we expect eventually."
>
> SENATOR GEORGE NORRIS

SHORTLY after our entry into the war, Robert Noble, Ellis O.
Jones and Herman D. Kissenger were arrested by F.B.I. agents
for "alleged seditious utterance," and a few weeks later were
suddenly exonerated with the official statement "free speech
as such ought not to be restricted." It was obvious the Department of Justice had not yet formulated an official policy
regarding sedition.

Attorney General Francis Biddle adopted the democratic
view that "at this time every reasonable attempt should be
made to maintain both free speech and public safety, and that
freedom of speech should be curtailed only when public safety
is directly imperiled."

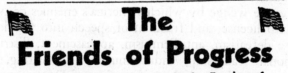

The Friends of Progress

Invite You to HEAR About the Amazing Experience of

ROBERT NOBLE
CALIFORNIA'S FEARLESS ORATOR

ELLIS O. JONES AND OTHERS
(EMINENT JOURNALIST)

Who will tell you about our F.B.I. findings.

ARE WE REALLY IN A WAR?

Remember: The U.S. Attorney General Says we have a PERFECT
RIGHT To Talk — AND WE WILL!

| ALL FREE | Come Early — and TELL EVERYBODY | ALL FREE |

America's enemies within took this as blanket permission to resume the work only temporarily interrupted by Pearl Harbor, and after the disbandment of the America First Committee. Ellis O. Jones wrote me exultantly: "We have already arranged to resume weekly meetings. We have a lot of ideas, are not in any way terrified and will not pull our punches."

"Biddle ain't a bad guy after all," I heard my "friends" say.

But a few months later—when Attorney General Biddle cracked down on those who had abused the privilege granted them under a Democracy—he was vilified bitterly, called a Jew, a Communist, a "tool of the internationalists." Until that time, however, America's vermin press took advantage of the green light to committing sedition. The Nazis and their camp followers wrapped around themselves the folds of the Constitution and the American flag. Kissenger's example was typical. This Bund patriot wrote me on January 14:

The only restriction I recognize was laid down by Alex Hamilton: "The Liberty of the press consists in publishing the truth FROM GOOD MOTIVES and FOR JUSTIFIABLE ENDS, tho it reflects on the Government, on magistrates, or individuals." I am a citizen of the Republic and not a subject of the Chief Executive! . . .

During December, 1941 and January, 1942 the Bill of Rights was heiled as lustily as had been the swastika at Bund rallies. It became the wedge by which America's enemies converted liberty into license; and freedom of speech into freedom to propagate defeatism, anti-Semitism, appeasement, distrust of the national leadership, indiscriminate Red-baiting, anti-British propaganda, and the defamation of Democracy as a way of life. Far from ending subversive action, the war merely served as a signal for redoubled effort—for another Pearl Harbor attack on the psychological front at *home*.

Lip service was rendered to placate the Department of Justice, and satisfy the technicalities of law, while all-out sabotage was aimed at national morale. That became the war-time "party line" of former America First-ers, Bundists, Christian Front-ers, Mobilizers and followers of various "shirt" movements. Pelley took the initiative and blanketed the nation with confidential wartime bulletins:

THIS WAR IS QUITE ALL RIGHT! It is going to work the economic and social miracles that never could have been otherwise, and all of us are going to be a personal part of them. . . . Get over your doldrums if you have them.

Hitler's friends took heart. Some of them became so bold that they lost all semblance of decency. George W. Christians sent out a series of leaflets threatening violence:

When the MAD MOB gets in MOTION make sure that they dig all of the blood-sucking banksters out from under their piles of rock and steel. Line them up against a wall and SHOOT them. . . .
Franklin Delano Roosevelt, the World's Greatest Humbug. . . . Now we are to give up our LIVES for the delusions of Grandeur of a Merciless Monster, FRANKLIN DELANO ROOSEVELT. SOME NECK—for a ROPE.

Waiting till the all-clear signal had flashed, Kullgren released the January issue of *The Beacon Light.* Kullgren "saw in the stars" wishful omens of "grave danger of assassination" of the President during 1942:

Which of the two courses [death or impeachment] will take place I am not prepared to say. I prefer to paint the picture to show you the forces in operation, and to leave the responsibility with you. . . . And you will reap as you have sown: and the sins of omission are as deadly as those of commission.

Those Coughlinites who had suspended individual activity in order to join effort with the America First Committee, now

To the
Attorney General of the United States:

        I am well aware that your Secret Political Police can rub me out whenever you say the word but just remember that unless THE ECONOMIC LIBERTY MOVEMENT has sufficient aggressive and capable leadership to STAB it through the coming confusion and chaos you will get a REIGN of TERROR that will make you scream for the Japs to come and save you from your own insanity.

              Geo. W. Christians.

THE WORLD REVOLUTION FOR ECONOMIC LIBERTY MARCHES ON

went back to their individual cells and set up shop to do business precisely as before. In the name of post-Pearl Harbor "patriotism" they added to the worries of a nation mobilizing for war.

Mrs. Agnes Waters, a professional mother from Washington, branded sugar-rationing as a Jewish plot to "Communize America." Warming up to her subject, she screeched: "There are 200,000 Communist Jews at the Mexican border waiting to get into this country. If they are admitted they will rape every woman and child that is left unprotected."

Mrs. Mary Tappendorf of the ultra-patriotic Chicago Mothers became greatly excited over the plan to raise a women's army auxiliary for war duty. "What do they want to do with girls in the front lines?" she demanded. "I'll tell you—it's SEX —and that's Mrs. Eleanor's idea, too. They teach it to the boys in the army. They tell them they'll go insane without it. The Administration has sold out the flower of our womanhood. . . ."

In Chicago, the Citizens Keep America Out of War Committee which under William J. Grace had sponsored Lindbergh, shortened its name to Citizens Committee and continued its routine of agitation against the war effort.

I went to see Horace Haase and found him busily at work on the next issue of his organ *Americans for Peace*. With his New York unit already functioning, Haase was contacting former American First-ers in cities throughout the country for the formation of secret cells, and had sent two urgent letters to Lindbergh who on December 19 had already addressed a gathering of former America First Committee officials at the swank New York home of Edwin S. Webster.

"We can't win this war," Haase kept telling me over and over. "What is the use of trying? Japan could capture Hawaii if she wanted to. I hope none of our boys get killed, but at the same time I hope we lose every ship in the Pacific."

Haase set me to work filing name cards of those to whom he had already written. I filed about a hundred and was not surprised to see a large listing of America First-ers, including the name of the notorious Boris Brasol. Haase told me he had visited Joseph P. Kamp, and had also been received by America's leading intellectual fascist, Lawrence Dennis.

"How did you get to see him?" I asked.

"I just called him up, told him who I was and he told me to come right over."

"Were you with him very long?" I asked.

"More than two hours."

Haase asked me for the present whereabouts of Cathrine Curtis and I told him all I knew about her, recounting my experience in Washington.

Shortly after my visit Haase apparently obtained enough funds to print, instead of mimeograph large quantities of *Americans for Peace* and sent out bundles of it to cell leaders in key cities. While not yet a dangerous organizer of appeasement and defeatism, Haase worried me greatly. I looked upon him as a symbol of a resurgent and even more sinister nationalist-fascist movement than any we had had so far. Such a disruptive and revolutionary force hacking away at

AMERICANS FOR PEACE

*An organization of rank and file Americans united for effectiveness in voicing
their desire for peace, freedom and independence for all mankind and
for the preservation of American institutions through the establishment
of the security only a just peace can bring.*

7165 Broadway
New York, N. Y.

HORACE J. HAASE
Temporary Chairman

Mar. 27, 1942

Dear Mr. ████████

Our idea is to get the organization set up so that when events and conditions make a more specific program possible we shall be there to jump in, whereas if we were not organized the opportunity would be lost while we set about getting members and leaders. As things are we cannot expect any outstanding person to lead us now. But if we build up the organization and have it ready we shall always be able to get the leader we want when we what him. I don't have anyone particular in mind but there are several amongst whom we can choose when we are ready.

Of course we must be very careful what we do and say these days. We must avoid the errors America First made. So far we have been mighty careful as you can see from our literature. We must continue to be cautious but firm. We must use our rights without exceeding them and without fear.

Yours most sincerely

Horace J Haase
Horace J. Haase.

Appeasement lives on. America First-er Haase lays the groundwork for another A.F.C. which, he cautioned, "must avoid the errors America First made."

the heart of a nation at war could conceivably shatter our morale, and help Hitler win his most decisive victory.

And in Congress, the obstructionists whom we dignify by merely calling them "isolationists," jumped back to their old dissensionist tricks.

"Perhaps nothing but a march on Washington will ever restore this Government to the people," said Clare E. Hoffman.

Representative William P. Lambertson gave an American voice to Nazi lies broadcast nightly from Berlin: "I voted for the declaration of war. Nobody would have told me that I would on the sixth of December. . . . We were maneuvered into it."

"Let us save America for Americans." Thus on February 28 John E. Rankin ended his speech with Stahrenberg's fascist slogan.

Discord, dissension and defeatism had not died down. My findings showed that unity on the psychological front was still a myth. Those who had been its vehicles prior to Pearl Harbor were still at it, prompting the venerable Senator George Norris to declare in the Senate:

Little things, little by little, every day and every hour, coming from somewhere, the finding of fault with something that is immaterial and which does not amount to anything, no matter which way it is done, are hurting us, are injuring our cause, and making it more difficult for our brave men to achieve on the battlefield the victory which we expect eventually.

I was by no means the only one to worry. The Americanism Committee of the American Legion in Los Angeles, had investigated the resurgent fascist groups and summed up the national picture in a brilliant report, concluding with:

All up and down the vital Southern California coastline there still exists a shrewdly laid network of enemy propaganda activity, eating away at civilian and military morale, and attracting subversive-minded individuals, amongst whom recruits for espionage and sabotage are most readily found. While the public is apathetic, lulled by a false sense of security into the belief that we are a 100% united people, enemy propagandists grow in numbers and boldness. Their public meetings are multiplying and their inflammatory speeches are delivered before an audience of increasing size and growing bitterness. . . . They must be stopped now.

I was burning to tell America what was going on, but as an investigator there was little I could do. Of course I turned in the evidence to the proper authorities but at this time it was essential I should remain an under-cover worker.

Then one morning in March I received an urgent telephone message from Russell Davenport of *Fortune* and found that he, too, had been worrying. He asked me to see Roger Butterfield, national affairs editor of *Life*. Roger wasn't convinced until he had been shown stacks of the printed evidence of seditious activity. I helped Roger with the preparation of his splendid article *Voices of Defeat* which appeared in the April 13, 1942 issue of *Life*, and helped awaken official circles to the menace of psychological saboteurs.

At the same time I was asked to do a similar piece for *The American Mercury* which seemed to be one of the few "highbrow" magazines willing to publish an article which would "name names" and withhold no punches. *Our Fascist Enemies Within* appeared in the March issue. As with my article on the America First Committee in the January issue, I had again decided to risk exposure in order to tell America of the scandal of treason parading as "patriotism."

As I had anticipated, some of the data in the article was

LIES - Made in Japan (via short wave)

Americans breaking into the homes of Japanese citizens have pointed their pistols at young Japanese girls and assaulted them before the eyes of their aged and helpless parents.

LIES - Made in Germany (via short wave)

Whatever Japan's aims are toward the Southwest Pacific, these aims concern Americans only as far as F.D.R. has tried to bully Japan into giving up these aims... Thank Roosevelt. It is his war.

LIES - Made at home (via the vermin press)

Were it not for the unwarranted interference of Mr. Roosevelt in foreign affairs... the Japanese Government would have no incentive to attack us. - FRANCIS P. MORAN, December, 1941.

I think history is going to convict him [the President] of being personally and individually responsible for this war... With the Nipponese controlling our western coast, mayhap Hitler will be welcomed not as an enemy but as a friend. - WILLIAM DUDLEY PELLEY, January, 1942.

LIES - Made at home (via the Congressional Record)

The Commander-in-Chief, of course, got us into this thing, when he himself had failed to prepare to meet it. - CLARE E. HOFFMAN, January 27, 1942.

traced to me. I determined to continue my work outside New York in order to let the matter "blow over" hoping in the meanwhile, that the news of my investigations would not reach "patriots" outside the city. And it happened that the moment was auspicious for a trip West where a job was crying to be done.

On August 4, 1938, the *Deutscher Weckruf* published the following:

At the celebration of German American Day in Detroit, recently, Mr. Parker Sage advised German Americans to organize on "a nationalist basis" by which presumably he suggested, with well-meaning intent, that the basis of such organizations should be devoutly in harmony with American ideals and institutionalism.

Sage and his work had interested me and I had corresponded with him since January, 1941, when I first learned of him through Colonel Sanctuary. He headed the National Workers League, a Nazi front organization, but our correspondence was confined to mere routine—payment of my dues in the N.W.L. and to receiving the weekly *Nationalist Newsletter*. I was cordial in my letters and on one occasion sent Parker Sage a copy of a booklet reprinted by the Klan from the *Dearborn Independent*.

On December 27, 1941, I received a lengthy letter from Sage. In it he made overtures which immediately placed me on guard:

One of our greatest troubles here is to secure stable leaders. The war has terrified some of our list—to the point of leaving this part of the country. We need experienced men here badly, and have reason to believe that if suitable material is available that we could guarantee a position in *private* employment at an American wage.

Our needs call for an experienced, able speaker and organizer. Well qualified to handle the racial problem (both Jew & Negro). He must be versatile enough to handle any place in private employment that we find him at a satisfactory wage. Most of his spare time would have to be devoted to the Cause here. Must be American-born, and preferably without a German name.

If you are able to fill the place or places please do so. . . . I realize it is a mighty difficult task to locate such men, but . . . I know there are many such mob-leaders available. . . . You have never informed us whether you are American-born.

I did not answer at once. Instead, I began to ask myself: is this a trap to get me to Detroit? Has Sage learned that I wrote *The American Mercury* articles? Or is it a ruse to get me to leave New York State and visit the stronghold of the Black Legion?

You will remember the Black Legion from the movie and the numerous articles written about it. Its membership was composed of Klansmen, strike-breakers, convicts, rapists, released murderers and variously assorted thugs convicted of assault and battery. Functioning mainly from 1935 through 1936 and calling itself "patriotic," it was a secret, hooded, revolutionary terror-group. Organized along military lines and linked with Pelley's Silver Shirts, it had a membership estimated at more than 100,000 vigilantes pledged to an oath of secrecy. Its multiple units bore such names as Black Guards, Bullet Club, Silent Legion, Modern Patriots.

The regiments were divided into squads for special duty: death squads, arson squads, flogging squads. Each was given special "patriotic" assignments—bombing labor headquarters, burning the home of an "enemy" or murdering a political rival. Discipline squads supervised each job and recalcitrant members were disciplined with the lash and pistol.

Anti-Catholic, anti-Semitic, anti-Negro, anti-Labor, the Black Legion left a trail of lynching, flogging, arson and murder across a half dozen mid-western states. Fifteen murders were ascribed to it—many of them still unsolved. When finally an attempt was made to clean up the Michigan scandal, only a few of its members were convicted of murder. The real leaders were never brought to trial and the matter was mysteriously hushed up. Who was protecting the ringleaders?

I knew that when the National Workers League was founded by Parker Sage in 1938, remnants of the Black Legion gang flocked to it. In addition, the N.W.L. attracted assorted strong-arm patriots from the local Bund, Silver Shirts, Klan and Christian Front. Since its founding, the League had earned a high reputation in "patriotic" circles for its anti-union, anti-Negro, anti-Semitic, anti-British, anti-Administration, anti-Democracy and avowedly pro-fascist and pro-Klan leanings. It was obviously arranged along the lines of the Black Legion, and now Parker Sage wanted me as organizer of the N.W.L. I had no illusions about the job—it was dynamite! My strategy was to get as much information as I could from him, for the purpose of turning it over to the proper authorities. On January 6, I wrote Sage:

I agree with you that it is difficult to find capable leaders. Your letter interested me greatly. I shall certainly keep your request before me. Let me think over the whole thing, if you will, and I'll write you again very soon. In the meanwhile, perhaps you would be willing to tell if the wages involved for such a leader are anything a man can hope to live on.

What would the estimate be? Will there be any legal protection? Would the job entail any travel? Does your "private employment" offer include factory or office work? A person who can do office work cannot always work in a factory, or vice versa. I think this is easily understandable. I'd like to have the above information so I may better classify.

In regard to your question as to whether I'm native-born, yes—definitely native-born. My mother also was born in this country, but father came over while a mere infant. We do not even use our language at home, hence I myself do not speak it well. We're as Americanized as the native-born American. Col. Sanctuary knows me pretty well. By the way, I think you ought to get hold of his new book. . . .

Sage did not reply as promptly as I had hoped, and I began to worry. When he finally wrote on February 22, he explained the reason. The Dies Committee investigator had called on him for questioning. "Our Dies Committee hearing went off satisfactorily everything considered," Sage explained, and went on:

The newspapers here stated that you were in charge of the Christian Mobilizers. Is this correct? Have you any connections official or otherwise with German or Italian societies? I ask for a special reason.

Regarding the work contact. . . . We need a good strong type. The work would be more of the factory type than office. Could get at least $40 a week, if hours could be handled. Much of the factory work here is 7 day work. A man has got to be healthy enough to work in private employment at least 10 hours a day, still have enough energy left for organizational work.

Do you think organizations such as ours should co-operate with the Klan? They are very decidedly a strong factor here and have, as far as we can learn, confined themselves to the Racial Problem—Jew & Negro. . . . E. J. Smythe wants to come out here and talk. What do you know about him? Is he anti-Catholic. . . . Hope you are passing on our N. L. (*Nationalist Newsletters*) to McWilliams.

I answered all of Sage's questions as he expected me to answer them, and asked for the clipping which had described me as being "in charge" of the Christian Mobilizers. I had a hunch that news of my correspondence with him had leaked out, which made me doubly cautious about going. And Joseph McWilliams definitely suspected me of writing for the magazines. Sage's next letter made it clear that this was no tea party, and I was in no position to expect any help from McWilliams in solidifying my position with Sage.

Enjoyed your letter of March 6th very much. *The job awaits your arrival* & as far as we are concerned the sooner you get here the better. Would like to have you bring or send direct credentials from McWilliams. Also send in advance your picture if possible—or snapshot fairly recent. . . . Bring all your old clothes. On arriving here come after 8:30 P.M. to 5144 Canton (rear porch entrance).

Not only would McWilliams refuse to give me such a letter, but I felt sure he'd write Sage that I was not to be trusted. At any rate, I had made up my mind against going to Detroit and wrote Sage a discouraging letter. But he hung onto me like a leech and a few days later I received another letter, sent by air mail, postmarked March 26:

Judged entirely by the information you have sent us, will definitely say that I consider you *very well* qualified to fill the place we have for you both in private employment & political work. . . .

Your real value to us is probably greatest due to your years of experience and your connections in the East. More than one person here has heard of George Pagnanelli. . . . A fictitious name would destroy much of this, & besides sooner or later would be found out & be turned against us.

Dies does have a large nuisance value BUT we feel that the real reason he is against us probably is because he is a politician. Hell, we found that Dies is or was a Klansman. *We* have nothing to fear from him. The F.B.I. have never bothered us & we never concern ourselves about them. We expect no trouble from them unless we break a Federal law.

If you can't reach McWilliams or Sanctuary have Brasol send a letter of endorsement direct to me . . . and a snapshot. . . . We hoped to have you here April 1st and I certainly hope it will be for the meeting April 10th. The doubtful draft situation makes it appear in our eyes wise for you to get here at once. Our work contact for you happens to be of draft age. . . .

Would also rather talk than write to you. I think you are safe in coming if your personal qualifications ennumerated are 51% accurate. You can start your private employment the day following arrival here.

His words now made me think in terms outside my own personal safety. Newspapers were filled with reports of sabotage in factories, in railway terminals, of mysterious plane crashes, and ships burning at sea. How much of the sabotage was going on in Detroit's own factories? What was the connection of the Klan and the anti-union, slow-up activity of the Klan and the National Workers League? What were the links between the N.W.L. and the local Bund? Where did Gerald L. K. Smith enter the picture? To what extent was defeatism and appeasement rife in the vital war city? How strongly had Father Coughlin influenced his sheepish followers? Was Mrs. Rosa M. Farber of the Detroit Mothers still active? Why did Sage whitewash Martin Dies? A thousand questions ran through my mind. I wanted to find the answers, but I was still hesitant. . . . Sitting down at my desk I reread Parker's taunt, still greatly puzzled by his insistent letters and what really lay behind them.

Just a line to say that we hope the Administration's war of nerves against Nationalism, as evidenced by their arrest of Pelley and others, has not undermined your morale. Your job is still waiting for you. . . . Are you coming?

Late that night I wrote him:

Just received your letter. You undoubtedly have received mine.
No. It'll take more than the F.B.I. to tamper with my morale. It's
just that I have to start a new life in a new world, so to speak,
and having obligations and things it'll take a bit longer to settle
my affairs here. One must be ready for any consequence once he
comes out there, and prepare for everything. Once my affairs
are in order, I won't give a damn what happens.

I wasn't lying about putting my affairs in order. With the
help of an attorney I made a will. I cleaned out my desk of
all my personal papers. In the meanwhile more letters from
Parker:

Your letter of April 10th at hand. Now about work. . . . The
best place here for one would be in some branch of machine shop
work. Dirty, hard, etc., but there lays the best money. . . . In
what branch of the nationalist work do you feel best qualified.
How about speaking ability, organizing work, conducting meetings, etc.? Saw your future employer yesterday and he seemed as
anxious as I that you get here. . . .

Who was he? Parker wouldn't tell. Instead he asked:

Will you care to make a special address here for us at our
meeting May 1st? We might get a respectable little crowd. Would
need information about your background of value in advertising
the meeting.
We have started a Pelley Defense Fund here for him since we
think he has an excellent chance of beating the charge. We want
to throw a Nationalist Rally for him, bring him to Detroit &
perhaps bring in at the same time a couple of other nationally
known figures—say McWilliams or Deatherage. All for the purpose of helping him fight, as well as try to develop a little solidarity in the cause. What do you think of the idea? . . . Can you
definitely make it May 1st?

I began to pack for the trip.
Just as I was about to leave, I read the news of Sage's arrest
and indictment with Garland Alderman, Secretary of the
N.W.L., on charges of complicity in the rioting against the
attempt of Negroes to move into a federal housing project.

Newspapers reported that 1200 people armed with knives, clubs, rifles and shotguns were at the project grounds on moving day. Scores were hurt. Many, seriously injured, were taken to hospitals. Was the Black Legion riding again?

I wrote Sage anxiously about coming. . . .

He explained that both he and Alderman were out on bail, that the N.W.L. was not involved officially, and closed curtly with:

If you are going to come please do so without further delays. I simply cannot find time to continue writing every week. The job is waiting.

I left for Detroit on the six o'clock bus, on April 22.

CHAPTER III

INNER CIRCLE OF THE N.W.L.

> "The peace will be negotiated by Hitler, Musso-
> lini, the present Japanese Government . . . and by
> patriotic Americans such as General Moseley, Wil-
> liam Dudley Pelley, Father Coughlin, Colonel Lind-
> bergh, and Senator Nye. It will be a just peace. . . ."
>
> GARLAND L. ALDERMAN

THE NATIONAL WORKERS LEAGUE was one of many Nazi-
front organizations operating in America. It wasn't the largest.
But its influence was far-reaching, and its work of sabotaging
the war morale was effective. It struck at the most vulnerable
sector of America's war effort—Labor.

The League organized an extensive campaign to sow dissension among factory workers of vital war industries. It
flooded Detroit with Nazi literature. Its publicity director,
William R. Lyman, made his own reprints of the literature
originally issued by Colonel Sanctuary, Stahrenberg, the Bund,
Klan, Edmondson.

It held frequent meetings, addressed by a choice selection
of rabble-rousers who offered to speak "on any phase of the
Nationalist movement for private gatherings in homes. . . .
There is no charge for this service in the Metropolitan area,"
according to the *Nationalist Newsletter*. The League promoted the appeasement drives of the America First Committee by distributing its own seditious literature at America First
and American Mothers meetings and urging "all patriotic-
minded" members to attend the "nationalist rallies" at which
Burton K. Wheeler and Gerald L. K. Smith spoke.

I arrived in Detroit at three o'clock Friday afternoon with
no credentials other than those for George Pagnanelli, publisher of *The Christian Defender;* "associate" of Joe McWilliams and August Klapprott, the professional merchants of
hate. I had neither my social security nor draft card. In case
of trouble I would take the rap as George Pagnanelli.

I had arranged to correspond with my "sister." I had no sister, but would keep in touch with a middle-aged lady whom I trusted implicitly with my mission. I would write addressing her as "Jeanette" and Jeanette was to write me in care of Parker Sage. I left with her samples of letters she was to write in longhand and mail from our "home" at 100 West 86th Street, New York. As a matter of precaution, she was to begin writing immediately that "mother's illness" was becoming worse.

It was almost eight o'clock when I walked up the squeaking stairs of the back porch of the ill-kept, corner house at 5144 Canton Street and knocked on the door. A burly man with a fierce countenance and wild black hair opened the door.

"I am George Pagnanelli," I said. "Mr. Sage asked me to see him."

"Come right up. He's expecting you," said the man.

I passed through a shabbily furnished living room, climbed the side stairs and found myself in a small lobby, with a large round table at one side, and a half dozen chairs lined against the wall. Standing at the entrance of one of the rooms was a tall, gaunt man, dressed in blue shirt and black suit. He was more than six feet tall, with a wiry frame, rugged features, thinning blond hair.

"Where is Mr. Sage?" I asked, looking first at the burly man, then at the immobile figure in the doorway.

"Hello, George," the man in the black suit called out suddenly. "I am Sage."

"Who is this other guy?" I asked.

"Otto Fritz. He's okay—lives here with me."

I shook hands with Sage and the German and laid down my suitcase.

Sage's face was that of a zealot. His mouth a mere thin slit, eyes cold-gray, his face clearly reflected characteristics I had seen often in New York: hate-frozen determination. Parker spoke in a cold, unemotional, deep-throated monotone. A grating voice. He impressed me as a man utterly without feelings, without warmth, unyielding and unbending, an uncompromising machine devoted to a fanatic cause.

He showed me a large batch of clippings from Detroit newspapers publicizing the investigations of the League.

Among them was a clipping describing George Pagnanelli as a leader of the Christian Mobilizers. I had just finished reading the clippings when Parker suggested that we go to Gerald L. K. Smith's meeting. I welcomed the idea.

"Take your suitcase along," he ordered. "You'll meet your future employer at the meeting. You'll go to his place with him tonight and start work tomorrow morning."

"Who is he?" I asked.

"You'll find out tonight," Parker said mysteriously.

I checked my bag at a near-by hotel. Smith's meeting at Maccabee's Auditorium had already started, and close to 2000 people were on hand. Parker seemed to have many friends there and kept nodding continually. Anxious for my first look at Smith, I found him a tall, well-built man, the evangelist type; a continual dynamo of motion. His voice rose and fell —bellowed and whispered—in rabble-rousing of a high order. He impressed me as a master salesman of ideas, a Joe McWilliams type but infinitely more cunning and more intelligent.

Smith praised Representative Roy Woodruff of Michigan as a "patriot beyond reproach." With great pomp and long-winded build-up he read good-will messages from Senators Nye and Reynolds on the publication of *The Cross and the Flag.* Senator Nye had said: "I have received issue number one of the new magazine. It is excellently done." And Senator Reynolds, who had permitted the publication of an article from his *American Vindicator,* had written as follows:

Let me congratulate you with my full heart upon your first edition. It is well you did it in black and white. It is just the right size; it hits the bull's-eye with every paragraph; it is straight from the shoulder; it is gotten up in a conservative manner; it should have its appeal; it speaks the truth. We have arrived at the hour when we must have more "two-fisted" talking and real action. America must be saved and America must be saved for Americans.

Smith's magazine automatically replaced *Social Justice* which had been banned from the mails by Mr. Biddle, who by this time had become a "Communist Jew." Heir to the Coughlinite following in his own bailiwick, Smith made an eloquent plea on behalf of the "persecuted, Christian Father Coughlin." Then he bellowed: "I would rather die tonight, rather be disemboweled tomorrow, or hung at dawn, but let me have my say in the Spirit of Christ. Give me liberty or give me death."

The mob howled at this technique. The familiar device of a demagogue exploiting the name of Christ for political purposes has always disgusted me. But the mob swallowed the entire hook when Smith proceeded to paint a tender picture of himself as a mother's boy. His "Christian mother seventy-six years of age" had allegedly told him: "Son, I don't want you to go into politics. I want you to serve Him as your conscience dictates and carry on your crusade without running for public office." But circumstances, Smith hinted broadly, may compel him to go against his mother's advice.

"Ain't he good?" Sage nudged me.

"Swell," I answered. "He's even better than Joe McWilliams. He's got more heart-throb stuff that goes over with the women."

Smith reached the heights of emotional appeal just before a well-trained corps of ushers passed the plate.

After the meeting Sage and I went out to the lobby. A big, flabby loose-mouthed tub of a man stretched out his hand. His eyes were greenish. His face dull and vacuous, riddled with whiteheads and blackheads. A dirty, gray felt hat flopped over his head. He wore a gray mixture suit, a bizarre blue tie; both his shirt and tie were askew. He reflected weakness and infirmity and confusion and seemed held together by loose, flabby flesh, not bones. Garland Leo Alderman was a mess.

"Shake hands," he said. "I sure am glad to see you."

I grabbed a limp, moist hand and dropped it quickly to shake hands with Russell M. Roberts, my future employer. I was also introduced to his wife, to a little German fellow named Otto and another German named Zimmerman.

"I'll be back in a minute," Garland yelled and disappeared.

On my way to the hotel to pick up my bag, I saw Garland talking to Gerald L. K. Smith in a darkened section of the street. I was surprised to see them talking together. Garland introduced me to Smith. In parting, Smith cordially shook Garland's hand and nodded to me.

"I know Smith well," he boasted. "I've met Smith before. He knows us at the N.W.L. He is with the League in spirit, but he can't come out with it in the open."

"Look at this," Garland interrupted suddenly and held out the May issue of *The American Mercury*. My heart missed a beat.

"Look! They published the letter I wrote in answer to an article by a guy named Carlson. They even made it better by cutting it down a little. Here, George, read my letter." I maintained a poker face as Alderman pushed *The American Mercury* into my hands. His letter read in part:

The F.D.R.'s, Peppers, McNutts, Churchills, Stalins, Edens, Winchells, Dorothy Thompsons, Rabbi Wises, Morgenthaus, Carlsons, Hulls, Kaltenborns, fan dancers, movie actors, and other warmongers who brought this war to America are not worth the life of one American boy, even if they throw in "campaign orator" Willkie for good measure.

The peace will be negotiated by Hitler, Mussolini, the present Japanese Government, and by Sir Oswald Mosley of England, and by patriotic Americans such as General Moseley, William Dudley Pelley, Father Coughlin, Colonel Lindbergh and Senator Nye. It will be a just peace for all and not a peace for the benefit of international parasites and traitors.

Garland L. Alderman
National Secretary, National Workers League

Alderman and I walked together back to the lobby. Sage, Roberts, Otto and Zimmerman were waiting for us. Roberts took charge of me from then on, and with Mrs. Roberts I followed him to their car. We drove swiftly away.

Roberts knew all about Pagnanelli. He had read my letters to Parker and had agreed to give me a job in his machine shop. He explained that Otto (the one I met at Smith's meeting) had been in charge of a Bund Camp outside Detroit and Zimmerman was linked with the Christian Front. Both were German-born.

Roberts lived eight miles out of Detroit at St. Clair Shores, a suburb. We had left the city behind by this time and had turned off from the main road. It was past midnight and unlike New York, the lights in most homes were out. After negotiating a series of turns and twists, we took a bumpy dirt road which was inky dark. Roberts slowed down the car, and as it stopped he said: "Well, George, here is where we work and plot against the powers that be. It's safe. No one bothers us out here." The location was grim and desolate and all I heard was the barking of dogs echoing eerily in the night. Preceded by Roberts' searchlight, I walked into the house.

I found myself in a tiny room which seemed to be the interior of a shack. At one end was the kitchen consisting of a gas range, sink and icebox. Near the other end was a davenport. At the extreme end of the "enlarged piano box"—as Mrs. Roberts later called it—was a curtained door. This proved to be the entrance to the sleeping quarters of Mr. and Mrs. Roberts. A large, sleek Doberman was spread on the davenport. Several Doberman pups were curled in a basket near the stove. The place—living room, bedroom, kitchen—stank like an unkempt kennel.

"Here is where we live," Mrs. Roberts said.

I asked where I'd sleep.

"On the davenport," she answered, cheerily. "We'll take Spottie in our room."

Roberts suggested we have beer. I still was not sure that I was among "friends"—that is, fellow "patriots." Lurking in my mind was the suspicion that I was being led into a trap. But I took a chance and drank down the beer. Roberts dripped and breathed hatred. As we talked on, it became apparent that he was essentially a violent man. He loved violence. He spoke continually of it. He cited the instance of beating up a laundry delivery man.

"What happened after that?" I asked.

"Nothing," he said. "Only twenty-five per cent of assault cases are ever prosecuted. The rest are let go. And only one out of every ten murders is solved. When the cops can't find the guy who did the murder they call it a 'suicide.' "

His conversation implied that it was not so risky to commit murder after all. I added that a good lawyer was a help. "All you need is some brains of your own," Roberts corrected.

I observed Roberts more closely. He was tough. A former sailor in the merchant marine, he was thick-set and bullish, with watery eyes, and florid face. He had a "beer nose"—red-purplish in color, spotted, the shape of an elongated potato. He chewed snuff and spat it out. He swore continually in the presence of his wife. His attacks on Jews were much more vicious than most I had heard during my investigations.

"What we need is a secret nation-wide organization to teach those sons of bitches the first lessons in Americanism," Roberts cursed. Bending over, he breathed in my face: "The only way to get at these sons of bitches is to bore from within in the F.B.I."

He expressed disgust with Americans and "this thing they call the American way." Hesitating momentarily, he added that the "nationalists" of Europe "know what this is all about. What we ought to do," Roberts asserted, "is to place some American nationalists in office."

He now began telling me of his own part in the founding and promotion of the National Workers League. He had paid for the distribution of thousands of leaflets. He had helped it financially. He had visited George Deatherage and induced him to join its Advisory Committee. He had bailed out Alderman and Sage. "Why we've done more for the League than anybody else."

But Roberts had remained completely in the background. "The reason I stayed away from meetings was because Parker was operating in the open," he said. "You're not going to win this thing by sticking your neck out. You've got to learn to work underground."

In other ways, too, Roberts had boosted the cause of the League. William R. Lyman whom he called an "ambassador of ill will"—due to his effectiveness as "publicity director"—had worked for Roberts and earned a livelihood while blanketing Detroit with vicious Nazi propaganda tracts. And when Garland Alderman was refused a job by every other concern, Roberts had taken him on. And now, he was harboring what he thought was a fascist who was expected to devote his spare time to the promotion of the "nationalist" cause in America's key defense city.

I realized with a shock that while Sage, Alderman and Lyman acted as the "fronts" and took the "rap," he remained in the background and pulled the strings. Roberts impressed me as the brain truster behind the N.W.L., and member of that inner circle I had come to expose. He gained recruits for the nationalist cause, to replace those who were indicted or exposed, by giving them employment. I recalled how Sage had urged me to bring with me anyone else for whom I could vouch. Roberts would harbor them—in return for work for the N.W.L.

Roberts and I finished our beer and retired for the night, he and his wife going to their tiny alcove and taking Spottie with them. I sniffed at the davenport and quickly pulled my face away. I threw a sheet over my "bed." I had no alternative but to place my head at about the spot where the Doberman's hind quarters had nestled. I was anaesthetized to sleep!

I was awakened at seven-thirty. As we ate breakfast, I learned the Roberts' home and machine shop were located on a three-acre plot of farmland. Roberts had been the first to move into the wild region. Nestling in a clump of trees only a few hundred yards from Roberts' domicile was Bund Camp Schwaben. Roberts and I walked to the machine shop adjoining his home. It was built sturdily of cement blocks, at one end of which was a shooting range. "We do our target shooting on Sundays," Roberts said. "Stick around. You'll see it."

Roberts already knew that I had never worked at a machine. But he was willing to train me under conditions of my bargain with Sage and I spent my first day puttering around the shop. Unable to find a room for myself, I spent Saturday evening again with the Robertses. I went for a walk after supper and when I returned I found Roberts seated at the kitchen table, a large green tool box filled with cartridges of various sizes in front of him. He was cleaning a gun, an ugly looking thing with a long barrel.

"Sit down, George," he invited, as I wondered if the gun was loaded.

"Things are getting to be so bad," he started, "that we'll have to have a conference about them niggers." He was referring to the Sojourner Truth Defense Housing Project and the rioting which followed when Negroes tried to move in. "The more I think of it the madder I get," Roberts exploded.

He held the gun in the light. It was a Luger automatic, with an unusual twelve-inch barrel. He had bought it from a German whom he suspected of having smuggled it out of Mexico.

"What do you think of this one?" he asked.

Reaching over to a yellow, canvas mackinaw jacket, he

pulled out a Colt-45 and handled it gingerly. The bullets had thick, blunt noses.

"The bullets from this baby will blow a six-inch hole in you," he said. "I'm ready if anybody makes trouble. . . . Now coming back to the niggers."

He outlined a plan which would "raise hell with the niggers." Drawing up his chair, he explained how pelting the roofs of the Project homes with rocks would break windows, keep the tenants awake and make a veritable no-man's-land of the Negro community.

"You do it at night and raise hell with their nerves. It's been tried elsewhere, under similar conditions and it has worked."

The missiles would be fired from the open windows of an adjoining white neighborhood, Roberts explained, and the barrage would continue systematically until dawn. I asked if he would use a rubber slingshot.

"No," he said, "better stuff." I presumed that he meant steel springs. "That's strictly off the record," Roberts warned.

"Oh, sure. Don't worry about that."

Roberts had other firearms. Pointing to the bedroom he said he kept two rifles there. "I'm short of ammunition," he added. "But I'm stocking up. I expect a shipment soon."

He said he could make shells right in the shop.

"We can make the molds in the shop, and after that it's easy."

"How about gunpowder?"

"All those things can be made in the shop when we have to." After a while Roberts added: "You know, George, the only thing to do is to organize rifle clubs. Then we can teach those sons of bitches a lesson."

On the kitchen table were copies of Representative Thorkelson's and Senator Nye's speeches, both from the *Congressional Record;* copies of the *Protocols* and Ford's *The International Jew.* These were Roberts' reference books.

Sunday afternoon a Mr. and Mrs. Darling arrived in a lumbering large green Packard. They brought along a pile of *Social Justice* magazines for the Robertses to read. Roberts introduced me to them.

"This is Pagnanelli from New York. He's here to help us do some Jew-baitin'."

"Tsk, tsk," Darling said with mock seriousness. "How can such things be!"

Darling was in his sixties, with a crafty face, and was said to be a close friend of Father Coughlin. His wife belonged to one of the Mothers groups.

"Let's go to the shop," Roberts suggested.

It was time for their Sunday afternoon shooting. They fired several rounds, after which Darling bent over to Roberts' ear and whispered something.

"Sure, he is okay," I heard Roberts say, looking at me.

The reason for caution became apparent when Darling declared that he wanted some ball bearings for "experimental purposes." He did not amplify, but Roberts remarked: "They'll come in right handy for making guns." The two walked off to the cabinet where the ball bearings and small tools were kept. They returned in a few minutes and I saw Darling fondling eight small ball bearings in his hand. If his experiment worked, he explained, he would have to get larger quantities.

After the Darlings had left, Roberts—who apparently was taking a liking to me—said:

"Now, Georgie, we'll go meet one of the other boys. Everybody around here who knows things knows that 'Slim' was a member of the Black Legion."

We drove over to the service station kept by Leroy "Slim" Hampton. Slim was tall and rangy. His complexion was sallow. His face was long and lean, reflecting secretiveness and an air of conspiracy. His language matched Roberts' unprintable quality and his political ignorance was equally venomous. "The Goddamed Jews run this country from top to bottom," was his theme and he, too, urged a "damned secret" organization as the only solution.

On leaving, Roberts remarked: "It's nice to have a fellow like Slim. When things get too tight we can always count on some parts for the car. He can even steal some gas for us."

With Slim's help I found a comfortable room only a few blocks away from his garage, and a mile from Roberts' machine shop. Ready for my first serious assignment on Monday, April 27, Roberts set me to work on a lathe. My job was to polish off small metal tubes from the inside and outside. I had never worked on a lathe before and the whirling metal tubes bothered me at first, but I soon caught on to it and surprisingly enough, finished off more than 100 tubings, each measured down to a fraction of an inch, in record time. It pleased Roberts immensely, and it surprised Garland Alderman who was operating the milling machine.

But I wasn't called to Detroit to work only as a machinist. Sage wanted me to organize and I had to make a show of some interest. Monday night I called at Parker's home and learned that he was employed by the Active Tool and Manufacturing Company. He boasted how his comparatively small organization had raised "more hell than many of the big ones." It was quite true and I was eager to find out what had made it tick so effectively. I was quietly formulating a plan which would not only answer the question, but at the same time give me the excuse to investigate all affiliated groups and individuals. Most important of all, it would delay—for the time being at least—Sage's insistent demands that I start to organize. That night we worked together on the new issue of the *Nationalist Newsletter*. One paragraph Parker inserted interested me greatly:

Friends of the N.W.L. have rallied. Contributions to the Defense Fund are being received. The Michigan branch of the well-known independent union, Society of Tool and Die Craftsmen at a general mass meeting on April 22nd passed a resolution to give moral, financial and political support to the THREE defendants, including Virgil Chandler, in the Sojourner Truth court case.

I wanted to know more about a union which according to Sage had pledged "moral, financial and political support" to three men indicted by the Department of Justice of a grave offense against Government property. I asked Parker to tell me about the Society of Tool and Die Craftsmen.

"I've been a member of it for three years," Parker said. "It has a membership of more than 15,000 in the tool and die works. It's an independent union and a damned good one. The best there is."

Then I asked Sage to tell me about those he knew in the

Detroit "patriotic" movement. I averted his suspicions by saying that I was keenly interested in my work as organizer, and
wanted to get the background so as not to approach the wrong
people or make the wrong move. Parker readily admitted
knowing Mrs. Rosa M. Farber and Mrs. Beatrice Knowles of
the Mothers groups; Robert Vietig, Alfred P. Adamo, John
T. Wiandt and many others. I asked him how important each
was in the movement.

"Why do you want to know that?" Parker asked.

"I'm thinking of organizing an advisory committee which
will remain in the background," I explained. "It would be secret so that if they catch us guys, the committee can remain
intact." The argument appealed to Parker and I followed it up
quickly with an adaptation of Roberts' own views:

"Look Parker," I said. "You and Alderman have been indicted. You've got your necks out. You want somebody to
organize for you to get the old members back and new members in. You asked me to come down to do the job. But we've
got to work it differently because the enemy is on our trail.
You can't afford to be seen with me, and I can't afford to be
seen with you. The minute they spot me as Pagnanelli I'm no
good as organizer. The brains of the N.W.L. has got to remain in the background."

"You're right there," Sage nodded. "If they get Russ [Rus-
sell M. Roberts] we can't go on, that's sure. He's everything."

"There you are. Roberts is underground. We're at war.
That's the only way to work it now. I want to know who is
important in the movement, so I can get them on the secret
advisory committee."

Parker agreed: "But you'd better not take too long," he
warned. "You can't let this thing stretch out indefinitely."

I won an initial victory by postponing the date of our next
meeting to a full week ahead. From this point on this, in brief,
became my counter strategy. I'd work for Roberts as machinist and try to keep him pacified. After work I'd attempt
to look up Parker's friends without necessarily letting him
know whom I had interviewed. At the same time I must impress him that I was earnestly engaged in organizational work.
It was my job, too, to "pump" Alderman for all the information I could get out of him, and eventually get him to arrange

NATIONAL WORKERS LEAGUE
Founded 1938

Nationalism is love of one's own nation - the readiness
to sacrifice everything to it's interests.

Detroit, Michigan, April 15, 1942

Vol. 3   NATIONALIST NEWSLETTER   No. 35
131

By order of the Central Committee, April 10, 1942 authorization
is given to raise a Wm. Dudley Pelley Defense Fund. Citizens not
acquainted with their district representative are requested to mail
funds direct to Box 701, Detroit, Mich., % Pelley Defense Fund.
Folks, keep in mind every day that a great nationalist, (Gerald
L. K. Smith), will be a candidate this fall from Michigan for the US
Senate. Talk a bit every day about him to some new face. This
sterling American may be behind the bars when voting time comes
Charles A. Lindberg is indeed the man of the hour, unafraid of
abuse and criticism, and most worthy of patriotic praise. He alone
has placed his finger upon the real cancer in American life - the
Jewish element. Lindberg names the Jew as one of the principal
The well-known commentator, Blair Moody, headlines the past week
war proposals of one of the NWL's national committeemen, George E.
Deatherage of Va. Mr. Deatherage ably proposes to organize our defense workers for war by putting them in uniform. The plan is worthy.
Indignation is sweeping over the country at the accusations level-
ed at Cong. Hoffman of Mich. We urge all citizens to obtain a copy
of his speech "Don't Haul Down the Stars and Stripes" - the same speech
Senator Gerald P. Nye's address in the Masonic Auditorium here on
the 2nd, under the auspices of the Committee of 1,000,000 resulted in
the most successful Nationalist Rally in recent years. Full credit
must be given Detroit's present ranking nationalist, the Hon. Gerald
L. K. Smith.
The personal hatred shown Senator Burton K. Wheeler of Montana,
our fellow-nationalist, by F.D.R. aptly shows the dictatorial nature
of our President. The Senator is an able American, and most emphati-
cally pro-American in the sense that he has small patience

Parker Sage defends those whom he regards as champions
of native fascism. Sage claims Senator Wheeler as a "fellow
nationalist."

a personal meeting with Gerald L. K. Smith. The success of
my plan depended on perfect co-ordination and timing.

After I finished at the shop, this became my daily routine.
I walked a mile to my room, dressed, then took a tedious
eight-mile bus ride into Detroit proper, after which I traveled
about in an unknown city to the home of the individual I
wanted to interview—spent several hours with him, another
hour in taking down notes while my recollection was still
"hot," after which I rushed to the post office to mail my precious notes home. The long bus ride back to my room was the
final step. And when I missed the last bus, which was not in-
frequent, I hitch-hiked home. I rarely got to bed before two
A.M. and I had to be up early and report for work at seven.

CHAPTER IV

OUTER CIRCLE OF THE N.W.L.

"By the time you receive this letter, I shall be on
the road to St. Louis and parts north together with
a uniformed squad of young men composing what I
believe will be the first Silver Shirt Storm troop in
America."

GERALD L. K. SMITH
TO WILLIAM DUDLEY PELLEY

GARLAND ALDERMAN spoke to me with uncommon candor
during our lunch hours together. He bared the secrets of the
N.W.L. while sitting on the lawn or, on rainy days in his car,
and told me how as chairman of the Pontiac chapter he had
used the America First Committee to do the "dirty work of
the League."

"I used the anti-Semitic stuff put out by the League, and
turned it over to America First members for distribution," he
said.

Garland loved flattery and I had no difficulty in "pumping"
him for information. I learned from him that the "William
Randall" punching the time clock at late hours was a policeman. To make sure, I asked Roberts if Randall really was an
officer. "Sure he is!" Roberts answered. And from Garland
I learned that Roberts' most profitable customer was a large
Jewish manufacturing concern. Tactfully I asked Roberts if
this was true.

"Sure it is," he said. "And I'm charging the sons of bitches
twice the money I would charge others."

Here was the strange spectacle of an important Jewish concern innocently promoting Roberts' anti-Semitism. But Roberts had contrived to keep his underground secret so well that
few knew of his connections with the N.W.L. Garland was
my informant for the fact that it was Roberts who had paid
bail for him and Sage when they were threatened with im-
prisonment. It was Garland who loaned to me overnight a

copy of Sage's financial statement of the League, enabling me to have it photostated on one of my daily visits to Detroit. From Garland I learned that both he and Sage had associated with Max Stephan, the Detroit Nazi and member of America First, who at this writing is under death sentence for having aided in the escape of a German aviator from Canada early in 1942. From Garland I learned that during the past month alone Roberts had purchased 4,000 pieces of "patriotic" literature, and turned over most of it to him for distribution.

Garland was impressionable and extremely gullible—an ideal and typical tool of fascist operators. He had been graduated from Ohio State University in 1936 with a B.S. degree in agriculture, but he permitted himself to be used as a dupe. In off moments he confessed his fear at the publicity following his indictment, and how neighbors in Pontiac where he lived shunned him. Thoroughly opposed to his views, his German-American wife had threatened: "If one more F.B.I. man comes to my house I'll go back to mother." As to his in-laws—also fine, patriotic German-Americans—Garland said, laughing:

"They went to the draft board and told them they'd take care of my wife and kid if they'd put me in the army. They said a patriotic guy like me ought to be in the army."

I asked Garland how he had got his start. Pelley's *Liberation* and Coughlin's *Social Justice* had been his primers and he had attended special lecture courses given during the winter months by Father Coughlin. He had become involved with the N.W.L. a year ago and become its secretary while serving concurrently as chairman of the Pontiac chapter of America First.

"The work wasn't much different as far as I was concerned," he said. "My home was full of literature of all kinds. I gave out America First stuff at League meetings, and League stuff at America First meetings. The two worked together nicely. We had people from both crowds attending each other's meetings."

The collaboration had not ended with Pearl Harbor. Garland was now visiting his old A.F.C. contacts to collect money for the N.W.L. defense fund.

With parrot-like consistency, Garland remarked daily: "This is a Jew government. It's part of their plot to rule the world. It's the internationalist banker capitalists and the Communists who are doing it all. Ain't that right, George?"

Garland wanted to be reassured constantly. I sensed that he was paying mere lip service to the routine Nazi ritual, and decided to test him. "Garland," I said one day as we were lunching in his car, "would you be willing to kill a Jew?"

He looked at me surprised: "No, not in cold blood. Not unless he attacked me first."

"And if he didn't attack you first, would you kill him?"

"I'd have no reason to kill him," he said simply.

"But suppose he was a nice big, fat, international banker, Communist Jew," I insisted. "Would you enjoy killing him?"

"No," he said with finality. "I couldn't kill a man in cold blood."

That reaction was not a Nazi reaction. It wasn't the spirit of the Christian Mobilizers, the Bund, the Christian Front. It simply wasn't the "kosher way" of being a Nazi. I regarded Garland as the most perfect symbol of a Nazi dupe, the most impressionable sucker for Nazi guile I encountered in all my four years as investigator.

Together with Garland one day after work we drove over to see Robert Vietig, former chairman of the Detroit chapter of the A.F.C., and supervisor to many near-by chapters. He had worked closely with Garland. Garland recounted that while speaking for the Pontiac chapter Vietig had advised his audience to "buy a gun and keep it well oiled" because they would "need it some day."

"How does he live?" I asked Garland.

"He is an insurance salesman," he answered.

As we knocked on the door of Vietig's home on Tennyson Avenue, he came out stripped to the waist. Athletic and in his late thirties, Vietig welcomed us into his home. He told us how a few months ago Parker Sage had come to him for advice. Vietig had urged him to lay low. But Sage had insisted on sticking out his neck.

"Look where he is now!" Vietig observed.

I asked him if the America First Committee was dead.

"You can't take Americanism out of the hearts and minds of the people," he said sharply. He had placed in a vault a set of the America First membership lists for future use. Vietig told us of his ambition. It was to found a political unit in Michigan with sufficient strength to hold the balance of power. It was his intention to have a speakers bureau and train speakers who were "one hundred per cent American like Garland here."

"Would you train those speakers along nationalist lines?" I asked.

"That's Americanism," he answered. "Nationalism is Americanism."

Vietig was the type of person I wanted to investigate more thoroughly. He was in the respectable class and seemed to be an important cog in the Detroit machine. I made an appointment to see him a few days later "to talk insurance." Vietig said nothing about having addressed a closed meeting of the N.W.L. in September, 1941, regarding which Sage had told me: "Boy, he sure opened up on the Jews—for the first time in public."

A peculiar "insurance salesman," Vietig seemed not at all interested either in talking or selling insurance. Instead we talked about "nationalist" politics and he told me that he enjoyed receiving the *Nationalist Newsletter*. Sage had offered him the editorship last February, but Vietig had refused pending the outcome of events after Pearl Harbor.

"What should we nationalists do now?" I asked.

"Tread water. That is all we can do," he answered.

Vietig described himself as a promoter. "I represent men," he said, "and I promote ideas." As to his personal future: "I expect to work less and less with the years. Why should I work hard?"

He told me of his close friendship with Laura Ingalls, and of an America First Committee meeting at Lansing, Michigan, where the two had spoken together to a labor audience. He recounted how she had said: " 'I can't say everything now because I do not want to go to jail.' Then she stopped," Vietig resumed, "because she was afraid to go on. But I stepped on the platform and said: 'I'll tell you what, men. If we go to war your unions will be shot. Labor will be under a dictatorship. You'll have a revolution eventually—why not have it *now!*'

The F.B.I. framed Miss Ingalls," [1] he exploded. "She was a fine person."

Vietig also thought that Pelley and Coughlin (both of whose sheets had just been banned from the mails) were being "persecuted." He expressed admiration for both and asserted he was "one hundred per cent for Gerald Smith." Vietig's importance on the Detroit scene became apparent when he admitted associating with two top-rank industrialists whom he mentioned by name.

Vietig was extremely conceited, greatly over-rating himself and I carefully nurtured his vanity to make him talk. He told me of the stunts he had pulled on America First platforms. He had "buried political issues" in a coffin. He had brought bent old mothers and cripples in an attempt to emotionalize the audience against war. Then he said: "I myself talked indirectly and by innuendo, by hinting but not actually saying it. I trained my audiences to understand and interpret me." In New York this was known as the "weasel word" technique.

"I'll tell you the inside story of Senator Wheeler the next time you come around," he said, as I arose to leave. "And I'll tell you about John L. Lewis, too. He is with us now you know." I was not surprised to hear this from Vietig. Lewis was no longer the "Public Enemy Number Two" of Christian Front days. Consistently for the past year Lewis had been lauded by Father Coughlin until *Social Justice* readers were finally urged on November 24, 1941: "Now is the time for labor to stand by John L. Lewis."

Why did Father Coughlin suddenly decide to become friendly toward a man he had hated so violently? What is the inside story, if any, between Coughlin and Lewis or their mutual representatives?

After a particularly hard day's work at the shop, I travelled some three hours by various buses to reach Mrs. Rosa M. Farber's home at 14634 Schoolcraft. Unwilling to talk at first, she finally gave me one of the most vivid interviews of my Detroit trip. Mrs. Farber remembered me from a letter I had written her in Washington. A large, energetic woman, in her early

[1] Laura Ingalls was convicted of being an unregistered Nazi agent on February 13, 1942.

forties, she had a sandy face and fine reddish-brown hair. She spoke calmly and forcefully.

I talked with her for two hours and despite her associations was beginning to believe I had misjudged her. She told me she had worked with Mrs. A. Cressy Morrison, Mrs. Catherine Baldwin, Dr. Maude DeLand, and had read *Social Justice*. Mrs. Farber confirmed my impression of Cathrine Curtis: "I regard Miss Curtis as the most capable woman in the country today. She not only knows politics, but she also knows Washington." Mrs. Farber was also well acquainted with Robert Vietig and was impressed by his abilities.

President of the Mothers of the United States of America, she had known as early as May, 1941, she confessed, that Laura Ingalls was on the Nazi pay roll. "There was a lot more about her than appeared in the newspapers," she said mysteriously. "What was printed was only half the story."

How did she know that?

And *why* had she continued to associate with her?

It was nearly ten o'clock. So far I had learned little from Mrs. Farber that was worth while. Then, as the hour hand on the living room clock pointed to ten, Mrs. Farber suddenly came out with: "There is no other way out for us than through a revolution."

"You mean a revolution with bloodshed?" I asked, surprised at her sudden remark.

She nodded: "It's the only way."

"I was going to start an underground organization last fall," she explained, "but they [meaning gossipy women] would not have been able to keep it secret and I gave up the idea. It's the only thing left to do now—start an underground movement." Mrs. Farber wasn't holding meetings of any kind now. "You only make yourself a target," she said. "They'll shut you down. The only way to work now is through conversation."

She called it that. What she actually did was to outline a whispering campaign. She gave me her formula as she practiced it day by day. She recounted how she had spread defeatism at the local school. One of the teachers giving out ration cards had said that rationing was necessary for psychological reasons. But Mrs. Farber had argued back: "If they want us to know that we are in the war then let them publish the casualty lists and also send the bodies back." One of the teachers had commented, "Yes, come to think of it, those lists haven't been published, have they."

Mrs. Farber boasted, "You see? I planted an idea in her head, now she'll think of it again."

Thoroughly warmed up to her subject, she went on: "I just plant seeds like that every day. They are little ideas which I put in my conversations day by day. I do it all the time. That is all I do. That is all you can do now. Here, let me show you something." She got up from her chair and went over to the bureau. From it she pulled out a large pocketbook and drew out a newspaper picture of Attorney General Francis Biddle. "Look at that face," she said. "It's one hundred per cent Jewish." [2]

From another folder in her pocketbook she took out a picture of a child whose grand-uncle was captioned as being General MacArthur. She said that his face, too, was Jewish. And then this statement from Mrs. Farber: "People say that MacArthur's little son looks like a little kike."

"Should we, in these conversations you suggest, use anti-Semitism?" I asked innocently.

"What do you think I'm doing when I show Biddle's picture and tell people he looks like a Jew?" she exploded. "Preach anti-Semitism all you can, the more the better."

After this Mrs. Farber lost all self-composure and all reason. Having controlled herself all through the early evening, she now let go and subjected me to a half hour of fantastic delusions. One of these was the amazing statement that Polish Jews had willingly and wantonly encouraged Hitler's attack on Poland. The *Sanhedrin*, or a mythical world Jewish Council (existing only in the imagination of Jew-baiters) had decreed this in order that Hitler devastate all of Europe.

"How would the Jews benefit from this?" I asked incredulously.

Mrs. Farber explained that it was to further a plot of world ruin so that Communist elements might be in a position to offer Communism as the only antidote for National-Socialism. "Hitler," Mrs. Farber said, out of all reason, "is being kept

[2] Attorney General Biddle is a member of the famous non-Jewish Philadelphia family.

alive as a hate object by those who want our civilization destroyed in order to set up an international world order."

I could hardly believe my ears, for here was a woman, hitherto rational, whose blind hatreds and fanaticisms led her to believe and propagate the most fantastic lies. She became just like the crackpots I had met on countless occasions. In her defamation of Jewry, in her attempt to lay the blame of war at the feet of persecuted Polish Jews, Mrs. Farber may have been attempting to absolve Hitler of all blame. In her lumping together of Hitler, Stalin, Mussolini, Churchill and Roosevelt Mrs. Farber followed another favorite Nazi device used to discredit the national leadership, and sow mistrust toward the national war effort. On leaving, she loaded me down with a huge stack of pre-Pearl Harbor isolationist literature.

I learned from Mrs. Farber that Mrs. Beatrice Knowles, president of American Mothers, was holding underground meetings. Phoning, I told her of my visits to Mrs. Farber, Vietig and Parker Sage. "Come right over," she invited.

Mrs. Knowles lived in a beautiful home in an expensive section of Detroit's suburbs. Vivacious, energetic, I also found her to be a determined and forceful woman, but not blindly fanatic. She was more poised than Mrs. Farber due, perhaps, to the presence of Mr. Knowles, though he proved to be a tame yes-man and agreed with everything his wife said.

Mrs. Knowles admitted she was holding secret "movement meetings" every second Monday in the homes of mothers. When I asked why she referred to them as "movement meetings," she explained that American Mothers no longer had any officers. Her new policy was to have a board of "advisers" who set the policy and passed it on to about thirty subordinate women leaders who, in turn, held meetings in their homes. She explained that her purpose was to make it impossible for authorities to investigate individual officers or to crack down on her organization.

A man's auxiliary to her feminine movement also functioned, and the menfolk met together with the women—just as during the pre-Pearl Harbor era. She and her women had carried on missionary work continually since December 7.

Mrs. Knowles thought highly of Gerald L. K. Smith and said that her lieutenants had distributed American Mothers leaflets at his meetings. Although Mrs. Knowles referred to the "terrible boys" of the N.W.L. she was no stranger to them, and admitted that William Lyman had not only attended many American Mothers meetings but that she had allowed him to distribute the subversive literature of the National Workers League. Mrs. Knowles had worked with Dr. DeLand, Mrs. Baldwin, Cathrine Curtis and Mrs. Morrison. She "admired" Mrs. Dilling's "courage" and thought Father Coughlin was a great American.

"We don't want any internationalists to dictate at the peace table," she said, and with a shrewd eye to winning the peace, added significantly: "Our real work will begin after the war is over. We patriots must be ready for that day."

I observed that I had met considerable anti-war sentiment in Detroit and that "nationalists" here were militant in the expression of their views. "That's what education has done," she explained. "Millions of copies of patriotic literature have been poured into Michigan. My Mothers are still engaged in such a campaign of education."

In my interviews after work I did not overlook John T. Wiandt, a tool and die maker working at the Ford plant, a veteran in the movement who had received literature from Colonel Sanctuary and Stahrenberg. He told me that he had been a member of the Klan and was also a member of the N.W.L. He had distributed League literature not only at meetings of Gerald L. K. Smith whom he admired, but also at the Ford plant. "I have an audience every lunch hour," he said.

I placed Wiandt in the category of a crackpot. None the less, his hot fanaticism, his tireless tirades against the Administration, and his voluble defeatism among defense workers branded Wiandt as one of the many cogs functioning unobtrusively, but effectively, in Detroit's native fascist machinery.

Among others whom I interviewed was an Italian-American real estate operator, Alfred P. Adamo. Adamo flooded Easter Sunday churchgoers with a vicious little leaflet entitled, "April 5, 1942—Happy Easter" in which the Administration was described as being composed of "poisonous Snakes and Rats that are the Professional Internationalists, Communistic and Foreign Refugees."

A former America First-er and member of the N.W.L. Adamo had received Hudson's, Pelley's, Sage's and Smith's bulletins regularly. He had promoted Mrs. Farber's work. Adamo's views had not changed in the least after Pearl Harbor. He regarded Father Coughlin as the ablest man in the country. He attended Smith's meetings, he told me, and hoped to see Lindbergh and Nye "come out in the open." He told me of "many hundreds of dollars" he had spent for "patriotic" literature.

I was working against time—trying to squeeze in as many interviews as I could before Sage became infuriated at my negligence of my official duties as organizer. It was with considerable difficulty that I placated him when we met again.

"When the hell are you going to go to work for us?" he demanded.

I pleaded that I was still tired from overwork, from lack of sleep, from the exhaustion of a new environment.

"But you're not too tired to see these other people."

I couldn't deny that. But I had to be firm with him.

"Look here, Parker," I said. "I've done organizing for the American Nationalist Party in New York (I had not), and I organized for Joe McWilliams (I had not). Go on and ask Joe (no one knew where he was) about the first-class job I did for him. But the methods I use ain't the methods everybody else uses. You gotta use different methods in different places. I use original methods and my methods always work."

I could tell that he wasn't convinced.

"Here I am in a strange city. I didn't leave my home and sick mother just to get a lousy job that don't pay anything. I've been here only ten days and you want me to go to town for you. I came here to stay permanently and to work for the Cause. Give me a break and leave me alone for a while. If you didn't trust me, you shouldn't have called for me."

"Now, now, George, don't get excited," he placated. "I was just anxious to see you get started. I've read all about you in the papers. We all know here you're a good man, but I was just hoping that you would. . . ."

I was waiting to be appeased some more before I spoke again.

"Look here, Georgie. Here are two tickets for the annual

ball of the Society of Tool and Die Craftsmen. We're going next Saturday. You'll meet some young men there and you can start recruiting for the League."

"Now you're talking turkey," I said enthusiastically. With some authority, I added: "Now let's go to work on the next issue of the Newsletter. First thing we got to do is to build up circulation!"

Sage looked upon me as a shining white knight come to re-organize ranks which had suffered through official investiga-tions. Encouraged by my supposed mission, he started off the Newsletter:

The N.W.L. is determined to carry on its legal activities. It will continue to serve the real interests of the American worker to the best of its ability and despite all efforts of the Jewish-Communist interests to destroy it. . . .

In the meanwhile, I had by no means overlooked my inves-tigations at Roberts' shop. I went frequently to the washroom to jot down notes of my conversations with Alderman and Roberts. The shop served as a clearing house for un-American literature. Garland circulated copies of Pelley's *The Mustard Seed*. Roberts gave Alderman a stack of Hudson's bulletins to distribute, and also a copy of Thorkelson's book, *We Must Save the Republic*, published by Pelley. When copies of *The X-Ray* and *Publicity* arrived they were passed from hand to hand. Roberts also bought a huge batch of reprints of Repre-sentative Hoffman's "Judas" speech and passed them to some of the male workers, urging: "Just pass them on to some good people you know, not to everybody."

"How about giving some to the women?" I asked.

"No, we don't bother with them," Roberts said. "Women and politics don't mix."

One hundred copies of the *Protocols* arrived from the American Publishing Society, Bremerton, Washington, a notorious American Nazi publishing house. They cost Roberts $18.80. He offered me a copy and I began to walk away with it, thinking it was free.

"That'll cost you fifty cents," Roberts called out. They had cost him nineteen cents each. The profits went into the

National Workers League defense fund. Roberts turned over twenty-five copies to Garland for re-sale. Thus, the sale of a Nazi propaganda booklet became the device by which Garland and Sage reduced their bail-bond obligation to Roberts and at the same time helped along Hitler's cause.

As my room was only a few blocks from Slim Hampton's garage, I stopped there frequently for a chat with the reputed ex-member of the Black Legion, now a member of the N.W.L. Slim was more vituperative than ever at reports that the State militia was helping Negro defense workers move into their new homes.

"Those Goddamed niggers. We'll have to kill those bastards. Kill thousands of the sons of bitches. Fight the militia! Sure, fight the Goddamed Jewish militia. Smoke out the nigger sons of bitches." Slim was a coarser edition of Roberts—if that were possible.

I was accomplishing my mission. My investigations were giving me a clear picture of the inter-relation between the America First Committee, the N.W.L., Smith, the Mothers, Vietig, Adamo and Wiandt, whose co-ordinated efforts had made Detroit such a ripe plum for subversive propaganda.

But my days here were numbered, as I couldn't keep up much longer the sham of being a "nationalist organizer." I worked conscientiously at my lathe. But Roberts was giving me work which became progressively more difficult for an inexperienced operator. At the same time, I was rapidly nearing a point of exhaustion caused by the abnormal hours I kept. Beginning to think of a graceful way to make an exit, I showed Alderman and others in the shop the letters I had been getting from my sister "Jeanette." They were so plaintive that they sounded real even to me. One of them read:

I sure was glad to hear from you and that you have such a fine job and like the boss, because I think it makes a difference even though any job is good these days. We are all fine here but Ma. Sunday was such a beautiful day Dr. Gardini said he thought it wouldn't hurt if she sat by the window a little while in the big chair, but it was too much for her. Poor ma, she couldn't even get that far and she had to go right back to bed and nearly had a collapse.

Pop and all of us are worried sick about her. I don't want to

worry you too much, George, but I promised to tell you the
truth so I guess I'll have to . . . I must go and fix up ma now.

Love and kisses from your
Sis

My major remaining tasks were to arrange to meet Gerald
L. K. Smith, and attend the Tool and Die Craftsmen's Ball.
Garland volunteered to arrange the introduction to Smith.
But we didn't have his private telephone number which was
unlisted. Even then, Smith changed his number frequently.
Garland and I determined to go down personally to his office
and arrange for an appointment.

Immediately after work on Friday, May 8, we rushed to
my room to change and arrived at Smith's offices just before
five P.M. Unlisted in the directory, Smith was located in room
No. 2006 of the Industrial Bank Building. Garland introduced
himself to Bernard A. Doman, Smith's office manager, as an
officer of the National Workers League. Doman smiled and
stretched out his hand. Garland then said he'd like to talk
with Smith personally.

"I have a large list of America First Committee names,"
Alderman said to my surprise, "which I want to turn over to
Mr. Smith."

At the mention of the mailing list, Doman's face lighted up.
Garland said the names numbered between "three and four
thousand." Doman's face beamed to the heavens. He would
be delighted to arrange a meeting immediately after Smith's
meeting next Tuesday at the Maccabee Auditorium. "But be
sure you write him a letter explaining all this, so I can show
it to him," he suggested.

Doman shook our hands warmly. Highly pleased and
loquacious, he accompanied us to the door.

"You never told me you had those lists," I said to Garland
in the elevator.

"That was the first time I told anybody," he whispered.
"I'll tell you more when we get out to the street."

Sitting at a quiet cafeteria, Garland explained that he had
refused to surrender to the Dies Committee his America First
Committee lists, saying he already had destroyed them.

"Keep it quiet, will you, George," he begged.

"Oh sure, don't worry," I answered. "But why do you want to turn them over to Smith."

"Because I heard Smith is going to run for the Senate and I'm thinking of campaigning for him, I want him to use those lists," Alderman explained. "They're all good names. . . . Now here is where you come in, George. . . ."

The lists he had at home were scattered, some typewritten, others on pledge cards. Garland wanted me to assemble them and type them out uniformly. Could I get a typewriter and finish the work over the week end?

"I'll do my best," I said, delighted at the opportunity.

"I'll bring the lists tomorrow morning and pick them up Monday," Garland said. "But remember, only two copies, no more. On Monday we can also write the letters Doman asked about."

Who was this Gerald L. K. Smith I was so anxious to meet?

Smith was no tyro at politics, for his career as a politician began with Pelley's Silver Shirts the year Hitler got into power. On August 5, 1936, H. E. Martin, then executive director of *Pelley's Weekly*, wrote the Reverend L. M. Birkhead the following letter on official Pelley stationery:

Answering your letter of the 3rd regarding Mr. Gerald L. K. Smith's connection with the Silver Shirts, which you say he denies, we have on file certain letters and telegrams from him received during July and August 1933. The letters are all written on Silver Shirts of America letterheads and signed by him. His registration number as a member of the Silver Shirts was 3223 and his wife's number was 3220.

The enclosed extracts from these letters will undoubtedly serve your purpose.

        (Signed) H. E. Martin
                  Executive Director, The Pelley Publishers

Among the extracts sent the Reverend Birkhead was the following from a letter which H. E. Martin declared Smith sent to Pelley on August 15, 1933:

By the time you receive this letter I shall be on the road to St. Louis and parts north together with a uniformed squad of young men composing what I believe will be the first Silver Shirt storm troop in America.

Two days later, according to Martin, Smith wrote Pelley from Hot Springs: "We have held three mass meetings, two street meetings, and appointed key men for literature in six towns; no, seven towns." And some of the lecture topics Smith used in promoting Pelley's cause were: "Some Day 100 Million Americans Will Hide Behind the Silver Shirts for Protection," and "Why I Left the Conventional Pulpit to Join the Christian Militia of the Silver Shirts."

Shortly after this Smith gave up Pelley and went to Louisiana. It was in Shreveport that Smith, then pastor of King's Highway Church, met the late Huey Long. Following that meeting Smith formally severed himself from the pulpit and turned politician by championing Huey's plan. After his assassination, Smith tried to take over the machine but was pushed away by another henchman, Earl Christenberry. Smith turned north in search of greener pastures.

In 1936 when his friend, Father Coughlin, sponsored William Lemke for President on the National Union for Social Justice ticket, and Dr. Francis E. Townsend ran for office on his own version of Share-the-Wealth plan, Smith again found himself in the thick of unorthodox politics. He described himself as a "contact man for the Union Party, director of the Townsend organization, a keynote speaker for Father Coughlin and supporter of Lemke for President." Smith was that kind of a man—a super promoter! In addition, Smith also turned up as speaker at a "grass roots" convention with his friend, Eugene Talmadge, governor of Georgia.

At the same time Smith became ambitious to run for office himself. He set to organizing the Committee of One Million, boasting that it would combine the best features of the Townsend-Coughlin-Long machines for a "nationalist front against Communism." According to a *New York Times* report he set out to "seize the government of the United States," making no secret of his strategy:

You've got to be in a state of crisis to do things well. That means you've got to look over men and events, convince yourself that there is a crisis. Then you've got the mentality of a soldier in a trench. Nothing stops you. You're ruthless. When you're right and know you're right, you should be ruthless.

PELLEY'S WEEKLY

Published By

The Pelley Publishers

P. O. Box 1776   Asheville, N. C.

August 5, 1936.

L. M. Birkhead,
3425 Baltimore Ave.,
Kansas City, Missouri.

Dear Mr. Birkhead:-

Answering your letter of the 3rd regarding Mr. Gerald L. K. Smith's connection with the Silver Shirts, which you say he denies, we have on file certain letters and telegrams from him received during July and August 1933. The letters are all written on Silver Shirts of America letterheads and signed by him. His registration number as a member of the Silver Shirts was 3223 and his wife's number was 3220.

The enclosed extracts from these letters will undoubtedly serve your purpose.

Sincerely yours,

The Pelley Publishers,

H. E. Martin

H. E. Martin,
Executive Director.

Aided financially by lesser Detroit industrialists, retired stockholders, wealthy dowagers, as well as the nickel-and-dime contributions of his believing rank-and-file followers, the Committee of One Million supported the America First Committee party line to the limit. Senator Nye and Congressman Day spoke for Smith's Committee and Sage's *Nationalist Newsletter* approved:

Senator Gerald P. Nye's address . . . resulted in the most successful Nationalist rally in recent years. Full credit must be given Detroit's present ranking nationalist the Honorable Gerald L. K. Smith.

Appeasement, obstructionism, a "negotiated peace," all-out campaign against the Lend-Lease Bill and against national defense; the breeding of defeatism and distrust of our leader-ship—these were the cornerstones on which Gerald L. K. Smith operated in Detroit. Speaking over radio station WJR he took up where Father Coughlin's hate messages left off—and this in America's most strategic city, the center of our war industries, the home of tens of thousands of war workers.

This was the man I was so anxious to meet personally.

CHAPTER V

DETROIT IS DYNAMITE

"You talk to the men every chance you get, in the washrooms, during working hours, while going home on the bus. One good nationalist can do a lot of good work, even in a large shop."

PARKER SAGE

SATURDAY NIGHT, May 9, I met Parker and together we went to the annual ball of the Society of Tool and Die Craftsmen's International Union at the Danish Temple.

"I'll introduce you to Tony Bommarito, one of the organizers for the Society," Parker said. "You ought to get along with a fellow Italian."

I can't easily forget Tony Bommarito. As we approached him, he was leaning against the entrance to the dance floor, serving as a bouncer. He had the build and temperament for it. More than six feet tall, powerfully built, with muscles bulging from the folds of a tight-fitting dark green suit, Tony reminded me of the tough guys on New York's East side. His lips were thick and sensual. His hair was kinky and his thick, leathery neck bulged over his tight-fitting collar. Tony's shoes were orange in color and had pointed tips. He wore a stiff-bosom shirt striped horizontally near the neck and vertically lower down. His necktie was a nightmare of color. His accent was a mixture of low Italian and gangsterese and he spoke from between tight lips out of the left corner of his mouth.

Parker wore his "America First" button and introduced me to Tony Bommarito as "Joe McWilliams' right-hand man."

"Glad to meet'cha, kid," Tony grinned.

"How'ya, Tony."

Tony rattled off the names of a dozen New York gangsters and asked if I knew them. I said I knew all "dem boys" and Tony seemed pleased. Characteristic of the petty gangster, Tony loved to talk about himself. He explained he was one of seven brothers. Two had been killed "in action"—dying glorious gangster deaths; two were "in the clink" (serving prison terms).

"Three of us is out."

As for himself, Tony told me he had been "in the clink" twice—once serving a term in San Quentin for manslaughter. His former associates had been the Gillette Boys, "Lucky" Luciano (convicted white-slaver) and "Dutch" Schultz—ex-bootlegger (riddled to death). "I wuz there when a million dollar deal crossed hands between 'Lucky' and 'Dutch.'" Tony's specialties before going in for labor organizing had been hijacking, bootlegging, and "bumping off the boys."

"How's bumping these days?" I asked.

"Not so good, not so good," Tony said in disgust. "You can't do no killing now. The C.I.O. is too big to buck that way. You gotta work quiet."

I asked Tony how he worked as organizer in the face of stern C.I.O. opposition. He answered in typical gangsterese: "We don't need many guys. We just send one or two in a shop. It takes five or six weeks to organize a joint. Our men talks to the right kind of a guy, den dis man gets a friend to come in with him. You wine 'em and dance 'em a couple nights in a hotel. When you get about twenty you hold a meetin'. You wine 'em and dance 'em some more and say 'how about organizin', boys.' That gets 'em."

I listened attentively.

"You begins your woik by talking against the Jews and the nigger. The Jew got us into the war. You tell 'em that. The Jew is keeping labor down by controlling the money. It's the Jew who hires niggers and gives them low wages. There is angles, see; there is angles. When a guy in a shop gets up and talks against the kikes, and some other guy in the shop don't like it, we call on this second guy. . . . There is angles. You gotta loin 'em." Tony summed up his technique: "You ties in the niggers with the Jew, den you call the Jews Communists. That gets 'em. Catch on, kid?"

Under the guise of fighting Jews, Communists and Negroes, it was apparent that Tony was introducing Nazi gangster methods in the labor field.

"Does Griffin know the way you fellows are working?" I asked. Jack Griffin was president of the Society.

"Of course he don't. Keep 'im blind. Keep 'im blind, is what I say. He don't know nuthin', and you'd better tell Parker to keep 'im blind. Don't tell 'im nuthin'."

Somehow or other the conversation turned to Gerald L. K. Smith and I asked Tony if he knew Smith.

"Do I know 'im? I bodyguarded for 'im back in 1939."

I asked if he had been paid much for the job. "Did you get as much as $25 a week and board?" I wanted to know.

"I wouldn't guard a dog for dat a week. I got $100 a week, with expenses." Tony then made this remark: "I don't know if he still gets money from the manufacturers like he used to. Boy, oh boy! The big dough sure used to roll in."

I reminded him that Smith claimed his contributions did not go over $20. Tony laughed: "I seen plenty of money comin' in. I used to see checks for $2000 and $3000. Woikers don't send them in. No sir, it was de manufacturers."

I asked Tony why he hadn't continued to work for Smith.

"He wuz too tight. He don't let nobody cut in. I don't want to tie up with nobody that don't let you in on his racket. There ain't no future in that."

"I like the way you talk, Tony," I said. "You got guts, I wanna see ye again. Got a little deal I wanna get your advice on."

"Sure ting, kid. Any time, any time. You can get me any time at the office before ten." Tony gave me his calling card. On the back of it he inscribed his home address: "100 Davenport. Apt. 212."

"Listen, kid. If any Jews is interferin' let me know and we'll pay dem a visit."

Tony had not read *Social Justice* nor any other subversive organ. He was not political-minded. Labor organizing on a racial basis was just a convenient new racket for him. Since there was no more bootlegging, killing, or hijacking, a fellow had to make an honest living.

After my talk with Tony, I went looking for Parker. As Parker did not dance, we spent the evening talking. He thought it time for me to learn the methods he had used.

"Whenever I go to a shop, I go to work on the fellow next to me. If he is a nigger I don't talk to him. If he is a Jew I don't talk to him either. I let them know I care nothing for them. I do everything I can to get them to leave me. You can't get anywhere with niggers and Jews."

This was essentially the same technique that Bommarito had been preaching. Though struck by its similarity, I was not surprised, for I had found that Nazi techniques varied only in the performance of detail. Fundamentally they ran true to the pattern created in the inner sanctums of Nazi propaganda bureaus and projected *im Ausland* (overseas) as "American." Parker went on:

"But if you are working next to a white man, begin by sounding him out. Size him up and ask key questions—Ask him what he thinks of Hitler. You can always tell if a man is a nationalist."

If the victim showed promise, Parker coached, my next step was to cultivate his friendship. In due time I was instructed to give him mild anti-Semitic literature and watch for reactions. If favorable, I was to give the would-be victim a stronger dosage.

"You work on him some more, and then ask him to drop in at our meetings. That's how you do it. You talk to the men every chance you get, in the washrooms, during working hours, while going home on the bus. One good nationalist can do a lot of good work, even in a large shop."

I listened closely, keenly aware that the poison of one man could easily permeate an entire shop in the course of a few months.

"As soon as you learn the trade at Russ'," Parker said, "I can get you a better-paying job with another shop. We have the contacts. Later on I'd like you to join the Society of Tool and Die Craftsmen."

I made arrangements to meet Parker again Monday night.

I spent all day Sunday typing for Garland Alderman a list of about 2,500 names of America First-ers in Pontiac, Royal Oak, Birmingham, Lansing and Detroit. I made a third copy and sent it home by registered mail.

Monday morning—fifteen minutes after starting time—I received a jolt when Roberts approached me at my lathe. Up to this time I had been calling him "Russ." I have never liked the stiffness of formality, even in my dealings with fascists.

"None of this Russ stuff anymore," Roberts began in a hostile voice. "I don't want to be high hat, but from now on you call me Mr. Roberts."

I looked at him silently and said: "Yes, Mr. Roberts."

But my mind was feverish. I was trying to reason just what had brought this complete about-face. It scared me. I knew that Sage and Roberts had intended to meet Sunday. Had Parker said something derogatory, or had Roberts stumbled on to the truth? I wondered if Roberts was giving me a hint that he would deal with me more directly later. Or, I reasoned, was it possible that like so many fanatics I had met in the past few years he had the erratic temperament which at one moment might be friendly and the next violent and cruel? At any rate, I took comfort in the fact that I had already purchased a return ticket which I carried on me, and could leave instantly—in my work clothes if necessary. I had nothing of value in my room.

However, I kept on at my lathe, turning out "pins" which were to be used in the assembly of machine guns. It was a delicate job, and I had to have the arms of the "pin" polished down to a hairline measurement of .873. I was allowed to vary the measurement only by .004 (4/1000th of an inch).

But Roberts' reception had upset me. The lathe jammed. I spoiled one of the "pins" and dulled the edge of the fine tool which cut the whirling steel "pin." Roberts rushed over and took the opportunity to bawl me out severely. It was without provocation. Even the most expert lathe operators are known to jam the machine and manufacturers allow for a certain number of "spoils." I didn't reply to Roberts' fury, but sharpening the tool, went silently back to my machine. I still had work to do here. Just before closing time I went over to Roberts, as Garland had suggested.

"Mr. Roberts," I said, "may I use your typewriter to type an important letter which Mr. Alderman wants me to do for him?"

"Can you use a typewriter?" he demanded gruffly.

"Yes, sir," I said.

He looked at me sullenly and cleared his desk.

I wanted to type the letter which Doman had suggested we write Smith. Alderman had dictated it during lunch hour and

I improved only the English. Garland stood over me as I typed from the hand-written copy. Then borrowing Roberts' fountain pen, he signed the letter.

I am writing you at the suggestion of your office manager, Mr. Dohmer [Doman], whom I visited last Friday, and asked to have an appointment made.

You may recall my name from our previous meetings, the last immediately following your address of April 24. You may also recall my name in connection with my chairmanship of the Pontiac Chapter of the America First Committee. More recently I have been smeared in the papers due to my former association with the National Workers League. I worked closely with Mr. Robert Vietig, chairman of the Detroit chapter of the A.F.C., and refer you to him for further information about me and my work.

In speaking to Mr. Dohmer [Doman] last Friday I mentioned my background and suggested that I had several thousand live names of America First Committee members in Pontiac, Royal Oak, Birmingham, and outlying districts. These names may well serve you in your campaign for the Senatorship. Mr. Dohmer [Doman] seemed immensely pleased with this idea, and urged that I be sure to write you, addressing you personally, and said he would arrange a brief meeting after your meeting on Tuesday, the 12th.

Tuesday night I should like also to have you meet a trusted associate of mine who is employed in the same machine shop with me at St. Claire Shores. I have worked with him, and can vouch for him fully.

We shall be glad to volunteer our spare time in whatever capacity you deem us best qualified. Wishing you the success which you so well deserve in your Senatorial campaign, I remain.

Respectfully yours,

(signed)   Garland L. Alderman

P.S. I am having this letter delivered personally at your office.

"I'll have to rush like hell to get to Smith's office before five," I said.

Garland drove me to my room. On the way over he asked to read the letter again. I gave it to him grudgingly, fearing he would change his mind about sending it to Smith.

"Gee, that reads nice," he said. "Be careful with it, George."

"You bet I will," I answered.

I rushed to Detroit, had two photostatic negatives made of the letter—as well as of the mailing lists Garland had refused to give the Dies Committee—and sent them home separately by registered mail. By the time I finished, Smith's offices had closed and I addressed Garland's letter to Smith's post office box. With the documentary evidence safely on its way home, a sigh of relief swept through me and I treated myself to a hearty meal at one of Detroit's expensive restaurants.

That night I saw Parker Sage again. He didn't know it was to be our last encounter. I outlined an elaborate plan of re-organization of the League, which made his dull and listless eyes shine with anticipation. I outlined three branches of the League in Detroit—each in a vital industrial sector and told him I had induced Garland to start a chapter in Pontiac (I had done nothing of the kind).

"That's swell, George. I've been after Garland to do that for a year!"

"Now this week, Parker, I'm starting to visit new men. I've got the lay of the land now. I know my way around town. I'm ready to go to work for you, and give all I got for the Cause. I'll speak at the next meeting of the League, and we'll soon be hitting on all cylinders again."

"That's swell, Georgie, that's swell." That's all Parker could say. That's all I wanted him to say.

"Now I'll tell you what I've been doing all week," he said. "I've been selling the *Protocols* at my shop. Roberts gave me a batch and I've already sold a mess of them."

"How much are you selling them for?" I asked.

"Sixty-nine cents. That leaves a profit of fifty cents which goes into the defense fund. I want to sell a hundred copies this summer. It's one hell of an easy way to make money if you know how to go about it."

Sage was delighted with the turn of events. I had made a good impression on Tony Bommarito and I had, so he thought, finally begun to work as organizer. He would arrange a lot of speaking engagements for me from now on. Even though he was under indictment, he would arrange it for me to speak for the Seven-Mile Fenelon Improvement Association—the group charged with creating the rioting in the Sojourner Truth Defense Housing Project.

"Wonderful," I said. "That's wonderful. You have no idea how happy I am. Now let's go to work on the *Newsletter*." Sage was in high spirits and he wrote:

Folks, keep in mind every day that a great nationalist, Gerald L. K. Smith, will be candidate this fall from Michigan for the U. S. Senate. Talk a bit every day about him to some new face. This sterling American may be behind the bars when voting time comes around, and if such should be the case, let us fight all the harder. . . .

"Good night, George," Sage shook my hand.

"Good-bye, Parker," I said, looking straight at him.

Tuesday, May 12, *Mr*. Roberts was again in a surly mood. By this time I was certain it was an indication of an innate cruelty in the man. If he suspected me, Parker would have reflected it last night. But Parker had seemed completely cordial; I reasoned that Roberts had not quite figured me out, so he was set on showing me that he was boss.

On Wednesday Roberts humiliated Garland shamefully, then came over to do his bit on me. In order to prevent an explosion, I suddenly remembered Garland's advice: "Whenever he gets sore at me I talk against the Jew and he softens up." I crowded more rapid-fire anti-Semitism in the next two minutes than Joe McWilliams had ever done in a two-hour speech. It pacified *Mr*. Roberts and he went away without bothering me.

He was never too busy to indulge in vituperative anti-Semitism. He seemed to revel in his hatred of the Jew and time and again I had seen his surliness disappear at the end of an anti-Semitic tirade. He had been surly Friday morning but when the *Protocols* arrived that afternoon he began to beam. His abnormal capacity for hatred seemed pacified with anti-Semitic jibes, he seemed to experience some kind of perverted emotional orgasm through the medium of hate.

I have said before that Roberts had impressed me as essentially a violent man. He was also the type that had to have a scapegoat for his failings. He had to have somebody to bully continually. A world without hating someone was a world intolerable to Roberts. He had to humiliate and bully and feel superior in order to live. Then, too, he lived in constant fear of the unknown and carefully scrutinized every passing automobile. His yellow canvas-lined mackinaw jacket always hung conveniently on a chair or near his desk, and he took it with him wherever he went. He felt safe only when the loaded Colt-45 was within reach and his vicious Doberman hounds within call.

My sojourn at his shop had proved to be a valuable laboratory for me! I had not only investigated the fascist scene in Detroit, but I had also studied the very epitome of native American fascist-mindedness. Roberts had the most perfectly developed fascist mind it was my ill-good fortune to study at such close range.

How to pacify Roberts for a few more days without bursting into a rage at his bullying, became a vexing problem. As I was determined to make a graceful exit, I tactfully showed to my fellow workers the letter I received from home, hoping the news would eventually get to Roberts. "Jeanette's" letter read:

Please excuse me for not writing sooner, but we have had such a terrible time with Ma all week. She never seemed to pick up after that last attack, just lay there getting weaker and weaker. It was just awful to see her and she couldn't be left alone for a minute, of course.

And then her mind began to wander. Yesterday afternoon she went into a coma. Dr. Gardini has been wonderful, he did everything he could, but now he says he can't do anything more. He says she may come out of this now but it is no use trying to deceive ourselves and that the end can't be far off. . . .

I miss you so much, George. Bud and Alice have been wonderful, but after all they are just kids, and Pop—well you know how Pop is—

Love and kisses from your
Sis

When Garland and I drove to my room Tuesday afternoon in order to dress for Smith's meeting, I gave him two neatly typed copies of the A.F.C. names and he was immensely pleased. We had dressed and were getting into his car when I suggested taking Garland's picture, (I had already photo-

graphed Roberts' shop and home). I was undecided about
Garland's pose, when he called out:

"Take my picture giving the Hitler salute!"

Alderman was serious, and I was naturally delighted at his
suggestion. I asked him to stand next to his car so as to include the license plate, and snapped two pictures of him in
the act of giving the Nazi salute.

We got into the car and drove off. In the rear were quantities of the *Protocols*, leaflets entitled *Awake, America, Awake*,
stacks of Hudson's bulletins, copies of *The X-Ray* and *Publicity*, as well as reprints of Roy Woodruff's insertion in the
Congressional Record of Gerald L. K. Smith's leading editorial in *The Cross and the Flag*, Hoffman's "Judas" speech
and a pile of the *Nationalist Newsletter*. Garland had taken
over Lyman's job of "publicity director."

Armed to the teeth with "patriotic" literature, we drove to
Smith's meeting. I asked Garland to tell me more about the
America First Committee. He told me such an astounding
story of collaboration between the Committee and Nazi interests that I would never have believed it if I had not seen its
duplication in the East.

"We had Bundists and Silver Shirters in the Pontiac Chapter," he began. "We didn't care who got in as long as they
spoke America First. Ward spoke [Louis B. Ward, one of
Father Coughlin's associates] four times for us and we paid
him for it. Sage used to come and put a dollar in the plate. I
used the meetings to make anti-Semitic speeches," Garland
said.

"Why did you have to make them at an America First
meeting?" I asked.

"I wanted to keep America out of war," he answered, "and
I thought I could do it better by spreading anti-Semitism."

If Alderman were more articulate he would have said that
he furthered isolationist views by rallying the mob around a
central hate theme: the Jews! Those were his instructions.

"That guy Lyman got me sore," he said. "He went around
to my America First contacts, collected their money and gave
them League literature. I suppose it came to the same thing
in the end, but just the same, he had no business going around
collecting from my own people. Did he, George?"

"Of course he didn't," I answered. "But how did he get to know your contacts?" I asked.

"I gave him my A.F.C. list," Garland said, with complete naïveté.

Garland told me more about his activities as America First chairman. Last summer he had spoken at the picnic of a "German social group." I asked him what he had talked about.

"I just built up Germany and knocked down the Jews." Garland's formula was as simple as that. "Hell, I don't want to talk about the past," Garland said after my insistent questioning. "Let's talk about tonight."

He had sold six copies of the *Protocols* over the week end and had also collected nine signatures on Smith's petition for nomination as Senator. He showed me the petition and laughing at his cleverness, remarked:

"Every time I sold a copy of the *Protocols* I also got a signature for Smith's petition."

"To whom did you sell the *Protocols?*" I asked.

"Oh, the America First contacts I still have. They're always good for some money when it comes to a patriotic cause."

Garland parked the car, and we walked to the Maccabee Auditorium. In his pocket was the petition and the America First list I had typed. We weaved through the crowd, Alderman greeting those he knew. Doman called us over and shook our hands cordially. I asked if Smith had received Garland's letter:

"Mr. Smith read it," he said in a guarded voice. "Everything is okay. He'll see you after the meeting."

Garland and I sat down next to German-Americans he knew from Pontiac. Their name was Geliske. They had signed Smith's petition and had bought copies of the *Protocols*. "They gave me $2.50," Garland whispered. "They're good people."

Smith's meetings no longer held a novelty for me. Smith displayed his wife and son and exploited his family ties, then, in a saccharine voice, told how he had gone to his aged Christian mother for advice, more alleged advice. He had asked if he should run for political office in order to save "this glorious Republic from ruin." And his bent old mother, looking her stalwart son wistfully in the eyes, had said: "Yes, son. The Lord knows best. Go and follow Him." [1]

Sweating and panting, Smith closed in a burst of wild cheering, as he reiterated his intention to run for the Senate, and screamed: "I will defend Father Coughlin all this summer."

As the crowd began to thin out, Garland and I walked down the main aisle to Smith. I watched every move closely. From his inner pocket Garland took out the petition and the America First lists. With these in hand, he approached the smiling and expectant Smith and introduced me as his friend. Smith greeted us cordially, took both the petition and the list and placed them in his coat pocket. Garland stated that he would very much like to work for him in his campaign, but he did not want to be conspicuous because of his background in the N.W.L. Smith smiled knowingly and said: "We can take that up later."

As we finished, Garland went back to talk to Doman while I went backstage to talk to Smith. My object was to get the petition back. I had tried all day to borrow it long enough from Garland to have it photostated. Backstage in the presence of a burly bodyguard, Smith talked pleasantly, but was too smart to part with the petition. Frustrated, I went back to Garland and I found him still talking to Doman. He gave us Smith's confidential telephone number—Raymond 9547. Do-

---

[1] The Lord apparently did not side with Smith, for Smith lost the primary election. Running as an independent Republican he also lost in the general election.

★ America First Committee ★

PONTIAC CHAPTER,	553 S. JESSIE STREET,	PONTIAC, MICHIGAN
NATIONAL HEADQUARTERS Chicago, Illinois		GENERAL ROBERT E. WOOD Acting Chairman
GARLAND L. ALDERMAN Pontiac Chapter Chairman		

Mrs. John Dawson – 166 N. Perry, Pontiac
Mr. Evans – 167 Stanley, Pontiac

Two of more than 2500 names and addresses of assorted America First-ers and Coughlinites which Gerald L.K. Smith accepted from Garland Alderman.

man then asked Garland and me to visit him at the office and talk "for a couple of hours."

"What did you think of the meeting?" I asked Garland after we had left.

"That crowd is with us. And whether they want to admit it or not, they're nationalist," Garland said. He was driving and I was taking verbatim notes with my pencil stub against several sheets of folded note paper. "Nationalism is the same thing as fascism," Garland continued. "That crowd don't want Hitler or Mussolini, but they want the same thing here —an American type of the same thing."

"What do you think of Smith personally?" I asked.

"I think he is doing the same thing Hitler did. He is trying to join all the nationalist groups together. The only groups he does not mention or want are those groups that'll smear him—like the N.W.L." Garland turned to me. "But he'll meet us on the outside," he said winking.

I had seen an illustration of this and needed no further proof of Smith's actual, not *professed*, leanings.

"Smith has the right idea. He wants to win the war for America. He wants to keep our boys right here defending America. Smith is smart. He doesn't stick his neck out like we did. You must think me terrible," Garland said suddenly. "I haven't invited you to dinner or anything. But honest, George, it isn't my fault. It's my wife. I told her about you and she thinks you're a Nazi. Just like me. She doesn't want to meet any new Nazis, she says."

"I guess your wife doesn't know me at all," I said, feeling sure the meaning would escape Garland.

"I was thinking of having some Bund guys and Silver Shirters and you up this week end, but I guess I'll have to let it go for a while."

I reported for work as usual the next day, which was un- eventful except for the doubled viciousness of Roberts. But I did not let him "get" me, however. I had laid my plans and wanted to follow them through. . . . Late that afternoon Roberts set me to work on an extremely difficult job. He showed me a sample of it.

"Randall did it last night," he said. He did not explain that

William Randall, the policeman who worked on the night shift, was also a trained lathe worker.

My new task consisted of shaving down a cylindrical block of steel to a specified dimension. That step was comparatively easy and I experienced no difficulty. But after this I was required to bore an extremely fine cone-shaped nipple at one end of the block while it whirred at top speed on the lathe. An expert could do it, but measuring down the nipple to hair-splitting measurements was beyond my limited experience. I had no confidence in myself and frankly asked Roberts if there was not something easier I could do.

"You'd better do what you're told and stop asking questions. I don't want anybody telling me how to run my business."

I tried desperately hard to round out the conical nipple to precise measurements. I failed. The lathe jammed with a roar. I shut the motor off instantly. Roberts came running over, and began to scold me severely before the other workers. I was getting fed up.

"Don't talk to me that way," I said. I did not want to say more because I did not want to spoil my extremely well laid plans for a getaway by losing my temper.

"Why shouldn't I?" Roberts bellowed: "You have been here three weeks and still haven't learned how to use the lathe." With this he turned and walked away.

I tried again. I performed the first step easily enough. Then I checked the tool and sharpened it in order to make sure it would cut smoothly. I formed the nipple successfully and was nearly finished with the final step—the nerve-wracking coning process from the base out—when the lathe suddenly came to a groaning stop. The tool broke. The machine jammed. I turned off the motor and slumped over—completely tired and dejected with it all. . . .

As I heard Roberts running toward me I grabbed a wrench and waited for him ready to smash his face and take the consequences. He came to an abrupt stop a scant six inches from my face. I grinned sardonically as he glared at me, bewildered at having his bluff called.

He backed away slowly, and I went back to the lathe. I disengaged the broken cylinder, laid aside the broken tool, started the motor to see if it still worked and busied myself with sweeping. It was almost time to quit work and Roberts stayed away from me until I left.

Garland had left his clothes in my room and we drove back to pick them up.

As I entered my room the housekeeper handed me a telegram. I knew what it said because I had sent instructions and specified the exact hour it was to be despatched from New York.

"It may be bad news," Garland said.

"I don't think so," I replied bravely. "If it was they would have 'phoned. Here read it yourself." I tossed him the telegram.

I watched Garland's face. "It's bad news," he said, sadly.

"Let me read it. What does it say?" I grabbed it from his hand. I must have given a convincing performance.

"I guess that means you'll be going home, George," Garland said softly, feeling genuinely sorry for me.

"I guess it does," I answered. "Tell Roberts and Sage, will you, Garland?"

Early the next morning, I left St. Clair Shores—unusually cheerful for a person who had received a telegram reading: "MOTHER WORSE LAST RITES ADMINISTERED COME HOME AT ONCE."

Thanks to my "sister Jeanette," the timing was perfect.

My trip had far outstretched its original purpose and for the first time I could present to authorities a true, all-around picture of the way the gears meshed in Detroit's native fascist machinery.

I succeeded in showing the common denominator between the respectable groups pleading appeasement and defeatism, and the outright Nazi frontists striving to achieve those same goals under identical slogans of "patriotism" and "Americanism." I succeeded in showing the common meeting ground between the America First Committee, the National Workers League, Smith's coterie of followers and the leaders of the Mothers groups I interviewed. From the evidence I had seen it was my conviction that the ringleader of the N.W.L. was Russell M. Roberts.

While shouting "win the war" our enemies within strove by subtle means, when other methods failed, to slow down the march of a mighty nation at war. Through the medium of whispering campaigns, through the dissemination of tracts avowedly seditious, through mass rallies and lone-wolf tactics, their purpose—whether they realized it or not—pointed to the way of greatest aid to Nazi Germany. Whether Mrs. Farber or Vietig admitted it to themselves or not, their course was the course which Hitler would most readily approve and gladly recompense. Multiplied a hundred thousand fold, their tactics could help Hitler win his greatest victory!

In his long-range planning for world-domination, naturally Hitler did not overlook this nation's key industrial city. Evidence that Nazidom's brains and millions had been poured into Detroit to cripple America at her most vulnerable point—Labor—was all too apparent. Production at the assembly lines, and outbound trains filled with armaments, readily showed that we were doing a grand job, but it was conceivable that Goebbels might succeed in Detroit and other cities like it. That's what frightened me. The Silver Shirters, Bundists, Klansmen, America First-ers, Coughlinites, Sages and Robertses had set into motion forces which could only hope to increase America's tensions and anxieties about winning the war. Working underground I knew what harm these vicious forces could in time do to our defense machinery through slow-downs, absenteeism, strikes and other sabotage. I could not stifle the feeling that Detroit was dynamite.

CHAPTER VI

FAKE YANKEES

"The only thing we can hope for from now on is for America to lose this war—to be smashed completely. That's the only way to get rid of Democracy. Yes sir, the only way to save America is for Hitler and Japan to smash us."

EDWARD HOLTON JAMES

I ARRIVED HOME exhausted and I had to rest completely for several days before resuming work. I put my notes into final shape, presented them personally over a period of days to the proper authorities and began to catch up with local investigations which had been interrupted. And peculiarly enough, my first two investigations showed that, like cancer, the Nazi plague knew neither race nor creed, poverty nor wealth. Take the case of Edward Holton James.

James came from a distinguished and wealthy New England family. His uncles were the eminent psychologist Professor William James and the famous author, Henry James. Edward Holton James lived in historic old Concord. He was an elderly man with a small round head, a fuzzy growth of white hair and something of the "aristocrat" about him. He was in fact a man of good breeding and correct manners.

As confirmed a fascist as Lawrence Dennis, James was a classic example of how Nazism can pervert and reduce to a Nazi dupe the most unlikely victim. James broke into the headlines in April, 1942, when he was charged by the Boston District Attorney's office for criminally libeling the President in a leaflet he circulated, demanding:

1. The immediate resignation of Mr. Roosevelt.
2. Immediate peace with Germany, Italy and Japan.
3. Immediate annulment of all Lend-Lease Laws.

James branded the policy of Franklin D. Roosevelt as "subversive of Yankee tradition." Even more: "He plotted wars against nations which had done us no harm. We brand and denounce him, and all his chore-men and yes-men and syco-phants, as wasters of the people's money, as wreckers of the Republic, as the bloodstained assassins of our soldiers and sailors."

Voiced less than four months after Pearl Harbor I consid-ered this the act of a traitor. Attorney General Robert T. Bushnell of Boston questioned James' sanity. (Joe McWil-liams and Adolf Hitler had also been called insane.) Two psychiatrists, one of the Jewish faith, the other Gentile, ex-amined James—and both pronounced him sane. James was let loose while still under the original indictment of criminal libel.

James' case intrigued me. Eager to establish his status in the American fascist movement, I wrote him while he was in jail, inclosing a copy of my *Christian Defender* and asking about his group, the Yankee Freemen. I received a reply as soon as he was freed on bail:

If you are thinking of joining our movement, please get in touch with Norman H. Wilson, 32 Rockland Avenue, Yonkers, New York. One must belong to a movement, otherwise one does not count for much. . . . I sincerely hope you will join.

I got in touch with Wilson, with whom I had already cor-responded. He relayed my qualifications as a "patriot" to James and James sent me my membership button—a large, blue Maltese cross. In my mail a few months later I was startled to receive a post card:

Will be at the Hotel Lexington, Lexington Avenue, Saturday and Sunday. If you are in New York, please give me a ring.—E. H. James.

Edward Holton James awaited me in Room number 2028. I found a man with a healthy, tan complexion, deep blue eyes, dressed in a white shirt, checkered trousers and sport coat. He sized me up quickly, and grabbing my hand, said: "You are a fine Italian type. I can tell by looking at your face."

But James seemed unwilling to talk about the things I

wanted him to talk about. We parried, and I missed every time, as James glossed over my key questions, and kept saying we ought to go downstairs for beer. High above New York's noisy streets, the room was quiet—a good place for an interview—and I tried to dissuade him from going to the bar. Finally, James said authoritatively that he wanted to have a glass of beer.

Once seated at a quiet corner table of the hotel bar, he opened up.

"I'm against the Government," he said earnestly. "I'm for totalitarianism. I stand for a totalitarian form of government." James went on, as if talking about the weather: "I don't like to call it nationalism because they call it that in Italy and in Germany. I call it Yankee-ism."

He spoke in a soft voice, bent over his glass of beer. I asked what he thought of Democracy.

"I have no use whatever for this thing called Democracy," James started. "I want to see a Yankee aristocrat rule this country. Democracy is finished. It gives the drunk and the heroic person the same rights and privileges. It places them on the same footing. Hitler is the prophet of the ages!" he called out. "Hitler is fighting for an ideal. The principle of leadership is there. The people are behind him. The Japs also are fighting for an ideal—but we in America have no principles to fight for."

I asked James if I should join the army when drafted or worm my way out. "You can't do anything alone," he advised. "Join the army. Become part of a national movement. Whoever rules the streets rules the country!"

"Our purpose, then," I asked in order to get him straight, "is to join a mass movement so that when conditions get bad here we can jump right in?"

"That's right," he agreed, shaking his fist. "Get right in and fight. We should have storm troopers just like Hitler did. They must be brutal. If they aren't, there is no use of having any. They've got to be brutal to crush all opposition! We've got to defy the Government, not by publishing leaflets, but by holding secret meetings of four and five persons all over the country."

James told me he was leaving for Indianapolis that night to study the Pelley trial, with a view to helping in the defense of other "patriots."

"George," he said suddenly, "you and I are revolutionists." Then he added: "All we can do now is to help those who are in trouble."

I looked around stealthily. "Yes," I said, waiting for more.

"The only thing we can hope for from now on is for America to lose this war—to be smashed completely! That's the only way to get rid of Democracy. Yes sir, the only way to save America is for Hitler and Japan to smash us." He said it coolly, as if ordering the waiter.

Peculiarly enough, James was not anti-Semitic. He could not be he explained, because it violated the dream of the founders of the Republic. Furthermore, it would not work in America. "You buck your head against a stonewall when you turn against the Jew," he said. James substituted the corollary common to the totalitarian mind: anti-Catholicism. James was violently hostile to institutional Catholicism, and particularly bitter against Boston's Catholic population.

He condemned Jew-baiters and gave me a laudable lecture on the benefits we had derived from the diversity of our immigrant stocks, emphasizing that exclusion based on racialism was un-American. He conceded that Jews as well as Negroes could be good Americans as long as they remained *Yankee* in spirit. His viewpoint made sense with respect to a Democracy —which James wanted to *destroy*. His perversion, politically, lay in the belief that it could work under an American Hitler.

Strongly influenced by *Mein Kampf*, James' passion was to see Americans live the heroic life and die the heroic way. He wanted "heroic Yankees" to rule, and through "heroic self-sacrifice" die for their country. I was curious to know if he had met Lawrence Dennis, for James' ideas were strikingly similar.

"I used to have lunch with him every time I came to New York," he said. It helped explain who had been his mentor.

We finished our beer, and James accompanied me to the door. The large Maltese cross stood out prominently on the lapel of his coat. "Wear the membership button I sent you," he urged. "It is our symbol. We've got to have a symbol, just like Hitler did." He shook my hand warmly. "I want to see you again, George, so we can go deeper into this thing."

This was the man who Attorney General Robert L. Bushnell had tried on grounds of insanity. Possibly it is *we* who are insane to allow such a man to be free. It is *we* who are insane for not recognizing the fascist mind, for not understanding its fanatic vigor and its revolutionary ardor. To me, James was a shrewd, intellectually inclined fascist, all the more dangerous because he did not mouth the usual trite phrases of anti-Semitism, which most of us have come to accept as shibboleths of Nazi doctrine.

Robert Jordan, my Negro "Aryan friend" was in trouble. His pro-Japanese tirades had got him into hot water and he delegated me to find him a "good white" lawyer. This was my motive in visiting John Wise, a New York attorney who had defended Robert Edward Edmondson. I traced him to his apartment on West 16th Street, and after I had introduced myself as a friend of Colonel Sanctuary and Edmondson, he received me warmly. Wise wasn't interested in defending any Harlem "Aryans." He was occupied with the defense of White, equally staunch "patriots."

As I was leaving, he tossed over a copy of Pelley's most recent booklet. "Spiridovich sent it to me. He is working with Pelley." I was surprised to learn this, as I thought he still lived at his ramshackle home on 9 Sheriff Street.

"Where's his wife?" I asked.

"She's still on Sheriff Street. Spiridovich hasn't seen her in months and she's pretty sore about it."

I had seen Lieutenant-General Count V. Cherep-Spiridovich's name frequently at Stahrenberg's. The "Count" deemed himself quite an authority on anthropology, announcing that "the Asiatic-Jew Bolshevists" had crossed "orangoutangs with white Russian women in an effort to produce a hybrid-elemental servant lower than their masters."

In 1939 when I first visited him, I found this eminent scientist living in the squalor of a grimy tenement in the heart of New York's slum district—an emaciated, coarse-featured man, toward whom I experienced an instant dislike. The "Count" had worked closely with Edmondson and Pelley; he knew

Henry Curtiss and Colonel Sanctuary. He boasted of having
helped Mussolini in his march on Rome.

But I knew better. To begin with, Spiridovich was not his
legal name and he was neither a lieutenant-general nor a
count. He got the titles from a White Russian officer who
allegedly had adopted him as a foster son. The original Major-
General Spiridovich had been a veritable Svengali in his world
intrigues against Jewry, his most infamous book being *The
Secret World Government*. His "adopted son" was an im-
personator—an ex-patent lawyer from Indiana, named Howard
Victor Broenstrupp, alias the Duke of St. Saba, alias Colonel
Bennett, alias J. G. Francis.

At one time Broenstrupp collected $87.50 monthly from
the United States Government for his W.P.A. job as research
worker on the Aeronautics Index project. When his work
was over, he hurried home to his multigraph machine to turn
out Nazi-line leaflets. One of them titled, *Intelligence*, included an attack on the President and called the W.P.A. a
"Mongol-Jewish Project."

Declaring himself "a soldier fighting under Major-General
George Van Horn Moseley," promoting subscription sales
for Hudson's *America in Danger* and distributing bulk copies
of the infamous cartoon *Your Crucifixion*, Broenstrupp also
flooded the mails with enormous quantities of his own literature. One of them claimed a circulation of 800,000 copies
while another, devoted to the "Revolution in America," issued this direct call:

Every pure Aryan American to his post, to save the Country
from apathy, hesitation, jealousy, all the elements of utter unfit-
ness to win, and bring to fulfillment the ancient prophecy that
"from the North will come a man to save our Country and Civilization."

And now in the summer of 1942 I knocked again on
Apartment 24, on the fifth floor of the drab, walk-up tenement near the heart of the New York slum section. The door
was flung open in my face. I confronted a large, fleshy woman, her hair, in disarray, hanging in little wet ringlets about an
ample neckline. She wore a bathrobe. Water trickled down

her ankles into her slippers. She had evidently just come out of the bathtub.

"I remember you," Mrs. Broenstrupp said gruffly, as she opened the door. She did not invite me in, but I walked in— keeping up a chatty monologue. I had hardly seated myself, facing the wild-eyed woman, when she burst out in a torrent of words: "I'm finished with him. I'm finished with all of you. I'm going to turn him in. He's nothing but a racketeer, a cheap racketeer. All you men are racketeers. I'm finished with you all."

She made a move toward the door, a hint for me to leave her premises. I began to calm her down. It was obvious that she had quarrelled with the "Count," and I had a hunch that she might furnish valuable information on his contacts. If I could only placate her to get her full story. . . . Rapidly I began telling her that I, too, was finished with all the racketeers, that I had not been impressed by her husband at all— which was the truth.

"That's the reason I haven't been around in three years," I said.

This seemed reasonable, but she grumbled on for a while longer, after which she settled back and told me the story of her life with the bogus "Count." He had left her last September and she had not seen him since, even though he had come to New York four times. He had not sent her money, and had not cared whether she lived or died, whether she was ill or starving.

Her complaints poured out of her in a torrent. As she spoke, the mop of stringy wet hair shook in all directions, at times hiding her eyes and sticking to the sides of her jaw. "My husband neglected me completely. I got along as best I could. I sold the typewriter. I sold the multigraphing machine. I sold some of his books. I had to live. I had to eat. For almost ten months he hasn't given me a cent."

I began to pity this woman, for she seemed sincere and was not putting on an act. Where had the "Count" been all these months I asked.

"He's been with Pelley in Indianapolis," she replied in passionate anger. "He and Pelley are both in New York now. He was within six blocks of this house Thursday night and he didn't even come to ask if I had enough to eat. God knows how I've been getting along since September."

Her face broke into a sneer as she went on: "Don't worry. I'll make him wish he had never treated me this way. I'll make it so hot for him that he'll never be in a position to treat anybody the way he treated me."

When I asked her how she knew of Pelley and Broenstrupp being in New York, she said the two had spent the evening at the home of a friend and this woman, also abused by her "patriotic" husband, was likewise ready to turn in her spouse to the authorities.

"My husband and Pelley have been living royally, going around in a car driven by a chauffeur."

In a voice that seemed to explode at me, she said that he dressed expensively and carried on with women, while he let her rot in a cockroach-infested tenement. I sat back, carefully taking mental notes and letting her talk. She recounted how Pelley had used her home as a hide-out. "He's slept on this davenport many times," she burst out.

I asked Mrs. Broenstrupp how Pelley got his money.

"From rich women," she answered. "He and my husband and others in the gang went around to rich old women, played up to them and got their money. That woman who is supposed to be Pelley's secretary. . . . She's with him all the time."

As her attack on Pelley grew, her wrath against Broenstrupp subsided for the moment. "He's gone in for a cheap brand of mysticism that fools some people. But it can't fool me. I know Pelley. I know what he is. I know his racket."

She came back to her husband. "He is the most self-centered man in the world and does not care anything about anybody else." I asked if he had ever been brutal to her, since Broenstrupp had impressed me as cruel.

"Of course he was brutal to me," she answered bitterly. "He slapped me once with his ringed finger and I was knocked out for an hour. When I came to, there was a two-inch gash on my face. I've done more for my husband than any wife could. I went around begging for money so that he could carry on his work. I believed in him and believed in his work at the time. I tortured myself for him. I even invested my own money in his work."

"If he was so mean," I asked, "why did you do all this for him?"

She shrugged her shoulders. "Why does a wife do things for her husband? I loved him at first. As the years wore on and we became more and more separated in body and spirit, I still stuck to him, hoping he was going through a period in his life and would reform. But he didn't. He became worse with the years."

I asked Mrs. Broenstrupp bluntly if their love life had been satisfactory in view of their differences otherwise.

"How could it be satisfactory?" she replied frankly. "He showed me neither kindness nor consideration. He treated me cruelly and selfishly. How can a wife love such a husband?" She looked at the collie sprawled at her feet. "That dog has shown more affection than my husband." Pausing she burst out: "He played me dirty, and he's going to pay for it."

I could not tell her I was an investigator, but upon leaving, I said: "Please let me know if I can help you in any way. You have my address. Write me if you need me."

"God bless you," she said. "It has already done me a lot of good talking to you."

I ran to a telephone booth and informed the proper authorities that Pelley was in town, and that Mrs. Broenstrupp was in a mood to "talk."

I hadn't seen Ernest Elmhurst (he changed his name from Hermann Fleischkopf) since the night he spoke at the Christian Mobilizers meeting and sold copies of his book, *The World Hoax*. I was eager to see him in order to gauge his "patriotism" at a time when the Allies were threatened by Japan's early attempts to invade Australia.

Elmhurst was held in high esteem by the Nazi hierarchy of America. He had spoken at countless Nazi meetings the country over since 1934, and he was a close friend of Stahrenberg, Deatherage, Hudson. In August 1937, Elmhurst was sent as delegate to the International Congress of *World Service* and showered with honors. Elmhurst was a prime factor in the psychological agitation against America's war effort.

The man was fantastic. All his teeth were capped in shining bright gold so that when he talked near a light or in bright

THE WORLD HOAX

A Protocol of 1935

based on a careful study of the Present Day Jewish Activities

By
ERNEST F. ELMHURST

With an Introduction by
WILLIAM DUDLEY PELLEY

❧

DONE INTO A BOOK FOR AMERICA'S GENTILE
PATRIOTS BY THE PELLEY PUBLISHERS WHOSE
ADDRESS IN THE YEAR ONE THOUSAND NINE
HUNDRED AND THIRTY-EIGHT IS POSTOFFICE
BOX SEVENTEEN HUNDRED AND SEVENTY-SIX IN
THE CITY OF ASHEVILLE IN THE STATE OF
NORTH CAROLINA · UNITED STATES OF AMERICA

Published by THE PAN ARYAN ALLIANCE

Two of "patriotic" Elmhurst's "patriotic" books. *The World Hoax* circulated widely among Pelley, Coughlinite and Park Avenue circles.

---

sunshine, his mouth seemed to glow with a lurid radiance. Barrel-chested, with squarish features, Elmhurst had a set, stubborn expression. I met Elmhurst at his home on Staten Island where he shared a cozy apartment with one Thomas Quinlan who knew Broenstrupp intimately. Quinlan told me he was a member of the Christian Front, had been active with the American Nationalist Party and attended Bund meetings. Elmhurst was engaged in writing a book that would "expose the Jew for all time."

"Will Theresa Holm help you edit it, as she did *The World Hoax?*" I asked.

"I don't know," Elmhurst replied. "I haven't made up my mind."

On the wall of Elmhurst's apartment was a calendar, the top showing an American Indian facing a Minute Man. Beneath them was a pair of bold swastikas. On the opposite wall was a coat of arms, decorated with a swastika in Nazi colors. Copies of Mrs. Dilling's and Sanctuary's books were on his shelves, in addition to a large assortment of Nazi books in

German and English. A stack of Sullivan's book, *The Road to Victory* and Dilling's and Hudson's current bulletins lay on his desk, with copies of the "patriotic" *Protocols* and Henry Ford's *The International Jew*.

I noted that his desk was unusually clean.

"An F.B.I. agent was here last week, and he may come again unexpectedly," Elmhurst explained. "I don't want them to go through my papers."

I was sure that the swastikas would not be on the wall then.

"What have you boys been doing lately?" I asked.

"We just returned from a trip we took together seeing patriotic friends," Quinlan volunteered.

Touring in Quinlan's car, they had visited Deatherage, Hudson, Charles W. Phillips, Elmer Garner, editor of *Publicity*, and Reverend Winrod's offices. In Indiana they had visited Pelley, and in Chicago paid their respects to Newton Jenkins, the Bund headquarters, and the "Julius Streicher" of Chicago.

"What was his name?" I asked.

Quinlan did not remember and Elmhurst would not tell. "We just went around to see what the boys were planning to do," he said.

"What is your line of work, Quinlan?" I asked.

"I'm a plumber, but I ain't working at it now," he answered. "Ernest and I are digging clams."

"You'd be making good money if you were working as a plumber," I said.

"That's right, but they'd put me to work on a defense project, and I'd be fighting against those who believe like I do. I wouldn't fight against the nationalist countries of Europe," Quinlan answered.

"Why aren't *you* in the army, George?" Elmhurst asked suddenly.

My draft board, of course, had determined my status. But in my investigations I had found it expedient to acquire a series of maladies. "I have a bad case of hernia," I answered, "and a very bad sinus, but they'll be calling me and I guess I'll have to go."

"Don't you do it," Elmhurst urged.

"How can I get away with it?" I asked, curious to know his reply.

"Tell them that the Dies Committee has influenced you and persuaded you against Soviet Russia and you cannot, therefore, fight on her side. Or else, you can tell them you read the Jewish *Bible* and learned to love your enemies. You love the Italians, Japanese and the Germans. Tell them that. They'll think you're a religious fanatic and leave you alone." Elmhurst was deadly in earnest.

Another bit of choice advice from Elmhurst was that I impersonate a soldier or officer. When caught I was expected to say: "I just wanted to know how it feels to wear a uniform."

"They'll put you away and you won't be drafted," Elmhurst explained.

Quinlan joined in with other schemes. "Don't let them take you into the army," he said. "Find some way to get out of it." As to his own plans Quinlan said: "I won't go into the army. I'll find a way to avoid it. Let them look for me."

Elmhurst assured me that he never overlooked an opportunity to "talk to soldiers and sailors." I asked him for more details.

"Since we can't work in the open we've got to work quietly. I just pick conversations with soldiers and sailors and ask them how it feels to be fighting a fake war."

"Aren't you apt to get into trouble that way?" I asked.

"Not if you go about it carefully. If the soldiers don't like it, you just leave them alone, but if they don't say anything you just keep on talking. I'm going to the city and we'll try it on the ferry."

Quinlan brought up the subject of the Catholic Church. "It's taking the side of the Jews and the Administration in fighting this war. Why some of the leaders of the Church are actually criminals. What is Archbishop Spellman but another guy who is looking out for himself?"

Elmhurst moved in. "That name Spellman sounds Jewish to me. He was born and raised in New York's ghetto and has absorbed the Judaic philosophy. Spellman smells kosher to me," he insisted.

"Maybe the Church is against Hitler because of the persecution of Catholics," I observed.

Elmhurst jumped on me. "Nothing of the kind. Germany is not persecuting the Catholics. It is the Jews who are making this propaganda. Jews in Germany became Holy Ghost Catholics, and Hitler told them to shut up but the Jews would not shut up, so Hitler cracked down on these. . . . Jews, not Catholics."

This was the most insanely ingenious explanation I had yet heard of Hitler's universal persecutions of religionists.

"We'd better be going," Elmhurst said. "I've gotta meet Bruno Richter."

Richter was a bartender who worked on Long Island. He and Elmhurst intended to visit a German lady named Munk whose son had been imprisoned for practicing the instructions Elmhurst had given me, and refused to bear arms. En route to the ferry, I asked Elmhurst if he knew General Moseley. "I've never met the General," Elmhurst said, "but he sent me some nice letters which I've locked up."

"Now here is how we work it on the ferry," Elmhurst began. "We go sit next to a couple of sailors and I begin by telling you that the Jews started the war and it is all a plot of the internationalist Jew bankers."

"Then what do I do?"

"You agree with me, and build up on that. Make sure you are talking loud enough for the sailors to hear you. But be careful, George. When they show you they don't like it, just stop talking."

"I get you," I said.

"After we finish with one group, we move to another, and another. Since we can't work in the open as before we'll work quietly," Elmhurst added.

But when we tried to follow out his plan in practice and made several efforts to engage service men in conversation, I felt like a traitor and couldn't go through with it. Elmhurst was furious with me.

"I'm disappointed in you, George," he said in disgust. "How in hell do you expect to win the war for us if you can't do better than that?"

"Give me another chance," I pleaded. "Let us try it again when we get out of the boat."

We tried it again at Battery Park. Elmhurst did not ask for

my co-operation this time. He picked his victim, a clean-cut young chap sitting on the bench, and declared bluntly that the Jews had started this war. The man took it calmly and said it was a matter of opinion. Opinion, hell, Elmhurst countered, the facts proved it. What facts, the man asked. Elmhurst came out with the sweeping generalities which I had heard at countless Bund meetings.

The man was unconvinced. "Those aren't facts," the man said quietly. "You are prejudiced. You are speaking emotionally. I can see you don't like the Jews, but that's no excuse for blaming this war on them. Stick to the facts and be logical about this if you want to get anywhere with me."

"Anyway, America can't win this war with all the Jews here," Elmhurst took off on another tangent.

"I think America will definitely win this war. It'll take us a little while to get started. But once we get going we won't stop till we crush those Nazis!"

This enraged Elmhurst but he controlled himself.

The man said German morale would break down first. Elmhurst said that was impossible. America would crack first. The man said America was as tough as any nation on earth. Elmhurst said it had become soft through movies and women. (Elmhurst did not associate with women.) The man said we were fighting a war to make the world a decent place to live in. Elmhurst said we were fighting for a dying Democracy. The future of Democracy lay in the years ahead of us, the man said, while the future of Nazism was death.

"Democracy is Jewish," Elmhurst raged, his face turning purple. "Democracy is nothing but the political system of the internationalist Jewish bankers. Baruch, Brandeis, Rabbi Wise, Lehman, Frankfurter—all Jews and all of them for Democracy. That proves Democracy is Jewish."

"Then fascism is Catholic," the man said quietly.

"Why do you say that? Look at Hitler. . . ."

"Yes, Hitler is a Roman Catholic. So is Goebbels. Mussolini, Franco and Petain are all Catholic. Does that prove that Nazism and dictatorship are Catholic just because some of the leaders are?"

Elmhurst lost his temper: "Come on, George, let's get the hell away from this guy."

We walked away. I looked back and slyly winked at the man we had left behind. "I guess we didn't pick the right man that time," I said, trying to hold back a smile.

"You're bad luck, George. You're the jinx. That's the first time I've met a son of a bitch like that."

"I guess he's one of Archbishop Spellman's Christians," I said.

"Yes, and he smells kosher to me."

We agreed to meet again. "I want to talk to you about some anti-Jew stickers," Elmhurst said.

When I had left Detroit I was not sure of Roberts' and Sage's reactions to my taking French leave. Immediately upon my arrival in New York I wrote both saying that my "mother" was in a "coma" and that the end might be expected momentarily. A week later I announced that "mother" had "died" and received the condolences of both. On June 14, Parker wrote:

All your letters have been safely received by myself, R. [Roberts]. We are all sorry to hear your mother passed on. As to the job it is still awaiting you. Why not transfer your draft registration here? Machine-shop experience might make it easier to get into non-combatant work. We hope to see you in person instead of hearing from you again. I can't go to bed & keep things moving too.

Roberts, too, wanted me to come back. "If and when you are able to return we'll welcome you to St. Clair Shores." He wrote a second time:

Garland left this week to take a job in Pontiac. . . . Bob L. [William Robert Lyman] sent me a wonderful book "The Secret World Government" by Major-General Count Cherep-Spiridovich. . . . They also list some other books on the cover. Could you drop around and find out if they are still in business and if possible if the Count is still alive? If you can get out here (should you decide to come) we can put you on and would like to have you but no one knows your problems better than you . . .

And with typical candor, Garland wrote:

The fight for an independent America still goes on. I am boost-
ing for Rev. Smith, a fine man . . . and am distributing thousands
of pieces of American literature such as Congressman Hoffman's
"Don't Haul Down the Stars and Stripes." . . . Smith is going
hot. . . . Please keep up the fight and write often. Best wishes for
America.

I was delighted to know that I was not suspected. It meant
that I could keep up my investigations of the N.W.L. by mail,
and, if it ever became necessary, could return to Detroit. I
hoped not. I took stock of my earnings while working for
Roberts. He had paid me sixty cents an hour and I earned a
net total of $91.30 during my three weeks' stay. I invested the
money in war bonds.

Awaiting me one morning after my return from Detroit
was a mimeographed leaflet from one George E. Hornby. It
was an announcement that a convention of "patriots" was to
meet at Boise, Idaho, on the Fourth of July. Hornby's leaflet
emphasized James' Yankee Freemen theme.

It's our last chance to get together on a definite, unifying program and plan of action before our traitorous, Constitution-
violating administration and its fellow-traveller Union Now, pro-
Russian, anti-American powers . . . succeed in selling down the
river to the British-Yiddish empire. . . .
What more justification do you need, what other incentive is
necessary to move you to join other Yankee American Freemen—
Ultra Americans all—for the purpose of issuing a re-Declaration
of Independence, and to pledge our all for the redemption and
purging of our U.S.A.?

I was not sure whether Hornby was in earnest about the inflammatory plans which his mimeographed leaflet indicated.
But subsequent events showed that he was serious, and the
convention was set to meet almost exactly seven months after
Pearl Harbor:

This rally of Real Yankees is to start at 10:00 o'clock the morning of July 4th and end the evening of July 6th in Boise, Idaho.

No noise—no advertising—is being put out about the conclave. We are going about the business in hand quietly and earnestly; . . . Come praying and singing, "God, Help America."

I had first learned of George E. Hornby from an advertisement he inserted in *Publicity* in January, 1942 offering a bargain selection of "patriotic" literature at the special price of fifty cents. I sent him $1 and asked for a double bargain. To my amazement, I received a letter written on the *official* stationery of the Disabled American Veterans of the World War, Canyon County Chapter, Caldwell, Idaho. Hornby's name appeared as "State Executive Committeeman."

I cultivated Hornby's "friendship" by mail, for I felt that the injection of the Nazi spirit in an organization of disabled war veterans could be a serious matter in war-time. Hornby wrote back cordially saying that he had enjoyed reading my fine letter, and was sending me under separate cover an "assortment of Ultra-American publications." He apologized because copies of the *Protocols* were sold out.

Upon receipt of his material I found that Hornby was promoting Mrs. Dilling's *Octopus*, Sanctuary's *The Talmud Unmasked* and Charles Hudson's bulletins. He had also reprinted in its entirety Stahrenberg's infamous leaflet *Why Are Jews Persecuted for Their Religion?* The same Nazi doctrine of hate was being used to arouse dissension in the Far West at a time when internal unity was paramount. Hornby also directed the Ultra-American Party, an offshoot of the American Service Brotherhood which "was originally organized and built around the issue of the American HOME." It believed in dealing "with the Jewish Question in accordance with the best American traditions."

The Ultra-American Party . . . is fighting your battle, and not in Europe either. . . . We would hate to think the American people were unworthy of the struggle we are making to preserve our Constitutional form of Government and true Americanism—*Ultra-Americanism*. Read, think, live, act and be Ultra-American. To be **ULTRA-AMERICAN** is to be **AMERICAN** and for the U.S.A. 100 per cent—only more so.

Hornby issued a series of Ultra-American books and tracts and spread them in a network throughout the country long after Pearl Harbor, in addition to peddling Sanctuary's, Hudson's and Dilling's outpourings. On June 15 I received a personal invitation on the stationery of the Disabled Veterans:

> We hope that you and any of your friends, who are dependable, trustworthy Yankee Americans ("Yankee" is a localism, a term that originally meant "first-rate" or "top-notch"), will find it possible to come to the convention as per the enclosed S-O-S announcement, which I trust you will take care to see that none of the enemy even gets a glimpse of.
>
> Now with F.D.R. cracking down and telling Biddle to "get tough" with such as us, it is getting to be hard to know how far you can trust some people. . . . Hoping to see you here. . . .

It was comforting to know that Hornby regarded me as a fellow "first-rate" Yankee. I answered him immediately:

> I was delighted to hear from you again. . . . I should tell that I'm not a disabled veteran. On the contrary, am not a member of the Legion, as I'm not old enough. I'm 100% American, born here, etc. . . . Are civilians about to go into the army acceptable at your convention? I'd like to know as I'd not like to spend the time and money to come out there and then find I'm not eligible to participate.

I got Hornby's reply by return air mail:

> Dear Brother Yankee—
> Don't worry about your welcome being in any way affected by the fact that you are not a World War Veteran. From what you say you stand a chance of being a more "seasoned" veteran than any of us and we only wish we could contact more who will be similarly situated before they have to face the horrors of this Jew-launched hell.
>
> Both my son and son-in-law are already in the "service," and of course, I have poured into them all that they seemed to be able to soak up; but now it is risky on account of the censorship to write to them the things I'd like to keep them posted on. . . . If you get to see Sanctuary tell him about the convention, or give him this S-O-S.
>
> . . . You'll find me calling the convention to order at 10:A.M. July 4th and you will learn the place of meeting after you get here, as you can understand WHY. Edward Holton James ex-

pects to come by plane. After the convention, before you start home, I'll load you up with literature, all you can make good use of.

. . . I feel that you will feel that it has been worth your while to take part in this before you get called. I hope you will find it possible to remain a while after the convention as *I'd like to post you on a code we can use for communicating when and if you are called*, & will be good for you to know it anyway.

My interest was considerably heightened by the secret "code" which Hornby proposed to teach me for our correspondence when I was drafted! Simultaneously, I heard from Edward Holton James who urged: "Go to the convention if you can make it. Anything is good that spells action."

I showed the correspondence and the convention leaflet to several official agencies of our government, and to the democratic group for which I worked. I also consulted Russell Davenport who was planning a comprehensive book on Nazi and native-Nazi forces. All were amazed at the boldness of an apparent group of war veterans brazenly defying the temper of a nation at war. I was urged to "get to the bottom of it."

I began to pack. But unlike the Detroit trip for which I had taken my old clothes and a battered bag, ready to decamp instantly, I felt I ought to dress more respectably. I purchased a khaki shirt, a pair of khaki trousers and took along my leather jacket, determined to look like a "veteran." I took my expensive view-camera. I slipped in a pack of special "process" film used by photographers for reproducing letters and booklets.

WHAT MORE JUSTIFICATION DO YOU NEED — WHAT OTHER INCENTIVE IS NECESSARY TO MOVE YOU TO JOIN OTHER YANKEE AMERICAN FREEMEN — ULTRA AMERICANS ALL — FOR THE PURPOSE OF ISSUING A RE-DECLARATION OF INDEPENDENCE, AND TO PLEDGE OUR ALL FOR THE REDEMPTION AND PURGING OF OUR U. S. A.?

THIS RALLY OF REAL YANKEES IS TO START AT 10:00 O'CLOCK THE MORNING OF JULY 4TH AND END THE EVENING OF JULY 6TH IN BOISE, IDAHO. NO NOISE — NO ADVERTISING — IS BEING PUT OUT ABOUT THE CONCLAVE — WE ARE GOING ABOUT THE BUSINESS IN HAND QUIETLY AND EARNESTLY; LOOK TO THE ONE WHO GAVE OR SENT YOU THIS ANNOUNCEMENT FOR FURTHER DETAILS. COME PRAYING AND SINGING "GOD, HELP AMERICA!"

I hope you will find it possible to remain a while after the convention as I'd like to post you on a code we can use for communicating when and if you are called & it will be good for you to know it anyway. Also, if you

Excerpt from Hornby's leaflet announcing his fascist convention and a section of his letter offering to teach Pagnanelli a secret code.

I had Mrs. Dilling's *Octopus*, copies of my *Christian Defender*, several membership cards and a small assortment of subversive literature distributed by East Coast Nazis.

As the train rumbled out of Grand Central Station, I fell to wondering to what extent the hate gospel had permeated the West, and to what extent Hitler's dissolvents were at work. I wondered to what extent the Great West would prove to be like the "narrow" East.

CHAPTER VII

SERPENTS AND VIPERS

"When the day comes to settle the score and I'm given a reward for my patriotism, I want to be made chief executioner of those guys who are now sticking up for Democracy."

FRANK W. CLARK

FOR THREE DAYS and three nights I travelled 2,500 miles across the heartland of America. Roared past the smoking chimney-cities, with their teeming millions working on twenty-four-hour shifts to forge shapeless metal into armaments of war . . . past the lush virgin valleys of Iowa and the spanless prairies of Nebraska, where Nature was working around the clock to feed a mighty nation in the throes of war, past the "cattle country," and past states rich in precious metals. Wealth! Boundless, immeasurable wealth: beneath the earth and above it, waiting to be tapped—America!

And this was the land of my adoption that Hitler and his agents, Goebbels and his American Quislings would shatter from within, and ripen for his political conquest—if they could. The West inspired me to fight on harder than ever.

As the train came to a jarring stop at Boise, I alighted and yelled a hearty good-bye to a group of soldiers and sailors who had been my companions during the long journey from Chicago. We had exchanged confidences, drunk wine and whiskey and played the harmonica together. They were boys who had been overseas and were home on furlough. I learned all about women in Ireland, England and Australia.

Early in the afternoon I telephoned Hornby's home and learned that he was at the G.A.R. Hall, campaign head-quarters.

"Come right over," he invited.

I met a man of about fifty-five, tall and rangy, with a brownish complexion and mustache. Hornby's face reflected the characteristic I had found common in my previous con-

357

tacts: that of a deep-seated hate frozen on immobile features; a face scarred with an inner, smoldering hate. Hornby had received a leg injury during the World War, and was compelled to use a cane.

I registered as a delegate and asked who else had arrived. The turnout was disappointing, Hornby said. News of the convention had somehow leaked out and he was worried. But two of the staunchest "patriots" in the West, Frank W. Clark of Tacoma and Mrs. Lois de Lafayette Washburn of Seattle, Washington, had both arrived.

"Where are they?" I asked, eager to take a room in the same hotel.

"They've registered at the Grand Hotel, but not under their right names. Clark has registered as William F. Gibson and Mrs. Washburn as Terese N. Thurlow. You'd better use another name, too: the enemy may be watching us."

I registered under the Yankee name of George Paige.

I asked Hornby if the convention were under the auspices of the Disabled War Veterans. It wasn't, he answered with some embarrassment, and he was no longer the Veterans' State Committee Executive.

"How about the letterheads?" I asked.

"I swiped a lot of them and have been using them for my correspondence," he explained. "It makes a good impression and it gives the movement dignity."

"I understand," I said, burying my emotions at the duplicity which had caused me to come out to Idaho.

"The Veterans don't know what it's all about," Hornby went on. "They're dumb about nationalism." He added that there weren't many Jews in Boise (population 30,000) but the Jews "run the city just the same."

Hornby introduced me to his associate in the Ultra-American Party, Joseph P. Spencer. I decided to work on Spencer and suggested having dinner together. Spencer proved to be a travelling missionary of hate and had lived variously at Briggs and Portland, Oregon; and Alexandria, Virginia. In 1939 he had toured the country in an auto, visiting such "patriots" as Deatherage and True. He had carried a load of "patriotic" literature, dropping it on his calls and receiving other tracts in exchange.

"We sure spread that literature around," Spencer boasted. "My wife and I carried that stuff from one end of the country to the other. No one can say I haven't done my bit for my country."

I asked Spencer how he had got his start in the movement. He had studied for the Baptist ministry and insisted that our churches were "outposts of the Jewish Empire." He told me he had been closely connected with the American Publishing Society, Bremerton, Washington, publishers of the *Protocols* and originators of the text for *Why Are Jews Persecuted for Their Religion?* I asked Spencer if he knew Stahrenberg. I explained that I had known him well.

"I've never met him, but we used to get a lot of stuff from the Nationalist Press," he answered.

"Do you know Edward Holton James?" I asked.

"Of course I do. Hornby and I both get his stuff and I agree one hundred per cent with him."

After dinner Spencer invited me to his home, six miles from Boise, where he kept a chicken and goat farm. Here he gave me some of the literature he had published. Its pattern was identical to that in the East. Spencer had a copy of *The Octopus*, quantities of Hudson's bulletins and an assortment of subversive literature already familiar to me. As we sat in the yard, munching fruit, he exploded:

"We'll have to have a revolution. I see no other way out."

It was a familiar cry, expressed in identical terms in the East. The word he used, "liberate," also had a familiar ring. Hitler used it to "liberate" Czechoslovakia. And Hitler "liberated" Poland, Belgium and France. "Liberate America" one of Stahrenberg's leaflets screamed. "Join the American National-Socialist Party."

Spencer outlined his plan for the revolution. It would start from the West, and roll eastward, gathering in force until it reached Washington. This, too, had a familiar ring, for it had originated with Nazi Consul Manfred von Killinger and the idea was promoted by Deatherage and his fascist friend, Mrs. Leslie Fry.

"But it's going to be a legal revolution," Spencer continued: "We don't want to do anything that's out of the way. We'll follow a strict Constitutional course."

"Yes, yes," I said, somewhat bored. I knew what was coming next.

"We'll have a second Declaration of Independence, elect a brand-new Congress and move the capital from Washington to Denver. We'll reshape our Republic and start from the beginning."

I asked Spencer if he would welcome Hitler here, knowing in advance that the answer would be an emphatic NO.

"No, siree, no Hitler here. We don't want any foreign *isms*. They belong in Europe. We want an America for Americans. We want a Yankee American government to rule Yankee Americans! America for the Americans. That's my ticket!"

Spencer showed me the letter he had received from Senator Reynolds, written on the stationery of *The American Vindicator*. On the bottom appeared the line "America for Americans . . . Our Citizens, Our Country First." The letter, dated March 1, 1940, read:

Thank you immensely for your fine letter of February 20, which has just reached my desk, and in appreciation of which I am hastening a response at the earliest possible moment. I do wish we had more full-blooded Americans like yourself in this country today who are actively engaged in helping America. . . .

I also thank you for the folder enclosed entitled *U. S. prospers attending to own affairs*. It is fine. I read it with much interest and appreciation.

With every good wish, my dear Mr. Spencer, and reassurances of my deep appreciation of your fine patriotic American cooperation, I am,

Most sincerely yours,
(signed)   Robert R. Reynolds

Whenever something about Senator Reynolds came up I found it difficult to reconcile the fact that he was actually a Senator, and Chairman of the extremely important Committee on Military Affairs at that!

I went back to my room in the Grand Hotel and readied myself for the convention the next day. The presence of Mrs. Washburn and of Clark was a godsend. Even if no one else of importance attended, my trip would have been worth it to learn just what these two co-conspirators in the American Nazi cause had been doing since Pearl Harbor. Hornby had said: "They've been very active, but working quietly."

Himself a World War veteran, Clark was formerly a lieutenant in Pelley's Silver Shirts. But he broke away from the "Goateed Fuehrer" and established his own storm-troop outfit known as the League of War Veteran Guardsmen. Clark had served as underground contact man with important fascists and travelled widely on mysterious secret missions.

Mrs. Lois de Lafayette Washburn, claiming to be a descendant of the French hero, was a veteran worker in the fascist cause. Although she, too, had operated from many parts of the country, she performed her greatest voluntary service to Goebbels' cause in Chicago by founding the American Gentile Protective Association, with Clark as national organizer. She maintained an extensive correspondence and had a mailing list of several thousand key cell-leaders throughout the country. Mrs. Washburn circulated a pledge which included the startling declaration: "I solemnly swear that never again will I vote for a candidate of either of the amalgamated Republican or Democratic parties."

Instead, she urged pledgees to:

. . . help support [the] organization of a NEW POLITICAL PARTY that will help stop this world holocaust, outlaw Communistic, Bolshevistic Judaism, smash the capitalism of international finance . . . and put a military man in the White House as Commander-in-Chief of our Army and Navy.

With Clark, Mrs. Washburn had helped found in 1938 the National Liberty Party with a typical American fascist platform. It wasn't her first experience with Nazi-inclined groups, for she made the following admission in writing:

. . . So I cast about me for male leadership. Finally I hit upon the idea of asking Father Coughlin to undertake to organize the forces of decency—since he was already on the radio battling the money-changers. Thus I really was the original sponsor of the N.U.S.J. [National Union for Social Justice]. I organized Unit No. 15 of the Tenth Congressional District, and helped to organize other units.

Her climaxing effort was the publication of the *Second Declaration of Independence,* in which she urged that "patriots":

> . . . utterly dissolve and break off all political connection that may hitherto have subsisted . . . and work out our own salvation . . . along Fascistic lines under the existing Constitution, which we will fight to defend and preserve.

As I went to bed in my hotel room, I put the light out and pulled up the shade. My eyes stared at what I saw in the room a scant twenty feet across from my window. The shade of the other room was up, and before the mirror in the room was a woman with her back to me. I believe that in such circumstances most normal young men would keep their shade up and await developments. But in this case I had an especial reason. I had never seen her, but I had a hunch that the woman was Mrs. Washburn. I waited till the woman with the shapely spine turned around so I could see her face. She turned around and I looked. Was it Mrs. Washburn? I wouldn't know until I saw her at the convention.

As I went to bed on the eve of Independence Day, I looked forward to meeting the following day those bogus "patriots" who were dedicated to the shattering of the United States in order to leave the pieces for an imported Hitler or a native Laval to piece together in a New Order, with a Second Declaration of Independence, and the "election" of a puppet New Congress.

Yes, the woman who undressed with her shade up *was* Mrs. Washburn.

The convention was called to order at ten A.M., on the Fourth of July after Pearl Harbor. It was a convention in name only. In a sense I was glad to see only fifteen assorted "patriots" present, and except for the principals, the rest were of no consequence in American Nazi politics. Although disappointed at the turnout, I was glad to see that the big-time "patriots" had finally learned to respect the might of the F.B.I. and the Attorney General's office, even though their reactions toward the Dies Committee remained mixed.

Hornby set the pace by reading a long-winded *Re-Declara-*

tion of Independence which he had composed in longhand on a thick pad of yellow paper. He had tried to model it after the immortal document but his attempt was a sickening plagiarism of Jefferson's inspired prose. Hornby didn't even know how the Declaration of Independence began and had to refer to a history book he had brought along.

The "convention" started peaceably enough with Mrs. Washburn giving an emotional harangue about the role "we patriots" were expected to play on behalf of "Christ and Country." She confided to us that she had been in constant touch with Edward Holton James and had evolved a Yankee Minuteman plan of action which would incorporate James' basic idea but avoid its libelous content.

The Yankee Minuteman proposal started the fireworks. Spencer had his own pet scheme to further and the two fell to squabbling. Too jealous to let the initiative rest with a woman, Spencer expostulated about a "necessary national leadership composed of such men as Lindbergh and Nye" to lead a Yankee Minuteman idea. Clark jumped to Mrs. Washburn's defense, and from then on the fireworks began to pop off in every direction.

Hornby sided with Spencer. Clark-Washburn began to woo me to their side. But I played the strategic role of a neutral. My task was to get as much data about each as I could and I could ill afford to antagonize them. The first day of the convention ended amid noise and confusion and we adjourned without having accomplished anything. That night I had supper with the Clark-Washburn clique and found that we had a lot of "friends" in common.

Mrs. Washburn was a short, plump woman of middle age, a veritable shrew in politics. Clark proved to be a rough type with large, jutting jaw, bull-like stance, an air of thorough aggressiveness. He was dressed in a khaki suit, with shoulder straps and wore a ring of opal with the Germanic initial "D" mysteriously imposed on it.

"There's nobody of any importance in the patriotic movement that we don't know," Clark began. True, Sanctuary, Edmondson, Moseley, Deatherage—he was a friend of them all and a hundred others of their kind.

Clark spoke of having had contact in the past "with German boys" but he was reluctant about details. He said these "patriotic Germans" had been "ready to come in" on a storm-troop movement in the northwest, but the plan had leaked out and they had been scared off. Clark talked freely of the need for revolution.

"I'm organizing patriotic bands in the Northwest," he said. "My job is to act as co-ordinator between different groups throughout the country. The revolution has got to get going in the West first."

I asked about the supply of arms and ammunition.

"That's being taken care of right now. Almost everybody has a rifle and they are putting away other firearms. The guys that prefer the silent method are stocking up on knives."

Mrs. Washburn interjected that Clark's organization of vet-erans had many thousands of members. Clark refused to name any specific figures, but merely said: "We can only get this thing rolling with the help of the vets on a nation-wide scale. That's what I'm doing now—organizing them underground."

Clark was one of the most bloodthirsty Turks I had ever met in my work as investigator. He talked incessantly of mas-sacre and murder and pogroms. "The sons of bitches ought to be pushed into the Pacific," he said time and again. He talked continually of "killing, hanging and gouging the enemy." He had but one ambition: "When the day comes to settle the score, and I'm given a reward for my patriotism, I want to be made chief executioner of those guys who are now sticking up for Democracy."

Sitting at the table, Mrs. Washburn kept repeating: "Those serpents and vipers ought to be smashed underfoot." It was her favorite expression and she interjected it on every oc-casion.

That night Clark invited me and several of the local men to his hotel room and bombarded us for two hours with a ha-rangue against Communism. His speech was based entirely on the fantastic reports of Mrs. Catherine Baldwin, New York director of the Defenders of the Constitution of the United States of America, and author of an eery Jewish-Liberal-Masonic-Communist-Capitalist plot to ruin the "Republic."

I had breakfast with Clark, and when I learned that Clark would not attend the second session of the convention because

he might get into a scrap with Spencer, I suggested we go
back to the hotel and "talk things over." The two were planning to leave on the one o'clock bus, thoroughly disgusted at
Spencer's sabotage of their proposed domination of the convention. Back in the hotel Mrs. Washburn expressed great admiration for Jeremiah Stokes, a Salt Lake City attorney who
had published a booklet, *The Communists' Plot to Purge
American Patriots From Congress.*

"If you go down to Salt Lake City be sure to give him my
regards," Mrs. Washburn said. "He's doing a fine job against
the serpents and vipers."

I wanted to get Clark's views on Hitler.

"I respect him one hundred per cent," he said without hesitation. "Of course, I would not like to see Hitler here, but we
can adopt for America those measures which would work in
America."

Mrs. Washburn had already expressed Japanese sympathies,
and I asked what she thought of Japan's attack on Pearl
Harbor:

"The New Deal worked secretly with Japan to bring it
on," she said. This was the wildest tale, the choicest Nazi lie
I had yet heard on the trip, but I acted as though I had suspected the same thing all along. She continued: "Japan is helping us fight off the Jew and the Jewish capitalist system. They
are fighting the nationalist cause with us. They are our allies
and not our enemies as those internationalist serpents and
vipers would have us believe."

I asked Clark if I should join the army or work my way
out.

"If I were to advise you as I want to advise you," he said, "I
might be held for it." He went on to recite how some of his
best friends among the Silver Shirts were being locked up by
army authorities. "You can do what you want to do," he said
winking.

"The Jews and the F.B.I. have been on my trail," he continued. "I'm having a helluva a time getting my mail. I got to
use all sorts of blinds and phony names. Sometimes it takes
me a month to get letters." I wondered why a staunch "patriot" should have to resort to such subterfuges.

Clark told me of an attorney with whom he had corresponded in Salt Lake City: "His name's McKnight and he's an okay fella. If you go down mention my name. Before you leave us, George," he said, "let me give you this."

Clark went over to a box on his desk and took out a small white eagle. He seized the lapel of my coat and decorated me with it.

"It's the symbol of the Yankee Minuteman," he said solemnly. Duly "impressed" at the "honor," I observed that the eagle was also Germany's emblem.

"Yes," Clark said, "the American eagle has his head up. Germany's eagle is crouching."

"In order to jump on the serpents and vipers," Mrs. Washburn put in.

Clark remained behind, while Mrs. Washburn and I walked over to the G.A.R. Hall. The crowd had increased by several more local men. It was Sunday and Spencer started off with a "prayer" which lasted a half hour and was filled with invectives against Democracy, Jews, the British, the Administration, the Communists and capitalism. Only Hitler was left out. The harangue was no sooner over than Spencer and Mrs. Washburn who had almost walked out during the "prayer" nearly came to blows over a discussion of the Yankee Minuteman. She moved that the convention be closed.

"That may be a wise thing to do," Hornby said. "News of the convention leaked out and a reporter called up my home for a story."

"I'd better run back to the hotel and pack up," Mrs. Washburn said in alarm. "The serpents and vipers are after us."

This officially ended the Boise fascist convention. From stacks placed on tables, the delegates helped themselves to "patriotic" literature. They went away loaded down with copies of *Publicity*, Jeremiah Stokes' booklet, *The Program of the National Liberty Party*, the vicious leaflet *Your Crucifixion*, copies of *The Ultra-American* and tracts advocating the "Ultra-American Way."

From Mrs. Washburn and Clark I had already received leaflets urging the sale of the *Protocols*; pledge cards urging the formation of a "new political party"; tracts advocating impeachment against the President; the platform of James' Yankee Freemen advocating immediate peace with Germany and Japan; and a lengthy mimeographed tract entitled *The Coming Civil War, Strife and Bloodshed* by Frank W. Clark.

Overwhelmed by the weight of the "patriotism" I had witnessed on this Fourth of July week end, I decided to walk off by myself to digest it all. I sat in the park facing the State Capitol and I reviewed events of the last few days. My trip had not been entirely fruitless. I had gathered some very incriminating facts against Clark and Mrs. Washburn, both of whom had camouflaged their underground work effectively since Pearl Harbor. I felt sure that their strong Axis sympathies, the literature they had distributed and the tracts they intended to publish would deeply interest the authorities.

Then, too, I had received introductions to "patriots" in Salt Lake City. In New York I had already seen evidence of Jeremiah Stokes' work and knew of the Nazi leanings of another "patriot" in Salt Lake City, Ernest Hollings. I felt that a nest of pro-Axis Americans was functioning quietly there which ought to be investigated. I wrote letters to McKnight, Stokes and Hollings, saying I expected to arrive in a day or two. My round trip ticket allowed me to return by way of Salt Lake City at no extra cost. I had just finished writing when Hornby phoned me at my room.

"I've been expecting you all afternoon," he said impatiently. "Don't you want to learn that code?"

"The code, yes. I almost forgot. I'll come right over."

Hornby and I sat with our chairs pulled up close. On a letterhead of the Disabled American Veterans he began to sketch the code letters. I watched him intently as he drew the symbols.

"What'll we use the code for?" I asked.

"For messages. We can exchange secret information when you are in the army. I can send you confidential stuff and you can send me some without the censors being any the wiser."

"What secret information would you want from me?" I asked, suspiciously.

"I have inside information that the Jewish officers will kill all the Gentile ones and put Communists in their place. I want you to write me when the plot begins to take shape."

I looked at him in amazement. The West certainly produced liars! Hornby must have sensed my disbelief.

"I'm telling you things, George, that very few people know. When you get into the army I want you to send me the names of the Jewish officers and all the information you can get on them."

"What'll you do with the information?" I asked.

"I'll send it along to the proper people." Hornby refused to elaborate and went back to the code.

"You'd better not mail me the code letters from the army post. Wait for week ends so you can send them from some small town. Later on we'll arrange a blind you can send your letters to."

Hornby asked me to listen carefully as he explained the figures, symbols and numbers he had put down on the letterhead.

"Now this first one is the Playfair Code, used regularly in the army. I've put it down so you can contrast it with the others, but we won't use that. This one," he pointed to a dual column with symbols resembling Egyptian hieroglyphics, "is real secret, but very hard to remember. You can use it after a while, but for the time being I'd suggest that you use the simplest and one of the cleverest codes I've devised."

Hornby pointed to the top row of letters he had grouped as follows:

ZYX	WVU	TSR	QPON
MLK	JIH	GFE	DCBA

"That's the alphabet spelled backwards," he explained. "To write the word 'Disabled' we begin by putting down the symbol letter for 'D'—here it is," and Hornby pointed to the first column of modified hieroglyphics. To write 'i' we take the second column and read down five letters to 'i'—that gives us code number '25.'" To write the code number for 's' we go to the third column, second letter—which gives us '32.'"

"Let me find the code number for 'a,'" I said. I found 'a' in the fourth column, and counting from the first letter of the column I found 'a' to be the eighth letter. The code number was 48.

"That's right," Hornby said, and worked out the rest of the word "Disabled." "It's simple. But it's a sticker if you don't know how."

ZYX WVU TSR QPON
MLK JIH GFE DCBA

▶ 25 32 48 47 15 36 45 △ [500 ℴℴℴ] 𝔇

[2] *quotes* 66 — 99

◁◫▽△▷◇⊡□−⁄∖⟍◖◖◗◗◗𝔇⊕⊖⊘⊗⊕

◁◫▽△▷ ⌣⌐⫶−⁄∖⟍∈⊂◗◖◖◗⊖⊙

Spacing figures 1 to 9; end of sentence 50, 70, etc.

comma 9, ?7, 2 to, too, two; 4, for, four, fore, 91

Z𝔜X WVU QPON MLK KLM NPQU VWX YZ

SHORT ABCDEFGIJ

Hornby's codes. Bottom rows (letters upside down) illustrate the
Playfair Code. The dual rows of hieroglyphics above it show
complicated codes devised by Hornby. The top row (alphabet
in reverse) was the basis of the code most frequently used
by Hornby, with the word "Disabled" written out below it:
(D) 25.32.48.47.15.36.45.

"Oh, I'm a photographer, too," Hornby said, "and I do sketching. I'm especially good at maps and copying interiors to measurements. By the way, when are you leaving?" he asked.

"Tomorrow. I'm going back by way of Salt Lake."

Early the next morning Hornby came to my room, greatly excited.

"What's the matter?" I asked. "You seem worried."

"Yes, about that code. Listen, George, do you think somebody will find out about it? I've been thinking all night. Somebody might come around and search this place. You'd better give the code back."

"I sent the code home by registered mail yesterday," I lied. "I'm always one step ahead of the enemy!"

Hornby seemed relieved. "I've heard from Hudson and McKnight," he said, taking out of his pocket a copy of Hudson's bulletin and a letter from the Salt Lake City attorney. The letter excited me because of its inflammatory contents. I determined to get either the letter or a copy of it. But how? I had to think fast.

"Look, Hornby, that's a mighty long and interesting letter McKnight has written you. Why don't you leave it here and let me read it at my leisure. I'd like very much to enjoy every word of it."

"I'll wait here while you read it," he said. "I have plenty of time. I don't have to be at the W.P.A. Project till one o'clock."

"If you don't mind, I'd like to copy down a short paragraph or two," I blurted. "The man is a poet as well as a patriot. I'll give it back to you as soon as I finish with it."

As he hesitated, I said: "C'mon. Let's not hang around here on this beautiful day. Let's go out and have a drink."

I took the letter and tossed it on my bed. After a while I returned alone and locked the door carefully behind me. I went immediately to my suitcase, took out a large photoflood bulb of 1000 watts and placed it in the light socket over the wash-basin. Then I set up my camera, and stretched out the bellows to within a few feet of the letter which I propped up against the wall with adhesive tape. I was taking critical focus under the burning photoflood lamp when in my excitement I tipped over the camera. With a pounding heart I dove after it and I caught it just before it hit the ground.

I set it up, again taking critical focus so that every comma and period showed clearly in the reflecting mirror. Holding my breath so the camera would not move, I counted fifteen and snapped the shutter. I made two copies of each page and also of the envelope with the date line. A section of Mc-Knight's letter to Hornby read:

I am filled with sore regrets, from the fact now confronting me; which forbids my attendance, at the convention of YANKEE FREEMEN. This will be a momentionous meeting, an historic gathering of the bone and sinue of true American liberty I verrily believe.

I would sacrifice a lot to be with you, so if I am absent in body I will attend in spirit and prayer. Oh, how I would love to strike hands with such nobelmen as Father Coghlin, Jearald Winrod, William Dudley Pelley, David Baxter, Frank W. Clark, and Edward Holton James from whose mighty brain was struck, like a living spark from the eternal alter of freedom, that statement of principles, equal in import to the declaration of independence: not to say Wheeler, Lindberg the incomparable, Senator Nye and Walsh, and others too numerous to mention here. Oh, what I would give to be numbered with them, what an honor, what a rare prevelidge. . . .

While not the best speller in the world, it was apparent that McKnight was no less a fanatic than Clark, Washburn, Hornby, Spencer. I was putting away the camera and film when the door handle rattled—accompanied by insistent knocking.

"Who is it?" I asked alarmed.

"It's me, Hornby."

I opened the door. "I came after that letter," Hornby said seeing it on the bed. "I got worried. . . . Say, what's that camera doing here?"

"This is a military zone, ain't it?" I asked. "And the enemy knows I was at the convention. Before packing, I'm sealing up the camera, the lens, and all my film with this adhesive tape so they can't frame me by saying I was taking pictures. A fellow's got to be careful these days. There's no tellin' what those Jews will do to a Yankee. . . ."

Hornby, whose intuitions seemed much more sensitive than I had imagined, seemed satisfied with the explanation. "I'll see you off on the bus," he said.

"Sure thing. It leaves in a half hour."

He sensed something was wrong somewhere, but couldn't quite make me out. Hornby wasn't a "big shot" fascist, although over the years he had done irreparable damage to the democratic cause in the Far West. What fascinated me was his soul-searing fanaticism. Hate had played such a crushing role in his life that he was completely subordinated to the delusions of a "Jewish plot to kill Gentile officers" which only a hate-oppressed mind could concoct.

CHAPTER VIII

THE MORMON CITY

"Japan and Germany will help us fight to preserve the Constitution by sending over whatever military aid becomes necessary. This is according to prophecy. . . . Hitler is the Redeemer of the Constitution."

ERNEST HOLLINGS

I WAS IN the room alone with two men. The one who had pumped both my hands in welcome was a small round man with a bald dome and rotund face. He had small, beady eyes and he peered at you from behind rimmed glasses. He was definitely of the single-track, uncompromising zealot type. Jeremiah Stokes had let his law practice slide and was devoting the major portion of his time to the writing of "patriotic" tracts.

The other man I faced was more than six feet tall, with powerfully sloping shoulders and a barrel chest. He had a large nose and blazing brown eyes. He was tanned a deep leather tan. His hands were veritable chunks of raw meat and bone, his wrists thick, his forearms—his shirt was rolled back to the elbow—were like those of a wrestler. All in all, James H. McKnight reminded you of a backwoods county sheriff, a man of action, tough as rawhide.

"By God, it's coming as sure as the sunrise," McKnight said, speaking in a voice deep and resonant. "The only way out of the mess is for an armed uprising to get going. Everyone here has guns and pistols. I myself have five—two pistols, two rifles, one shotgun."

I asked if the pistols were registered.

"They're supposed to be. Guys out here don't bother much."

Stokes, the cautious and careful one, said he had "heard" that guerrilla bands would be formed in due time which would raid adjoining towns, clean up the Jews and move on

during the night. Those from Salt Lake City would pounce
on adjoining towns, while vigilantes from adjoining towns
would "clean up" the Jews of Salt Lake City.

"That's so the patriots will not be recognized," McKnight
put in. "Yes sir, it'll be guerrilla fighting. It'll start in the
West and sweep to the East. Sure as the sunrise."

Memories of General Moseley, Fry, Deatherage, Spencer
—on July 7, precisely seven months after Pearl Harbor! Then
to my ears which by this time had become inured to the startling, came the sound of McKnight's booming voice:

"What we need is a Hitler in every state—a strong man
who will rule things the right way."

Stokes and McKnight had offices in the Atlas Building.
Both had read Pelley and Winrod faithfully. Both had been
active in America First Committee work. Stokes admitted being in touch with Hudson and Sanctuary. He knew Thorkelson personally. From Stokes I learned that he had been active
in the "patriotic" movement since 1933, the year Dashnag
henchmen killed the Archbishop and Hitler came to power.
Stokes had been writing extensively since then. Under the imprint of the Federated Libraries, Inc. he estimated that he had
distributed several hundred thousand "patriotic" tracts. American Women Against Communism in New York were eastern
distributors of his goods and Edwin Perry Banta was his main
contact.

Although I hadn't yet obtained a rounded picture of subversion in the Mormon City, I got the instant impression that
McKnight was ringleader. He had been "educated" from the
writings of Colonel Sanctuary, Stahrenberg, Snow, Edmondson, Asher (editor of *The X-Ray*), Baxter's Social Republic
Society, the various Mothers groups and countless similar
patrioteers.

"Let's get a bite to eat," McKnight said.

At lunch we met Ernest Hollings. I invited him to my hotel
room in the evening to "talk things over quietly. And bring a
friend with you," I added.

Hollings brought along C. F. Allen, Pelley's former representative in the Mormon City. A nondescript type, Allen's
face seemed to have been pressed through a wringer. His
mouth was tiny, his forehead was steeply sloping and he had

the eyes of a frightened man. Allen believed that Pelley's fascist plan as outlined in his book *No More Hunger*—richly praised by the Japanese—should prevail in America. "Pelley is the Jews' best friend," Allen said earnestly. "The Jews don't realize it."

Asked him about the "rich old woman" who I had heard had given money to Pelley.

"Oh, I think you mean old Marie Ogden. She lives in a wild part of Utah. She is a card, all right. Her sister died and she kept injecting fluids into the body for two years expecting to bring it back to life."

"Did it ever come back to life?" I asked, deadpan.

"No," Allen said seriously. "Marie Ogden was just a fanatic, and they say she gave all her money to Pelley."

Of the two, Hollings interested me more. A short, rounded man with a fine skin, fine features and silver, well-brushed hair, he had been instructor of physical education at the University of Utah, he told me. His distinguished accent belonged to South Africa, and from Africa he had emigrated to the Mormon capital. But Hollings proved to be a Dr. Jekyll and Mr. Hyde, for behind the small, philosophic, professorial face, was the tongue of a seasoned Hitlerite disciple.

Like McKnight, Stokes and Allen, Hollings also was a Mormon. He had started on his hate-mongering work by distributing bound copies of *The International Jew* during the twenties. Since then under the imprint of Christian Party Headquarters, he had sold the *Protocols*, distributed Pelley's, Edmondson's, Spiridovich's poison writings, particularly recommending Winrod's *Defender* and *Destiny*, organ of the Anglo-Saxon Federation. Hollings revealed that during the 1936 elections he had received $300.00 from the Republican Party for legitimate campaign purposes.

"I used the money to buy 40,000 pieces of patriotic leaflets against the President," he said. Among them, he confided, were thousands of copies of Reverend Winrod's *Revealer* which in banner headlines "proved" "ROOSEVELT'S JEWISH ANCESTRY" from authentic Nazi sources.

Hollings was a confirmed religious fanatic and believed implicitly in the "prophecies" of the Anglo-Saxon Federation. He was thoroughly steeped in the teachings of the cult. No matter that some of his beliefs were based on such forgeries as *Washington's Vision* and *Benjamin Franklin's Diary*. Blind religious fervor spurred Hollings to desperate missionary work. And enslaved by Nazi complexes he looked forward to an uprising by "patriots" simultaneously from the East and the West, to which the Axis powers would give direct support.

"What's that? What's that you just said?" I asked incredulously.

"I said," Hollings repeated calmly and with the conciseness of a professor, "that when the American people revolt from the East and the West at a preordained hour to battle Communism, we shall receive direct aid from the Axis powers. This aid will come both from Japan and Germany."

"Do you mean to say that Japan and Germany will intervene in a military way to establish nationalism here?" I asked.

"What I mean, precisely," Hollings continued, "is that both Japan and Germany will help us fight to preserve the Constitution by sending over whatever military aid becomes necessary. This is according to prophecy."

I leaned back limp against my bed, where I had been sitting.

"What's the matter. Do you feel weak?" Hollings and Allen both came over.

"No," I said. "It was your prophecy. I had a revelation myself."

"What was it? Tell me," Hollings urged.

"It was nothing," I answered. "It was abortive. It went away. Now, coming back to the Axis," I resumed, "I suppose you look upon Hitler as . . . a sort of guardian."

"Hitler is the Redeemer of the American Constitution!" Hollings said.

Hollings also predicted victory for National-Socialism, after which would arrive a millennium of peace, life eternal, the liberation of American Indians, etc., etc. It was taken verbatim from the Nazi dream bag. Hollings had read it so many times that he came to believe the prophecy to be his own.

"The Kingdom of God shall come," he said impressively, "but it will be preceded by a confusion, during which time this country will be torn by revolution."

"Let's be practical," I said. "What can you and I do to hurry along the Kingdom of God. I'm no good at waiting."

"There is a lot that you and I can do. The whispering campaign is a good method. Holding quiet meetings at homes or offices is another method. There are many ways you can do the work of the Lord. Today there are many groups with opinions which differ as to method but are unanimous as to the ultimate ends. Some of these groups are always battling each other. You tell me it happened at the Boise convention. That is a healthy sign. It shows that we are in a battling mood. But some day these groups will forget their differences and merge under one leadership and one common aim."

"What will that aim be?" I asked.

"The Kingdom of God, of course. The factor which will bring them together may be racial or it may be political, but they'll be united eventually. The America First Committee brought many of the groups under one leadership."

"But it was Jew-controlled," Allen put in. This was the Nazi party line which was evolved when the America First Committee disbanded, and thus ostensibly ended its career of appeasement and psychological sabotage.

Hollings answered Allen: "That made no difference. It united the large majority of the people under nationalist leadership, and that is what counted. If there were any Jews on it they would have been thrown out eventually."

I switched the conversation back to Hitler and Nazi Germany.

"Hitler wanted peace, world peace," Hollings declared. "It was Poland which first invaded Germany and naturally Germany had to retaliate. Hitler merely wants to unite the German people under one leadership. The Lord permits you to do that, you know."

I saw my guests to the door, after which I immediately took to jotting down my notes. It was a long time before I could fall asleep, before I could reconcile myself to the truth that what I had just heard had taken place in a city founded by a great spiritual leader who had fled from persecution and oppression! I wondered how many times the great Brigham Young had already turned over in his grave at the sight of his co-religionists planning and plotting an era of persecution and bloodshed which would far exceed the oppressions which his own followers had suffered.

"A group of the boys are meeting up in my room this afternoon," McKnight said on the second day of my stay at Salt Lake City.

"I'll be there," I said.

"And come to my office any time you want to. The door is always open during the day. Come in and use the typewriter. Make yourself perfectly at home," McKnight insisted.

I whiled away my afternoons, typing and making notes of letters and booklets which McKnight left loosely on his desk or closet. The temptation to make copies was great, but I had to be extremely careful for the "boys" dropped in unexpectedly. I trained myself to listen to the slightest footstep and instantly go back to typing innocent letters to mother.

Among the "boys" was Alfred F. Hust, the photographer, whose shop was a few doors from McKnight's office. Hust pouted perpetually against the F.B.I. "They won't let me alone. They always come around to my shop and my home and ask questions." A short beefy, belligerent man, with surly lips and volatile temper, he had been interned as an alien dur-

Hon. J.H. McKnight,   P. O. Box 1326,
Attorney-at-Law,   Tacoma, Washington.
207 Atlas Building   March 26, 1942
Salt Lake City, Utah.

My dear Sir:

     Through the kindness of one person in the name of Mrs. Lois de Lafayette Washburn, General Delivery, Seattle, Washington, your name, letter and copy of her latest reply to you, have been forwarded to the writer; same before the writer.

     So the Yankee element, and the Nationalist element, (it is understood that you are a nationalist - native born -) are PREPARING for the coming revolution. They are NOT interested in REFORMING anything. They are interested ONLY in revolution and ARE preparing for it. The Communists have prepared for revolution

     Therefore, an institution is afoot in the making. It shall, undoubtedly, be led by Yankees, with an expected following of millions of other good and patriotic Americans. They, these Yankees certainly know among other good Americans, that an American Second Revolution is inevitable, because they also know that the

                           Respectfully,

                           F.W. Clark

Enclosure.   FRANK W. CLARK.

Excerpts from the inflammatory letter "patriot" Clark wrote McKnight on March 26, 1942.

ing the World War. "They want to know if I've been taking pictures. Of course I have—that's my business. I take them in my studio every day."

Hust was a member of the Steuben Society. During a dinner tendered by Steubenites in honor of Nazi Consul and spy ringleader, Fritz Wiedemann, Hust had gone over "just to shake his hand, that's all," he asserted, and continued: "I never receive any literature or anything. But listen," he said softly, "if you send me anything do it through McKnight."

One of the regulars at McKnight's office was David Slider Richton, nicknamed "Hitler Richton." He had a colossal head, which seemed to be bulging in all directions, a large beet-red nose and frowsy white hair.

"Why do they call you Hitler Richton," I asked.

"Because of the poem I wrote *Hitler's Not a Bad Man After All.* I'll recite it for you. . . ." He did recite it, without waiting to be asked. The doggerel verse ran nine stanzas:

Hitler's not a bad man, the world must have him wrong,
So thought that I should tell you in the rhythmic verse or song,
He's trying to help the Have-nots
Cause the Haves claim nearly all,
Hitler's not a bad man after all.

Richton asked for my birthday and hour of birth and when I had told him, he said: "I've been watching you. You're a natural-born Mormon, and the date and hour of your birth show that you like adventure and like to work alone."

"That's true," I said. "What else can you tell about me?"

"You also like to investigate. You will make a good investigator." Then he asked sharply, "Have you ever done any investigating?"

"I never have," I answered, "but I'd like to try it some day."

Another of the boys visiting McKnight was Alvey C. Johnson, a former policeman. A powerfully built chap, Johnson was the silent type. He just sat back and listened.

"I sure like to see McKnight get mad," he said.

"I'll bet he makes the other guys look sick," I said.

"You bet he does," Johnson answered, and recounted how one day in court a witness whom McKnight was examining had called him a liar. "So McKnight just slams the witness on the jaw right in court. . . ."

"Yes?" I asked, curious.

"And breaks the witness' jaw. But that's nothing—he's beat up a lot of guys around here."

I wondered what might happen if McKnight knew that just before his arrival I had been going through his closet and found the speeches of Senators Nye, Wheeler and Charles W. Tobey; Congressmen William G. Stratton and Philip A. Bennett; copies of *The X-Ray;* Pelley's and Sanctuary's booklets; Winrod's *Revealer;* tracts from John B. Snow; We, the Mothers Mobilize and America First.

McKnight had kept the carbon copy of a letter he had written Clark, suggesting a "secret conference" at his mine "in the wilds of Nevada where there is no water but it would be an ideal place to go." There was also a letter from General Moseley: "Your good letter is appreciated. Our people are awakening to the dangers. . . . The campaign of education must go on."

"What did the judge do to McKnight?" I asked Johnson.

"He fined him $500 for contempt of court. McKnight paid it, then facing the judge he says: 'Your honor, I should like to have the privilege of paying another $500 if the court will allow me to break the defendant's other jaw!'"

Johnson shook with laughter. . . . Just then, McKnight strode in. He seemed unusually huge and bony and tough.

"Hello," I said and went back to my typing, while he went to the closet to hang up his coat.

"Hey! Who in hell has been playing around with my stuff," he roared.

I kept on typing, while he inspected the closet. "Maybe it was the washwomen who do the cleaning at night," I said.

"They never come into this office," he answered.

"In that case it must be the Jews," I said with finality. "You must really keep the door locked from now on, Mr. McKnight."

"I'll rip to pieces anybody I find fiddling around with my stuff," he bellowed in the loudest voice I had ever heard in an office room.

Luckily, the "boys" began to arrive for their mid-afternoon

chinfest in McKnight's cluttered law office. They filed in one by one: Hust, Hollings, Johnson, Allen and a newcomer named Rooney. Rooney was one of the most obscene men I had ever heard. Every other word was interspersed with a frightful oath. And oddly enough, he was a beautician—but business was understandably bad.

McKnight's offices in the Atlas Building served the purpose of the village general store with the potbellied stove of yesterday. Almost every afternoon his fascist cronies gathered around his desk to review current events with native fascist glasses. At these informal conclaves McKnight presided as the patriarch. He sat behind his desk, placed his huge ham-hands on the table or waved them majestically through the smoke-filled air and apostrophized his disciples in flowing, eloquent prose. I can see him this minute, as I saw him on the hot July afternoon, with his shirt-sleeves rolled up, and the winter underwear showing underneath. I was told that the Mormon religion requires full length flannel underwear the year round (for men only). On the most boiling hot day, you would see McKnight in his heavy underwear.

McKnight regarded himself as a man with a mission and believed that he would be called upon to lead fellow Mormons in battle to "save the Constitution." His disciples sat in a semicircle around him, in sturdy chairs you could lean back on, kick in the ribs and have them stand up under the beating. Tough men, these followers of his, fanatics all. Today they had met to do me special honor. I was a guest from New York. I had attended the Boise convention. I was a friend of such-and-such a "patriot." I had once published *The Christian Defender*. I was now touring the country, "co-ordinating" "patriotic" sentiment. I was a "patriot" they all looked up to. They had all come to hear me talk.

But I turned the tables—and I made them talk. I accomplished this by the simple device of saying that I'd talk after they had all had their say. By then it was nearly supper time.

Rooney started the session by mimicking the Jew. He had done it on countless occasions, but this time it was for my special benefit. "They are trying to get us to hate the Germans, the Japs, the Italians. But, by golly, they can't," he said.

I asked McKnight if he believed, like Hollings, that we'd

have to get aid from the Axis nations to "preserve the Constitution."

"No doubt of that," he said. "It'll be the same as it was in Spain. Spain could not have won unless the Axis had sent over help. And in this country, we'll have to get the help of both Germany and Japan."

"Then you look upon Hitler favorably," I observed.

"He is an agent of the Lord," were McKnight's exact words. I can never forget them.

"The only thing we can do now is to continue with our whispering campaign," Hollings put in. "Pressure will be brought upon the government in due time to create the necessary period of national chaos, then revolution, then the Kingdom of God."

He went over to McKnight's desk and pulled out a booklet entitled *Is God a Jew?* This was a new one on me. In the East I had heard the Hebraic ancestry of Christ questioned as a stock propaganda device of the Nazis, but this was the first time I had noticed any bother about God Himself. The thirty-six-page booklet was written by Hollings under the imprint of the Christian Party Headquarters, and illustrated with drawings from Pelley's *Liberation* and the *Deutscher Weckruf*. According to Hollings God was *not* a Jew.

It was about this time that eight Nazi saboteurs were caught by the F.B.I. after being landed on Long Island and Florida. Hust belittled the work of the F.B.I. "Nothing like it happened. It's all fake and humbug. What dumb people—these Americans are. They believe whatever they read." The arrest and conviction of Bundists on charges of espionage, too, was a frame-up, according to Hust.

I asked McKnight directly if we should really do our part to help bring about a condition which would necessitate Axis help.

"Yes, of course," he said. "That is what we should do."

"How can we best go about it?" I asked.

"The whispering campaign is one good method. Meetings like this are fine. None of the boys are buying defense bonds. There are a lot of ways we can go about it. The leaven is here, and will leaven the whole, spreading from mouth to mouth, from home to home. We'll have a revolution here, sure as the sunrise tomorrow."

"I'll remember," I said, and went to pay my farewell respects to Stokes. He was moving offices and had remained away from our meetings. I asked Stokes his opinion of the so-called crackpots in the movement.

"We have got to have the extremists to put our message across," he said. "There must be those who'll be so saturated with the message that they'll stop at nothing. We cannot minimize their role. They are the martyrs to the cause. They are the trail blazers, and guideposts. We can learn a lot from their mistakes. Then, too, they publicize our movement and bring it to the attention of the masses. Don't overlook the role of those you call crackpots. They're just as important to the patriotic movement as you and I."

"What should our job be from now on?" This was a stock question in my repertory.

"It's the job of people like you and me to keep things stirring. It's our job to educate the masses of the people and arouse them. Now when you go back East and stop off to see Hudson and Pelley, boost them up. They'll need encouragement. We all need it."

I said I'd do that. With this we shook hands and parted.

I had been investigating the Mormon City fascist cell for five days. I had seen only one side, the ugly side, of the Mormon religionists. I wanted to know to what extent the Nazi sympathies of McKnight and his gang had permeated the Mormon Church. I decided to attend services at the Capitol Hill Ward, Church of the Latter Day Saints. It was situated atop a hill and overlooked the rest of the city. In the early morning sunlight it shone like an etching against the azure sky.

I had never been to a Mormon Church and I was extremely curious to observe the ceremonies. But even more, I wanted to see how widely prevalent were the beliefs I had been hearing for the past few days. I reasoned that my impromptu attendance at one of the many wards would supply me with a fair test.

The interior of the Capitol Hill Ward resembled a little New England Church. The congregation of about two hundred youths and adults impressed me as being particularly clean-cut. There were no trappings, no ritualistic procedure, no vestments of any kind. The Bishop was dressed in his Sunday best and so were his assistants. The services—consisting of hymns, a brief reading from the Mormon Book of Prayer and the partaking of a tiny glass of water and a bite of bread —were extremely simple. The service was followed by an open discussion in which everyone was eligible to participate. The procedure was thoroughly democratic.

One fine middle-aged Mormon got up and said that in his spare time he was urging friends to invest in war bonds. He suggested the Ward launch a campaign to stimulate sales among the parish. "While our boys are fighting the enemy," he said, "we must remain good soldiers at home so that they won't be disappointed in us when they return."

The Bishop, a youthful man in his late thirties with a clear voice and earnest manner, asked whether anyone would care to express an opinion regarding the Soviet system of State control over a child's education. "I don't think that we ought to judge the Russian system too harshly," another Mormon spoke. "Right now the Russians are fighting heroically and I think that this can partly be traced back to their education. We ought to respect the fighting quality of the Russian peo-- ple at this time instead of being critical of them."

I listened as another Mormon got up to speak. She seemed to be a grandmother and had aged gracefully. "One of my sons and three of my grandsons are in the army and navy," she said with quiet dignity. "And I want to see them come back. But lately I have been hearing nasty rumors against such things as the morale of our boys and the way they feed them and treat them. Now I believe it is very un-American for anyone to spread around such gossip and I'd like to suggest that our Bishop look into it."

I could have taken leave of the Mormon City with the impression that *all* Mormons were like McKnight, Hollings, Hust, Stokes, Allen, Rooney and others I met. I could have been scarred by that image, and when asked back East what I thought of Salt Lake City, I could have said: "It's full of fascists," for it is the easiest thing in the world to fall into lying generalities. It saves you from thinking.

But as it was I took leave of Salt Lake City with my faith in its beauty, and its promise of the future fully restored by the random Ward meeting I had attended.

CHAPTER IX

MIDWEST ROUNDUP

"I was in Washington having lunch with Martin Dies and others on his Committee, when Dies turns around and asks me if I know George Pagnanelli."

COURT ASHER

I STOOD AT the corner of Grant Street in Omaha and looked at the rows of frame cottages. They were the kind of homes you see everywhere in America. I couldn't see the street numbers, but I knew instantly which was "Poison Cup" Charles B. Hudson's home. A lone American flag hung from the porch. Everybody else on the block took Americanism for granted. Hudson screamed it out.

An intimate collaborator with countless fascist operatives, Hudson had served the nationalist cause with uncommon fealty and was cited by *World Service*. After Pearl Harbor he redoubled his efforts and fanned the flames of national disunity through his organ, *America in Danger*. And he preferred to remain in contempt of court rather than reveal those who financed the publication of a tract which was so vicious and defeatist that Hudson added the line: "This card is intended only for Americans in possession of their full civic rights; it is not intended for the armed forces of the U.S.A."

Hudson's face was uninteresting, but his eyes, like the ostentatious display of the flag, gave him away. They burned with zealot fire. He was in his early sixties and fired with a dynamic energy in the righteousness of his cause. His wife, a pleasant-looking woman, believed implicitly in his ideas.

"My husband is fighting Communism," she said seriously. "I think the Government should subsidize him for the patriotic work he has done for the last seven years."

Hudson proved a difficult subject to interview. He had appeared before so many investigational bodies that getting information out of him was like pulling the proverbial tooth. At first he confined his answers to curt replies, but after three hours of clever dodging on his part and insistent questioning on mine, I exacted from him the admissions that he had associated with:

William Dudley Pelley	General George Van Horn Moseley
James True	
Reverend Gerald B. Winrod	Mrs. Leslie Fry
Colonel E. N. Sanctuary	Henry D. Allen
William Kullgren	Lawrence Dennis
Mrs. Elizabeth Dilling	Mrs. Lois de Lafayette Washburn
Court Asher	
Edward Hunter	Frank W. Clark
Jacob Thorkelson	Jeremiah Stokes
Edwin Perry Banta	George Edward Sullivan
Representative Clare Hoffman	National Workers League

"Do you know any Bundists?" I asked casually.

"The Bund is un-American," Hudson said with blazing eyes.

So far my interview had proved disappointing, but as in the case of super-super-patriot, Mrs. Farber, I had the feeling that Hudson would eventually unlock the door behind which he had barricaded himself.

"Let's take this stuff down to the post office," he said, pointing to bundles of *America in Danger* I had helped assemble. In the car, with a large box of envelopes on my lap, I was looking through them for familiar names when my eyes fell on an envelope marked "Personal" and "Confidential," and addressed: "Hon. Eugene Talmadge, State Capitol Building, Atlanta, Georgia." I looked at Hudson out of the corner of my eye. He was driving and his eyes seemed set on the road. I wondered what confidential letter Hudson was sending the Governor.

"Let's drive over to the park," Hudson said after we left the post office.

Sitting in the car, he started by expressing admiration for General Moseley and Mrs. Leslie Fry. I asked if her former plans could be carried out today.

"I don't think so," he said, "but I know a plan that will work. It's the Vigilante Plan."

He explained it had been inspired by the Associated Farmers

which under financial assistance by reactionary business men and anti-labor groups, had taken the law into their hands, resorting to terrorism toward anyone they regarded as "Communist." I asked Hudson for more details about the Associated Farmers—who were farmers in name only.

"In California they're a state-wide organization. They're composed of 'select men,' carefully chosen patriots. They're banded loosely and are available at a minute's call—just by phoning. We ought to have the same plan on a national scale in every state. I'm against a centralized leadership of patriotic forces at this time," Hudson continued. "What I'd like to see are small, tightly-knit groups in each locality."

"Poison Cup Charlie" was against the idea of joining an organization.

"You are always a target and the larger the organization the bigger the target. Then there's always the chance of being smeared with the bad ones in the lot. Large organizations are no good at this time and I'm too smart to join any of them. I'd rather work alone with my wife."

At midnight the next day I was at Lincoln, Nebraska, to interview Charles W. Phillips, publisher of *The Individualist* about whom I had been hearing considerable among "patriotic" circles. From the cool heights of Salt Lake City I came to the broiling hell of the Midwest. In Omaha I had seen the thermometer 112° in the shade. Lincoln seemed even hotter.

Phillips was a small, sharp man, wearing rimless glasses, with the familiar pallor of library workers. A lawyer by profession, he hadn't practiced in years. Instead, he had been devoting his time since 1935 to saving the Republic via the "patriotic" route. Phillips drove me to his home and I met his hospitable wife who shared his views. The reading of the *Protocols*, she said, "opened our eyes to the internationalists."

"I've known Hudson for many years," Phillips said, "and I think he is a fine fellow." But you can't dismiss Phillips by saying that he was like another Hudson. He wasn't. Although he had been investigated by Federal authorities, I had the conviction that Phillips would prove more dangerous in the long run to the cause of Democracy. He was the type who bored quietly from within, not noisily from the outside like Charlie "Woodpecker" Hudson.

Phillips confided that he was opposed violently to the present capitalist order, saying we were "victims of a system that cashes in on human greed." But when I asked him for a substitute, he fell back to the "need of a spiritual awakening" to solve our social, political and economic ills. He disclaimed anti-Semitism, but did make sweeping generalities against Jews.

As I sat in Phillips' home, with blinds drawn to keep out the scorching heat, I thought of the old saying: "A man is known by the company he keeps." To begin with, there were James True, Elizabeth Dilling and Colonel Sanctuary whom he knew personally. He had conferred with John B. Snow, Joseph P. Kamp and Fred R. Marvin whose book was recommended by *World Service*. Phillips had corresponded with General Moseley and fascist Seward Collins. He received Edmondson's and Gerald L. K. Smith's propaganda tracts. Phillips had also been needled by American Nazi Lawrence Dennis' bulletins; by fascist Nesta Webster's books and by other "patriotic" literature, issued by the pro-Nazi Boswell Publishing Company of London.

Opposing Lend-Lease, national defense and adulating Lindbergh and his nativist *ism, The Individualist* clearly reflected the extent to which Phillips had been influenced by his political associates. In it he recommended all of Japanese agent Ralph Townsend's booklets, saying: "These pamphlets should be in your files"; he quoted fascist Lawrence Dennis at length; he urged readers to buy Sanctuary's and Harry A. Jung's poison tracts and he based a series of issues of *The Individualist* on the mouthings of one Frank A. Parker, an obscure, self-styled economist who addressed many meetings of Kurt Mertig's Nazi front, Citizens Protective League.

Although he had read *Social Justice*, Phillips did not like Father Coughlin. "He is a rabble-rouser," he said, "and I don't like rabble-rousers." Phillips wasn't the type to like noise and thunder and bombast, but one who worked quietly and studiously, preferring to associate with "gentlemen fascists" like John B. Snow.

Riding in the train the next morning, I reviewed the events of the past few weeks. I had learned that the pattern of fascism in the West was identical with that in the East, but that the "wild" West emphasized direct methods, while the East was held down more by conventions and went in rather for propaganda scheming. I looked at the trainful of soldiers and sailors, most of whom were laughing and happy, carousing with their female acquaintances or kidding around with fellow soldiers. It was likely that none were aware of the existence of an enemy army on the home front, an enemy which did not drop bombs nor fly planes but worked stealthily underground, boring quietly from within at those pillars of Democracy on which their morale rested.

I still had stops to make in Chicago and Indianapolis before going home. I wanted to be home in time to see Steven, my youngest brother, off to the army. He had just been graduated from Fordham University and passed his State Bar Examinations. Steve was the first in our family to be drafted (eight months later John followed), and the event was comparable to the day mother and father received their citizenship papers.

In Chicago, I wanted to look up Harry Augustus Jung, who was friendly with countless "patriots." In fact, Jung was no small fry. His work had been subsidized by banks, by industrialists and by rich old women scared to death by the Communist revolution "around the corner." Harry Augustus Jung was director of the American Vigilant Intelligence Federation represented in the East by his collaborator, Colonel Sanctuary. He styled himself the "nation's foremost authority on subversive forces."

With his usual caution, Jung had written me a cryptic note in pencil: "Anytime you come in will be okeh. I am usually here from 9 A.M. to 6 P.M. Call up before you come—Superior 4618."

"I can't see you today," he said when I phoned.

"How about this evening or tomorrow?" I asked.

"Sorry, Mr. Pagnanelli. I've just been subpoenaed to testify before the grand jury and I'd better not see you—especially since you are going to go into the army.

"I hope I'll hear from you when you're drafted," Jung said and hung up.

In 1933, Jung made membership in his American Vigilant Intelligence Federation secret, with secret codes and mysterious rituals. And in 1935 its organ *The Vigilante* had so well served the fascist cause that *World Service* placed it on its honor roll. Jung also went into the wholesale distribution of the *Protocols* and wrote Harry F. Sieber, then treasurer of the Silver Shirts:

We can give you a price of sixty cents per copy in quantity lots of the *Protocols*. As for *Halt Gentile!* and *Salute the Jew*, same can be had at ten cents per copy, in quantity lots or fifteen cents a-piece.

Jung's associates in those days included Peter Afansieff, a White Guard Russian, born in Petrograd in 1893, who arrived in San Francisco in 1922. With three other White Russians Afansieff worked on a new translation of the *Protocols* in Jung's office, and soon after became affiliated with the New York and Chicago branches of the Bund. When he assumed the alias, Prince Peter Kushubue, the doors of society opened to him and the bogus prince almost succeeded in getting a wealthy heiress to marry him.

But when the scheme fell through, the frustrated "prince" changed his name to Armstrong and tried his hand at forgery. He was convicted of forging a United States Treasury check and Federal Judge F. J. Kerrigan sentenced him to eighteen months in the penitentiary.

Together with Captain Victor de Kayville (born Livok) a former officer in the Czarist Army who jumped ship, Afansieff helped publish *The American Gentile*. It was a "patriotic, American pro-Aryan" semi-monthly published "for the defense of Gentile culture and civilization." James True and Robert Edward Edmondson wrote for it and articles from *World Service* found their way in. *The American Gentile* became the filthiest Nazi-front sheet of its period in Chicago and deserved the praise which it received in *World Service*. In February, 1935, Jung accused Afansieff of withholding funds and the two parted company.

In the meanwhile and with uncommon "patriotic" versatility, Jung was "fighting Communism" by obtaining funds from both Jewish and Christian firms. Jung solicitors told wealthy Gentiles they were combating "Jewish Communism," while wealthy Jews were told that the Vigilantes were "combating Communism."

Among those seduced by Jung under the delusion that they were supporting a worthy cause (during 1931–1934) were the Rockford National Bank, First National Bank of Joliet, Illinois; International Harvester, William Wrigley, Florsheim Shoe Company, Sears Roebuck and Company and many others. The biggest sucker, however, proved to be the aged Mrs. Finley J. Sheppard, daughter of the late Jay Gould, who gave away millions. Scared out of her wits at the "coming Communist revolution," she was shaken down for $5,000 by Jung and his cronies. Jung was the first Park Avenue "patriot" to go after the big money boys, first to sell the *Protocols* and first to share offices with an Illinois Klan leader, Gale S. Carter, who was number 37 in Jung's super-secret membership list.

In addition to these samples of "patriotism," Jung had another profitable pastime. He maintained a labor spy and strike-breaking establishment and kept extensive files of persons and organizations he considered "radical." Jung sold this "confidential information" for high fees. The late speaker of the House, Henry T. Rainey, summed up his exploits in a letter he wrote Jung:

My files show that you are a sort of detective, worming your way into the homes of the most trusted members of labor organizations and obtaining information with which to combat the efforts of labor organizations to better their conditions, and that you obtain this information for the purpose of assisting "strike breakers."

The data I have show that you foment strikes in the districts where there is no union and then settle the strike for a price. The information I have with reference to you is that you are the man who does the slimy, stool pigeon work necessary for the purpose of destroying organized labor wherever it has contractual relations with employers.

This was the background of the man I wanted to see.

Jung had changed his tactics in recent years. He now spent lavishly to bury his past and put on the cloak of respectability. He became a specialist on "Americanism" and graduated to lecturing before the Chicago Athletic Association and the Racquet Club. He was befriended by Colonel Robert R. McCormick, publisher of the *Chicago Tribune* and had his office in Room 2212 of the Tribune Tower, dubbed the "Devil's Tower." My disappointment at not being able to see him was bitter for Jung was one of the "big shots," with a tremendous capacity for mischief to the democratic cause.

I realized that the Chicago grand jury investigating un-American activity would seriously conflict with my own work and I knew that my "friends" would remain underground until the storm passed over.

None the less, I phoned Mrs. Mabel J. Willard, whom McKnight had urged me to see and she, to my surprise, asked me to visit her at her home. I had seen evidence of their voluminous correspondence and it was apparent that some of McKnight's schooling was due to her efforts. In September, 1941, she had written McKnight:

Am enclosing an article written by an Ex-Col. in the last Worlds War—signature is his nonde-plume—[he] is limited on finances, so we try to get his material before the public with *no* signature. . . .

Did you read the Edmondson Case "Jews Vs. Christians in Court." If not, I'll send one to you. . . . "Roosevelt's Jewish Ancestry" gives a full chart. You may have it. If I make any suggestions which you know or have, forgive me—these come out of New York to me, and [I] keep sending them on. If you don't have *The X-Ray*, Muncie, Ind., get it, he's fearless. *The Herald* put out by Scribner's Lake Geneva, Wis. is new.

. . . Here is a party to get in touch with, a personal friend of Gov. Talmedge—Mrs. J. E. Andrews, 319 Pulliam Street, S. W. Atlanta. . . . Under separate cover am sending a bunch of data to Governor Talmedge.

I was not surprised to see Governor Talmadge's name reappear. Both Hudson and Mrs. Willard realized the former Governor's aptitudes to participate in the native American fascist movement. In another letter to McKnight dated September 3, 1941, she had written:

I find no one from Utah? Can you get a list of Utah names to me. I'll send them on to W. coast. I'm having a party, David Baxter, of San Bernardino, Calif. get in touch with you. He's in accord with our views but working them *very* quietly & in a different manner. A 3rd party is being fostered and you may be the key man in Utah for just that, and please do not give Mrs. Coleman that information. This place [Chicago] is the anti-war Capitol, also Peace Mecca. . . . Mrs. Dilling is the baby that has their goats, her *Red Network* sure pours it on them. That leaves the field clear for our work. . . .

Our fight *is now*. Nathan Hale didn't wait for an election. Some [day] these big wigs are going to find they will have to follow & bow to the masses—& soon. Lindbergh is a natural. . . . He was here to see General Wood.

We are putting on a luncheon September 9th for 300 at Sherman Hotel. I'm on the Committee, have speakers to contact, and oodles of work ahead—so am forgetting my Hebrew complex for a few days.

It was apparent from the look of her home that Mrs. Willard did not care for housekeeping. There were other things about which, however, she did care. "Every time a German is killed," she said, "it means there is one white man less to fight the Asiatics." By Asiatics she meant Jews, not the Japs.

"I hope every one of these Bundists is caught," she said and when, in surprise, I queried why, she answered: "Because you'll find them all to be Communists."

Mrs. Willard would not admit that a nasty man could be anything but a Communist, a Jew, or a tool of either or both. As our conversation progressed I gathered that she seemed to revolve in the center of nativist circles. She was a close friend of Mrs. Dilling and Mrs. Van Hyning, Clark and Mrs. Washburn. She had been active in the America First Committee, in We, the Mothers Mobilize and prided herself on the methods she had used to hide her tracks.

"We must not all stick out our necks," she told me in a confidential tone. "Somebody will have to do the work when others are jailed. Some of us must be left to carry on."

She told me of the support General Wood, chairman of the America First Committee, had given We, the Mothers Mobilize.

"The General helped us out several times." I pinned her down to whether or not he had given a specific contribution, and Mrs. Willard said: "Sure, he once gave us $100."

"Did that show on the books?" I asked.

"Not on your life," she answered. "I took care of that. I put it down in pencil. After Pearl Harbor I just erased it from the books and no trace remained of General Wood's contribution."

"That was pretty clever," I said.

"The America First Committee is the same today as it was before. But they don't know it." By "they" Mrs. Willard meant "the enemy"—anybody who did not believe as she did. "They think the Committee is disbanded. Far from it. It's active just the same, but it's working in other ways now."

Time and again Mrs. Willard broke off the conversation to investigate me with her own queries. I answered her to her satisfaction and she continued to give me considerable information. She had corresponded with Boris Brasol, the White Russian fascist; with Sanctuary, General Moseley and Mrs. Farber. She held Cathrine Curtis in great esteem and had worked closely with David Baxter, the California revolutionist who had been her guest.

"He walked around the block a few times to make sure he wasn't being followed, then he came in and slept right on that couch there. I haven't kept any of his letters," she said, "because they were dangerous. They can't pin a thing on me since Pearl Harbor. Why I'm so patriotic now that I'm even an air-raid warden and I do work for the A.W.V.S. The only thing for us now is to bore from within and show them a thing or two later on."

Mrs. Willard couldn't deny being in touch with Pelley because she had many of his booklets on the table. She kept her subversive literature all over the house, and for my benefit dug out pieces from under the davenport, from among the linen in the closet and made two trips to the kitchen.

"I have it all over," she said, "so that when they search the house they won't find it all in one place."

It was silly; none the less, Mrs. Willard was a symbol. From all I had seen and read, I gathered that there were a lot of women like her in the Chicago area, each engaged in tearing down what other Americans were trying to build up.

Even though I had cordial invitations from Mrs. Lyrl Van Hyning of We, the Mothers Mobilize (of which I, as Pagnanelli, was a card-holding member) and others, I knew that it would reflect on me suspiciously if I remained while the grand jury investigations were on. It was bitterly disappointing because I sensed that Chicago was the hotbed of a native fascism which was truly alarming in proportion and intensity. I had never had this feeling before. As I analyze Chicago, I can readily understand why. In addition to the Dillings, Jungs, Van Hynings, Willards, the America First Committee which had first festered there, there was the factor of the "Washington-New York-Chicago newspaper Axis," with the *Chicago Tribune* as the cornerstone.

Its publisher was a remarkable and profound man. He himself said so—and who should know better than Colonel Robert R. McCormick, "Bertie" for short. He thus appraised himself in a letter he wrote a correspondent on February 20, 1942:

You do not know it, but the fact is that I introduced the R.O.T.C. into the schools; that I introduced machine guns into the army; that I introduced mechanization; I introduced automatic rifles; I was the first ground officer to go up in the air and observe artillery fire. Now I have succeeded in making that the regular practice in the army. I was the first to advocate an alliance with Canada. I forced the acquiring of bases in the Atlantic Ocean. . . . I did get the marines out of Shanghai, but was unsuccessful in trying to get the army out of the Philippines.

Campaigns such as I have carried on inevitably meet resistance, and great persistence is necessary to achieve results. The opposition resorts to such tactics as charging me with hatred and so forth, but in view of the accomplishment I can bear up under it.

More serious was the damage to our morale which the influence of McCormick caused in the Midwest. He held up Jung as an "authority on Communism" and commended Mrs. Dilling for her "patriotism and devotion." Whereas the influence of the Dillings and Jungs extended among thousands only, "Bertie" reached millions (average daily circulation of the *Tribune* was 1,076,866) with a daily barrage of obstructionism and defeatism of the war effort, carping at the national leadership, berating Democracy and denouncing our military allies under the guise of "patriotism" and "freedom of the press."

His value to the divisionist cause in America was manifest as early as 1935 when *World Service* endorsed the *Chicago Tribune*, along with the *Chicagoer Weckruf*. In 1941, the *Tribune* as well as the Hearst chain of newspapers (Hearst was burned in effigy by soldiers in New York during the World War because he was pro-German) earned the plaudits of Nazi agent Viereck in a letter he wrote to his boss, Heinrich Dieckhoff.

Other partners of the "newspaper Axis" were the New York *Daily News*, published by McCormick's cousin, Captain Joseph Medill Patterson; and the Washington *Times-Herald*, published by Patterson's sister, Eleanor "Cissy" Patterson. Their combined audience was estimated at five million readers daily. The party line was the same for all three.

On December 14, 1938 under the by-line of its Washington correspondent, John O'Donnell, the *Daily News* honored an American Nazi, Pelley, by publishing in its entirety the contents of one of his booklets purporting to show the number of "Jews in Washington." Pelley's picture was inserted and the cover of his vicious booklet reproduced. The story was featured on page two under a screaming three-column headline and continued for nearly two and a half pages.

And the August 30, 1942 editorial in the *Daily News* broached this savage "explanation" of the war:

. . . Or perhaps Hitler was not wholly to blame for this war. Perhaps there was a subconscious conviction in the minds of

F. Y. I.   Aug. 21, 1942

Berlin in English, 5.26 p. m.

Berlin, commenting on the "so-called free press of America," today cited the Chicago Tribune, the New York Daily News and the Washington Times-Herald as typical examples of what the American press was up against under Roosevelt's dictatorship. These newspapers, being true American papers and representing the majority of American people, are being persecuted by the Roosevelt administration even to being accused as saboteurs of the war effort.

many Europeans that there were too many people in Europe anyway, and that a big blood-letting might help matters.

"Hardly a day goes by," wrote William Shirer, "that they [these three papers] are not cited by Goebbels to prove one of his points." And as I stood on the Chicago sidewalk and looked at the impressive office building of the *Tribune*, with McCormick sitting high up in his ivory tower I recalled the righteous indignation of Congressman Elmer J. Holland which he expressed so eloquently in the *Congressional Record*.

Despite their cloak of prosperity, their fine building . . . these three papers are in spirit and in conduct members of the "vermin press." Separate their editorials from the trappings of a large city newspaper, publish them as a separate book, and read them as a continuous theme. You will see their net effect is to preach defeatism among our civilians and mutiny among our soldiers, to spread dismay among our allies, and to create joy in the hearts of our enemies. . . .

This is no small matter. . . . This means that approximately 5% of the total population of these United States is being daily exposed to the virus of Fascist philosophy—to the direct assault of the enemy propaganda campaign. No propaganda broadcast of the Axis radio—no enemy leaflets—can reach so many Americans as do these Fascists of the native brand.

With deadly effect the corrupt Parisian press poisoned and paralyzed the spirit and morale of the French. And—when we recall that the total circulation of the most powerful members of this venal press reached less than one half of one percent of the total population of France—we can clearly judge the danger with which *we* are faced.

It is not necessary to be in contact with the enemy in order to bring him aid and comfort. It is only necessary to share a common hatred; to desire the same results; to think in the same patterns. . . . This is a foreign war, yet it is also a war of ideas. . . . To the end that this group consists of Americans, Mr. Speaker, this war is a civil war as well as a foreign war. It cannot be won until our enemies at home are conquered and rendered harmless.

Regretting my failure to make a thorough survey of Chicago's "patriots," I turned southward to Indianapolis to visit William Dudley Pelley. I knew Pelley was undersized, had a goatee, wore an oversize military hat and looked ridiculous in the uniform of the Silver Shirts. But what was it that made him such a dynamo of subversion? I was extremely curious to gauge the extent of the cunning with which he had side-stepped every effort so far to keep him in prison. Like Jung, he moved about secretly. None but his most intimate friends knew where he lived. I went to his attorney's hoping to find him in his office. It was my lucky day, for I found Pelley.

The most unforgettable impression was his hand shake—the sweatiest, unhealthiest, clammiest hand shake I ever hope to experience! I visualize him leaning against a desk, his striped shirt open down to his puffed-up belly. His undershirt was sweaty, stuck against a chest puny, narrow and sunk in. His lips were thick and the blood in them seemed to be sluggish and clotted. His hair was streaked with lifeless gray. His brows, jet black by artificial means—hung bushy over sunken eyes. His goatee and mustache, both of them white, stuck out of his small, wizened face. My initial impression was one of revulsion and disgust at the limp, dissipated grayness of the man before me. He smelled of decay.

And then I became aware of his eyes. They were like living coals buried in a heap of ashes. And in their light shone all the cunning and the wizardry which had led a half dozen investigating committees, including the F.B.I., a merry chase up to the time of our meeting. Pelley did not impress me as being fearless. His apparent nerve in defying law and authority was not one of courage and conviction in one's ideals as much as it was of contempt and derision. It was a combination of super-ego and disdain for the opinions and dictates of authority. Callous as a street urchin, Pelley impressed me as extremely ruthless and self-seeking. He was by no means a blind fanatic but on the contrary, a calculating and cold-blooded propagandist.

"Oh, yes, I remember you," he said. "You were with Joe McWilliams."

I was surprised at his memory. I hadn't written him in a year. He asked me immediately if I knew any "patriots" who would testify on his behalf as his trial for sedition was set for the following week. I suggested Ernest Elmhurst but he brushed him aside. I suggested Colonel Sanctuary.

"Oh, yes, he's coming down. We've got him."

I suggested John B. Snow.

"That's a thought. I know Snow. I'll talk it over."

"How about Carl Mote?" I asked, knowing that this wealthy Indianapolis utility magnate was his close friend.

"He'll be down. I've known Mote for ten years."

Pelley outlined his plan for the coming trial: "We are going to crack this thing wide open, this issue of free speech against dictatorship. This trial is a big thing and we're getting Lindbergh and Thorkelson to come down." Pelley expected to stretch out his trial in order to get national airing for his views. "We're going to make monkeys out of Biddle and his crowd," he boasted.

I tried to avoid it but I couldn't. Pelley stretched out his hand again. I had to take it and shake it. And as I looked into his malignant face, I wished there were some means of projecting to all "patriots" the nation over the picture of that decaying little Nazi. I felt sure that no one in his right mind could ever again look up to this mixture of malice, cunning and conceit as a missionary for "Christianity," "patriotism" and "Americanism."

It was not until I had interviewed George Henry, a prominent and respected Indianapolis attorney, that I understood how Pelley had successfully posed as a "patriot" since July 28, 1938 when he boasted in his vermin sheet, *Liberation:*

It is a fact which posterity will attest that Chief Pelley of the Silver Shirts was the first man in the United States to step out openly and support Adolf Hitler and his German-Nazi program. Hitler became German Chancellor on the 31st day of January 1933. This publication appeared on the 18th of the ensuing February openly and unashamedly endorsing Hitler and his program against the German Jewish "reds."

In contrast with Pelley, George Henry was one of the pillars of the community, a man of handsome appearance and honest convictions. But, I believed, he had developed a political blind spot which warped his sense of values. Henry admitted knowing Pelley "for some years," and said: "Pelley is a brilliant man, one of the most capable men in the country." It was his expressed opinion that Pelley was being hounded unjustly by the Department of Justice. "Sedition is what they want to make of it," he said. "There is no longer any constitutional interpretation of law."

I asked George Henry quite bluntly what he thought of Pelley.

"Of course I don't agree with everything, but I believe he has some fine points. We all have our opinions. You have yours. I have mine." On the whole, George Henry was more than favorably inclined toward Pelley. "If Pelley will handle his case right," he said, "he has a chance to do a lot of good."

Henry confided that he used to read *Social Justice* and Pelley's magazines before they were banned. The bogey of Communism was so deeply imbedded in Henry's mind, he was so hostile to the New Deal and so bitterly anti-Jewish, that he seemed completely unaware of the sinister symbolism of Pelley. The impression I got from my talk was that he condoned Pelley and condemned the Government for prosecuting a self-indicted American Nazi. If such an intelligent and respectable man—twisted, as I believed, by political hatreds—condoned Pelley's utterances, how much more gullible were apt to be the simple-minded and the less learned Pelley readers. The thought was frightening.

After seeing Pelley and Henry, I took the bus to Muncie to meet Court Asher, publisher of *The X-Ray*. It was afternoon, but that did not matter to Asher, for he was in his pajamas and with bare feet. On his arm was a tatooed nude woman with awesome bust and hips. He welcomed me into his home with a loud: "Howdy, George. Right glad to see you stop by. Martin Dies was asking about'cha."

Taken aback with the distinction of being paged by none other than the chairman of the Special Committee on Un-American Activities, I asked Asher for the details.

"I was in Washington having lunch with Dies and others on his Committee, when Dies turns around and asks me if I know George Pagnanelli."

"What did you say?" I asked.

"I told him I knew nothing about'cha. Dies is all right. I'd vote for him for President."

"Did you meet anybody else in Washington?" I asked.

"Hell, yes. Springer [Raymond S.] from Indiana was with

me all the time. He introduced me to a lot of the other boys. I met Rankin and Hoffman, both are fine gentlemen. They know the score."

"Do you know any other Congressmen?" I wanted to know.

Asher distinctly told me he had received small contributions from Congressmen Charles I. Faddis of Pennsylvania and Paul Shafer of Michigan. "Shafer sent me $10 and said to let him know if I wanted more."

Wholly unlike Pelley, Asher was on the surface, a likeable fellow, easy going, blunt of manner, candid. He told me he had met the Congressmen on one of his many appearances before the Washington grand jury. As I looked at this boyish man with the thick mop of hair, it was hard to believe he had become involved with such poison-peddlers as Pelley, Broenstrupp, Clark and the National Workers League.

"Sure I spoke for the League in Detroit and the America First Committee in Pontiac. Then I went over and had a talk with Gerald L. K. Smith. He wanted to buy out *The X-Ray*, but I wouldn't give it up. I saw Father Coughlin and asked him straight to his face if the Pope was one-fourth Jew. He sure seems to love 'em, I told Coughlin."

And yet this humorous Legionnaire had poisoned Muncie and Indianapolis with tens of thousands of copies of a defeatist weekly newspaper, a dangerous dissolvent of national unity.

"They all know me around here," he said laughing. "I'm a member of the Elks, the Eagles, the Moose and the American Legion. I used to be a member of the Klan but I gave that up. They know *The X-Ray* around here like they know their *Bible*."

Asher had reprinted freely from *Social Justice*, Hudson, Pelley, but most frequently from the *Chicago Tribune*. "When I didn't have the time to write the stuff I just took it from the other boys. They said it better than I did, so what was the difference?"

Asher had served in the World War and told me that he had been treated for what he described as "neurosis." He was highstrung, made grimaces without cause and burst into laughter without provocation. He reminded me of Verne Marshall, chairman of No Foreign War Committee who was declared to have become unnerved and was reported resting in a sanatorium. Asher also impressed me as extremely impressionable and, like Garland Alderman, was a type easily led.

Asher admitted knowing Carl Mote and said that Mote was "worth a half-million dollars." I asked if he had received financial support from the Indianapolis magnate, but Asher did not want to commit himself. George Henry, however, had assisted him.

"He sent me some money," Asher said, "but what I liked more was the two brand new tires he sent for the car."

Asher drove a handsome, gray Packard sedan, 1939 model. He owned his home. He was the first "patriot" I had met who did not complain of lack of funds. He claimed to be a close friend of George Ball, an official of the famous jar manufacturing concern at Muncie.

"George is worth $60,000,000," Asher said, "and a swell guy. I talk to him just as I'm talking to you now."

Asher was peculiar in many ways. He was one of the first "patriots" to admit candidly his friendship with prominent Congressmen and industrialists. Then, too, Asher's carefree attitude toward finances intrigued me deeply. His home, car and print-shop, were all paid for.

"Money? What good is money?" he asked. "What can you do with it? I don't know what worry is. Whenever I want money, all I have to do is to go to those boys and ask for it."

No "patriot" had *ever* talked that way to me.

Asher opened the pages of his newspaper to Edward James Smythe, the notorious American Nazi and liaison man between the Bund and the Klan, by permitting Smythe to run a weekly column in *The X-Ray*. And in the November 1, 1941, issue of *The X-Ray* Court Asher denounced Democracy in a long article:

The word "democracy" is the weapon of scoundrels and the refuge of fools. Every political pap-sucker seeking public office takes it to his breast—every war monger and public liar uses it as a shield to deceive the unwary. . . . No thank you. Before this matter is ended a great many Americans will not like the taste of "democracy."

David Baxter promptly reproduced the invective and circulated it as a preparatory "study course" for the American *der tag*.

Asher's half-literate sheet (except for the stories he lifted) could hardly provide the income to meet its current expenses, let alone maintain his home and automobile. I was convinced that big business interests must be promoting him and his defeatist sheet. Infinitely more shrewd and farseeing than Asher, these "big money boys" could be using Asher—a former bootlegger who obviously knew little about politics—as their front man to propagate anti-New Deal, anti-British, obstructionist propaganda. And Asher the crude, likable, simple-minded joiner was made to stick out his neck, and in the name of "patriotism" encourage political anti-Semitism and defamation of Democracy in Muncie, the city famed as Middletown.

Asher's friend, Carl H. Mote, is president and general manager of the Northern Indiana Telephone Company, the Commonwealth Telephone Corporation and has other utility business connections. He is an attorney and a former newspaper editor. Mote wrote at least three articles for Pelley's *Roll-Call* which appeared in the February 17, March 3, and March 24, 1941 issues. All were true to the Pelley pattern and one was so "good" that Pelley placed it on the front cover. Mote branded the President's message to Hitler at the time of the Munich appeasement as "an impudent telegram." And his apology for Hitler in *Roll-Call* was far from subtle:

Whatever may be said against the morals of Adolf Hitler, no one has ever dared accuse him of having had any part in the destruction of Germany which began with the Versailles Treaty and continued to the first months of 1933.

Judged purely by the amount of abuse and vindictiveness in his writings for Pelley's magazine, Mote hated the President and the Administration infinitely more than Hitler and National-Socialism. This note was implicit during my talk with him as we sat at the Antlers Bar in Indianapolis.

Mote was a cordial and affable host. This pleasant-faced man with the keenly piercing, sky-blue eyes and agreeable manner had associated not only with Pelley and Hudson, but had travelled to New York to meet Lawrence Dennis; the

notorious Boris Brasol and Siegfried Hauck, manager of
Viereck's publishing concern, in order to talk over the publication of a book he had written.

Mote could not deny these contacts because a New York
newspaper had already printed them. But as in all my investigations, I preferred to obtain direct testimony and I quizzed
Mote. I found him a difficult subject for several reasons: first,
because his friend Pelley was about to come up for trial; second, because he was wary after being called before the Chicago grand jury. Shrewd and often one step ahead of me,
Mote parried and dodged my questions during the three hours
we were together. But I wore him down as the night went on.
I asked and re-asked questions, in one guise or another, directly and by innuendo, till I had got all the answers I wanted.

He admitted knowing Colonel Sanctuary and John B. Snow;
he had worked closely with Mrs. Dilling; he knew Harry
Augustus Jung. He had met Seward Collins and had made
purchases at his bookshop. Mote knew Edward Hunter, the
veteran Boston pro-Nazi. He had conferred with General
Moseley, with Charles W. Phillips and with Cathrine Curtis.

"What did you think of Lawrence Dennis?" I asked Mote.

"He is a very able man," Mote answered.

Mote had the highest respect for the dean of British fascists,
Nesta Webster, whose books were distributed in America by
Snow, William Kullgren, Deatherage, Stahrenberg.

"She has taught every one of us," Mote said with fine candor.

Doubtless Mote thought himself on the right side when he
objected to peace-time conscription as a measure of national
defense. Whether he realized it at the time or not, Mote was
actually paraphrasing the Nazi short wave broadcasts when
he wrote in Pelley's *Roll-Call:*

We are spending billions for peace-time conscription, for airplanes and for ships, when most everybody suspects, though few
will dare say, that the "defense program," including peace-time
conscription, is the master hoax of the New Deal. It takes rare
impertinence and bold hypocrisy. . . .

Mote claimed he was not anti-Semitic, and yet he spoke
constantly of the "Jewish League of Nations," referred to

"money changers" and "internationalists"—popular Park Avenue terms for "Jew"; harped on Jewish surnames to the exclusion of others, and indulged in such cheap Pelley devices as ridiculing Willkie by calling him Vendell L. Villkie. Mote further insulted Mr. Willkie by calling him "more alien than American" and branded his repudiation of Father Coughlin's support (which Coughlin offered voluntarily during the 1940 elections) as "asinine," because Willkie had said: "I consider anti-Semitism in America as a possible criminal movement and every anti-Semite as a possible traitor to America."

Mote complained bitterly against the Property Seizure Bill, a measure to enable the Government to seize private property in the prosecution of the war (exercised only in rare cases). He appeared before the Senate Committee on Military Affairs, and incensed because no other business executives had publicly followed his line, he declared himself in these terms:

I think the foremost business executives and managers of America have betrayed their stockholders, their bondholders and their employees, and that individually and collectively they ought to be discharged for their indifference. . . . Such a measure as this ought to have brought every business in America to Washington with monkey wrenches and lead pipes, and it would if they were worth their pay as trustees for their stockholders. . . . There is not now, and there never has been, any necessity in America to compel our citizens to defend themselves.

Mote said this just six months before Pearl Harbor. It was inevitable that Hudson should urge his readers to read what he described as Mote's "masterpiece." Mote continued with his obstructionist tactics after Pearl Harbor. Just as he had spoken before the Bund re-enforced League to Save America First in California in 1941, he spoke in Cincinnati in July, 1942, under the auspices of the American Charter, a Coughlinite offshoot. He beat down our war effort—painted a national picture of dejection and ended with the call familiar to all revolutionary audiences: "I don't know when the American people will rise in their wrath and shout to high heaven 'We have had enough.' I do know that such a time will surely come."

In a vicious booklet he circulated *after* Pearl Harbor, Mote quoted Mrs. Dilling, fascist Lawrence Dennis and even the discredited *Protocols* to support his contentions. Mote looked upon all Jews as "war mongers," but he said nothing about Hitler's gigantic preparations for total war, or his extensive conspiracies for territorial and world ideological conquest.

And in the booklet quoting Dennis and the *Protocols* as authorities, Mote made "predictions" of violence and a military dictator I have heard a hundred times at Nazi meetings:

Unless there is a shortage of rope, at the end of five years human necks will be more talked about than bottlenecks. . . . If and when a Caesar appears, he is likely to come from the Army, the Navy, the Air Force, the Marines. . . .

If you had been there with me at the Antlers Bar, you would have found it hard to believe that these threatening and vengeful utterances could have been voiced by the mild-mannered man who faced me. It became all too apparent to me that Mote was the sad victim of a complex: the hate-

---

WEEKLY ROLL-CALL   Page 7

Life and Fortune Magazines Tout for Great Red Father on Potomac

Luce Publications Reveal Radical Backing by Clever Yammer for National Submission to New-Deal War-Defense Racket ..

REGARDLESS of the fate of H. B. 1776, there is increasing evidence that the "whole mass of deceits" practiced on the country since the Great Red Father began simulating a vicarious hysteria in 1937 are being penetrated. No revolutionist has been more steadfast in his devotion to the "new social order" than Henry R. Luce of *Time-Life-Fortune*. There are movie and radio fans, bundlers for Britain, uplifters and war profiteers who will accept his five-page essay in *Life* of February 17 as the most profound and convincing document *The American Century* has yet produced but others will discover in the maze of contradictions and imbecilities the most amazing and damning admissions from revolutionary headquarters since Professor Rexford G. Tug-

By
CARL MOTE

really knows. His admission that they were "men of common sense" is little short of a surprise. It is likewise surpris-

---

Carl Mote, president of the Northern Indiana Telephone Company, contributed signed articles to American Nazi Pelley's *Roll-Call*. In this article in the March 3, 1941 issue Henry Luce— long a bulwark of capitalist Democracy—is called a Communistic "revolutionist" and an "internationalist" because he spoke for a better world order.

In "The Rothschild Money Trust" at page 37, Andrew
Fabius stated that the TNEC[5] had disclosed that Lamont

> Early in 1940 some one else said that Congress had
> become as impotent and useless as the Roman Senate in
> the days of Tiberius Caesar. These observations are enti-
> tled to more than passing consideration since it was the
> much disputed "Protocols of the Learned Elders of Zion",
> as long ago as 1905, that first revealed the goal of invisible
> forces:
>
> " . . . we shall invest the President with the right of
> declaring a state of war," it was stated.

In his booklet, G.O.P. Fifth Column—circulated widely after
Pearl Harbor—Carl Mote, general manager of the Commonwealth
Telephone Corporation, quoted from Nazi-approved "authorities." One of these was Andrew Fabius who "respectfully dedicated" his book—based on and quoting freely from the Protocols—
to "Ford, Coughlin, Thorkelson, Winrod, Hudson, Edmondson,
True, Moseley, Sanctuary, Pelley." As to the Protocols Mote
thought these notorious forgeries were "entitled to more than
passing consideration."

Roosevelt complex. Hate the President at any cost. Hate
everything he does, hate them even before he does them. Hate
him more than you hate Hitler and Stalin. Hate the very
ground he walks on and curse the very bed he sleeps in. Hate
till you blind your own reason and reduce yourself to the
level of a Bundist who knows nothing but hate and sees
nothing but revolution and pogroms ahead.

As I left Mote I experienced a sadness which is difficult to
put into words. Sleep was out of the question. I had met
personally a fine man who doubtless loved his family and
country. What a shame, I thought, that a man of Mote's
calibre and interests should reduce himself to the level of a
vile Pelley. What a blow to Democracy to have Mote on
Pelley's side, rather than on the side of those who were fighting for a world of decency and equality and justice for all
men. I regarded Mote as a tragic victim of the most ruthless,
hateful, soul-searing propaganda machinery the world has
ever seen!

Chapter X

ATTORNEY GENERAL BIDDLE CRACKS DOWN

"My motives were born of a burning patriotism and a high idealism. . . . I am a truer patriot than those who convicted me."

LAURA INGALLS (Nazi agent).

THE DAY after I had seen my brother off to Uncle Sam's Army, July 22, Attorney General Francis Biddle and J. Edgar Hoover cracked down on the "patriots" in a move as sudden and thunderous as summer lightning. Combining the elements of surprise and careful planning, Biddle's blitzkrieg netted a sizable catch of twenty-eight related propagandists on mass indictments for sedition. It climaxed the work of the Department of Justice which had begun with the roundup of Nazi and Jap agents immediately after Pearl Harbor, and which had required seven and a half months to reach the propaganda dupes of the fascist hierarchy.

I took time out from my investigations to make a survey of the accomplishments of the Department of Justice and of its best known unit, J. Edgar Hoover's Federal Bureau of Investigation. Up to July 22, a total of 9405 Axis agents, both American-born and foreign, were arrested and legally dealt with. Countless others were being investigated behind the locked doors of grand jury rooms or quietly stalked by many bureaus of Mr. Biddle's Department of Justice. Slow and sluggish to start, Democracy was finally developing teeth that bit hard.

The grand jury hearings which resulted in the indictment of twenty-seven men and one woman for sedition began more than a year ago. Under Prosecutor William Power Maloney, dozens of witnesses were heard and their utterances analyzed by propaganda experts. Assisting Maloney in the gathering of evidence was Dillard Stokes, reporter for *The Washington Post* whose exposure and interpretation of native fascist activity earned for him the Heywood Broun Memorial Award.

The indictment alleged that the twenty-eight defendants committed conspiracy—

> . . . to publish, convey to, and urge upon members of the military and naval forces of the United States of America and the people of the United States of America for the purpose of obstructing, and designated and intended to impede, obstruct and defeat the preparation of our national defenses against aggression and invasion and the National War Effort.

It also alleged *conspiracy* to—

> . . . carry on a systematic campaign of personal vilification and defamation of the public officials of the United States Government and to that end would advise, counsel, urge, persuade and convince members of the military and naval forces of the United States that such public officials are traitorous, corrupt, dishonest, incompetent, un-American and mentally unbalanced. . . .

Of the twenty-seven men and lone woman, I was friendly with eighteen. I had corresponded with eight (*), while I knew personally ten (**) of the "patriots."

** Elizabeth Dilling	* C. Leon De Aryan
** Howard Victor Broenstrupp	* Robert Edward Edmondson
** William Dudley Pelley	* Ellis O. Jones
** Prescott Freese Dennett	* William Robert Lyman, Jr.
** Charles B. Hudson	George Sylvester Viereck
** Court Asher	William Griffin
** Eugene Nelson Sanctuary	Hans Diebel
** James C. True	Hudson de Priest
** Oscar Brumback	Robert Noble
** Edward James Smythe	Ralph Townsend
* Gerald B. Winrod	Donald McDaniel
* Elmer J. Garner	James F. Garner
* David J. Baxter	Otto Brennermann
* William Kullgren	Herman Max Schwinn

Not long after leaving Stahrenberg's I had become aware of the common methods used by Nazis and their American transmission belters. I knew that their sources of inspiration were the same. Their methods were basically the same, and the mediums to which they resorted to bring about discontent and defeatism and revolution were essentially common to all twenty-eight. Although not all knew each other well enough to work together, I had found that they were engaged in doing and saying the same things in slightly different ways, and on varying levels of society. Whether they knew it or not, they were all heading in one direction.

In addition, I had been acutely aware that many among them exchanged information, and met frequently in "Christian" conventions or co-ordinated their "patriotic" plans during informal visitations. Many exchanged mailing lists so that placement on the list of one resulted, in due time, in placement on the lists of many of the others. Most of them recommended each other, distributed one another's literature and kept in constant touch through intimate correspondence. The indictment expressed it in the vigorous language of the law:

It being the plan and purpose of said defendants, and divers other persons to the Grand Jurors unknown, to destroy the morale and faith and confidence of the members of the military and naval forces of the United States and the people of the United States in their public officials and Republican form of government . . .

. . . the said defendants . . . planning and intending to seize upon and use and misuse the right of freedom of speech and of the press to spread their disloyal doctrines, intending and believing that any nation allowing to its people the right of freedom of speech and of the press is powerless to defend itself against enemies masquerading as patriots and seeking to obstruct, impede, break down and destroy the proper functioning of its republican form of government under the guise of honest criticism . . .

. . . the said defendants . . . knowing full well and intending that a government bereft of the faith and confidence of the members of the military and naval forces and of the people is powerless to defend the nation or the people against armed attack from without or treachery from within and cannot long survive.

As I looked back at the accomplishments of the Attorney General's office, my amazement grew at the patience and efficiency. Many months were spent in checking and cross-checking data on a subject. The information flowed in from dozens of sources and was furnished by innumerable witnesses in addition to the testimony of under cover men. My own efforts were so puny by comparison that they were hardly worth talking about.

None the less, it was gratifying to see that some of my "best friends" had been caught in the dragnet. At no time working under the direction of any official agency, I had worked along for four years purely on my own intuitions and self-training as investigator. I had voluntarily turned in data I regarded important to at least seven Government research and prosecuting agencies. I was pleased to know that as an American I had been of some service to my adopted country.

And I was also happy to see our officials finally realize that a saboteur need not necessarily have to be a prototype of the sinister old-fashioned figure with bombs in one hand and blueprints in the other. Nor was it necessary for him or her to be on the Nazi payroll to serve Nazi ends. The conviction was permeating among our official agencies that most of the saboteurs of Democracy looked and acted like ordinary men and women, went quietly about their work of destruction, lived on Park Avenue as well as Yorkville, came from some of our best families, and the most efficient among them were American-born and boasted of their ancestry. The conception that a fifth columnist did not have to be a paid agent of a foreign power, that he could lurk in the pulpit and cocktail lounge as well as the factory, were revolutionary steps toward stifling Hitler's agents and his American dupes functioning on the psychological battlefront.

Miss Laura Ingalls, trophy-winning aviatrix and firebrand America First-er, was one of the first to be sent to jail. She was convicted of being an unregistered Nazi agent in the pay of Baron Ulrich von Gienanth, second secretary of the German Embassy, and reported head of the Gestapo in the United States. She had been paid ten times "thirty pieces of silver" a month to betray her country. It was shown that part of Miss Ingalls' expenses as America First speaker were met with Nazi money, and among many letters she wrote there was one to her friend, Cathrine Curtis, with the invitation: "I know you will visit me at my chalet at Berchtesgaden."

"The best thing you can do," Baron von Gienanth told Miss Ingalls, "is to continue to promote America First." And when overflow crowds filled the meetings which Laura Ingalls addressed, it was testified that the Baron "couldn't withhold his joy." It was testified that in her speeches for America First and other "patriotic" groups including those of Cathrine Curtis, "she was doing everything possible to prepare and pave the way for the time when Hitler would come over." Upon her conviction, Miss Ingalls faced the judge defiantly and began what appeared to be a rehearsed statement. Speaking in a crisp, defiant tone, she reverted to the stand-by of all American Nazis:

Your honor, one of the great fundamentals implicit in our Constitution is liberty of conscience. I felt I had a right to follow the dictates of my conscience. . . . I worked individually, and individualism is a real American trait.

She shifted her foot and after glaring at the audience, she faced the court again: "My motives were born of a burning patriotism and a high idealism . . . I am a truer patriot than those who convicted me." The final gesture was still to come. She threw back her head and with a final hysterical shout cried out: "I salute the Republic of the United States."

Cathrine Curtis' friend was quietly led away to serve her sentence for crimes against a Republic unappreciative of her brand of "patriotism" and the Department of Justice "went to work" on others of her kind.

George W. Christians, the one who advocated a "rope" for the President and was a chum of Edward Holton James, Mrs. Lois de Lafayette Washburn and Nazi agent Oscar Pfaus, was convicted for sedition in the record time of four days.

Francis P. Moran's offices in Boston were shut down by the F.B.I.

David Ryder, Frederick Vincent Williams and Ralph Townsend were convicted as Japanese agents in the employ of Jikyoku Iinkai, which paid out at least $175,000 to its American Quislings. The case of Ralph Townsend, a former American consular official, was most striking. Townsend offered no defense to the charge that he was an unregistered agent. It was shown that he had printed 60,000 copies each of *The High Cost of Hate; America Has No Enemies in Asia* and 30,000 copies of *There Is No Half Way Neutrality* urging that America remain strictly "neutral" and give Japan a free hand in the Far East.

Townsend pleaded the cause of complacency and defeatism as an editor of *Scribner's Commentator* and its pro-Nazi affiliate—*The Herald*, both of which served as unofficial mouthpieces of the America First Committee. It was testified that Charles Shipman Payson, New York financier, invested $110,000 in the magazine; and Jeremiah Millbank, a New York banker, $50,000. An additional $30,000 was provided in "bales of twenty dollar bills" and left anonymously on "living room windows and hall tables," according to the story officials of *The Herald* told Dillard Stokes.

Robert Jordan, the Harlem fuehrer, was indicted for promoting Nipponese "Americanism" among Negroes.

Social Justice, The Beacon Light, Publicity and other defeatist fascist sheets were barred from the mails.

Mrs. David I. Good, Philadelphia socialite, president of the Dames of the Loyal Legion and friendly with Baxter, Hudson and Kissenger, was questioned by the grand jury.

The army refused to give Lawrence Dennis a commission, while Secretary of War Henry L. Stimson refused an army post to Colonel Charles Lindbergh.

Public opinion ousted George Deatherage from a naval defense job.

Representative Hamilton Fish's secretary, George Hill, was convicted of perjury regarding collaboration with Nazi agent Viereck. Ham Fish was ignominiously dragged before the Washington grand jury and questioned on his Nazi affiliations in one of the most sensational cases involving a member of Congress. The testimony shows the amazing cunning of Viereck and the equally amazing gullibility of our so-called "patriots."

A bewildered man in a shabby brown suit, Hill told how he had been advised not to tell the truth on his first appearance in court. When he changed his mind, he told of being introduced to Viereck by Ham Fish, in July, 1940, in Fish's office and of receiving instructions to co-operate with Viereck. He told how Fish had momentarily left the room and how, in his absence, Viereck gave him two $50 bills.

While he continued his duties as Fish's secretary, Hill's first job under Viereck was to mail out 125,000 copies of a speech written by Nazi agent Viereck and inserted in the *Congressional Record* by Senator Ernest Lundeen, favorite of the Steuben Society. Hill received another $150 from Viereck and later $100 more. "Viereck told me not to write him," he testified. "He told me he would get in touch with me."

According to reports appearing in *The Washington Post* from then on Hill acted as purchasing agent for Viereck, buying speeches by those Congressmen and Senators who furthered appeasement, defeatism, dissension and the general Nazi party line. Some of these speeches were actually written by Viereck, others inspired by him and inserted in the *Record* by his lackeys in Congress. All told, there were at least twenty-one Viereck-approved Congressmen and Senators.

Upon instructions from Viereck and from funds supplied by Viereck, Hill had their speeches delivered to Fish's office, Room 1424 in the New House Office Building, along with franked envelopes. He then distributed them to the America First Committee, Women United, John B. Snow, Mrs. Beatrice Knowles, Ralph Townsend, Mrs. Flora Walker of the American Coalition and many others. Fish's office became a center for Viereck's agitations, and American taxpayers footed mailing charges of close to a million speeches intended to disrupt national unity and hasten the collapse of Democracy.

"What Viereck was doing," declared William Power Maloney, "was to put words in the mouths of the legislators on Capitol Hill who were duped . . . while he laughed at them in secret reports he sent to Berlin."

During this time Prescott Dennett walked in and out of Ham Fish's offices, conferring with Hill, relaying instructions from Viereck, carting away bagsful of defeatist speeches for mailing to Viereck-approved lists. Hill testified that Dennett paid for more than a half million items. When Dennett was hauled before the grand jury, Fish sent a frantic call to Dennett's home and did away with eight bags of speeches bearing his frank. None the less, an additional ton of defeatist propaganda was unearthed in his home: the hoard from which Dennett had given me selections on my visit the year before.

When Ham Fish was dragged before the grand jury he claimed not to know that Viereck was a Nazi agent. On the contrary he considered "Mr. Viereck an American citizen of long standing and good standing." Fish was highly evasive in his answers. "I have no memory of that at all," was a standard answer.

"Is it a coincidence," asked Prosecutor Maloney, "that his views as a German agent coincide so closely with your views as a Congressman at this time?"

"No, it is not," answered Fish. He became flustered: "How do you mean it? I don't understand that question at all. What do you mean by it?"

A few days after my return from the West, Pelley was convicted. Informed of his plans to gain notoriety, the prosecution made quick work of the goateed fuehrer. Sanctuary and Thorkelson testified on his behalf and Charles Augustus Lindbergh also made an appearance. Pelley wailed "persecution" and howled he had been "mistreated." But a jury of farmers and business men from the environs of Indianapolis found him guilty on all eleven counts. It deliberated only three hours and fifteen minutes. The trial lasted seven days and Pelley was sentenced to fifteen years in prison. Pointing his finger at Pelley, United States District Attorney J. Howard Caughran shouted in eloquent summation:

> You are a traitor to your country, the arch-Quisling of America parading under a false flag of patriotism while you stabbed your country in the back. You will go down in history with Benedict Arnold and Aaron Burr.

A few months later his daughter, Adelaide Marian Pelley, was arrested by the F.B.I. with four others charged with harboring Broenstrupp, alias Spiridovich, as a fugitive from justice. While it was true that many other Nazi tools were still at large, it was comforting to see our various law-enforcing and fact-gathering agencies co-ordinate their machinery and, together with an aroused public opinion, run down some of those who were actively opposing and seeking to subvert our war effort through Nazi methods of psychological warfare.

Chapter XI

PROSELYTES OF THE "NEW ORDER"

> "As far as the Fathers of the Republic are con-
> cerned, they were nothing but Masonic hoodlums.
> They were all Masonic monkeys. . . . We could do
> a lot of things without committing high treason."
>
> OLOV E. TIETZOW

THERE WERE TWO fascist operatives I wanted to see. One was
Olov E. Tietzow, endorsed by *World Service* as a "patriot,"
and the other, Edwin Flaig, of the Flaig Brothers Hunter's
Lodge in the mountains near Pittsburgh, where Tietzow now
made his headquarters after operating from Minneapolis, Chicago, Boston, Buffalo, New York and Charleston as American
Nazidom's travelling emissary.

So far as Flaig was concerned, I was sure he needed investigation. My cue was an interview I had once had with Paul
M. Winter, a Legionnaire of Shavertown, Pennsylvania and
distributor of Nazi pamphlets direct from Berlin. Winter had
told me that he, together with Mrs. Dilling, had visited Edmondson. During our conversation, he had mentioned that he
knew a "big German" who had returned from Germany a
few years ago. This man, whom he named as Flaig, was a
specialist in the manufacture of guns.

"He makes rifles and pistols on order," Winter said, and
told me that Flaig had sold James True five rifles. "Whenever

Pro-American

THE AMERICAN GUARD

Freedom   Justice

"THE WHITE MAN'S PARTY"

UNITE UNDER THE SWASTIKA
SYMBOL OF LOYALTY TO AMERICAN IDEALS

417

you want anything in firearms, get in touch with Flaig. He'll fix you up. Be sure to use my name."

Olov E. Tietzow was a Swedish-born "patriot" whose passion was to promote Americanism through the credo: "Unite Under the Swastika—Symbol of Loyalty to American Ideals." He was fuehrer of The American Guard, "The White Man's Party," and a tireless pamphleteer who had flooded the country for many years with Nazi tracts, each headed with a design showing an American eagle clutching at a swastika. His book *Aryan Americanism*, specifically recommended by *World Service*, pointed "the way to a sane political development of my adopted country." I had once read a letter of Tietzow's which said in part:

> The coming struggle here in America will, I believe, be fought not with ballots but with bullets, and ladies should therefore stay out of it—it is a man's struggle and not a ladies' picnic, a struggle wherein ladies will be of value only as—spies.

As soon as I reached Pittsburgh I phoned him and because of our previous correspondence had no difficulty making an appointment to see him at his home. Tietzow was unmarried and was engaged as an engineer in a defense plant. At night he worked on a book which outmatched Bund literature in virulence. I could see that he was applying what he had written to me in a letter shortly after Pearl Harbor: "We could do a lot of things without committing high treason."

Tietzow told me about himself. With Oscar Pfaus, now in Berlin, he had started a Nazi group in New York, then become involved with the Friends of the New Germany. Speaking freely as to a co-worker, Tietzow confessed that he had received money from the Chicago branch of the German-American Bund to help finance his pamphlets. When I asked how much he had received, and how frequently, he became evasive but reiterated that he had got "pretty good money."

Tietzow spoke highly of Senator David I. Walsh of Massachusetts, who about the time of my interview was the victim of a public airing of an alleged personal scandal. According to Tietzow, the Senator saw eye to eye with him politically and had received, and thanked him for all his literature. When Tietzow had got into trouble with the Post Office, Senator

Walsh had interested himself in his problem because of personal friendship, Tietzow asserted.

"I've been in one revolution," he said, referring to his military service abroad, "and I wouldn't mind being in another. That is why I hope Hitler w . . ." He changed his mind and did not finish. "I have no faith in constitutional methods," he resumed. "Nothing will work here but a military coup d'état. And as far as the Fathers of the Republic are concerned, they were nothing but Masonic hoodlums. They were all Masonic monkeys."

I did not wait to listen further.

I also received a cordial welcome when I called on Edwin Flaig. Hunter's Lodge was perched atop a wild, picturesque, heavily wooded knoll, sixty acres in extent, at Millvale, eight miles outside Pittsburgh. The Lodge itself was built of logs, and included a spacious meeting room on the main floor, two large rooms above and a sizable cellar. A large residential home adjoined the Lodge. Only Edwin Flaig knew the secret buried in those inaccessible hidden acres.

As I walked up the steep hill and knocked on the door, I had a feeling that I was going to meet a man who would be different from the usual run of native fascist or Nazi sympathizer. I entered the gun shop and found it extremely well stocked with rifles, revolvers, ammunition and sundry hunter's goods.

Edwin Flaig himself came forward to meet me, dressed in a khaki shirt and dark trousers. His bearing was distinctly military. Six feet tall, with well-built, powerful shoulders, he gave the impression of being in active military training. His complexion was ruddy, his gestures dynamic. Flaig's manners were authoritative and at the same time ingratiating. The first question Flaig asked was whether I knew Paul Winter and Joe McWilliams personally. It was then my turn to ask if *he* knew Joe.

"I know pretty nearly everybody who has done work against the Jews," he answered. This set the atmosphere for what followed. Flaig offered me wine and after we had finished we placed the empty glasses on the mantel over the fireplace. The logs crackled, sending out showers of warm sparks. As we sat facing each other on the small benches, our relation was one of complete chumminess. Perhaps this will explain the startling disclosures which Flaig made.

He was of German ancestry, American-born, and spoke German fluently. He told me he had served as a lieutenant in the American Army during the last war after which he had toured the world and stopped for an extended visit in Germany, attending many meetings of the Brown Shirts which had been addressed by Hitler personally.

"Sure I went to his meetings," he said. "I heiled Hitler like everybody else. He used to tell us [and here he injected a German phrase which he translated] 'I have a plan,' and I used to wave back at him that he was crazy. Hitler *was* crazy," Flaig emphasized. "He *is* crazy; no one but a crazy man would have dreamed of doing the things he has done."

Flaig told of his friendship with Goering and Ernest Udet, the Nazi flying ace and a commander of the *Luftwaffe*. He recalled how Udet used to be a stunter in Nazi air shows and how Goering and Udet used to engage in smuggling operations. Flaig also claimed to be a personal friend of Wilhelm Frick who in 1933 was appointed Minister of the Interior by Hitler. Flaig foresaw Hitler using mustard gas on New York city and said gleefully: "Those bombs will kill thousands in the subways. Three Christians will die for every Jew."

He suddenly motioned to me to keep quiet. He had seen someone approach. Flaig put on a professional smile and walked to the door. The man who entered was not formally introduced to me, but before he joined us, I heard him whisper to Flaig: "Is this gentleman all right?" Flaig vouched for me and the man joined in the conversation, which became progressively more anti-Semitic, anti-British, anti-Administration, anti-Democracy, pro-Hitler. The newcomer had also travelled in Germany and was now employed as a supervising engineer. Flaig addressed him as "Charlie."

"I talk in my shop just as I am talking here," Charlie said. "We all believe the same way at the shop and I tell them just what I'm telling you here now."

He told of meeting hunters who allegedly had continued shooting after the hunting season because "Jew hunting is go-

ing to be pretty good soon and we are practicing." Charlie confided that he had hidden several guns near his home. His son was in the army and had supposedly told his father before leaving: "Dad, hide them guns so when I come back we can use them."

Then Charlie made this statement, "By golly, if Federal agents visit me and I know their intentions ain't nowhere being near honorable, I'm going to give them a dose of my own poison gas." As I listened, startled, he explained that it left no trace except for a slight mark which looked like a tiny burn.

Again the door opened and we stopped talking. Whenever interrupted by a visiting customer we talked about the price of food. Our intimate conversation was resumed as soon as the customer left.

Before divulging the formula for his homemade poison gas, Charlie again observed: "I hope this gentleman is all right." Upon being reassured by Flaig that I was, Charlie went on. "You take cyanide and any other acid and put them in separate vials. When you're ready mix the two, give the snooping Federal agent one whiff and that'll be the end of him."

"Now I want to show you fellows something you've never seen before," Flaig said. He went into an adjoining room and returned with a magnificent rifle. He handled it tenderly and displayed it with considerable pride, taking apart several sections to show how easily the telescopic lens could be detached. He then gave the gun to Charlie and asked him to look through the sights. Charlie was speechless with praise. I handled the gun myself and was amazed at the efficiency of the telescopic lens.

"It's the latest model from Germany. There are only a few in this country!" Flaig said, as I wondered how he had obtained one.

Just before leaving us, Charlie paid for the cardboard targets he had come to buy. "I haven't bought a single damned war bond," he said, closing the door.

Flaig and I were alone again and Flaig, who had urged me to buy a gun and lay it aside for future use, now coached me on the technique of burying a gun without exposing it to rust.

"First grease the barrel, then wrap the gun in heavy canvas. Dip the whole thing in a light coat of paraffin and bury it. It'll last you a long time."

In view of Flaig's Nazi sentiments I naturally pondered on the number of guns which might have been buried on his wild wooded acres.

Flaig launched a tirade on the invulnerability of Germany to invasion and the inevitability of Germany's triumph. "England has already lost the war," he boasted. "Germany and Europe are impregnable. England would have been conquered last summer, but Germany discovered just in time that Russia had made a dishonorable pact and she had to turn around and teach Russia a lesson. But by July 1 (1942) Russia will be pushed beyond the Urals," Flaig prophesied with typical Nazi wishfulness. "America can't win. And some of the munitions we are now making are going to be left behind and used by the boys here. They'll dynamite Detroit, Pittsburgh, Chicago —paralyze transportation and isolate whole sections of the country. There'll be a purification. A blood bath is the only way out."

We were seated in front of the fireplace and had finished our second glass of wine. Flaig was so aroused that his eyes took on a wild glare. His hands began to gesticulate violently. I asked if he looked forward to National-Socialism here.

"Not only here, but the world over. It is the only way out. This damned system of Democracy has got to end."

Flaig then told me of being visited by two Federal men the week before, and he complained: "You can't tell the truth these days without being called a Nazi or a fifth columnist. You can't be a patriot today without somebody coming after you."

I asked why they had visited him.

"They wanted to know if I knew anything about some machine guns in Pittsburgh."

"What did you say?" I asked.

"I told them I knew nothing about machine guns," Flaig said. "But there *are* machine guns in Pittsburgh all right," he added laughing.

I asked if those he knew about were new or old models, whether there were only a few or enough "to count for something when the day comes." But Flaig was too smart and he wouldn't bite.

"I don't know," he said, becoming evasive. "But there *are* some. I know that. A machine gun is a terrible thing."

It was getting late, so I asked Flaig if he could see me again tomorrow and take a walk through the wods. He agreed readily. I wanted to visit him again for two reasons. First, to bring my camera along; second, to see if I could discover the hideout where guns might be buried—particularly those latest, deadly telescopic models from Germany.

The next day was perfect for picture taking and I spent some time photographing the locale from the road. At the foot of the hill was a roadhouse, with some of the side windows grated with iron bars. I noted mentally that the roadhouse could be used as a lookout post for those who entered or were inspecting the Flaig estate from the outside. As I went about taking pictures, I automatically considered myself under observation. If questioned, my excuse would be that I was a "tourist" taking "souvenir" shots. That is the way a horde of Nazi agents had got away with photographing our industrial plants, harbors and air fields.

Flaig was mowing the lawn as I walked up the steep flight of stone steps. I pitched in and helped. After we had finished Flaig himself suggested going for a walk. In addition to the gun shop and the large residence adjoining it, there were several other homes on the property. He intended to build more homes and eventually found a settlement.

Flaig now told me a bit about his personal life. He had been married in France and had a son there, a strong nationalist. Flaig couldn't get along with women: "They make a lot of trouble for me. I prefer the company of men."

About two years ago he had been desperately ill and penniless. "But I got on my feet again," Flaig said. He did not explain how he had obtained the finances to buy this magnificent estate. But he did tell me that he had always had inside information on Hitler's plans, and had actually marked on a calendar the day of Hitler's invasion of Poland. He divulged other information which indicated that he was not merely boasting.

"If I knew you better, I could tell you lots more," Flaig said.

I asked about Edmondson.

"I knew him and sold him a gun with a sight. His wife was very helpful to him," he reminisced. "She wore the pants in that family."

I asked about James True. He admitted knowing and meeting him at Winter's home in 1939, but apparently suspicious, said nothing about the sale of five guns, and I did not press him. I was content to have learned from Winter that the deal had been transacted in his home "right before [his] eyes."

I asked Flaig if he knew Pelley. He had never met him personally, but one of Pelley's men had visited him, and they had exchanged views about founding a settlement wherein each tenant would share the work co-operatively. "Of course, all would have to see eye to eye politically," Flaig said.

As we walked about the estate I kept a sharp lookout for mounds and freshly dug earth. But Flaig refused to take me up into the woods. He had sold a lot of regular United States Army rifles, 30.06 calibre. He explained that these guns were best because ammunition was standard. "They can always get the ammunition without trouble. I told my customers to buy them and lay them aside for use against the Jews."

One of Flaig's customers was driving part way to Pittsburgh, and I agreed to go along. It was past noon, and my bus left shortly after one P.M. While Flaig went back into the gun shop, I questioned his friend and learned that Flaig was a member of the North Side Sporting Club, and other rifle clubs. He was well-liked and contributed generously. He told me that in Allegheny County alone there were more than seventy gun clubs with a membership of 12,000. "Babies are born with guns," he said. "Everybody owns a gun here."

I asked Flaig's friend if the rifle clubs were politically conscious about the Jews, for example, and national politics. I emphasized anti-Semitism and politics. His denial was prompt. "No, we don't bother about politics. We just get together and shoot, but we fight back when they try to seize our rifles. Practically everybody around here is a member of the N.R.A. (National Rifle Association)."

It was apparent to me that this man knew nothing whatever

about Flaig's revolutionary ideas. He regarded Flaig as a good, neighborly fellow. I did not learn the man's name, but I jotted down in my notes the license number of his sedan.

Flaig came out of the gun shop. "Let me show you what's upstairs before you leave," he said. We re-entered the gun shop and climbed the stairs. There were two large rooms, one of which was filled with hunters' equipment. The other, long and spacious, could have served admirably for meetings. Flaig read my thoughts.

"This can be used as a meeting hall," he said.

Downstairs, I asked Flaig to pose for me. He posed once, but suddenly decided he did not like the idea and refused to face the camera a second time.

"You'd better take this along, as a souvenir," Flaig said, handing me the catalogue of his gun shop. It was a sixty-four-page book, with numerous illustrations, expensively printed. It advertised countless items which obviously required considerable capital to stock. How, from his confessed poverty of a few years ago, Flaig had been able to build up an enormous and profitable business puzzled me greatly. It may have been uncommon business acumen. On the other hand, I felt that his Nazi preachments, admiration of National-Socialism, contempt for Democracy and the national leadership; his defeatism and defamation of the war effort—all these on the part of a man who described himself as a former lieutenant in the United States Army—would distinctly interest the proper authorities.

As soon as I had got back to New York I made it a point to see Elmhurst and keep my promise to visit his friends in Brooklyn.

"You'll meet them all tonight," Elmhurst said: "The McDonalds, the doctor, Steve Sylvester and Roy. Roy's been a cop for sixteen years."

"What's Roy's last name?" I asked.

"We just call him Roy," Elmhurst said.

I hesitated about visiting a veteran policeman as I felt he'd see through me and tip off Elmhurst. If "Roy" discovered my work, a man in his position might easily employ counter measures, some of them not pleasant to contemplate, and when it came to a showdown it would be a cop's word against mine. I thought it over carefully and decided that inasmuch as my investigations were nearing an end, my exposure would not matter. As to a cop's testimony against mine, I determined to get so much evidence against "Roy," both written and oral, that if things ever came to a showdown he could not possibly refute my testimony or stack a coterie of witnesses against me.

I decided to go, despite my feelings that I should not. But I wanted to know if this Brooklyn cop had been negligent in his duty toward checking acts of vandalism against synagogues which at that time were rife in Brooklyn and the Bronx. I wanted to know how large was Elmhurst's "patriotic" gang and I wanted to know why "Roy's" name was being kept a secret from me. It was with the expectation of high adventure that I went to this policeman's home.

Elmhurst had not misrepresented. "Roy" admitted visiting Stahrenberg's to "buy literature." He admitted helping sponsor meetings of the Mobilizers, Nationalist Party and to having Sanctuary, Russell Dunn and the Bundist "Reverend" Herbert Lewis, as speakers.

Together with Elmhurst, Steve Sylvester and "Roy" comprised the ringleaders. In addition, there were Tom Quinlan, five or six other men and a half dozen women in the room. In the circle was also a Brooklyn physician who served on the local draft board. They were old-timers and knew many of the standard Nazis in the movement. "Roy's" son had sold *Social Justice* for four years and his home was filled with the subversive literature of Flanders Hall, Edmondson, Broenstrupp, Smythe, Hudson, Dilling and others. He subscribed to most of the "patriotic" services.

The informal "family gathering" began with a lot of pro-Nazi talk in which Elmhurst assumed the role of a savant and final arbiter of all questions of dispute. But the last thing I had expected to hear was a vicious anti-Catholicism on the part of men (except Elmhurst) who were churchgoing Roman Catholics.

It started innocently enough with Sylvester's comparison of Christ to Hitler, followed by the statement that like Christ, Hitler was re-establishing pristine (he pronounced it "priestyne") Christianity by cleaning out the "Catholic doctrine" (he pronounced it "doktreene") of the dead weight it had accumulated. And, like Christ, Hitler was being crucified for opposing the "money changers." Sylvester then launched into a vigorous attack on the Reverend Robert I. Gannon, president of Fordham University, who repudiated his isolationist stand by declaring: "It is humiliating, but many of us are ready to stand up and confess that we were wrong and he [the President] was right. It was our war from the first." In Nazi eyes, this placed Father Gannon as being on the "Jewish side of the war."

It was also Sylvester's preposterous notion that Myron Taylor, who had just left as special envoy to the Vatican had taken over a "certified check" to "close the Jew Deal with that man, the Pope. This is a bad Pope," Sylvester declared. "He loves the Jews."

From then on the Church hierarchy and the "Jeevies" (as the draft board physician alluded to the Jesuit Order) received such a searing and unremitting attack that I could have imagined myself in a Klan gathering. The talk degenerated into bitter invectives and, as with all Nazi-minded men, ended in the threat of violence. "Roy" observed that five or six of the "big shots" in the Church ought to be lined up with a blackjack and—he illustrated by drawing back his right fist, then coming down swiftly with it on his knee—"hit right on the mush."

The physician recommended "hard labor for them Jeevies," and "Roy" countered with: "Sure, make them work for their living."

"Yep, they are a menace. They're always asking for money," the physician agreed.

I was appalled. When I recovered I realized that Americans who turn Nazi-minded lose all respect for decency and humanity, for true religion and for God. Hate so obsesses them that turning on their Mother Church is as natural as turning against anything else. For hate is a Nazi cancer that devours the soul and from which no one is immune. In his booklet *Dare We Hate the Jews* Father Daniel A. Lord observed sagely: "Anti-Semitism rots the soul. . . . Hatred is a form of self-poisoning. Physically it creates an auto-intoxication. Mentally it throws a man completely off the level of sanity."

Complementing Father Lord's writing was an article by Father J. Elliot Ross in *The Ecclesiastical Review* for May, 1939 which every anti-Semite regardless of his denomination should read:

There is another selfish reason why Catholics should not take any part in anti-Semitic orgies: those who succumb to such persecution hysteria inevitably suffer a spiritual degeneration. One cannot play with pitch without becoming tarred, one cannot practise sadism without becoming sadistic. . . . When finally he reaches a point where he can experience pleasure in the most barbarous cruelty against human beings, who are equally with himself children of one common Father, God, he has himself become a barbarian.

Elmhurst had invited me to go clam-digging with him and I accepted, hoping to get evidence to show that while clam-digging off New York Harbor he might be in a position to relay messages to enemy interests.

Riding along on the bus to Prince's Bay in Staten Island, I watched Elmhurst keep a tight grip on a long thin package. We walked down the street toward the bay with the map-like package held tightly in his hand. We crossed a bridge and knocked on the door of a brown, weather-beaten house. The door opened, and a wizened, wrinkly woman with a hard face and sharp, suspicious eyes opened it cautiously.

"Hello, Mrs. Schmitt." Handing over the mysterious package, Elmhurst added: "any time tonight, yes?"

I burned with curiosity, and while Elmhurst talked quietly with Mrs. Schmitt I wandered around the premises. The pigeons interested me. There were fifteen or more. I kept looking at their legs in a way which would not arouse any suspicions. Could these pigeons be used to carry messages to outlying boats? The thought burned feverishly, and I could do nothing to quench it.

Elmhurst kept his clamming paraphernalia at Mrs. Schmitt's. We put on our old togs and jumped into the boat. "Yes, sir, George, America has as much chance of winning this war as the Jews had against the Bund," he began. I recalled another of his wishful "predictions"—the fall of Stalingrad. "It'll take one more week," he said on September 10, 1942.

We rowed out. The tide was low—a good time for clamming. We dug all afternoon. Elmhurst seized the clamming rake, a scissors-like affair with large curved prongs, and lifting it high in the air plunged it into the sea bottom, then scooped the tongues together and brought up clams, rocks and mud. It was my job to pick out the live clams and throw the junk overboard.

I asked Elmhurst if ship movements could be observed from where we were. The ship lanes were out several miles, he said, and guessing my thoughts added that the waters were patrolled by the coast guard. This, however, was no drawback to an ambitious Nazi agent. Throughout the afternoon only one coast-guard vessel passed by. Elmhurst was a close friend of Paul Scholz, the Nazi spy, at the Germania Bookstore.

"I tried to tell him to be careful, and how to do things, but he would not take my advice. He knew it all."

"They've let you pretty well alone, haven't they?" I observed.

"I was too smart for the F.B.I.," Elmhurst boasted. "They didn't touch me. I was too clever for them. I am always careful whom I talk to."

"Maybe you behaved yourself," I said, fishing for information.

"I'm a sixth columnist," he answered.

Laughing to throw off suspicion, I asked if a sixth columnist was "a guy who manufactured defeatist talk."

"I have my own conception of that. They will yet find out," he said mysteriously.

Elmhurst also knew Max Blank, the spy at B. Westermann Bookstore who was convicted with Scholz, but he was unwilling to talk further and hinted we drop the conversation. And Elmhurst definitely balked at telling me Roy's last name.

"Why don't you forget it, George?" he said peeved.

Another indication of Elmhurst's dawning suspicion was manifested at our next meeting. I went to it with some hesitation and fear. I did not know why, but I felt that I was under Roy's constant scrutiny. He had offered to drive me to Elmhurst's home, but I was suspicious of his friendliness. When I arrived at Elmhurst's, purposely late, I made sure no one lurked in any of the cars parked near-by.

Roy and Sylvester with their womenfolk, Tom Quinlan, the physician, and a newcomer, John Thornton, were all present. Roy had brought a batch of Sanctuary's propaganda, instead of Edward James Smythe's seditious leaflets he had promised and told me he had at his home. Elmhurst showed around the letter he had received from Adelaide Marian Pelley, another from Tietzow asking to quote from *The World Hoax.* Mrs. Dilling's and Hudson's latest bulletins were on Elmhurst's desk. After looking at the swastika, the literature and the war maps, Mrs. "Roy" observed smartly:

"With all these maps and things, Ernest, this place looks like Nazi headquarters."

Elmhurst had worked hard on the copy for a series of seditious stickers and leaflets and showed them around for approval. One of them read "Jews caused this war. Make them pay for it." This Nazi bromide was to be printed on adhesive paper and taking advantage of blackout regulations, stuck in public places. Another sticker entitled "The Four Freedoms" propagated the Nazi canard that Jews were refusing to join the army. One virulent bit of Nazi poison was signed by a non-existent League of National Jewish Organizations.

"There they are. All we need now is a printer," Elmhurst said.

"I want you, George, and Roy here to go tomorrow and find a printer. You do the work from now on. I've done my share."

Elmhurst was shouldering the seditious act on a policeman of Irish lineage and on an American he presumed to be Italian. He made sure no German-Americans were involved, least of

Dear George:

Mr. Drew likes to see you next Tuesday evening at his home, 2152 Stuart Street, Brooklyn, regarding Sanctuary and Starhemberg.

Best Regards

Ernest

all himself. "Go ahead and change the writing any way you want to," Elmhurst added. "It's your job from now on."

Roy and I agreed to meet the following day to get Sanctuary's advice; Stahrenberg was out of business, another Nazi printer had died and Hackl Press, printers for the Bund and the Mobilizers, was closed down by the F.B.I. It was long after midnight when the "patriotic" chinfest broke up. Bus service had stopped and trains to the Staten Island Ferry ran at long intervals.

"I'll drive you to the ferry," volunteered Roy.

"You're filled up," I said. "I'll go over with Doc."

"Sure, there's plenty of room in my car," the physician said.

Roy drove his car behind ours and as I alighted at the ferry I jotted down the license number of both automobiles.

"Hey, what are you doing?" the cop called out.

"Nothing," I said stiffly. I did not care what he thought of me from now on. *I wanted to know who "Roy" was*. When I met him in the drugstore of the New York Times Building the next day, I sensed his coolness. He had come with John Thornton, former member of the Christian Front Sport Club, and twice a deserter from the army, he confided.

"Those stickers are too hot to handle now," he began.

"But last night you were all for it. What happened overnight?"

"I've thought it over and I don't think we'd better do anything now."

"Then there's no use of going up to see Sanctuary," I said.

"We may as well go up," Roy answered, "so that if we change our minds we can get the job done."

When we saw Sanctuary he suggested we try the William S. Brewer Printing Company, 169 Duane Street.

"Are you going there?" I asked Roy.

"No, George. I'm through with this thing. A fellow has to be careful nowadays."

A week later I checked with the Brewer Printing Company, presenting myself as a friend of the Colonel. I ascertained that Roy had visited the plant but his proposition had been turned down as too risky.

"Have you done any work like that before?" I asked Brewer.

"You're damned tootin' right I've done that kind of work before the war. Here, look at this."

From under the pile of rubbish on his desk, Brewer tossed over the June, 1939 copy of the *Christian Free Press*, Mrs. Fry's propaganda sheet. "We printed that here," he said. "We also did a lot of work for Edmondson. We printed 4,000 copies of *The Secret World Government* by Spiridovich. And we did a hell of a lot of work for Sanctuary. Just before he was indicted, Pelley was over here trying to buy some type. I guess we've done enough for the patriotic cause. But can't handle anything hot now."

Thanks to Roy and Elmhurst I had stumbled upon one of the important New York presses which specialized in fascist literature!

In the meanwhile, I checked with the vehicle bureau the registration of the twin license numbers. I learned the full name and address of the Brooklyn physician. I also learned that "Roy" was James Le Roy Drew and that his 1942 black Ford sedan was registered in his wife's name, Blanche. His shield number was 7998. In my possession, also, is Drew's unlisted home telephone number. Furthermore, I've received letters from Drew and Elmhurst. In his letter Elmhurst involved Drew's name with Stahrenberg's. I've kept detailed notes of many interviews with Drew which I've not recorded here and have put them away for safe keeping. I believe that if I'm put to it I can fully prove my case against him as an accomplice of Ernest F. Elmhurst, the American Nazi.

I began to get letters from Mrs. Lois de Lafayette Washburn. She addressed them as "My Dear Fellow Sufferer" and "Friend Pagnanelli," and signed them "T.N.T." She had lost no time in getting started on her Yankee Minute Men leaflet upon her return from the fascist convention at Boise. "No name, no address will go on the stuff I send out—nothing, so they will have a hard time trying to hang me," she wrote and kept me informed of the "secret" developments. "No releases whatsoever will be made," she wrote—

until everybody is all set to do his part, so that they will be flying so fast in all directions all at once that the enemy will be

flabbergasted and confused and will not know in which direction
to start the bloodhounds on the scent. . . . You can be getting
your lists for mailing lined up. That's the way I work ahead of
time.

Her next letter, in September after Pearl Harbor, informed
me that the pamphlets were ready, but—

I can't set any date for the release—not until my Chief [Frank
W. Clark] turns up. He is lost, or at least I've had no word for
3 weeks. Don't know whether he is off on some secret mission,
or what. He told me a while back that there would be a time I
would not hear from him; but I wrote him all was ready and
that we were waiting and raring to go; but I never make a move
of any kind without his approval and authorization, for it might
prove fatal to some of his plans. . . .

Her next letter said: "Just held consultations with the Chief
who says to go ahead, open up both barrels and let 'em have
the full volley of our guns." She continued:

Your request "please keep my name confidential from all"
shall be respected. . . . Rest assured that no lists will ever be kept
in reach of the snoops. That part is all taken care of in advance
before we start. Neither will any quantities of the material be
kept on hand for the snoops to break in upon. That too had been
taken care of in advance. We're all distributors, and pray what
can they do about that? Not a damned thing! So have no fears.
Five hundred of my own will go forth this week, and I don't
know how many the co-operators will get out for nobody knows
what the other fellow is doing; we are expecting good returns;
and those will lead to more, and those to more, etc. I'm busy
today notifying the advance contacts to let 'er go.
  God bless you for the fine work you are doing, and I hope it
will be rewarded with much success. If every young man your
age had the brains and integrity you have, we would soon end
the racket. . . .

Mrs. Washburn's Yankee Minute Men tract was clearly inspired by Edward Holton James' leaflet on Yankee Freemen.
It was equally seditious, demanding "immediate annulment of
all so-called 'Lend-Lease' Laws" and "immediate armistice
with all nations against whom we are arrayed at war, and a

YANKEE MINUTE MEN

Think Yankee,   Talk Yankee,   Act Yankee

RESCUE THE REPUBLIC! Defend the Yankee Tradition and Restore Social Justice, Christian Culture, and the Rights of Mankind!   Preserve our

negotiated peace, and with an all-Yankee cast on our side of the conference table. . . . We champion and will fight for the rights of Yankee nationalists."

In addition, Mrs. Washburn branded "the policies of the present administration of our governmental affairs—both foreign and domestic, in peace and in war time—as subversive of our Yankee tradition. We brand and denounce all these secret plotters . . . and we hold them responsible for the tragedy at Pearl Harbor."

In her next letter early in October Mrs. Washburn urged me to dodge army service.

I was talking to the Chief again about the conscientious objectors. . . . The Chief says it is best to do your objecting at the start. They are sending the boys who object to the insane asylum because they haven't prisons to put them in; but damned if I wouldn't rather be at large among the lunatics who, after all, are not any more luny than the ones who put them there . . . so stand on your Constitutional rights and tell 'em to go to hell. I'm passing this to you for what it is worth. That's exactly what I would do were I a man for I could carry on my crusade from the insane asylum. . . .

Oh, boy! Was I busy jamming the mail Saturday night. We're opening up to let 'm have a volley from both barrels. . . . Fine man went from here to Texas not long ago, and he is calling on clergymen in the principal cities of that State, and has promised full co-operation.

I decided that it was about time to let a bit of firing be done from New York. Preaching sedition and urging me to stay out of the army exhausted my patience. I published an article, under a false Chicago date-line, and carefully camouflaging those facts which might give me away, I exposed Mrs. Wash-

burn and Clark as co-authors of the seditious leaflet. Her next
letter dated October 13 told the story eloquently:

> Of course we expected to be fighting the serpents out in the
> open before very long, but I hardly expected such quick work.
> . . . So I didn't go to bed last night but stayed up folding and
> getting my supply of literature in shape to taxi out with it early
> this morning to a place of safety. . . . I will defy the devils and
> taunt them with it and ask them what they are going to do about
> it. They will soon enough find out what we Yankees are going
> to do. . . . F I G H T !

Mrs. Washburn's next letter revealed interesting ties with
Governor Talmadge, and also showed that she continued to
trust me implicitly:

> I am cautioning you not to give my address to anyone. . . .
> The order may be filled from Texas, California or Michigan. I
> have taken the precaution to see to it that if the supply is shut
> off here, more can be planographed right in Chicago; so they
> will never succeed in stopping the flow. . . .
> The response continues to be satisfactory, and I am filling
> orders all the time, receiving some anonymous contributions with
> lists to be circularized. . . . An air mail from New York brings
> me the good news that ex-Governor Talmadge of Georgia and
> his bodyguard, a military man, are organizing a new White
> Man's secret society in that State. He is a fine man with whom I
> used to have some interesting correspondence. He has had our
> platform and perhaps they will decide to co-operate with us. . . .

I answered Mrs. Washburn sympathetically, expressing
"painful shock and surprise" at the publicity she had received.
I asked whom she suspected in Chicago. In answer she sent
me a copy of the vile letter she had written a blameless Jewish
professor in Chicago. Professor Julius Jonathan Steen must be
wondering what on earth brought the wrath of an enraged
woman on his shoulders. My article had scored for in her next
letter Mrs. Washburn wailed:

> I bragged too soon. The F.B.I. stooges have since located me
> through my Social Security (Bolsheviki identification tag) and
> phoned me at my office, thereby muffing their assignment; for I

talked them out of investigating me. Had they swooped down on me at my hotel, as I expected, I might not be here. But I'm boasting no more.

The rest of the letter was occupied with the "military trial" of her "Chief." Clark had been called to Washington to testify, and had been locked up. "It's a frame-up, of course," she wailed.

When you are able to do so, I wish you would contact Edwin Perry Banta, 215 East 17th Street, Apt. 8. He is a prince. He has been keeping me posted on all fronts, and he contacted Sanctuary's lawyer. . . . The only Willard I know in Chicago is a Mabel J. Willard, 816 E. 57th Street, who put me in touch with Lawyer McKnight in Salt Lake City, but surely she is on our side of the fence. She signed one of my pledge cards.

I wrote her a reassuring letter, telling her that everything would turn out well, that her "Chief" may soon be released. Then I received an air mail letter postmarked November 18:

Just a hurried note as I am packing up, to advise you to direct no more mail to this address, as I am journeying to parts unknown. I am moving out to the country someplace, thus to lose my Bolsheviki identification tag—that "Social Security Number." That's how they tracked me here and hounded me. So, until you hear from me under another name, adios.

The *Chicago Tribune*, "World's Greatest Newspaper," is rallying to the defense of Colonel Sanctuary, and Sanctuary's lawyer will work for the release and exoneration of Frank too. . . . Colonel McCormick and Colonel Sanctuary are fellow Colonels and comrades. . . . So until you hear from me under another name, adios.

T.N.T.

I was about to write her again to her post office box when a newspaper item a few days later told me what had happened. The story bore a Washington date-line and read:

Mrs. Lois de Lafayette Washburn of Seattle was ordered to appear before a Federal Grand Jury understood to be investigating seditious activities. Mrs. Washburn, author of a pamphlet,

Yankee Minute Men, was subpoenaed by William Power Maloney, special assistant to the Attorney General. Officials declined to discuss why she was summoned.

That was not the end of Mrs. Lois de Lafayette Washburn. On November 19, I received an embittered and venomous letter in which she addressed me as "Your Honor of the Jewish Gestapo." Someone had apparently tipped off Mrs. Washburn that I had been investigating her. But surprisingly enough, on December 31 I received another letter from Mrs. Washburn addressed to "Dear Pagnanelli":

You tried to communicate with me after I left Seattle. The letter got to D. C. but never reached my hands. A fool woman tore it up. She was one of those who insisted you were a spy. I have since learned that this is not so. I am very sorry I went off on a tangent and bawled you out. . . .
Am spending the holidays in Chicago. Then I shall leave for "parts unknown." . . . Hope to see you again some day when the smoke has cleared away and the blood of the "vipers and serpents" is washed up.

On March 27 she wrote again addressing me as "Honorable Sir" and again cleared me of all blame, stating: "I trust you will pardon my former hallucinations. . . . Thus I pray for your forgiveness." She signed it T.N.T. On the upper right hand corner of her letter was her new return address: "Cell 217, Women's Division, 200 19th Street, S.E., Washington, D.C. Jail."

CHAPTER XII

TREASON IN LIBERTY'S CRADLE

"A whispering campaign is the best thing now.
Mrs. Murphy tells Mrs. Duffy and she tells Mrs.
O'Toole who tells it to Mrs. Smith. . . . It's the safest
thing to work nowadays."

FRANCIS P. MORAN

I CARRIED ON a correspondence with Edward Holton James.
He was on a nation-wide tour contacting and co-ordinating
the efforts of fellow fascists who had not been apprehended
by the Department of Justice. "Yankee Comrade," one of his
letters to me began, "Here is our program. Germany for the
Germans. Yankeeland for the Yankees." It went on:

The Germans under the swastika have had a revolution which
has brought liberty to their people (*das volk*). . . . Germany is
nearer to democracy than we are. Churchill and Roosevelt understand nothing about democracy.

The Yankee Freeman will see to it that the "Atlantic Charter"
goes to the bottom of the Atlantic Ocean. Our course is marked
for us by George Washington and '76. The Germans have organized the Hitler elite. We shall see in this country the George
Washington elite.

I was now working feverishly against time and against being discovered as an investigator. Mrs. Willard of Chicago
had already written James and others that I was not to be
"trusted." Fortunately disbelieving her, James gave me the
opportunity to "explain" my integrity as a "patriot" and I succeeded in convincing him that I was loyal to the American
Nazi cause. Mrs. Washburn's arrest would further throw the

YANKEE COMRADES   *Leaflet No. 2*   YANKEE COMRADES   *Leaflet No. 26*

I Stand With Germany   I Support Petain

439

weight of suspicion against me. Then, too, Edwin Banta had been partly responsible for my "losing face" as investigator in the New York area. This informant for the Bund had no direct proof, but while mixing widely among "patriotic" circles he spread the rumor that George Pagnanelli had "sold out to the enemy."

Nor could I forget that Drew was also wise to me, and it worried me because I had no means of knowing what he was doing about it. Between these and others who also suspected me, I found myself in such hot water that I decided to leave town. I wanted to investigate Boston fascists and I wrote James—who had just returned to his home in Concord—that I intended to visit "my Italian fishermen relatives in Gloucester." James wrote back: "When you come up to Gloucester, why not spend a night with me?"

I packed and left hurriedly on an early morning train.

Edward Holton James lived on 26 Lexington Road, Concord—on the same historic road over which British redcoats retreated after their stand at Concord Bridge. Historic markers and historic homes and historic landmarks dotted the road all the way to Lexington six miles away. Adjoining James' home was the square, white picket-fenced home of the immortal Ralph Waldo Emerson. James lived on ground as hallowed as Valley Forge and Bunker Hill.

Inside his home I found the walls studded with mementos of his historic forebears. There were photographs of Professor William James and the writer, Henry James. Antique colonial furniture adorned the room of this veritable museum of Americana. I was swept to those days only a few generations ago when patriots had died on that very spot in order that Democracy might live. But Edward Holton James had other thoughts. He placed in my hand the latest copy of his *Grapevine Letter*:

He would be a fool who pretends that there is any patriotism in the war now going on. . . . As regards political revolution, a people's movement here must do precisely what the Germans did. It must get rid of the two-party system known here as "democracy." In reality, this system is a sham. . . . Either Hitler will take over this country, or the Yankee Freeman will take it over on a one-party basis.

James was talking to me: "Hitler did away with the two-party system, and that's what we've got to do here. What we should have here is a government by the elite, with a boss at the head—an American Hitler. Whoever starts the movement and keeps it going will become boss—just as in Germany."

I realized with a start that I was not on hallowed Concord earth, but in the home of Concord's Quisling!

"Our type of revolution is more potent than arms. We use ideas as weapons. That is the way Hitler first worked it."

"Yes," I said absently: "The American people are sovereign."

"Nothing of the kind," James snapped back. "They are nothing but cattle. They are stupid. Only a handful, only the elite are capable." Then he added sternly: "George, I want you to get away from that red-white-and-blue idea. It belongs to the past. A New Order means making a clean sweep of the ideologies of yesterday. It means a New Life, a New Outlook entirely. Hitler's *Weltanschauung* (world vision) was worldwide in scope. The Yankee Freemen are the American arm of that world revolution."

I sipped at my cider and looked into the blazing logs in the fireplace. They lighted up James' face, ardent in its intensity. I wanted to look into the fire and dream, but James would give me no peace.

"You haven't read your *Mein Kampf* carefully, George," he admonished. "It's our *Bible*."

His copy lay next to *The Diaries of George Washington*. He got up and went to the bookshelf, and brought over a sheaf of letters he had been receiving from fellow Yankee Freemen. There were several from Rudy Fahl, of Denver, who had been indicted for sedition, also letters from Margaret Norton and Norman Wilson, both of whom had helped formulate the Yankee Freemen platform.

"Of course I know the *Grapevine Letters* conflict with the Law," James said. "And I know what it means if we're caught. But I'm within my Constitutional rights in putting them out. It's the sedition laws which are unconstitutional."

It was late and I asked to be excused. In reality, I wanted to be alone to jot down my notes. James led me up a quaint series of steps, past a hall dotted with historic photographs. Books on American history lined the shelves in my bedroom, adjacent to copies of *The Talmud Unmasked* by Sanctuary and *The Octopus* by Mrs. Dilling.

James was downstairs when I awoke the next morning. Silently I tiptoed to his room in search of Nazi literature and Nazi books. I did not think he'd hear me, as he was playing the violin.

He stopped playing suddenly.

"George," he called out.

I managed to get back to my door and had just entered my room when he came around the corner. "I'll be right out," I said.

Mrs. James was away and I expected that for breakfast we'd slap together a few eggs, make our own coffee and leave the dishes in the sink. On the contrary, a delicious breakfast—and later, lunch—was served us by a maid. After breakfast I went back to my schooling. It was Sunday morning. James opened the pages of his well-marked *Bible*—and read from pages 328-329 of *Mein Kampf*.

I asked whether the revolutionary plan of Yankee Freemen was to be confined to the *Grapevine Letter* and personal missionary work.

"For the time being that is all we can do."

"But how about storm troopers and arms and organization?"

"In due time all that, yes. You've got to meet violence with violence. But what's the use of talking about that now? When you have 60,000 men, or at least 20,000 in one section and rule the streets—then you can think about the storm troopers."

"And would the movement include the use of arms and munitions?"

"Why, of course," the Concord Quisling answered.

James told me of the visit he had had with Norman Wilson. "Wilson wanted to see this thing end by assassination," he said. "I'm for assassination, if it would work. But it won't solve anything. Besides, we are doing the assassination the way it ought to be done. Assassination by words. These are our weapons now—words. They penetrate deeper than bullets."

James continued, carried away by his own fervor, his face florid. "Our job right now is to hamstring the war effort. If Roosevelt puts this war over with the people, we're through. The world revolution will be through."

"How about reform?" I asked.

"You can't have reform without revolution," he stormed, "and you can't have revolution without blood. You can't create anything new without destroying the old. And you can't destroy the old without killing off those who support it. A New Order means a New Order in every respect. Reform is out completely."

This climaxed my course of instruction. As he drove me to the station in his new auto, I thanked him for his hospitality.

"I've been watching you, George," he said. "You are a go-getter. You don't do a thing and then stop. You have determination. You make a good Yankee Comrade. I wish we had a few dozen more like you."

I thanked him for the compliment. Before leaving, James gave me copies of thirty-six inflammatory leaflets he had published, most of which had originally appeared in the *Concord Herald*. One of them, *Hitler in Concord*, read:

The reason I am for Hitler and the Germans is because I honestly believe that Hitler and the Germans are interested that we should save our-way-of-life against the British. The Germans have a stake in this country. . . . I see no reason why Japan's friendship would be a harm for us. I favor Hitler coming to Concord. I hope he will come soon. . . . Together, we shall work out something good.

My first stop in Boston after I left James was to call on Conrad Chapman who was related to James by a marriage tie. I found Chapman literally hiding in a tiny, off-the-road house at 17-A Branch Street. Even Bostonians in the vicinity did not know about Branch Street. Chapman was unusually tall, with a small head and delicate features. His face had the look of a studious laboratory worker. A moment later he told me he was taking courses at the Massachusetts Institute of Technology.

Chapman was unwilling to talk. When I tried to make an

appointment to see him the next day, he said: "One of my friends has got into trouble. He was framed, of course. But I don't want to see anyone or do anything else until I settle this matter. They can easily get something on you nowadays."

Chapman's background was familiar to me. An extremely clever operator for the Goebbels cause, Chapman was the man behind Mrs. Fry: he gave the orders and had charge of the funds. He had many contacts high in the Nazi Ministry of Propaganda and was involved in the abortive American Nazi *putsch* engineered by Consul Manfred von Killinger. He used the alias Warren Weston, but never associated publicly with known members of the Bund, Silver Shirts and other pro-Nazi groups on the coast many of which he guided through his lieutenants: Mrs. Fry, Henry D. Allen and Ivan Gorin. When Allen was subpoenaed to appear before the Dies Committee, he turned over more than 1000 letters incriminating notorious Nazi operatives in America and many of the letters involved Chapman. Chapman quietly left the country and was followed by Mrs. Fry. I had got the tip that he had quietly slipped back into the United States. This was the man I faced.

"How did you learn my address?" was the first question Conrad Chapman asked.

I mentioned my "friendship" with Deatherage and implied that I had got it from him. Then I asked: "Have you been visited by the authorities?"

"No," he answered. "And I don't want them to. They are usually very thorough."

I remembered that phrase and it haunted me during the rest of my interview. Why was he afraid of a "thorough" investigation? What had he to hide?

"I haven't been doing anything since December," he said, referring to Pearl Harbor.

"Do you ever hear from Mrs. Fry?" I asked.

"Oh, no," he answered, "she went back. . . ." He was unwilling to say that she had fled to Germany from the F.B.I.

I asked if he was in touch with James True or George Deatherage, with both of whom he had worked in former years. He denied recent contacts with them and he also denied communicating with an extremely close collaborator of his,

Henry D. Allen, the ex-convict who had also served as liaison man between General Nicholas Rodriguez of the Mexican Gold Shirts and Herman Max Schwinn, West Coast Bund leader.

I asked Chapman if he saw Lawrence Dennis.

"No, but I used to get his magazine, *The Awakener*. Dennis worked on it and Joseph Kamp used to be the editor."

His memory was excellent. But Chapman was unwilling to talk further. I did not think at the time that my interview had been productive. But in the light of later developments in connection with Mrs. Fry, it proved important to locate Chapman, alias Warren Weston, at his sequestered home at 17-A Branch Street.

I found Boston seething with anti-Semitism, defeatism and rumor mongering. Evidence of Christian Front and Coughlinite activity was rife. The fascist spirit had permeated the "cradle of American Liberty." It had even penetrated the American Legion. I made it a point to interview William F. Campbell, Commander of the Norfolk County Post, who had circulated widely the vicious anti-Semitic charge that "the situation of Draft-dodging has become so flagrant, that large numbers of a *certain racial group* are coming from New York to this section where they are getting defense jobs and keeping out of the Draft."

I faced the undersized, fanatic-faced man and demanded proof.

"That's what I wanted to see you about," he countered. "I wanted to get your proof from New York. The F.B.I. is after me for the proof. What have you got?"

"But I haven't any. I came to get the facts from you," I said, my anger rising.

"Well, I'll tell you. It's this way," Campbell began, halting: "We have a lot of proof, see, but we can't give it out because we got to protect the defense workers. These men have jobs and they can't talk in the open."

"Have they talked to the F.B.I. and Army Intelligence?" I asked.

"I myself talked to them. But I tell you my men are afraid to talk to anybody. They're afraid of their jobs."

"You know damned well," I said heatedly, "that the F.B.I. and the Army Intelligence will protect your men. If you can't trust them you can't trust anybody."

It was my impulse to smash this gossip monger square in the face, regardless of the oversized dimensions of a "witness" he had brought along. Campbell apparently had no proof to the tale that "Jews" were evading the Draft by going to Boston. Through a close friend of mine in the Boston Army Intelligence office I ascertained that no "proof" of any consequence had been presented. I am prevented from elaborating on my friend's fuller answer.

Legionnaire Campbell's rumor mongering was merely another tongue of flame from Boston's native fascist fires. I predict that unless it is curbed, Boston's clerical-fascist stench will some day cause national nausea. Even now—Hitler has much to be proud of in Boston!

At Daddy's and Jack's Novelty Shop on Bromfield Street, I found that with every dollar's worth of goods you received a handful of anti-Semitic poison.

John Joseph Murphy, publisher of *Save America Now* a Boston edition of *Social Justice*, boasted that he had been the first man in the country to raise the cry of impeaching the President.

"Yes, sir, I was first—back in 1938."

Murphy had been a leading light in the America First Committee and regarded Father Coughlin as a "sterling American, the finest man America has produced." He dedicated an issue of *Save America Now* to the Reverend Curran, Coughlin's agent in the East and had used regular *Social Justice* channels of distribution.

"I was never a member of the Christian Front here but I spoke for them," Murphy said. "I know Moran and I like him very well."

"Were you in sympathy with the Christian Front principles?" I asked.

"With its program of Americanism, yes. But they also had a radical program. I wasn't for that. I was strictly for their Constitutional methods."

I went to see Edward H. Hunter, a failure as ex-detective

and labor spy, a stand-by on the *World Service* honor roll and a "patriot" with a distinguished pedigree.

Hunter set up shop in 1932 "to inculcate the principles of Americanism in industrial, religious, fraternal, and educational circles" under the high-sounding name, Industrial Defense Association, Inc. That same year he was contacted by Kurt G. W. Luedecke, a Nazi agent with whom Hunter became friendly and introduced at the Exchange Trust Company. Here Luedecke opened a bank account then tried to induce Hunter to found a chapter of the Swastika League of America. The League actually functioned for a while, but was denied a state charter. When Hitler came to power a year later, Hunter mysteriously began to receive $300 a month which he devoted to the publication of an extensive line of pro-Nazi tracts.

Even though the Boston Better Business Bureau branded him an anti-Semite, it did not hamper Hunter. But when his role of a Nazi party-line follower took an ominous course, the Massachusetts Legislature investigated him in 1937. Hunter proved to be an evasive witness. Senator Thomas M. Burke finally asked:

Q. Isn't it true you attempted to create a corporation of the Nazi League in Massachusetts?
A. Yes.
Q. Then I say, is it true you are a Nazi . . . ?
A. Yes, I am.

Even though the Committee concluded that he carried on "the most vicious activity clearly intended to incite racial and religious hatred," Hunter was released to take up from where he had left off. I dug out a letter he wrote in 1938 to a correspondent:

I am acquainted with Bund members . . . and do not want to know any finer or cleaner Americans than they are. I can assure you 99.9% of the propaganda against the Bund originated in Communistic circles. . . . I would advise you to send a couple of dollars to *World Service* and George Deatherage [the addresses of both were given], asking them to place your name on their mailing list.

He wrote again:

I cannot understand how any student of Radicalism can be misled by the Jewish cry of Fascism and Nazism. . . . Fascism is made out of whole cloth by the fathers of liars (St. John's 8-44). There is no such animal in America.

In 1941 Governor Saltonstall signed an act dissolving Hunter's Association, but the patrioteer with the nine lives bounced back with the Industrial Defense Service. Member of the American Coalition, Hunter's contacts with American fascists were countless and the damage he rendered to the democratic cause can best be computed by its direct beneficiaries: Luedecke and his kind.

On my first visit to him in 1941, I found the grizzled "patriot" who had hoodwinked Boston's sleeping citizens, seated quietly behind his desk. He had crafty manners, sharp eyes and was given to rapid-fire questioning. When I survived the clumsy inquisition Hunter put me through, I switched the conversation to the Bund.

"The Bund is Nazi," Hunter exploded. "They are all for-

The Industrial Defense Association, Inc.

136 Federal Street, Boston, Mass.
Telephone Connection

President
EDWARD G. JAY
Consulting Engineer

Treasurer
ROSS H. CURRIER
Active in Military, Naval
and Insurance circles.

Organized to inculcate the principles of Americanism in Industrial, Religious, Fraternal and Educational circles.

Vice-President
MISS EVVIE F DALBY
Genealogist

Executive Secretary
EDWARD H. HUNTER
Lecturer and Organizer

necessary. The main paragraph in your letter of August 19, surprises me. I cannot understand how any student of Radicalism can be mislead by the Jewish cry of Fascism and Nazism. Those two words were coined as a Smoke Screen to cover up the dirty work of Communism.

What they are pleased to call Nazism is nothing more nor less than an open demonstration on the part of Germans and other Nationals that this country can not be overthrown by Communism or any other "ism". A visit to any of the German groups will conclusively prove that statement to you. Fascism is made out of whole cloth by the fathers

Very sincerely yours,

Edward N Hunter

EHH: Executive Secretary

Hunter is one of many American Nazis who infest Boston, once the cradle of Liberty but now the cradle of a sinister developing native fascism.

eigners. They call themselves American, but that's only to cover up their Nazism." But I doubted if he had really reformed. "We don't want no Hitler here. We don't want no Bund to run our country. We want one hundred per cent Americanism. Of course," he added earnestly, "Hitler is doing an excellent job in Germany. We ought to be doing the same here, but . . ." he winked, "we want to do it our way, the American way, the one hundred per cent American way, strictly according to the Constitution."

Hunter's viewpoint had merely changed from an adulation of Nazism to a species of American Fascism, from a red-white-black swastika to the red-white-and-blue. Regarding me as one of the boys on the inside, he explained his current line of work in these terms:

"If you were a factory owner and wanted to know everything about 1000 employees, you'd come to me, and ask me to find out how many Communists you had working for you. I hunt down Communists in factories. That's my business now."

This was the same business which Harry Jung had once practiced in Chicago—and Jung was a director of the Industrial Defense Association. Hunter's next query was startling. He asked if I knew any "patriotic hotheaded Italians" who could be relied upon to do a little sabotage, or some Ukrainians who were angry enough to "blow up a factory."

When I visited Hunter the second time in the fall of 1942, I found his new office at 40 Central Street quiet as a morgue. He was no longer hunting for "Reds" in America's factories, and business was bad. Hunter was now locating missing persons. But his pet themes were revolution and bloodthirsty anti-Semitism. I asked what would expedite the revolution.

"Lay low, is the only advice I can give. With that Jew Biddle in office, you can't do anything now."

I told him about a New York "group" which was considering the distribution of anti-Semitic stickers. He advised against the idea.

"If the leaders of your group were Yankees it would be all right. But if Germans, Italians or Irish do anything like that it won't work. They'll put the finger on you right away. Lay low right now. Everybody ought to lay low. Why haven't I been picked up?" he boasted. "I've done more than Edmondson or True . . . I worked carefully and knew who I talked to. I wouldn't talk to anybody unless I knew he was okay."

Hunter was a subscriber to *Destiny*, organ of the Anglo-Saxon Federation. Copies were stacked on his desk. His preachments subscribed fully to the Anglo-Saxon drivel.

"Armageddon is coming. All the Jews except those chosen to live will be exterminated. The Kingdom of God shall come soon, then the millennium of a thousand years of peace."

I asked Hunter if he knew Howard B. Rand, president of the Federation. "Of course I do. He comes here almost every week. He is preparing a chart for me giving the family tree of Israel. As a matter of fact, he is speaking tonight. Why don't you come along. . . ."

I turned to Francis P. Moran, fuehrer of the New England Christian Front. I had first visited him in the summer of 1941 at his office at 108 Massachusetts Avenue. A black sign on the door read: "Sociological Research." Inside, a discolored American flag drooped in the corner. Small cubicles were stuffed with the poison tracts of Edmondson, Stahrenberg, True, Sanctuary, Pelley. A stack of Joseph P. Kamp's *The Fifth Column in Washington* was laid next to a pile of leaflets from the American Coalition of Patriotic Societies. Copies of *Social Justice* rested above the folds of the *Deutscher Weckruf*. On the wall was the emblem of the Christian Front, "C. F.," superimposed on a cross.

Moran sat at the desk, tight-lipped, coarse-textured, fanatic. He represented a new type of Christian Front fuehrer. He neither gushed out with "Christianity" nor did he heap abuse on the Jew. He was a calculating and cold-blooded propagandist of the Bund's Gerhard Kunze type. When I told him that I belonged to the Christian Mobilizers he sneered, looking upon McWilliams as an amateur.

"You can't win this fight with terrorism, with storm troopers, or just by yelling 'Jew.' You've got to lay the groundwork first. You got to be subtle about it so they can't pin down anti-Semitic or fascist labels on you. We're all working for the same end," Moran confessed, "it's the tactics that are important. You can lose this fight with the wrong tactics. McWilliams isn't using the right methods."

He explained how he worked—quietly and without fanfare, through the medium of unobtrusive underground cells throughout New England. His open forums were dignified, he said, and no booing or hissing was permitted. But his technique of injecting the racial issue paralleled Father Coughlin's.

Moran instructed his henchmen to approach strangers in a "tolerant" vein. As their education in Hitlerite propaganda progressed, the recruit was introduced to a more advanced state of anti-Semitism. In final stages of his conversion the victim was handed Stahrenberg's and Sanctuary's literature.

"After that the fellow is in the bag," Moran smiled. "It's the only way to operate in New England. The people are conservative around here and you gotta give it to them in gradual doses. You gotta take it easy with them."

Moran confided that he received *Fichte-Bund* and *World Service* literature regularly through "blind" addresses—that is, to mail aliases throughout Boston. I asked Moran how he had come to decide on the technique which he apparently had worked so successfully. Moran's answer was blunt:

"Mr. Scholz and I worked it out together."

"Who is Mr. Scholz?" I asked.

„SIEG IM WESTEN"

ist kein Film im üblichen Sinne. Es ist der

Original - Bildbericht

des Oberkommandos des deutschen Heeres über die grösste militärische Operation aller Zeiten.

Der Film wurde zusammengestellt aus 2,700,000 Fuss Material, aufgenommen von Kameraleuten, die den deutschen Armee-Einheiten in vorderster Front eingegliedert waren. Er enthält ausserdem Bilder, die von den englischen, belgischen und französischen Streitkräften aufgenommen wurden und beim Vormarsch in deutsche Hände fielen. Sie sehen z. B. bisher unveröffentlichte Aufnahmen von der Bemannung der Maginot-Linie.

Christian Front *fuhrer* Francis P. Moran sponsored this Nazi film in Boston, obtaining it through the medium of his friend, Dr. Herbert Scholz, Nazi consul.

"Dr. Herbert Scholz is the German Consul in Boston," he said.

And through the good graces of the Nazi consul, Moran sponsored showings of *Sieg Im Westen*, the Nazi propaganda film whose purpose was to cow Americans before the invincibility of the Nazi war machine. Moran corresponded with the American Nazi, George Deatherage, kept in close touch with Father Coughlin and was a personal friend of clerical fascist Reverend Edward Lodge Curran.

Moran spoke with Father Curran at the Friends and Neighbors Club of Pawtucket, Rhode Island, shamelessly called the President a "Jew" guilty of "treason," and charged that the "White House sold military secrets to England and France." Father Curran looked on smugly as the audience applauded. State Supreme Court Justice Francis B. Condon, who had been invited as a speaker under false pretenses, denounced Moran: "I would not be on the same platform with that speaker if I knew he would make those radical statements," he said.

When I met Moran again in November, 1942, the F.B.I. had closed down his "Sociological Research" office—not, however, before he had distributed thousands of Viereck's propaganda books from Flanders Hall; not before he had permeated Boston and its environs with a systematic campaign of defeatism, anti-Semitism, anti-war and fascist virus.

I spoke with Moran at his home in West Roxbury. By his confession unemployed for several years, while engaged in voluntary work for the Christian Front, Moran had just purchased a sturdy three-story home. I could not ask him his source of income. Instead I asked if he was still active in the movement after his appearance before the Washington grand jury.

"Whatever I do now," he said, "I do alone. I know I'm being watched. Just the same, I keep in contact with what is going on. I still control them all in Boston. I've told them to lay low right now. Only the Citizens Constitutional Committee is holding meetings. They're made up of women and the F.B.I. won't bother these women."

Moran continued to receive subversive literature from his former associates. "They keep sending stuff and I'm glad to get it." I saw the evidence on the kitchen table. Kamp's stuff was prominent. Moran's predictions about Boston's former Mayor James M. Curley, now in Congress, interested me. "He's been to Congress before and he knows Washington inside out," Moran said. "Now that he's back he'll raise a lot of hell and he'll make Ham Fish look like an amateur."

"A lot of hell is being raised right here in Boston," I said.

"I guess I had something to do with that," Moran boasted, his thin, bloodless lips barely parting as he spoke.

"The only thing you can do now, of course, is to talk about Communism and the Jews. You can't touch the war. A whispering campaign is the best thing now. They'd have a hell of a time tracing it. Mrs. Murphy tells Mrs. Duffy, and she tells Mrs. O'Toole, who tells it to Mrs. Smith. Yes, these women

HITLER, THE "PROTECTOR" OF CHRISTIANITY

The mission of German nationality in the world is to free this world of Jews and Christians. When the meaning of national freedom is recognized by all other unfree peoples, they will also recover from the illness that besets them by following the example set by the German spirit ∿∿∿∿∿∿∿∿∿∿∿∿∿ Through the German soul and through unadulterated German blood, the world will be able to return to a state of health, but only after it has been freed from the curse of Judaism and of Christianity, and only when races shall

ground for all the peoples and nations of **Europe during the Thirty Years war.** This was a religious war of that supra-state power, the **Roman Church. It was started and carefully nurtured by the Jesuits in order to force Protestant Germany once more under the yoke of Rome.** (The Counter-Reformation!) (See E. U. M. Ludendorff: "Das

Holy Roman Church remained true to its mission as a supra-state power and killed off the best German racial stock in the most terrible war of all time. Not long before that, the Church had murdered millions of the best stock through its insane holy persecution of witches.

Jewish-Christian morality in general and in every particular. **If we wish to create something new, we cannot permit the existence and operation of disorganizing factors such as Christianity.** If we wish to do a thorough job, we must overthrow and shatter all opposing and destructive forces—unsparingly and without compromise. **Germanic blood and Christian baptismal water can never mix!**

These excerpts are from *Defilement of Race*, a book written by Dietrich Hutten and published in 1937 by *Deutsche Revolution* of Duesseldorf, Germany.

can certainly dish it out, and by the time they end up they've got something which everybody believes. It's the safest thing to work nowadays." Moran boasted how he himself had set several rumors into circulation in order to reach "the ears of certain people.

"Revolution by bullets not ballots," Moran said, "is the only way to clean house and get back to the Constitution. I'm within my Constitutional rights in saying this."

I regarded Boston, headquarters of the Dashnag, as a smelly political monument to the spirit of Francis P. Moran and Edward H. Hunter, and the subversive forces they had so loyally and freely served for so many years. Someone was protecting Moran. I did not know who it was, but Moran boasted—and he is not the sort to boast without some foundation: "The movement has friends all over the city. A lot of people here think the way I do, but they're not coming out with it—not yet. Our friends go up, all the way up!"

What did Moran mean by that?

Unlike Detroit and Salt Lake City and New York, I saw little in Boston which might give me a glimmer of hope that the poisonous atmosphere there would clear. The same public apathy which permitted Hunter to "come back" time and again and establish himself is indicative of the "I don't care" attitude of Bostonians in continuing to permit the cancer of fascism to gnaw shamelessly at the cradle of Liberty.

The American Irish Defense Association, under the direction of Miss Frances U. Sweeney, the Rumor Clinic maintained by the *Boston Herald*, and the *Christian Science Monitor* with its magnificent exposé articles were doing commendable work, but I was not convinced that their efforts alone could quench the fires of nativist-fascism enveloping Boston. Almost singlehanded Miss Sweeney succeeded in barring from the large newsstands copies of *Catholic International*, a near-seditious organ berating our war effort, defaming Democracy and championing clerical fascism. It was issued by a former publisher of dirty sex magazines, an American-born Jew who had been converted to Catholicism. In a peppery issue of her *Boston City Reporter* Miss Sweeney raked its editor, David Gordon, over the coals with telling effect.

None the less, I felt that her efforts in the Boston area were akin to digging at a mountain with a hand spade. For whoever was protecting Moran and patronizing Hunter was dedicated to the defeat of the American democratic tradition and the American war effort. No one who knows the fascist pattern can remain impervious to the native American Fascist fever that has enveloped Boston and its environs.

Should it ever come to flame, Jew, Protestant, Catholic alike will be scorched—just as Jew, Protestant and Catholic alike were scorched at the disastrous night club fire which, like an avenging hand, struck at Boston for its political iniquity a scant few weeks after my visit, resulting in the death of about 490 Catholics, Protestants and Jews. Death knows neither race nor creed. The Nazi cancer knows neither race nor creed. It devours all. First it devours the mind, then the heart, then the body.

On March 17 Hamilton Fish spoke among his elements and urged the founding of a Third Party composed of disgruntled, like-minded, anti-New Deal elements, and named James Farley and Senator Wheeler as vice-presidential candidates. Father Curran also addressed Bostonians under the auspices of the South Boston Citizens' Association. On his way to the hall Father Curran fondly greeted Francis P. Moran in the lobby of the Hotel Gardiner.

Unholy race riots, too, shook Boston on holy St. Patrick's Day.

In Chelsea, Brookline and Dorchester Jewish boys and girls were set upon and severely beaten by "patriotic" bums glowing with Coughlinite "Christianity," but the matter was hushed up, and no action taken—even the Boston press unanimously suppressing any mention of it.

Bostonians remained smug in their "patriotism."

Chapter XIII

GRAVE DIGGERS OF DEMOCRACY

> "If you find any organization containing the word 'democracy' it is probably directly or indirectly affiliated with the Communist party. . . . It is time to brush aside this word 'democracy' with its connotations."
>
> MERWIN K. HART

ONE HOT SUMMER NIGHT in July, 1940, at the Franziskanner Hall in Yorkville, McWilliams was threatening to raze to the ground the Democratic and Republican parties if and when elected to Congress. After the meeting, as the "patriots" were streaming past the table of poison literature sold by "Pop" Eibach, "Pop" called me over.

"George, I've got something good for you," he said. Handing him fifty cents I pocketed the volume. In the subway I began to read *Communism in Germany*. It was copyrighted in 1933 by Eckart-Verlag, Berlin. The author was Adolf Ehrt, and it was sponsored by the General League of German Anti-Communist Associations. It was prefaced with a quotation by "Chancellor Adolf Hitler." One section of the book was entitled "Why Americans Should Read This Book," and carried the notice:

The value of this German exposé as an object lesson to other countries has led our Committee to place it in the hands of leaders of public opinion throughout the United States.

Appearing above the caption "For the American Section of the International Committee to Combat the World Menace of Communism," was a roster of approved "leaders" as follows:

Walter C. Cole
John Ross Delafield
Ralph M. Easley

Elon Huntington Hooker
F. O. Johnson
Orvel Johnson

Samuel McRoberts   Harry A. Jung
C. G. Norman   Walter S. Steele
Ellis Searles   Archibald E. Stevenson
Josiah A. Van Orsdel   John B. Trevor
Hamilton Fish, Jr.

The first ten on the list apparently became convinced that the Nazis' cry of "fighting Communism" was actually a sham. Of the other five whose names appeared, grand juries are familiar with Ham Fish and Harry Augustus Jung; John B. Trevor's American Coalition was mentioned as a "factor" in the indictment of twenty-eight persons charged with sedition, while Walter S. Steele must share morally whatever honor befalls the Coalition because of his intimate collaboration with Trevor. As to Archibald Ewing Stevenson, he is employed as public counsel by the New York State Economic Council, a super-patriotic group whose chairman since 1936 has been Merwin K. Hart, a devout propagandist for Franco.

"There is no longer any distinction between Fascism, Nazism and Falangism," said Franco, belatedly, in December, 1942.

And the world had no greater devotee of the Spanish Falangist cause, alias Spanish Nazism—along with Hitler, Mussolini and Franco—than Merwin K. Hart, Stevenson's employer. During the Spanish Civil War Hart travelled to Spain, spoke over the official Franco radio, and on his return wrote a glowing book, *America Look at Spain,* raking Democracy over the coals and heaping upon it abuse and scorn. After this, Hart recommended to the Falangist propaganda office, his friend, Miss Jane Anderson, who had once declared at an Economic Council meeting that "America is morally and mentally ripe for a revolution." After Miss Anderson finished her work on behalf of the Spanish Nazis, the German Nazis hired her for short-wave broadcasts to America. The Department of Justice has declared Hart's American-born, absentee Quisling friend to be a traitor to her country.

Upon his return from Franco's Nazi-Spain Hart, who admitted being received by high Falangist officials, denounced the ideals and principles which had motivated the French and American revolutions. He justified the intervention of Nazi and Fascist armies in Spain. In his book *America Look at*

Spain, Hart lauded Primo de Rivera's career as dictator and praised his suppression of "free speech and free expression of opinion." Hart directly approved Franco's type of government in these words: "If one wishes to be a stickler for the theory of pure democracy . . . or if one wishes to see virtue in the constant policy of compromise . . . one may find fault with the proposed government of Spain."

During the winter of 1938–39 Merwin K. Hart founded the American Union for Nationalist Spain, which attracted the Christian Front elements in droves. On Hart's committee were Lester M. Gray, a founder of the Manhattan unit of the Christian Front; John Eoghan Kelly, its organizer; the Reverend Edward Lodge Curran, its promoter in the East; Patrick F. Scanlon, its publicist in the Brooklyn *Tablet*; Mrs. Catherine P. Baldwin, a correspondent of Frank W. Clark; Joseph P. Kamp; and Robert Caldwell Patton, editor of the fascist *Patriot Digest*.

And when Hart decided to hold a "Pro-American mass meeting for Americanism and neutrality"—in the Seventh Regiment Armory—he appointed Bernard T. D'Arcy, *Social Justice* distributor as promoter and put Allen Zoll in charge of showing *Spain in Arms*, standard movie for Christian Front audiences. It was only appropriate that Father Coughlin's picture should be carried down the aisle amid the tumult of his idolaters.

Hart claimed for his Economic Council, founded in 1931, a membership of 2,000, and a circulation of 17,000 for its biweekly letter. Hart is a Harvard graduate, member of a half-dozen exclusive clubs and his scorn for Democracy is deep-rooted and missionary. "Democracy," Hart said, speaking before the Nassau Club, Princeton, New Jersey:

. . . is the rallying cry under which the American system of government is being prepared for despotism. . . . If you find any organization containing the word "Democracy," it is probably directly or indirectly affiliated with the Communist party.

And before the New York Union League Club, composed of influential business men, he spoke on *The Alien Influence in Our Midst*, asserting: "It is time to brush aside this word 'Democracy' with its connotations." "In the interest of true

Americanism," he distributed thousands of copies of his speech. From Mrs. Flora A. Walker of the American Coalition came this letter of appreciation:

The box of your speech on "The Alien Influence in Our Midst" arrived and we are extremely grateful for your generosity. We shall "plant" them in fruitful spots.

As for fascist propaganda, Hart dismissed it: "The fact is that while Communism infests the country, fascism is almost nowhere to be found. Nobody heard of it until Communism came along. That is the real danger. So much for the fascist bogey."

The record shows that for the past fifteen years Hart has been engaged as a professional propagandist for one cause or another. With an annual salary fixed at $10,000 he has sought to influence legislation, both local and national, in the interests of clerical fascism (Falangism) and ultra-reactionary businessmen, using the bogey of Communism as an operating base. Supreme Court Justice Robert H. Jackson has denounced Hart as "pro-fascist."

In a professional capacity, Hart opposed the forty-hour week. He fought against the Unemployment Insurance Act, and he fought the Child Labor Act, insisting that it was an "inspiration from Russia . . . a Russian law for American youth." Hart's unsavory record also shows that he advocated the disfranchisement of poor and homeless Americans by demanding during the depression years that only those be permitted to vote who were not on relief.

Member of the America First Committee and a close friend of William R. Castle, who was chummy with Viereck, Hart fanatically opposed the Lend-Lease Bill and battled against aid to England and Russia. In his appearance before the Senate Committee on Military Affairs he sought to whitewash Japan by declaring that "an unfriendly attitude on the part of the United States drove Japan into the arms of the Axis." A few months later came Pearl Harbor.

On June 3, 1937 Hart presided as chairman of the Congress of American Private Enterprise, and among those who were listed as speakers were Gerald L. K. Smith, Mrs. Elizabeth

Dilling, Miss Cathrine Curtis, Congressman Clare Hoffman and Harold Lord Varney, who was an associate of Lawrence Dennis.

Hart's friendship among reactionary big business men is wide. James H. Rand Jr., president of the Remington-Rand Company has been his chief contributor. Other donors have been Lammot DuPont, president of the E. I. DuPont de Nemours & Co.; A. W. Erickson, chairman of a large New York advertising agency; Alfred P. Sloan, president of General Motors; J. H. Alstyne, president of the Otis Elevator Company. I am sure that these important capitalists helped finance Hart in good faith, and are totally unaware that clerical fascism, like authoritarian Nazism, is committed to the destruction of capitalist Democracy. The difference is merely one of method: clerical fascism works more subtly and proposes to strangulate capitalism by slow stages, rather than by guillotine methods.

In addition to John Eoghan Kelly and Reverend Curran, promoters of the Christian Front, Hart's acquaintanceships extended to other fields. General Moseley wrote him: "I sympathize with you one hundred per cent on what you are doing." John B. Snow arranged an introduction for him to H. W. Prentiss, Jr., of the Armstrong Cork Co.; and it was Seward Collins who wired Hart: "Much honored by invitation to join your general committee. Will be delighted to serve and to aid Union [for Nationalist Spain] in every way possible."

His other friends were the anti-Semites Harry A. Jung, Mrs. Dilling and Verne Marshall. Martin Dies, in whose honor Hart gave a luncheon at the Biltmore Hotel, was greatly embarrassed by the presence of Fritz Kuhn and James Wheeler-Hill as guests at a reserved table. Hart and Juan F. de Cardenas and Jose G. de Gregorio of the Spanish Embassy exchanged cordial letters with him, and Hart was extended the official thanks of Franco's Nazi regime for the "great and enthusiastic help you have extended to the Nationalist Cause in so many ways." The point was well taken because James True, another of Hart's friends, endorsed *America Look at Spain*, as a:

. . . broad and accurate vision of appraisal . . . intensely interesting eye-opening and ear un-stopping book, one that is startling in its revelations and impressive in its obvious honesty.

I tried repeatedly to interview Hart, but could not get beyond his secretary, and when she finally asked if I'd care to see Archibald Stevenson, I jumped at the opportunity, posing as a "patriot" from Detroit named Rudolph Eibers. Stevenson proved one of the shrewdest men I had interviewed and whitewashed his employer loyally.

Whereas Hart had boasted "I am proud to call Lindbergh a friend," Stevenson damned Lindbergh for his "racist" views. Whereas Hart's name had appeared over articles in *Social Justice* and Zoll's magazine, and had been endorsed by Coughlinites, Stevenson ridiculed the Catholic priest. Whereas Hart's acquaintances included anti-Semites, and his office during the Spanish Civil War was visited by many Christian Front-ers, Stevenson condemned anti-Semitism and said some of his best friends were Jews. But Stevenson's "cleverness" became laughable when he denounced Hitler, Mussolini and Franco, but kept mum on Stalin, whereas Hart had always denounced Stalin and soft-pedaled the others. Hart damned Democracy, but Stevenson swore by it and said he'd fight for the American way of life.

When I asked Stevenson—who up to this time had been talking glibly—if he knew Edward Rumely, agent of Imperial Germany during the World War, and still active in "patriotic" circles, he stopped, sputtered and coughed nervously. His mouth opened, then closed. I asked again. He said:

"Mr. Rumely, you know, was charged . . . and justly mind you, I'm not saying he wasn't, with being pro-German during the last war. His organization is apt to be criticized for it. Yes, I know his group."

Even though he had avoided definitely answering my question, it was quite a confession for Archibald Ewing Stevenson. He changed the subject after that and went into a peroration about some of his best friends who were Jews, about his Americanism, and how he'd fight like hell to preserve the American way of life.

This is the story I learned when I tried to probe the reason

the Nazis selected Archibald Ewing Stevenson to serve on
their committee, and *why* Merwin K. Hart, who serves as
backbone of America's reactionary business brains and bank-
books, hired Stevenson as public relations counsel.

Hart admitted in the public record his correspondence with
Lawrence Dennis, the "dean" of American intellectual fascism.
And my investigations of Dennis convinced me once again
that no breach exists between those who are dismissed as
"crackpot" and the Park Avenue grave diggers of our Democracy. I visited Lawrence Dennis at his stuffy office in New
York in the fall of 1942.

"Where's Joe McWilliams now?" Dennis asked, looking
up from the typewriter.

"Why, he's in Chicago," I said, surprised that "the brains"
of American Fascism should profess interest in the Yorkville
rabble-rouser.

"Oh, no," Dennis answered. "I met him twice only a few
weeks ago and we lunched at an Italian restaurant around the
corner."

Dennis told me that he had been meeting McWilliams for
"two or three years." Joe had made some mistakes, he admitted, but he was learning and Dennis believed that he had
benefited "from the advice I gave him just before he went to
Chicago." Somehow I was certain that Dennis had been coaching McWilliams personally while he ran for Congress. Taking
me for a Christian Front variety of "patriot," Dennis tossed
over a letter.

"It's from Deatherage," he said. "I made copies of it. I'm
typing an answer and will show it to you in a minute." While
he typed, I read Deatherage's letter, sent from Nashville,
Tennessee:

Since leaving the Naval Base job I have had one job with an
Ordnance plant—but . . . the officers in Washington over that
plant had to order me removed. Next week, unless something
else turns up I will go on an army job further south. . . . I spoke
in Charleston day before yesterday before the Exchange Club.
. . . I meant it only to clear the atmosphere in my home area.

Have made several trips in the South recently and have been
rubbing shoulders with the rustics. They are up in the air over
this poll tax business and there is liable to be trouble. Both sides

are arming themselves and a check on the wholesale hardware sales show considerable increase in the demand for ice picks, shotguns and shells.

"Here is a copy of what I wrote back," Dennis said. "You can keep it, but don't let it get around." I read his answer. It was a five-page letter ending with "Thanks for writing me. Do it again." Except for the statement that Mrs. Dilling had been on the mailing list of Dennis' bulletin, it was taken up with personal matters. Amazing to me was that Dennis kept in close touch with leaders of the so-called "lunatic fringe" and at the same time worked with those in his own class, such as Seward Collins.

"I haven't seen Collins in some time," he said, "but I keep in touch with him."

I switched the conversation to Viereck, and Dennis instantly became cautious. I reminded him that I had read his articles in *Today's Challenge* and had also heard him speak at Viereck's American Fellowship Forum.

"I do not think Viereck was a good man to advise the German Government," Dennis said. "None of them were. I always used to argue with them."

We spoke of the Bund, and Dennis criticized its use of uniforms and swastikas. "Americans do not like that sort of thing. It's too bad. The Bund could have done a good job." He followed with the amazing statement: "The Nazis haven't spread any propaganda here. That's just. . . ." Without finishing the sentence, Dennis resumed: "No, the Bund didn't bring about any anti-Semitism. It worked among German-Americans only."

Born in Atlanta, "of a long line of American ancestors," Dennis' hair is woolly, dark and kinky. The texture of his skin is unusually dark and the eyes of Hitler's intellectual keynoter of "Aryanism" are a rich deep brown, his lips fleshy. Graduated from Harvard, Dennis worked seven years for the State Department. After spending six years in Wall Street, Dennis went to Europe in 1936, and was honored in Italy and Germany. He conferred with Mussolini for an hour and dined with Count Ignazio Tahon de Revel, secretary of the Fascist Party Abroad. In Germany Dennis met Baron Ulrich Von

Gienanth who later became pay-off man to Laura Ingalls. Dennis lunched with Dr. K. O. Bertling of the Amerika-Institut, who later endorsed Dennis to Manfred Zapp, manager of the Nazi *Trans-Ocean News* by writing:

I propose that you visit right away Mr. Lawrence Dennis, with whom you have already perhaps become acquainted in the meantime. . . . All you have to do is to contact him on the telephone and mention that I am sending regards.

And from General George Van Horn Moseley came this:

I enjoy reading your weekly letters and generally agree with you. In your letters dated January 11th, I think there is a lack of frankness in regard to the S.C.B. Hore Belisha. . . . This is my personal opinion expressed to you and I ask that you destroy this letter after you have read it.

Dennis' three books: *Is Capitalism Doomed?*, *The Coming American Fascism* and *The Dynamics of War and Revolution*, together with his rabid *Weekly Foreign Letter* bulletin ($4 a year), considerably influenced fascist thought and he became known as "America's leading intellectual fascist." Dennis minced no words:

I do not believe in democracy or the intelligence of the masses. This book is addressed not to the masses but to the elite or to the ruling groups, actual and potential . . . the governing minority of wealth, prestige and power, economic and cultural, present and future. . . . I am in favor of the revolution here. . . .

Speaking as he thought to a fellow fascist, Dennis was more specific during my interview: "I am for National-Socialism in America," he asserted, just the way Joe McWilliams had said it.

Would it take the form of a military dictatorship? I asked.

"I do not think so," Dennis answered. "I have friends in the army and I know their mentality. They are not mature politically. But they'll follow a political leader, the same as in Germany. As to a future leadership, Nye and Wheeler are both politicians, rather than leaders. There are many potential leaders and they'll step forward when it's time for them to do so."

"How about Lindbergh?" I asked.

"Lindbergh is excellent, but he is not well versed in politics. Surrounded by a circle of advisers of the nationalist type, Lindbergh would make an excellent nominal leader. But this is a battle not so much of personalities, as it is of ideas. The propagation of *ideas* is the important thing. The personalities will take care of themselves."

"Will wealthy Jews be exempted from persecution under American National-Socialism?" I asked.

I have remarked previously that fascism knows neither race nor creed. And in asking Dennis that question I had in mind a wealthy American Jew who boasted of his "friendship" with Dennis and denied that Dennis was anti-Semitic or that his philosophy was detrimental to the interests of American Jewry or America itself. I do not know whether this American Jew was politically stupid or whether he was trying to be "smart."

Dennis laughed at my query.

"A long, long time ago," he began, "some of the rich Jews in Germany got away with a few things. But that was a long time ago. American National-Socialism will begin with a wave of anti-Semitism in which both rich and poor Jews will eventually suffer. The process will be completely reactionary."

I listened attentively as this champion of American National-Socialism spoke with thorough knowledge of Nazi techniques.

"Such slogans as 'America for the Americans,' 'White Supremacy,' 'Strict Isolationism,' 'Europe for the Europeans,'

882   My New Order

"I could continue to cite examples indefinitely. *The fact remains that two worlds are face to face with one another. Our opponents are quite right when they say:* Nothing can reconcile us to the National Socialist world.' How could a narrow-minded capitalist ever agree to my principles? It would be easier for the Devil to go to church and cross himself with holy water than for these people to comprehend the ideas which are accepted facts to us today. But we have solved our problems.

Hitler, the "protector" of capitalism. Excerpt from Hitler's speech on December 10, 1940 at the Rheinmetall-Borsig Works, Berlin.

'Keep Our Army and Navy at Home' will become popular. Reactionary feeling will become rampant, followed closely by anti-Semitism. I guess that answers your question fully," Dennis said laughing. "I am prejudiced against the Jews," he continued, "but I have a good friend in George Sokolsky. He is the best friend the Jews have." [1]

Dennis was "disgusted" with the way Pelley had handled his trial, but he thought better of Mrs. Dilling. "She phoned me when I was in Chicago, and I met her," he said. "She didn't know anything politically about National-Socialism, but she admired Hitler for cleaning up Communism."

Dennis brought up Gerald L. K. Smith and asked if I was familiar with his work. I merely said that I received his magazine, and explained Smith's policy.

"He is on the right track. The only thing to do is to declare yourself for the war now, even though you were against it before. After you say this," Dennis coached, "begin to explain that we're fighting for Communism."

The door suddenly opened and at the threshold stood a tall man with Nordic features, a scar running from ear to jaw. He was dressed in the uniform of a private in the United States Army. The soldier hesitated as he saw me.

"Oh, Mr. Pagnanelli is all right," Dennis explained. "We were just discussing the national situation. Nothing confidential. Sit down, Bob."

The soldier's name was Dr. Robert Lorenz, a mechanic at Keesler Field, where a division of our air force is stationed. Formerly Lorenz had been an instructor in economics at the

[1] George E. Sokolsky defended Merwin K. Hart in his columns, and on October 21, 1941 showed the first of many similar instances of lack of insight into Jap double-dealing by predicting: "Of course, the Japanese will not make war on us." Five days before Pearl Harbor he prophesied: "In spite of bellicose talk, the Japanese want no war with us. . . . The Japanese would like a freezing of the present status quo until a way can be found for an end to her present escapades without too much loss of 'face.'" Lawrence Dennis was saying the same thing.

Sokolsky also whitewashed Gerald L. K. Smith by declaring: ". . . Now I know and like Gerald Smith and see him every time I go to Detroit and have yet to discover that he is more anti-Semitic than Rabbi Stephen Wise." Staunchly supporting the America First policy, Sokolsky's name appeared on the Board of Governors of fascist Allen Zoll's Emergency Council to Keep the United States out of Foreign War. Mrs. Dilling was also listed.

University of Alabama. He was an American citizen of German birth. He told Dennis he had been questioned three times by the F.B.I. and Army Intelligence and was contemptuous of their treatment. A subscriber to Dennis' bulletin, Lorenz had come for some back numbers. Dennis gave him a batch.

Once again the door opened. This time the visitor was a big, bluff man, with popping gray eyes and plump complexion— an attorney named Robert Dennis O'Callaghan. He knew Joe McWilliams.

"I helped him get a good lawyer for his case. And funny thing," O'Callaghan said, "only a couple of weeks ago Edward James Smythe [then a fugitive from justice] called up and made an appointment to meet me. But he never showed up." O'Callaghan was voluble: "I've been offered a job as Custodian of Alien Property in Washington. I don't know if I'll take it." [2]

O'Callaghan remained to talk with Dennis, while Lorenz arose to go. I accompanied him to lunch at a corner cafeteria. Seated at a secluded table Lorenz expressed amazement at Dennis' grasp of the "world revolution."

"Few Americans understand the nature of the war in Europe. It's a revolution, and part of a world revolution in the making. You have to have Prussianism to carry on the revolution. You cannot fight this war on sentiment. Hitler," Lorenz said, "is breaking down national barriers. He is de-nationalizing in order to make a United States of Europe with Germany as the technological and industrial center. The best workmen in Europe, the finest painters and artists will be brought to Germany after the revolution is over. Germany will become the political and cultural center of all Europe. The rest of Europe will look to Germany for direction."

Lorenz neglected to add that the rest of Europe, denuded of its artists, artisans and intellectual leaders would serve as slaves to the "master race."

During 1935 and 1936 Dennis was associate editor with another of Merwin K. Hart's friends, Harold Lord Varney, on

[2] O'Callaghan accepted the job and according to his former law partner is engaged in confidential government work with the Chicago office of the Alien Property Custodian.

the staff of *The Awakener*. Calling itself the "journalistic spearhead in the national fight against Rooseveltism," *The Awakener* championed "the Americanism 'of the right' and opposed 'the socialism of the left.'" Among its contributors were Harry A. Jung and John Eoghan Kelly. The editor was Joseph P. Kamp. It was held in such high esteem in Nazi circles that in 1935 *World Service* circulated a list of "Newspapers and Reviews Against Jewish Imperialism" and along with the *Deutscher Weckruf*, it recommended:

The Awakener, New York City, 11, West 42nd Street.

Chicago Tribune, Chicago (Ill.), Tribune Tower.

The Gentile Front, Chicago (Ill.), Box 526, Editor: Peter Armstrong.

The Vigilante, Chicago (Ill.), Department K., P. O. Box, 144 [Harry A. Jung].

In the face of severe criticism Kamp closed up the fascist sheet after two years, but he quickly reopened shop under the banner of the Constitutional Educational League, and since 1937 has issued tremendous quantities of defeatist and dissensionist tracts. When I asked Dennis what he thought of Kamp's current "patriotic" efforts, he answered:

"His approach is fine. I put him to it."

Kamp's efforts on the League were an extension of the policy of *The Awakener*. He conceded this by writing a correspondent in 1937:

The Awakener is dead, but the work is being carried on, and under separate cover, you will receive, in return for your stamps, some recent booklets and pamphlets of the Constitutional Educational League. . . . It is unfortunate that the patriotic element find it impossible to maintain one patriotic newspaper. . . . However, through the Constitutional Educational League and the patriotic organizations cooperating with it, an energetic campaign is now under way.

Yours for American ideals,
(signed)   Joseph P. Kamp

Leaving Dennis, Jung, Kelly and other fascist collaborators in the background, Kamp adopted the slogan "Our Constitutional Republic must be preserved" and set out to "smash Communism"—nothing else. He had not been functioning long

THE AWAKENER
A NATIONAL ORGAN OF UNCENSORED OPINION

Edited by

HAROLD LORD VARNEY

Associate Editors

LAWRENCE DENNIS
DEMAREST LLOYD

JOSEPH P. KAMP, EXECUTIVE EDITOR

Published Twice a Month by

WAKENER PUBLISHING CO., 110 West 42nd Street, New York

No. 11   MAY 1, 1935 $2.00 A YEAR

WHY WIN the WAR

. . .

and LOSE what we're fighting for?

When in November, the Red elements threatened to halt the Dies Committee, the League began a nation-wide drive on its behalf; secured over 400,000 signatures to petitions and deluged Congress with an avalanche of letters and telegrams from aroused patriots. As part of this campaign, Commander Edward E. Spafford, former national head of the Legion, and Chairman of the League's Award Committee, announced that Congressman Martin Dies had been selected to receive the American Legion Award for 1938. The Dies Committee expressed its appreciation and, at a later date, Congressman Hoffman at a public meeting in New York openly declared that but for the League's effective work the Dies Committee would not have been continued.

R.1022
A.A.V

"Auxilio Social"
OFICINA CENTRAL
DE PROPAGANDA

(Valladolid, noviembre 15, 1938)
(III año triunfal)

Mr. Merwin K. Hart,
New York State Economic Council, Inc.
17 East 42nd Street,

New York

Dear Mr. Hart:

Thank you very much for your letter of November the 3rd. We were very interested to read your article about "AUXILIO SOCIAL" published in the Herald Tribune of Oct. the 30th. and we are immensely thankful for it, as well as for having mentioned Our Work in your broadcast at Malaga.

As our need Mrs. Carmen Icaza de Montojo is away I have the pleasure of writing you and of sending you by today's post a pamphlet about "AUXILIO SOCIAL" and a newspaper of a series of 300,000 copies that have been published on October the 30th. the second anniversary of "AUXILIO SOCIAL" and sent to those who fight in the fronts.

We shall be very pleased to set Miss Anderson and to show her "AUXILIO SOCIAL" as well as to help her in any other thing in which we could be useful to her.

Thanking you again for your article and with kindest regards,

Yours sincerely,

JEFE DE LA OFICINA
CENTRAL DE PROPAGANDA
P.A.

Saludo a Franco!
Arriba España!

Left: Friendly letter written by the chief of the Spanish Ministry of Propaganda to Merwin K. Hart expressing desire to receive his friend, Miss Jane Anderson, whom he had recommended. An Atlanta woman known as the "Georgia Peach," Miss Anderson accepted the Falangist offer and became a Franco agent. She is now doing short wave broadcasting in English from Nazi Germany three nights a week, and has been adjudged a traitor to her country by our Department of Justice. *Right:* Proof that Kamp (who had served on one of Hart's Nationalist Spain committees) was intimately associated with American Nazi, Lawrence Dennis. Proof, also, that Kamp's organization has had close relations with Martin Dies and his Committee.

when the League was investigated by the Senate Civil Liberties Committee, headed by Senator Robert M. LaFollette. Kamp called the Committee "disloyal and un-American" and after the fashion of Mrs. Washburn, Hornby and Spencer, suggested "a new Declaration of Independence in self-defense." He screamed:

> We have not attempted to organize or dis-organize labor. We have taken no part in industrial conflicts. We have not engaged in strike-breaking. We have no spies in the labor movement. We have not organized vigilante groups. . . . WE serve only OUR COUNTRY.

In a long-winded statement Kamp branded the investigation as "the culmination of a conspiracy between John L. Lewis, representative of Communist and other Red organizations." A Communist was one who opposed Kamp's ideology and dared publicize his collaboration with a native Nazi like Dennis. Unappreciated at home, Kamp's self-styled "bona-fide, law-abiding, patriotic organization" was held in greater esteem by *World Service*. In 1938, three years after its original plug of a Kamp product, it again urged Nazi sympathizers "to obtain and read" the booklet *Join the C.I.O. and Help Build a Soviet America.*

Kamp claimed he distributed 2,200,000 copies of it from 1937 through 1940 alone and that in that same period more than "10,000,000 pieces of literature" were published by his organization. Fellow member of the *World Service* honor roll, the Reverend Winrod continually advertised and promoted Kamp's literature with especially printed appeals sent to *Defender* subscribers. Also among Kamp's closest associates was Martin Dies. In 1938 Dies was selected by Kamp to receive the League's "Americanism Award" and Kamp wrote:

> The Dies Committee expressed its appreciation and, at a later date, Congressman Hoffman at a public meeting in New York, openly declared that but for the League's effective work the Dies Committee would not have been continued.

In a folder entitled *The Fifth Column Conspiracy*, Kamp urged "patriots" to *withhold information* "regarding Communist activities" from J. Edgar Hoover's F.B.I. and submit it, instead, either to Martin Dies or to him. "If you are fearful of becoming involved, your information will be treated in confidence if sent to the Investigation Department" of the League, Kamp suggested coyly. It is natural that this apparent collusion between an associate of Lawrence Dennis and the Honorable Martin Dies should lead to suspicion, particularly when it followed on the heels of a Kuhn-approved luncheon tendered Mr. Dies by the Franco-ite Mr. Hart.

Equally odd is the extreme cordiality which exists between the League and many fanatic labor-baiting Congressmen. Reports have long been rife that the "research" for many of Hoffman's speeches and even some of the speeches themselves were written by Joseph P. Kamp. Kamp does not explain how he financed his extensive propaganda broadsides; maintained offices in Alabama, Wisconsin and Connecticut; sponsored Representative Hoffman and others on speaking tours in Alabama, Tennessee, Pennsylvania, Michigan and New England, and trained League speakers and leaders throughout the country.

The indications are that Kamp is financed by those ultra-reactionary and fascist-minded business men who have never forgiven the President's reform measures and continue to derive their greatest satisfaction from badgering him at every turn, even though the distrust and dissension created during war-time aid Hitler's cause. Kamp's Constitutional Educational League was named as a factor in the mass indictment for sedition on July 22.

I decided to visit Kamp under a different alias because I felt sure that he had already discovered Pagnanelli was not on his side. I found him one of the most disagreeable men I had met in my four years as investigator. His was the face of a man steeped in volatile, soul-consuming hate. It was pallid, with a solid jawbone, irregular features, flesh-colored moles and piercing gray eyes bathed in suspicion, distrust and venom. A conspicuous yellow-white stripe ran from the middle of his forehead up into the crown.

There were many questions I wanted to ask the arrogant Joseph P. Kamp as I sat in his large, untidy office. Kamp was reading a letter he had received from Charles Hudson. He read it attentively then put it away before turning to me. Unfortunately our conversation proved unsatisfactory to me. Too suspicious a person to talk freely to a stranger, Kamp spent half-an-hour in quizzing me intently instead of giving me a real opportunity to quiz him. I answered his questions easily, posing as a Wall Street office worker, and expected him to open up after I had finished. But he didn't.

As I sat there he tossed over a copy of his latest effort—one of many he had printed since Pearl Harbor. It was entitled: *We Must Win! We Will Win! But Why Win the War and Lose What We're Fighting For?* Both title and text followed *precisely* the line which Dennis had advocated during my interview with him. Kamp's formula to "win the war" and "preserve the Republic" was by "legislation to remove all Communists and fellow travellers from public payrolls" and by continuance of the Dies Committee. The only enemies of Kamp's "Republic" were the Communists, the "Communist" labor unions, the New Deal, the President and the Administration directing the nation's war effort. Nowhere was Hitler given equal prominence in Kamp's directory of national hate.

Through investigations too involved to narrate here, I traced the printer who did most of Kamp's work. He was John H. Mullen, printer also for John B. Snow, John Cecil and George Deatherage. Mullen confided that he had set up the type for *War, War, War,* by "Cincinnatus." As with Sullivan whom I interviewed in Washington, Mullen knew the identity of this mysterious author, but would not part with his secret. The mystery intrigued me. I determined to learn "Cincinnatus'" identity on my next trip to Washington.

As I continued my investigations among groups fronting for those "big business" interests who hated the President more than Hitler, I saw that they were often headed by men who had grudges that went as far back as the last war.

Take for example, the Committee for Constitutional Government which financed tremendous lobbying campaigns and collaborated with America First. In one instance alone it financed the printing and distribution of 16,000,000 pamphlets and conceded spending at least $209,859. Its program of "constructive Americanism" is directed by executive secretary Dr.

ARREST RUMELY; SAY GERMANY OWNS THE EVENING MAIL	GOVERNMENT OPENS DR. RUMELY'S TRIAL	GERMAN FUND BARED IN DR. RUMELY TRIAL	SHOW 'DUMMY' STOCK DEAL IN RUMELY SUIT	BOOKS FIXED TO HIDE KAISER IN MAIL DEAL
Government Charges Perjury in Statement That Paper Is Under American Control.	Defendant Accused of Concealing Purchase of Evening Mail for German Authorities.	Disposition of $9,000,000 in City Banks Inquired Into in Evening Mail Case.	Chemist Admits $75,000 Was Sent Him by Messenger to Buy Evening Mail Shares.	Lawyer for Two Dr. Rumely Co-defendants Admits $371,000 Payments Were Concealed.
$100,000 BAIL DEMANDED	TELL OF NOTES SOLD HERE	$390,000 IN CHECKS TRACED	LAWYER'S ACTIVITY SHOWN	WOMAN TELLS FIRM SECRET
Kaiser's Government Alleged to Have Invested $1,361,000 in the Paper.	Witnesses Describe Negotiations for Transfer of Paper in 1915 and Flotation of German Loan.	Prosecution Seeks to Link German Bond Drive Money with News-paper Purchase	Testimony Details Part in Transaction of Kaufman, One of Indicted Trio.	Reveals Facts Connecting Mysterious "Perez No. 1" Account with Newspaper's Purchase.
PAID IT THROUGH DR. ALBERT				
Whose Memorandum Shows the Cost Was Charged to His and Bernstorff's Joint Bank Account.				
Edward A. Rumely, Vice President, Secretary and publisher of The New York Evening Mail, was arrested late yesterday afternoon by agents of the				

VISITED GERMANY ON RUMELY MISSION	HUNT HENRY FORD AS RUMELY WITNESS	RUMELY CONVICTED; JURY ASKS MERCY	RUMELY SENTENCED TO YEAR AND A DAY
S. Walter Kaufman Tells of Trip to Baden-Baden to Discuss the Mail with Sielcken.	Government Agents, Searching for a Month, Unable to Find Him.	Verdict Finds German Government Furnished Money to Buy The Evening Mail.	Similar Penalty Imposed on His Co-Defendants, Kaufmann and Lindheim.
$150,000 MORE ADVANCED	MAIL WRITERS TESTIFY	HIS CODEFENDANTS GUILTY	GIVE BAIL, PENDING APPEAL
Attorney Also Says He Called on August Busch in St. Louis in Behalf of Newspaper	No Attempt to Influence Their Work in Behalf of Germans, They Assert.	Kaufmann and Lindheim Declared in Conspiracy to Defraud the United States.	Each Asserts Innocence of Concealing German Ownership of The Evening Mail.

The sensational story of Edward Aloysius Rumely as headlined in *The New York Times* from the day of his arrest on July 8, 1918, to his conviction on December 18, 1920, as an agent of Imperial Germany on whose behalf he bought the New York *Evening Mail* and operated it from 1915 to 1918.

Rumely's links with Count von Bernstorff, German ambassador; Dr. Heinrich Albert, the Kaiser's paymaster; and Bernhard Dernberg, chief of German propagandists in America during the World War, were shown in court. George Sylvester Viereck's name was also involved. It was further testified that Rumely founded the S. S. McClure Newspaper Corporation as a holding company and turned over $748,000 as an initial fund which he subsequently used to purchase the *Evening Mail*. Tried in November and December, 1920, Rumely *was not* a "victim of war hysteria" as tearfully alleged by the executive secretary of the Committee for Constitutional Government. S. S. McClure is still associated with Rumely.

Edward A. Rumely who served a sentence in the Atlanta Penitentiary as an agent of Imperial Germany.

Testifying before the Senatorial Committee to Investigate Lobbying Activities in 1938, Dr. Edward A. Rumely retold the sensational story of how he bought the New York *Evening Mail* in the early years of the war, with money supplied jointly by Herman Sielcken, a "great international merchant" residing in Baden-Baden, Germany, and the rabid Germanophile, Mrs. Adolphus Busch of St. Louis.

He told how Heinrich Albert, German agent, gave $200,000 for advertising in foreign-language papers urging "neutrality." And when Senator Lewis B. Schwellenbach read from the record of the Circuit Court of Appeals charging that Rumely refused to report to the Alien Property Custodian an indebtedness of $1,451,000 to the Kaiser's government, Rumely demanded furiously, "Is that relevant?"

Senator Schwellenbach: Yes; very relevant. When a man comes in and represents himself as a patriotic American it is relevant to see if it is the same campaign being conducted by you as was conducted by the German Government in 1915.

Mr. Rumely (interposing): There was not or is not one scintilla of evidence. . . . I thought we were here to discuss—

Senator Schwellenbach (interposing): When we find the same man, who, when trouble in Europe was going on between the German Government and other governments, is engaged in propaganda activity, trying to educate the American people today, we are interested in what he was doing the last time a similar situation was existing.

And when his treasurer, Sumner Gerard, was called to testify he duplicated Rumely's evasive tactics, pretending to be so "dumb" as to be unable to state where the account books were kept, how much had been received, who were the contributors and how the funds had been distributed. And when, in exasperation, Senator Theodore F. Green asked Gerard if he were a mere "figurehead," Rumely's treasurer replied: "Only so far as the actual expenditure of the money is concerned." In afterthought he added brightly: "I can't add up a golf score even."

Rumely is boss of the Committee for Constitutional Government and second in command to Frank E. Gannett, publisher of a string of newspapers and founder of the Committee in 1937. As soon as the Senatorial investigation was over, Rumely literally went underground and erased his name from the Committee stationery. But he continued to run it by appointing a docile Protestant clergyman as "acting chairman and secretary" who visited the office only occasionally. He was the Reverend Norman Vincent Peale, once a joint speaker with Mrs. Elizabeth Dilling and the Reverend Edward Lodge Curran at a "pro-American mass meeting sponsored by more than 50 patriotic organizations" at the Hotel Commodore in New York.

Rumely's other appointees also have interesting backgrounds. His vice-chairman, Louis J. Taber, an official of the National Grange, was also on the national board of the America First Committee. Amos Pinchot, a veteran with Rumely and on the board of America First, served in a liaison capacity. Rumely assigned Mrs. Morrison's American Women Against Communism to distribute Pinchot's defeatist propaganda bearing the imprint of the Committee for Constitutional Government—a variation of his work during the World War.

Rumely's friendship with Henry Ford dated prior to the summer of 1918 when Ford rushed to Washington in an unsuccessful attempt to save Rumely from being indicted. George Harvey, our ambassador to England, charged in his magazine, *War Weekly:* "Edward A. Rumely was for years

Sunday, Oct. 30, 1938
3 P.M.

INVOCATION:

Rev. Norman Vincent Peale, Pastor Marble Collegiate Church

SPEAKERS:

Mrs. Elizabeth Dilling, Author "The Red Network"

Rev. Fr. Edward Lodge Curran, Ph.D., President
International Catholic Truth Society

The acting secretary of the Committee for Constitutional Government was listed as speaker with Mrs. Dilling, under indictment, and the Reverend Curran, Father Coughlin's agent, at a "pro-American rally" at the Hotel Commodore, New York.

the secret paid agent of the German Government. Rumely's close, if not closest, friend during the past six years has been Henry Ford."

I tried to arrange an appointment by phone to see Rumely personally in order to ask him about Ford. When I failed in this, I decided to pose as a German-American from Detroit who was ostensibly travelling to New York and "upon the suggestion of interested patriotic circles" there who "recommended that I be sure to see you." I signed the letter "Rudolph Eibers" and had it mailed from Detroit. With the Germanic alias and an America First button on the lapel of my coat, I called at Rumely's offices.

The Committee was located at 205 East 42nd Street, Room 600—in the same building where Lawrence Dennis has his offices—occupying premises with S. S. McClure, formerly of McClure's Newspaper Syndicate; with Leaders and Events Syndicate, Inc.; with America's Future, Inc.; and also with the Committee for the Nation whose chairman was J. H. Rand, Jr.

I found myself in a large and businesslike office. Rumely kept me waiting half-an-hour and when he finally emerged he began to protest without a word from me. "We have no connection with any other organization. Just as a matter of policy we work alone." He acted like a man who had a guilty conscience and wanted to avoid meeting strangers. "You can have all our literature," he said, "but we don't work with any other organization."

He turned to the switchboard and asked the operator to get a "Mr. Becker of Chicago," and before disappearing into one of the many side offices, he ordered me to "just sit down and wait." When he emerged another half-hour later, he said gruffly: "Mr. Glen Hancock will tell you about our organization."

The assistant secretary was a tall, clean-cut man, with a small and extremely alert face. He was quiet-mannered in contrast to the blustery and energetic Rumely who conveyed the impression of being a dynamic and bossy super-promoter. At first Hancock was suspicious and tight-lipped, but after my "patriotic" spiel and a recitation of "patriotic" events in "Detroit, my home town," we met on common ground.

I asked Hancock if he knew Kamp. "You mean Joe," he said. "I know him very well. He is doing good work with his literature."

I asked him if he knew Merwin K. Hart. "I've known him for many years. Dr. Rumely knows him very well, too," Hancock volunteered and went on to tell me how Hart's organization functioned.

When I asked Hancock if he knew Cathrine Curtis, he laughed: "Of course I do. I've known her for a long time. She's been to this office many times."

When I asked if he knew Mrs. Dilling, Hancock nodded, but did not elaborate. It never occurred to me to ask him about Father Coughlin and the Christian Front. Hancock himself volunteered the information and I quote him verbatim:

"Back in 1937 when we first started, we solicited Father Coughlin's support in the fight against the 'Court Packing Bill.' He worked with us nicely. We supplied Father Coughlin with all the statistics and he published them in *Social Justice*."

When I asked if the Committee still maintained contact, he answered: "Not any more. He has too many enemies. But at one time the boys from Brooklyn used to come to our offices and get a lot of our literature." At about the same time, too, Christian Front-ers flocked to Hart's office for a like purpose.

While in Chicago, I had called on one of Rumely's close friends, George Washington Robnett, executive secretary of the Church League of America, the National Layman's Council and editor of *News and Views*.

A tall, graying man, meticulously dressed, he began at once a tirade of bitter invective against the Jews. "It will be very bad for them after the war," he said in summation. He then asked whether it was true that in New York *The Daily Worker* was sold only by "Jewish salesmen." Robnett's mental processes seemed identical with those of Elizabeth Dilling.

I do not know what possessed Robnett to start on anti-Semitism. My letter to him merely said that I had "been active in the patriotic movement for almost four years, and [was] acquainted with almost everyone here of any consequence." I did not enclose a copy of *The Christian Defender*. Clinging to anti-Semitism throughout our conversation, Robnett told me that his Church League had 200,000 names on its mailing list and that his Layman's Council was composed of "many notable business and professional men." Although he seemed intelligent, he was victimized by the Nazi lie that Judaism was synonymous with Communism.

He told me of informants throughout the country who kept him posted on the "Communist plot to Sovietize America" and specifically mentioned a Mr. Mulligan in New York. Upon showing me pamphlets which Mulligan had procured from the Reverend L. M. Birkhead's Friends of Democracy, Robnett urged me to "get its Jewish connections, if Birkhead's got any" as soon as I returned home and offered to pay incidental expenses from a fund he maintained for such purposes.

I listened without surprise as Robnett told me of his friends: Snow, Kamp, Hart, Walter S. Steele, Colonel Sanctuary. He described Representative Stephen A. Day—whose book had been published by Viereck's Flanders Hall—as a "fine fellow" and said "I hope to do all I can for his re-election." Phillips quoted widely from Robnett's *News and Views*, while Hudson urged his fascist readers to obtain from it their data on "significant trends." Among Robnett's closest friends were Harry A. Jung and Mrs. Dilling.

"Why don't you go up and see Mrs. Dilling now?" he asked, as he reached for the phone. "I'll call and tell her you're coming."

I had no intention of seeing Mrs. Dilling at this time, however. I left Robnett's office after he prompted me again to spy on the Reverend Birkhead. In the quiet of my hotel room, I read issues of *News and Views* he had given me.

Dreadfully upset at the "menace of organized radicalism," about the "Red cells in our schools," Robnett even called down the monthly *American Magazine* for publishing an article which "paints a gilded picture of Stalin." But while Robnett was denouncing "the Red Menace in America," he made no comment against American Nazis. In fact, Robnett's *News and Views* seemed to be merely another outpost of reactionary "big business" interests, mixed with a brand of hysterical Red-baiting and flag-waving paralleling those of Mrs. Dilling. Robnett was backed by important industrialists. General Robert E. Wood once sent him a personal check, followed by another substantial check by R. Douglas Stuart, Jr., youthful founder and a director of the America First Committee, according to reports which were then in circulation.

After I returned to New York Robnett sent me Mulligan's address with the suggestion that I plan my investigations with him. Robnett cautiously excluded Mulligan's name from the letter, with the comment: "I mentioned to you the name of an educator who sends me material from time to time. His name and address are on the slip of paper attached." He then outlined his requirements for spying on the Reverend Birkhead:

With whom does this fellow associate particularly? By that I mean whether or not he makes a habit of collaborating with Leftist groups of the extremist type—Communists, etc. How large an organization does he have? Where does he live? Anything at all that has a bearing on identifying his role. . . .

I showed the letter to the Reverend Birkhead and he suggested that I "play along with him." He gave me several mimeographed releases and a crumpled letterhead of the Friends of Democracy. I also sent Robnett Birkhead's home address. To cover up my work I invented a "girl friend" who had "wormed her way into the Friends of Democracy." In return, I asked Robnett to arrange a meeting for me with Rumely. There were a great many things I wanted to ask Rumely. Robnett wrote back:

I hope that you and Dr. Mulligan are able, through cooperation, to develop some of the information he seeks. I would suggest that you drop in to see Mr. E. A. Rumely of the Committee for Constitutional Government. I will drop him a note telling him that you have indicated a desire to talk over some things. . . . I hope your girl will be able to dig up more stuff out of the waste basket. That is always a mighty good place to get material.

When I met Dr. Arthur G. Mulligan (a teacher of speech correction with the New York League for Speech Improvement) mysteriously in a corner of the Hotel McAlpin lobby, he urged me to visit a man who had a personal grudge against Birkhead and who might "talk for us."

I had no stomach for such intrigues against a reputable minister of the gospel who had undertaken the thankless job of fighting Democracy's enemies, both Communist and Nazi and was damned by both camps, even though it might result in important information as to other operatives apparently engaged by Robnett to pry into the affairs of democratic organizations. I dropped Mulligan and Robnett.

On January 5, 1943, Rumely wrote me in response to Robnett's letter to him and asked why I wanted to see him. I did not answer and let the entire matter drop. I was finishing my book and several guarded queries about "Pagnanelli's real name and home address" had been reported to me. I determined to work at my book in my hide-out until the manuscript and documents were safely in the hands of the publishers.

Chapter XIV

LIBERTY'S HANGMEN

> "Our only hope from now on is Congress. I've
> been needling them in Congress and I intend to keep
> on needling them."
>
> LAWRENCE DENNIS

LATE IN THE FALL of 1942, I interviewed Edward Atwell, an
important official of the America First Committee who was
"on the inside" at the New York offices. He answered the
question which had been repeatedly put to me: "Is the America First movement dead?"

Atwell was having supper with his wife and daughter when
I visited him. A powerfully built man, with pink and white
complexion, Atwell impressed me as sincere even though he
had spoken four times with Nazi agent Laura Ingalls, written
numerous speeches, worked sixteen hours a day for the America First cause and shared the innermost secrets of the A.F.C.
Atwell impressed me as a sincere, anti-fascist isolationist.

"We were all ready to enter politics when Pearl Harbor
came along," Atwell said. "Our plan was to have every city
block catalogued by names of families and the number in each
family. We were already selecting our block captains."

"What did cataloguing have to do with politics?" I asked.

"Just this, each family was to be given a card and told that
if it needed anything—clothing, food, advice—all it had to do
was to visit the nearest America First office. Nobody had to
join it, but at election time our idea was to ask them to vote
for our candidates."

"They couldn't refuse to do that," I observed.

"Of course not. That's the way Tammany Hall worked it,
and that's the way we intended to get into power."

I asked the blunt and outspoken Atwell whether leadership
by America First would have been a good thing for the nation.

"I'm not sure. It may have turned out okay, then again it
may have become a Frankenstein of our own creation. That

office I worked in was a madhouse. There were Bundists and Silver Shirters and Christian Mobilizers. . . ."

"Don't forget the German secret service men," Mrs. Atwell put in. She had worked in the A.F.C. office with her husband, and I turned to her for information when Atwell seemed hesitant.

"To tell you the truth," she said, "I never thought that Laura Ingalls was the only German agent we had. You can call Germany anything you want, but you can't call her dumb. If she had one agent in such a big organization, she might have had a hundred. There was a fellow named Riepel whose brother was arrested by the F.B.I. as a spy. We always thought Riepel was a Nazi agent."

"There were also the White Russians," Atwell put in.

"Yes, that Czarist woman, the Countess. She told me she supported the Committee and wanted to keep America out of war in order to give Hitler a chance to clean up Russia so she could get back her property," Mrs. Atwell said.

"The office was full of men and women with selfish motives," Atwell resumed. "The Committee grew too fast. It took in everybody. It had no time to check up. It could have got out of control easily. There were many sincere ones, but there were a lot of people who had an axe to grind. Like the Bund fellows."

"What interest could the Bund have?" I asked naïvely.

"Plenty!" Atwell burst out. "It was to Germany's advantage to have us stay out of war. It was perfectly possible that in due time German agents might have got control of the whole thing by working in the background and using other people to front for them! A strong, well-knit minority can always put it over on the unorganized majority. And I wouldn't be surprised," Atwell said softly, "if some of the money we got in was German money."

"How do you know that?" I asked.

"I know that a lot of money came in anonymously. You just opened the sealed envelope and the money dropped out. I wouldn't be surprised if some of that money was German money. Yep, the Committee might have become a very dangerous thing."

Atwell looked me over speculatively.

"I did a lot of talking for the Committee. A tour of eleven states was mapped out for me, and I was all set to go when I got the notion to look at the Bundists and Christian Front-ers about me. I asked myself 'Where am I going! Where is this Committee going with all these guys on board?' " Atwell resumed, "I'm loyal to my country and I didn't go on that speaking tour."

My initial impression that Atwell was sincere seemed borne out. My respect for him grew.

"Did Lindbergh write that Des Moines speech?" I asked, referring to Lindbergh's sensational "anti-Semitic" speech.

"I can tell you the inside story on that," Atwell answered. "Lindbergh himself wrote that speech, but never showed it to anyone on the Committee. We were just as surprised as anybody else."

"Do you think Lindbergh is through as a leader?" I asked.

"Far from it," Atwell answered. "To a lot of people he is still the hero who flew the Atlantic. That toothy smile of his still gets the women. But he has no political mind and knows little about politics. He is a good man to get the people to come out, and he can be used by other men."

"How?"

"He can be used as a front, surrounded by such men as Wheeler and Nye on the board of strategy. This may happen in the future," Atwell said thoughtfully.

"Then you don't think America First is through forever?"

"Hell, no!" Atwell said spiritedly. "Lindbergh will come back and America First will come back whenever the time is ripe. All you have to do is to call a meeting, bring the old faces together again, give them a hero they can look up to, and they'll start all over.

"There are a lot of neurotics and frustrated people in the world. Old maids, missionary types, people who have to get a release for their hates, neglected people," Atwell continued, "they all want to become somebody by joining a movement. They'll all come back as soon as they get the signal."

My talk with Atwell late in 1942 was one of the most enlightening I had had. I quizzed Atwell on his personal anti-Semitism and found that the little he had was of the "harmless" type; social, rather than the sinister political anti-Semitism

—the spearhead against Democracy. Atwell feared mass anti-Semitism as a revolutionary device. He feared the "mob element" and he dreaded the consequences.

"I've seen the mob in action. Back in 1939 it was the Christian Front that went around beating up people. First it's the fist, then clubs, then knives, then firearms, then . . . I don't want to see innocent people killed. Mass anti-Semitism is bad business. It can end up in revolution as sure as you're sitting there."

Then, on January 4, 1943, the Department of Justice added the names of five men and women to the list of twenty-eight already charged with sedition. The five were Mrs. Lois de Lafayette Washburn, Frank W. Clark, Mrs. Leslie Fry (alias Shishmarova), George Deatherage and F. K. Ferenz, a Los Angeles Nazi operative. It also indicted the New York Evening Enquirer, Inc., whose publisher, William Griffin, had been named originally. The new indictment raised to thirty-three the number of those charged with sedition, and to thirteen those whom I knew personally. In addition, it named Lieutenant-Colonel Ulrich Fleischhauer of *World Service* as a factor and traced the beginning of the alleged conspiracy to 1933.

Mr. Maloney's determined attacks on saboteurs of our morale aroused the enmity of America First Congressmen and Senators, some of whom were involved with the defendants and did not relish the airing their record received. They defended America's alleged Quislings. The Department of Justice was smeared as a "Jewish Gestapo" despite the fact that Americans of the Jewish faith were *completely* absent from the handling of this particular case. The indictments were prepared and signed by these members of the Department of Justice: Edward M. Curran, Wendell Berge, William Power Maloney, John T. M. Reddan and Miss Jean R. Meyer, a Catholic who spent eight years in a convent. None the less, the cry of "Jewish Gestapo" against the mainly Irish attorneys continued to be raised by the "patriots."

"They are no more guilty than I am," Senator Nye told reporters, and proceeded to falsify the indictment as being based only upon pre-Pearl Harbor "isolationist activity." Falling in line, Senator Robert A. Taft asserted that the "indictments present a real danger to the continuance of freedom," and according to newspaper accounts he suggested the "disbarment of the Government attorneys." Senator Wheeler echoed Nye and Taft and spoke of the need of a "new leadership" and a new political party. Ham Fish joined the chorus. And when Congressman Hoffman, was charged with having sent 2000 copies of his "Judas" speech to Hudson, 1000 copies to Winrod, and 500 copies to American Nazi David Baxter, he absented himself from the chambers and made no reply to the scathing charges other than to join in the clamor in blanket defense of the alleged "persecuted Christians." Colonel McCormick raised a howl in the *Chicago Tribune* and termed it a "Moscow propaganda trial," while the "vermin press" of native fascists set up its own specialized squeal of protest.

Under these difficult conditions, Attorney General Biddle suddenly removed Maloney as chief prosecutor by elevating him to the post of Chief of the Trial Section. Maloney was then replaced by O. John Rogge, special counsel for the Securities and Exchange Commission, with an excellent record of convictions against the Huey Long machine. In the absence of an explanation by Mr. Biddle, ugly rumors of "appeasement" were voiced by the more emotional sector of the democratic press, while the fascist elements and America First Senators and Congressmen crowed over their "victory" at the "kicking upstairs" of Maloney.

Under these circumstances I visited Lawrence Dennis on February 8, 1943, and he gave me what I regard as my most sensational interview during my four years as investigator. I tell that story here without dramatics. As I opened his office door, I had no idea of the influence which this American Nazi wielded among our Senators and Congressmen. My motive in seeing Dennis was merely to ascertain whether he knew Gerald L. K. Smith, for I had seen a startling resemblance between the January issue of Smith's magazine and some of Dennis' writings.

"Of course I know Smith; I know him very well; I had lunch with him when he was in New York last," Dennis said. "Smith is a good fellow, he listens to me."

And when I called his attention to Smith's America First

Party, he added: "I wish him well with it. I hope he succeeds.
He has the right idea."

Then I asked Dennis if he personally knew Charles Lindbergh. His eyes settled on me before he answered: "I used to
talk to him often before he went to Detroit. Goodness, yes,
of course I know him," Dennis emphasized.

Dennis talked so easily and seemed to trust me so fully that
I asked if he knew Ham Fish. "Very well, very well," he answered. "But Fish has no brains. His sympathies are all right,
but he is dumb. His influence is in proportion to his brains."

"How about Reynolds?" I asked.

Dennis brushed Reynolds down with a gesture of the hand.
"Dumb. No brains. Reynolds is just a rabble-rouser. He is
chairman of the Military Affairs Committee, of course, but
he has no brains."

To say that I was startled at Dennis' bold statements is to
understate my feelings. In a nervous mood, Dennis fingered
objects on his desk as he talked, but his manner toward me was
cordial. Regarding me as a co-fascist, he spoke with a frankness which I knew he'd never display before the F.B.I. Our
conversation turned to the attacks of Nye and Wheeler against
the Department of Justice.

"You can give me credit for that," Dennis said suddenly.
"I've been talking to them all along."

"Talking to whom?" I asked, wanting to make sure I had
heard right.

"To Nye and Wheeler," Dennis said. "I told them that
after they got the patriots, they'd jump on them. I got a long
letter from Nye just the other day."

I was bursting with questions. Exactly when and where had
Dennis met the Senators, who else was present? What else had
they talked about? But all I dared ask was how he had met
Wheeler and Nye.

"Oh, I have many friends in Washington. They invited
the Senators to dinner and asked me to be there. I impressed
upon Nye that the indicted people were just crackpots. No
serious leader would ever follow them. They were just shooting their mouths off."

"But they're nationalists," I said.

"Oh, yes," Dennis agreed. "These nativist movements are

to the good. They keep things going. They've all been needled, but they are not leaders."

"What do you think of Wheeler and Nye personally?" I asked.

Dennis' answer was direct: "Nye is the best of them all in Washington. And he is nearest to knowing what it's all about. Wheeler is a good fellow, but he can't stand up to Nye. Taft is coming along, but he is still old-fashioned. Nye is a good man."

"We patriots are certainly thankful that a man like you can reach those distinguished Senators," I said, tongue-in-cheek, "and influence them in their actions."

"I don't mean to say I've done everything," Dennis said. "I've talked to them and they've listened. They're intelligent men, and they've used their own judgments. The scales are dropping from the eyes of some of our Congressmen, as the *Scriptures* would say," Dennis observed. "They are beginning to learn what it's all about."

The telephone rang. "I'm expecting an important call," Dennis said, and jumped to answer the phone. He spoke guardedly. "Very well. I'll be over in ten minutes," he said.

I arose to leave: "Wait, I'll go down with you," Dennis suggested. On the way down I asked if he knew William R. Castle.

"Oh yes. He's reactionary, but he is a good fellow."

I asked him what he thought of Colonel McCormick.

"Dumb. No brains," Dennis said. "I know a lot of the men in his office. I look them up when I'm in Chicago."

I decided to test Dennis' veracity and determine to what extent he knew Wheeler, Nye and Fish. I had repeatedly postponed a trip to Washington because of my book, but the rumors circulating against the Department of Justice, Dennis' allegations and the presence of several of the defendants in Washington, prompted me to drop my editorial revisions on *Under Cover* and undertake the trip.

I wrote Fish, Nye and Wheeler, establishing my America First connections, and professing friendship with the "patriotic L. D. who has spoken well of you." To James M. Curley, the Boston politician elected to Congress, I wrote saying I was a good friend of Francis P. Moran, the Christian Front leader.

Intending to make a roundup of America First Congressmen, I also wrote Representatives Hoffman and Dewey Short; Senators Taft and Walsh, Chairman of the Naval Affairs Committee.

Upon arriving in Washington, I decided first to look up Edmondson and Leon De Aryan, editor of *The Broom*, both indicted. Living at the Plaza Hotel, Edmondson avoided me for two days until I finally collared him with his attorney John S. Wise, Broenstrupp's friend. His face harsh and wrinkle-lined, neither bright nor friendly, Edmondson gave me no opportunity to ask him about Edwin Flaig, or about Lusenberg, Elmhurst's Nazi pal who allegedly fed Edmondson "factual" data for his *Vigilante Bulletins*.

Leon De Aryan—the fifteenth defendant I knew personally—proved to be more friendly. Born of Greek and Polish parents, he had changed his name from an unpronounceable Greek surname. The extremely crafty and tight-lipped De Aryan and I talked for more than an hour. I could not penetrate his protective armor other than to obtain the admission that he had been friendly and had worked, with Herman Max Schwinn, the West Coast Bund leader; Hans Diebel, Los Angeles Nazi worker, and Mrs. Leslie Fry. De Aryan told me that his religious preference was Zoroastrianism—a cult confined to only a few score adherents in America, which made use of fire in the course of its secret and mysterious rituals.

I looked up Dr. Maude S. DeLand and found her surrounded by her Nazi books and typewriter. "These are all I need," she said. She had met De Aryan. She told me she admired the Japanese because they always returned borrowed books. She then posed the syllogism: "They condemn Hitler because of his racist ideas. But the Jews also think themselves a superior people so they must be worse than Hitler. It was Jehovah who made the Jews a "chosen race" so God must be even worse than Hitler. Now what's wrong with that logic?"

I visited Mrs. Mabel Dennett, wrinkled mother of Prescott. "Viereck came to our home many times," she said, "and I always thought he was a perfect gentleman."

I had no difficulty in seeing Hamilton Fish. As I waited in the outer room, I speculated on those who had been there before me: Viereck, Dennett, Dennis, America First-ers, Chris-

tian Front-ers and Steuben Society members who had idolized
him. On the wall hung a plaque: "The U. S. A. First, Last
and all the Time." Underneath it were five framed pictures
of horses. Over the doorway to Ham Fish's office hung a
stuffed fish. Fish shook my hand cordially, and kept on sign-
ing letters, as I studied his face, spiked with crude and crass
fanaticism.

"Do you know Lawrence Dennis?" was the first question I
asked.

"Oh yes," Fish answered without looking up. "I saw him
only a month ago. His ideas are not my ideas, but they are
all right. Oh yes, Dennis is an able man. He is all right. He
looks me up every time he comes to Washington. I expect him
to come down again soon."

That is what I had come to find out.

Fish was in a talkative mood. The magic of my friendship
with Dennis was potent. Having told me he knew Joseph P.
Kamp personally, and having aired his plans to help found an
American Party to function mainly in the Southern states to
encroach on the Democratic Party vote, and to obstruct the
forthcoming sedition trials by introducing a new bill, he continued:

"That trial against those indicted men and women is shameful. Why, they have nothing on them. Those men and women
are just anti-Communist, anti-Jewish, anti-British, anti-New
Deal. That's all. Nothing wrong with that."

Fish deliberately evaded the more ominous issue of how
these slogans were used as the smokescreen to hide their fundamental objective of subverting Democracy, by impairing
morale and promoting distrust and dissension preparatory to
an American *der tag*.

"A few weeks before the trial starts I intend to go on the
air. Even if we can't do anything, we can certainly make a
lot of noise and put it up to them. We're not through yet.
There are twenty or thirty of us—Hoffman, Nye, Wheeler,
men who haven't done an evil thing in their lives. We're not
through, not by a long shot."

Fish expressed great interest in Dennis' appearance before
the Army Exclusion Board and seemed eager to help him.

"Why are they hounding him?" he asked. "I see no reason.

He hasn't done anything. He'll tell me all about it when he comes down," Fish said, shaking my hand cordially. "Remember me to Lawrence when you get back."

The week end of February 20 was gone before I realized it, with Ham Fish the only Congressman I had found time to interview.

On my return to New York I called on Lawrence Dennis and was warmly received. It was obvious that my Washington trip had boosted my stock as a fellow "fascist." I informed him of Fish's anxiety about his appearance before the Army Exclusion Board—which had the power to remove Dennis from seventeen states of the Eastern Defense Command—and his eagerness to be of help.

"I didn't tell Fish about it," Dennis said, "but I told Nye and Wheeler as soon as I was called. Wheeler saw the Assistant Secretary of War about it."

I no longer doubted Dennis' statements. He was not the boastful sort.

"Who else have you approached in Congress?" I asked boldly.

"Several others. These men, of course, know others. It's not necessary to know everybody. Our only hope from now on is Congress," Dennis asserted. "I've been needling them in Congress and I intend to keep on needling them. Congress is our only hope. . . . Nye is the best man in there now."

Dennis was uncommonly frank with me and believed my story that my trips to Washington were made in order to find "a civil service job in the Office of Price Administration." In the course of our conversation he phoned Ralph Beaver Strassburger, wealthy newspaper publisher of *The Norristown Times-Herald*, who had also helped finance the publication of *Germany's White Paper*.

"Do you know Strassburger?" I asked Dennis.

"Oh yes," he answered. "He is my friend. The F.B.I. has been investigating him for a year. That dumb F.B.I. They've been investigating me, too. . . ."

I had timed my visit so that if Dennis went out for a luncheon engagement, I'd accompany him again. It worked out as planned. Dennis left the office in charge of a red-haired man named John Howland Snow (not related to John B. Snow) who had commented: "Benedict Arnold saved his country three times. If he was a traitor, he was a good enough traitor for me." Snow proved to be an ardent American Fascist.

Dennis was bound for the Harvard Club. While walking together, it occurred to me to ask him for a letter of introduction to Senator Nye. I knew it was a bold request, but I determined on this as the ultimate test of his friendship with and influence upon this important Senator. To my amazement, Dennis said without hesitation:

"Sure, I'll give you a letter of introduction. Come around tomorrow morning and I'll write it on my stationery."

I called at his office with a pounding heart fearful that he might, in the meanwhile, have learned of my investigations and warned Nye. But there was no need for apprehension.

"Sit down, Pagnanelli," Dennis said smiling, as he took out a sheet of engraved stationery and envelope. He seemed to bend over the paper for a long while, and when he finally finished writing he handed me the letter. It read:

> Lawrence Dennis
> 420 Warwick Avenue
> West Englewood, N. J.

Dear Gerald:
   This is to introduce a friend of mine, Mr. Pagnanelli, who is down in Washington looking for a job with the Government. He is a great admirer of yours and wants to shake your hand.
>   With best regards
>   (signed) Lawrence Dennis

Two days later, I faced Senator Nye in his spacious office. Although I had met him at the America First offices in the summer of 1941, I don't think he remembered me. Though he was extremely difficult to see, I gained immediate entree on the strength of my introductory letter from America's leading intellectual fascist.

Nye laid his work aside, placed Dennis' letter in front of him, lit a cigarette and leaned back in his swivel chair in cordial welcome to what he regarded as the envoy of his Ameri-

United States Senate

COMMITTEE ON APPROPRIATIONS

February 16, 1943

Mr. Geo. Pagnanelli
100 West 86th Street
New York, N. Y.,

Dear Mr. Pagnanelli:

Thanks for your letter of the 10th.
It will be pleasurable to see you if you come this way.

Sincerely yours,

FROM NYE TO "PATRIOT" PAGNANELLI

can Nazi friend. I had been highly nervous while waiting to see him, but my nervousness vanished as I sat opposite Nye; it was like talking to Lawrence Dennis or Joe McWilliams, and I felt perfectly at ease. One of the first questions I put to the Senator was to ask his opinion of Dennis. I quote him verbatim:

"I respect Lawrence very much. He is fine stuff. I see him frequently. He always calls me up when he comes to Washington."

The tone of reverence in Nye's voice toward Dennis was distinct and unmistakable.

I succeeded in gaining the Senator's confidence during the half-hour of my interview.

"Do you think the America First spirit has died down?" I asked.

"Far from it," Nye answered. "I have it very deeply and I want to see the inner circle of the America First Committee come out in the open again."

Looking at me speculatively, he added: "I am going to Chicago to see General Wood and talk this whole thing over with him. A Third Party is the only solution."

Nye admitted receiving Douglas Gregory, America First leader, at his offices in recent weeks; and he confessed knowing Joseph P. Kamp personally. He then paraphrased Dennis in "explaining" why the thirty-three men and women had been indicted:

"The greater majority is just crackpot—nobody would follow them. It was really a move to get Wheeler, Lindbergh, me and others like us. But we made a few speeches on the floor and beat them to it." Senator Nye's hard, grim features broke into a smile: "The America First spirit is much stronger now. But there is a right time for everything. You can ruin a good thing by coming out with it at the wrong time. When the time is right we'll be out in front again, fighting. All of us who fought on the America First Committee will be together again. Tell that to the boys back home."

Senator Nye rose up from his swivel chair and leaned his powerfully molded body over the desk; his features were defiant and resolute. The impression I carried away was that Nye would be extremely difficult to down. The similarity of his

LAWRENCE DENNIS
420 WARWICK AVENUE
WEST ENGLEWOOD, N.J.

Feb 25, 1943

Dear Gerald:

This is to introduce a friend of mine Mr Pagnanelli who is down in Washington looking for a job with the Government. He is a great admirer of yours and wants to shake your hand

With best regards

Lawrence Dennis

Letter from an American Nazi to an American Senator introducing "patriot" Pagnanelli.

features to those of the late Kemal Ataturk haunted me. His admiration for Dennis and the probable influence of Dennis' American Nazi views on Senator Nye's own utterances on the floor of the United States Senate worried me. His anti-Semitic remarks about the "Jewish crowd" which he uttered during the first minute of our interview frightened me!

Senator Burton Kendall Wheeler was too busy to see me, his secretary said. That is, he was too busy until I uttered the magic words: "I am a friend of Lawrence Dennis." The secretary smiled and typed it on a slip of paper, along with my name and address. Senator Wheeler kept another caller waiting while he received me briefly. When I asked his opinion of the indicted men and women, he dismissed the query with:

"All these men are guilty of is anti-Semitism."

Wheeler impressed me as an extremely shrewd, frostbitten politician, capable of putting up a stiff and bullish fight. A bulwark of the America First Committee, Wheeler's "patriotism" may be gathered by his declarations in the *Congressional Record:* "Japan is one of our best customers. I see no reason why we cannot live at peace with her." And only three weeks before Pearl Harbor he was quoted in *The New York Times:* "If we go to war with Japan, the only reason will be to help England." Of eleven national defense measures, Wheeler's voting record was eleven times "Nay."

On leaving I told Wheeler that Dennis expected to be in Washington soon.

"Fine. That is fine," he said, chewing a long cigar.

As I entered Congressman Hoffman's office, Room 1204, the memory of Mrs. Dilling's thundering herd came to mind and I recalled how that wild mob had packed his office, then stampeded down to Roy Woodruff's office, Hoffman's colleague from Michigan. I called Hoffman's attention to the episode.

"I recall it very well," he said between tightened lips.

His florid face deeply burrowed with wrinkles, Hoffman was virtually impossible to interview. Dillard Stokes' phrase, "scowling isolationist," described him perfectly. Hoffman was suspicious—so much so that he received me in the presence of two secretaries. I asked if he intended to protest again when the conspiracy trial came on.

"It all depends on what they do," he said. "I'll have more to say on Maloney later on." His jaws clamped down tight.

Hoffman had good reason to be tight-lipped. He voted "Nay" against twelve major national defense measures. His "Judas" speech—of which 145,000 copies were printed—had proved to be the most popular item of American fascist consumption after Pearl Harbor. An article under his name appeared as early as May, 1938 in Allen Zoll's *American Patriot*. Winrod published a long article of his in a pamphlet called *The Constitutionalist*. George Deatherage sold his speeches in specially prepared booklets. William Kullgren sold them. Hoffman, however, was the special darling of Joseph P. Kamp who sponsored Hoffman on an anti-labor speaking tour which took in more than eight states. On Hoffman, too, was heaped the honor of "Secretary of Public Health and Morals" in a nationalist cabinet selected by Edward James Smythe, liaison man between the Bund and the Klan, in which Father Coughlin was listed as Secretary of the Treasury, Jacob Thorkelson as Secretary of the Navy, and appeasist Senator Wheeler as Secretary of State.

A large man, with a huge head, hanging jowls and prominent mouth, Senator David I. Walsh made a queer statement in the course of my interview with him when he asked:

"Don't you find that the more people you ask the more you hear that we should not have gone into this war. . . ."

Coming from the chairman of the important Senate Committee on Naval Affairs, the query struck me as indicating an ominous state of mind toward winning of the war. A staunch America First-er, he voted against every major defense measure, and when I asked him if he thought the America First spirit was still alive, he answered:

"It is very much alive, and is getting more so every day. You can't win the peace with this man in the White House."

The impression I carried away of Senator Walsh was completely negative.

James M. Curley proved to be a huge man, with silver hair, sharp features and formless mouth. His slogan was "What can I do for you?" and he seemed to be the perfect "boss" type. Although in Congress only a few months, Curley had already found a seat on the important Appropriations Committee and had made good Francis P. Moran's boast that Curley knew his way around Capitol Hill.

My object in visiting him was to ascertain the extent to which he deserved the praise heaped on him by the Christian Front leader. I couldn't probe into this during my short interview, but my impression was that this affable and shrewd personality whose regime in his native Massachusetts was marked by public scandal, was on the road to becoming a power in the House. Curley was not the type of man who would remain buried, or remain ungenerous to the pleas of friends. His office was already cluttered with a steady stream of callers and he greeted most of them with "What can I do for you?"

Curley's intense anti-British sentiments may some day be voiced openly.

On the table of Dewey Short's reception desk were copies of Kullgren's *America Speaks* and the Reverend Harvey H. Springer's (who was a staunch Winrod-Fundamentalist) *Western Voice*. Both publications shrieked the "Jewish Gestapo" theme used in smearing the Department of Justice. Short, whom I had already heard at a Brooklyn America First meeting, proved to be a chubby fellow with twinkling blue eyes and a disarming smile. But he was an America First nationalist to the core.

"The America First spirit is not dead," he said. "Lindbergh is still the hero. Every once in a while," Short confessed, "some of us with the America First viewpoint still meet to talk things over—Congressmen, Senators, and men like William R. Castle and Samuel Pettengill," who was spokesman for Rumely's Committee for Constitutional Government.

When I asked for the names of specific Congressmen, Short named Wheeler, Nye and Fish.

"I don't think we had to get into this war," Short continued, "and we wouldn't have if we had not called everybody dirty names and insulted them, if we had built our home defenses and minded our own business."

Short summed up all the deceptive arguments advanced by the ignorant sector of the so-called isolationists. In the first place, Short had voted against all twelve national defense measures introduced in the House by the Administration, including the bill to arm the Guam Naval Base, and he also voted "Nay" on the Military Appropriation Act and Conscription Bill.

Short denounced the President for suggesting a peace-time defense army. He denounced the Administration for its expenditures for national defense. His total ignorance of the world-revolutionary nature of National-Socialism matched his apparent ignorance of the motives of the baseball-loving, gadget-loving, bath-loving Japanese, as the editorial from the Washington *Times-Herald* he inserted in the *Congressional Record* on November 17, 1941 stated. That editorial, endorsed by Short, went on:

Of all the oriental people, the Japanese are the most nearly like us. . . . It is against these people that our war hawks are proposing that we fight a war. Again why? The Japs don't want to fight us. They have gone to the length of clippering a special envoy over here to make another bid for peace.

Short impressed me as the symbol of the willful and short-sighted politician whose Roosevelt-hatred had blinded him to the failings even of his own record to arm America against enemy attack. Unfortunately, his simplification of the causes leading to our entry into war and his abysmal ignorance of the global revolution initiated by the Nazis was shared by others of the Congress.

Those I visited urged neither a vigorous and two-fisted stand against America's Nazi enemies without nor against the enemies within our country. While the rest of the nation toiled and sacrificed, the impression I got was that these former America First-ers (with the exception of Curley who ran for Boston Mayor at the time of Pearl Harbor) were still America First Committeemen at heart, and were working behind the scenes to revive the defeatist and appeasist dogma of the America First Committee.

Far from giving up *The American Vindicator* for the duration, Senator Reynolds, Chairman of the Senate Committee on Military Affairs, had sought to popularize it even more by changing the name to *The National Record* and by cutting the subscription price in half. The Stahrenberg slogan "America for Americans" remained on the masthead. I felt, somehow, that the America First Senator, like the rest of those I had met was merely marking time. Nye's remark raced through my mind:

"When the time is right we'll be out in front again fighting. All of us who fought on the America First Committee will be together again. Tell that to the boys back home."

Doubtless the Congressmen and Senators I interviewed were sincere in their hearts. One cannot doubt their fervor and one cannot justly impugn their patriotism. But the impression I carried away was that these men would disrupt our Democracy rather than permit "this gang in the White House," as one of them termed it, to win a just, enduring and universal peace.

So subtle was the needling these Congressmen had received that they saw nothing wrong with the phrases "America First" and "Nationalist America." The patriotic connotation of these slogans would be difficult to attack were it not for the fact that "nationalism" is a trend toward an international "new order"—the grouping of reactionary forces against the individual freedom of Democracy.

Just as old notions of anti-Semitism have been altered to become a revolutionary Trojan Horse device, by the same token, the old notion of healthful nationalism has been warped by Nazi strategists to subvert Democracy and serve as prelude to revolutionary fascism. David Baxter, the California Nazi, proved the point by declaring in his *Tactics*: "In America the revolution will no doubt be staged by American Fascistic forces—patriotic American nationalists."

Mussolini's fascist system was first described as "nationalist." The French fascist organization *Croix de Feu* which developed into a Vichy instrument was called "nationalist." The Nazi party is the *National*-Socialist Party. The Japanese War Party is a "nationalist" party and Franco's Falange was first known as a "nationalist" party. All these countries had their "Germany First," "France First" and "Spain First" parties. Recall that the motto of Sir Oswald Mosley's Blackshirts was "Britain First" and Stahrenberg's slogan of the American National-Socialist Party was "America First, Last and Always."

"America First" can be no different in its connotation and ultimate outcome despite the sincere intents of some of those who mouth it. "America First" is a cry unwittingly used by Liberty's hangmen.

As to Lawrence Dennis who relentlessly promoted the America First cry and carried on the needling of Congressional members while his friend and collaborator, Viereck, was in jail, I regard him as one of the most dangerous men to our war-time unity. He towers above Viereck in every way. His circle of influential Americans is infinitely greater. He is smart enough to work underground and avoid publicity. Because of his native background and training in our consular service, Dennis is an adroit diplomat and makes expert use of well-meaning clergymen and a high official of the Civil Liberties Union to stand by him whenever he is brought before an investigating body. It enraged me to hear him boast how well-meaning and democratic groups had defended him, while in the next breath and in the name of freedom of speech he denounced Democracy and plotted to multiply its tensions. Goebbels' statement fitted Dennis' role perfectly:

We National Socialists have never maintained that we were representatives of a democratic viewpoint, but we have openly declared that we only made use of democratic means in order to gain power, and that after the seizure of power we would ruthlessly deny to our opponents all those means which they had granted to us during the time of our opposition.

Throughout this book I have refrained from commenting on the lack of action of our Federal agencies against those native-born saboteurs of Democracy-at-war who were still at large and who, I believed, did not deserve to be. But I have fully appraised Dennis' underhanded work. I am convinced he does not want Democracy to emerge the victor. I am convinced that he is a distinct liability rather than an asset to the prosecution of our war for survival.

Why is Lawrence Dennis given liberty to disrupt national morale? Why should he be exempted because he is a friend of important Senators, Representatives, businessmen, newspaper publishers? Is Liberty's chief hangman privileged any more than the lesser, and less influential promoters of American Fascism? Is the pretext of freedom of speech under whose protective folds he is plotting the slow strangulation of Democracy, of greater import than the welfare and unity of a nation? Why must America *at war* continue to be the victim of Goebbels' taunt:

It will always remain the best joke made by the democratic system that it provided its deadly enemies with the means of destroying it.

CHAPTER XV

DEMOCRACY MUST WIN
THE PEACE!

"It is necessary, first in time, to win the war. But, first in importance, it is necessary to win the peace which follows the war. To win the war and lose the peace would be a worse defeat for us [Coughlinites] than if we fought the war to a draw."

REVEREND CHARLES E. COUGHLIN

Now, IN APRIL 1943, as I work on the last chapter of my story, I pause to look back over those stirring years since October, 1938, when I hesitantly knocked on the door behind the barber shop on East 116th Street. I suppose young men all over the world today find it difficult to realize they are the same persons they were a short time ago. I know it is difficult for me, for when I first stepped into Stahrenberg's filthy little shop I had no idea of the magnitude of Hitler's world propaganda network and the world-shaking events which have followed in the wake of his revolutionary *weltanschauung*.

I have learned a great many things during more than four years of life in the Nazi underworld, and I want to sum up my impressions. In order to do this it is necessary to check and see what happened to some of the people who travelled with me through the revolutionary byways of American fascism. What are my "friends" doing now? How about Stahrenberg, Mrs. Schuyler, Boris Brasol and all the others?

As Hans von Stahrenberg, his real name, Pete worked for the New York Park Department while at night he did printing for Colonel Sanctuary and Japanese interests until the F.B.I. raided his shop. Since then he has disappeared completely.

James McGee is back to "respectable" printing of memorial cards. Father Coughlin's picture which greeted you on entering his shop has been replaced by a calendar. His son,

Arthur, was detained by the F.B.I. because of his friendship with the Nazi spy, Josef Klein.

Mrs. Schuyler's latest "patriotic" quirk is the "discovery" that the Episcopal Church is loaded with Communist and Socialist doctrine. Her Church Layman's Association is now fighting the pesky Reds on all fronts.

In his last letter to me Kurt Mertig wrote: "We hold our weekly meetings since two weeks in the homes of the trustees of our group, rotating weekly. Our motto is contained in the Pledge to the Flag." Since then Mertig has been ordered removed 300 miles inland by the Army Exclusion Board.

Allen Zoll is reported as being in the Canadian Army.

Merwin K. Hart's friend, John Eoghan Kelly, has been indicted by a Washington grand jury on charges of being an unregistered Franco agent. *He was convicted late in May!*

Bernard D'Arcy, distributor of *Social Justice*, was discharged from the United States Army. Back in civilian life, he asserted he had "no apologies to make for knowing Father Coughlin or being a friend of his."

Jack Cassidy of the Christian Front is a private in the United States Army, and was last stationed near Seattle, Washington.

While in Chicago, Joe McWilliams borrowed a large sum from one of the mothers of We, the Mothers Mobilize for America and at this writing hasn't paid it back. Joe published a book, *The Serviceman's Reconstruction Plan* "explaining what America must do for our servicemen when Johnny comes marching home." With the help of one Alice Rand, Barrington, Illinois, he is issuing the *Post-War Bulletin* promoting his ham-and-egg plan "for those now sacrificially serving in our armed forces." He is intent on winning the peace the McWilliams way. This American Nazi hoodwinked Chicagoans and spoke before the North Central Kiwanis Club. On March 3, 1943 he addressed a group of navy mothers.

I have learned that Joe plans to run for Congress in 1944, and is being sponsored by powerful native fascist interests. I have also learned that the former Alice Rand is Mrs. Alexis de Tarnowsky, wife of an officer in the United States Army.

Father Coughlin still keeps in touch with his former collaborators and is far from being "through." Appealing for funds for religious purposes in August, 1942, he injected politics by praising "authoritarianism" and denouncing "Democracy with its majoritarianism."

In the April 10 issue of *The X-Ray* Court Asher announced that according to "very reliable sources Father Coughlin will soon be on the air, broadcasting from a station in Mexico." Mexico is a stronghold of the National Union of Sinarchists, a species of clerical fascism describing itself as "hierarchically organized as soldiers in a spiritual militia" and dedicated to a "counter-revolution" to hasten "the end of the capitalist and liberal regime." The Mexican Chamber of Deputies has charged it as being "a shock brigade prepared by Nazi agents." Its members take an oath of "unquestioning obedience to the Sinarchist *Führer* and to the Church." Father Coughlin repeatedly praised sinarchism in *Social Justice*. Sinarchism is being lauded in other surviving American clerical fascist organs.

It grieves me to report that the flame of the Christian Front is being rekindled in New York by its former promoters in the *same* Church locale, under ingenious and secretive tactics. For the present it is known simply as The Committee, but the patrons and promoters represent the same old fascist crowd. Prominent as organizer is James O'Kelly, former chairman of the Paul Revere Sentinels, clerk in a New York district court, an anti-Semite and a Coughlin-worshipper.

General Moseley has been retired on a pension and since Pearl Harbor has kept out of politics.

Phalanx fuehrer James Banahan is working as a carpenter.

When I visited Siegfried Hauck I found him working at a gas station near Scotch Plains. Talking about the war, he observed that America might win the war, "but if America loses the peace . . ." Hauck laughed.

With the help of the *Chicago Tribune* Congressman Day was re-elected by voters who forgot all about Flanders Hall.

Prescott Dennett, under indictment for sedition along with Edmondson and Hudson and Baxter sent me a plaintive letter appealing for funds. I sent each a letter.

In a letter dated December 7, 1942 Kullgren, also indicted, offered to send (and later did send) one hundred free copies of the January, 1941 issue of *The Beacon Light*, which hinted at the need for assassinating the President.

Mrs. Dilling settled a divorce case with her husband and upon her indictment for sedition, screamed: "I am guilty only of pro-Americanism." Under the auspices of "Friends of George Washington Principles" and "Truth and Liberty Meeting" she has been touring the Midwest selling *The Octopus*, issuing her bulletins and recommending George Edward Sullivan's defeatist book. The *Chicago Tribune* has defended her staunchly, as has the Reverend C. O. Stadsklev of Minneapolis. Her monthly bulletins continue to heap unparalleled abuse on our Department of Justice.

Charles B. Hudson, indicted, has continued to call our war for survival "that fake war" and has carried on "patriotic" business as before. He still sells Mrs. Fry's book, *Planned Economy* for $1 and those by Mrs. Dilling and Sullivan.

As for Mrs. Fry, alias Paquita de Shishmareff, the Immigration Bureau caught her when she tried to re-enter the United States on the S.S. *Drottningholm,* which arrived in the summer of 1942 with members of the diplomatic corps and correspondents. She's now a guest of our vigilant Department of Justice and under indictment for sedition.

Robert Leonard Obidiah Jordan, the "black fuehrer," was convicted of sedition and received ten years in Federal prison, along with Lester Eugen Holness, the "Reverend" Ralph Green Best and an accomplice, James Henry Thornhill, who got lesser terms. The "Little Napoleon," Joe Hartery, met his Waterloo with six years. The Civil Rights Bureau of the Department of Justice under Assistant Attorney-General Victor W. Rotnem traced Japanese propaganda to the Black Dragon Society and cracked down on seditious cells in nine states.

The Reverend Gerald B. Winrod, under indictment, has resumed publication of *The Defender* and in his appeal for funds used Senator Robert A. Taft's letter to Attorney General Biddle urging that the indictments be withdrawn.

The Ku Klux Klan is resurgent and in January, 1943, advertised in the Maryville, Tennessee *Enterprise:* "WANTED —5000 or more of the 10,000 Klansmen in the following counties answer this ad: Knox, Blount, Monroe, and Loudon— there is work to do—Write Klansmen, Box No. 30."

The Reverend Joe Jeffers made the following statements against the Catholic Church in November 1942:

And here in the United States where does the Catholic Church have its capitol? It has it in Washington, D. C. And we sent an Ambassador to the Vatican. That was a disgrace to every American in a nation which our Supreme Court has stated is Christian.

In December Jeffers wrote me: "We have started a special fund for a coast to coast broadcast which we feel is divine order." I informed *America* (magazine) of his bigotry (previously I had sent in a full report of the Bund-Klan meeting at Camp Nordland). On February 3, 1943 I heard from Harold C. Gardiner, S.J.: "We are pleased to keep in touch with this activity in case an opportunity arises of doing some definitely constructive work against it."

Commander Edward Elwell Spafford is dead.

The citizenship of many Bund leaders has been revoked. Severin Winterscheidt, former editor of the *Deutscher Weckruf*, testified under oath that he was instructed by Berlin to smear "everything that was inimical to National Socialistic ideas" as "Communist."

As to Edward Holton James, he has become bolder with every *Grapevine Letter*. Calling the United Nations "United Hypocrites," and our leaders "madmen" who have made themselves the "blood-stained assassins of our soldiers and sailors," he defended Tojo's cause on January 14, 1943.

Grapevine Letter Number 88 was mailed on March 31:

He who resists the draft today, in the name of liberty, gains a place of honor by the side of the immortal heroes who founded this country. . . . They who resist the draft today are the heroes who will guard the Constitution, and build that army which is "necessary for the security of a free people. . . ." The Supreme Court has become not only a useless institution, but a subversive institution as far as the interests of a free government are concerned.

Edward Holton James was still at large as this book went to press and still in intimate touch with fellow "patriots" throughout the country. The *Boise Valley Herald* was publishing his writings. James is an example of how a so-called crackpot may continue to engage in coercing native Americans against the war effort.

After being ousted as an official of the United Service Organizations, John B. Snow retired to his home near Suffern, New York, where he now lives in self-seclusion.

Mrs. A. Cressy Morrison still permits Edwin Perry Banta, speaker for the Bund, to work in her office. Banta has turned into confidential trouble-shooter for native fascists throughout the country, receiving their mail at his home, assisting them with advice and doing contact work.

Seward Collins has closed the American Review Bookshop, rented the building and retired to his country home at New Canaan, Connecticut. Conrad Grieb is in the army.

John T. Flynn, chairman of America First, has returned to his writing work. William R. Castle, at this writing, is nursing himself in Florida. Lindbergh and Ford are together: Lindbergh is working for Ford. Chortled Gerald L. K. Smith:

The presence of Lindbergh in Detroit is one of the most inspiring events to take place since Pearl Harbor. The youthfulness of America's hero, alongside the wisdom of America's industrial sage, serves notice on the world that real Americanism still is, and real Americans are, still alive.

Parker Sage and Russell M. Roberts wrote me regularly until the indictment of the "ambassador of ill will," Lyman, for sedition. Alderman continued to write with unabated *Protocol* "patriotism." He was last working for Pontiac Motors in Pontiac getting $1.20 an hour plus overtime.

Ernest Elmhurst is carrying on quietly on Staten Island trains and ferries. Drew's invitations to his home became so insistent that I became suspicious and have avoided him completely. I still have the copy of Hudson's bulletin which he gave me. Both Elmhurst and Drew are under investigation.

Thomas Quinlan kept his promise. He became a draft-dodger and tried to hide out in the Midwest. But army authorities caught up with him. Quinlan was tried, convicted and is now serving three years for draft evasion.

Horace Haase, friend of Kurt Mertig, Lawrence Dennis, and staunch America First-er, surrendered as a conscientious objector and is now in prison.

On April 21, 1943, Major Alexander Cloyd Gill visited Birkhead's New York offices. He told Birkhead that Kamp was in constant touch with and frequently visited Martin Dies in Washington . . . Five days later Gill was found dead in the office of the Constitutional Educational League. Newspapers reported that Kamp had visited his office at 6:25 A.M. and found Gill dead at his desk. The cause was given as heart-attack.

From his luxurious apartment on Morningside Heights, Sanctuary (under indictment for sedition) has moved to a drab, walk-up brownstone tenement, taking with him his library of hate books.

The Reverend John Jefferson Davis Hall had been publicized so widely in newspapers and magazines as a devout preacher that on April 16 I called on him again. I found that he now had two assistants to help him in giving "blessings" over the 'phone. Placing my face against his beard Mr. Hall hugged me several times, then pronounced a special blessing. But he spent the next two hours in a violent tirade against the Catholic Church and the Jews.

Olov E. Tietzow legally changed his name to Anderson. At this writing he is in Chicago operating quietly, and will publish his book under his new name. I've written Edwin Flaig four times without receiving an answer.

George Hornby continues to be active as propagandist, although no longer with the W.P.A. whose equipment he used secretly to publish his poison writings. Collaborating with the "Reverend" H. R. Sickle, on January 27th he sent me a four-page leaflet "proving" that "the United States attacked first," not the Japs. His letter to me was on Disabled Veterans stationery.

I corresponded with James H. McKnight and he urged me to settle in Salt Lake City: "Work is plentiful here now, and big wages." He also apologized for the "war-mongering" speech of David O. McKay, a high dignitary of the Mormon Church. "I suppose our long friendship [with McKay] has terminated forever," McKnight wrote. "I will not follow a war-monger even tho he be my twin brother."

Charles W. Phillips has resumed publication of *The Individualist* after a lapse of some months. Mrs. Mabel J. Willard carried on her "patriotic" work in Oklahoma for a while; she has now resumed operations from her Chicago base.

Court Asher still lifts stories from other newspapers and continues to publish *The X-Ray*.

Carl Mote is spreading his "patriotism" among farmers by writing for the *Farmer's Guild News*. He sent me the announcement of his new magazine *America Preferred*. Mote intends to play a prominent part in Indiana politics and the formation of a Third Party following Gerald L. K. Smith's pattern of "patriotism."

The April issue of *The Cross and the Flag* referred to Senator Lundeen—some of whose speeches were written by Viereck —as the "late and much-beloved, fearless patriot" and divulged that Mrs. Lundeen is "speaking under the auspices of the America First Party" in the Midwest.

I lost my contact with Boris Brasol through the oversight of a fellow investigator, who, in order to cover himself, told Brasol I had been trailed to his office. It placed Brasol on guard against me. Brasol moved to a super-secret hide-out. It's located at 1841 Broadway, Room 901; telephone: Columbus 5-5934. He doesn't like to be disturbed.

As to the Mothers groups, Mrs. Beatrice M. Knowles wrote me late in December, 1942, from Detroit:

Your air-mail letter was awaiting my return from a trip through the state. . . . We have been meeting as always and much good is derived from this. The meetings also serve to help them keep their chins up . . . so they look forward to the meetings with much comfort.

Mrs. Rosa M. Farber refused to answer my letters, and I have wondered whether she was still engaged in promoting her peculiar "patriotism"—the whispering campaign.

The Chicago We, the Mothers Mobilize for America have completely changed their tune. They have gone in for "social reform," "slum clearance" and "old age assistance." Members are instructed in "The Mechanics of Voting" and "Why Parliamentary Law." Their organ is the *Women's Voice*, a chummy four-page monthly which carries its poison between the lines. Mrs. Lyrl Clark Van Hyning helps run it. Her sister, Mrs. Genevieve Campbell, laid down the policy of the sheet.

Rather than attempting to storm forts by brute strength, this paper is beginning as a mental gadfly, buzzing about to prick here and there, never revealing its plans. . . . By means of wit, satire, understatements and hints—lightning flashes rather than long diatribes—implant your sting, then buzz away. . . . Let your mailed fist be most often sheathed in the velvet glove.

The Mothers of America, under Mrs. David Stanley, have carried on a vicious rumor-mongering campaign in Cleveland, while the Minnesota Mothers act as sponsors for Mrs. Dilling. From Darby, Pennsylvania, Mrs. John Browne, of the Crusading Mothers of Pennsylvania, mailed me vicious defeatist leaflets and in one of her typical letters wrote:

You know, Mr. Pagnanelli, I have never given up the fight for our Republic. . . . We have a great work to do, and do it right away. In the near future you will hear from me on some concerted action. I have great hopes for the future, our torch will burn brightly again.

Mrs. Agnes Waters, professional Washington mother, still rampages at meetings. She suggested I send her $300, then urged: "Any time you are in Washington just barge in on us. If I am not at home my children will be." I've kept away from her and her children.

A particularly vicious Coughlinite Mothers unit still doing business as usual is the Mothers of Sons Forum, Cincinnati, headed by Mrs. Ethel Groen. Venomously anti-Semitic and anti-British the Mothers have asserted that "National-Socialism stands for positive Christianity" and propagated other choice lies originated by the German Library of Information. Cathrine Curtis addressed them and was quoted in newspapers as stating: "I don't blame Hitler for what he is doing. He wants to conquer for the German people."

Under the stimulus of mysterious financial backing the Anglo-Saxon Federation plans to broadcast "Kingdom Messages" over a national network of thirty-seven stations.

Walter Steele's *National Republic* continues to appear, and Mrs. Flora A. Walker continues to send out Steele's magazine and an assortment of "anti-alien" literature. Business as usual. As for Miss Cathrine Curtis, when I wrote asking if she were still active after Pearl Harbor, she answered: "I find many people just beginning to awaken to the real cause of our Republic and more interested than ever in preserving its traditions, institutions—and Constitution."

Recent issues of Robnett's *News and Views* are blazing, demagogic displays of star-spangled Americanism, dedicated to answering "What is the American System?" They emit fire against the Reds, make no comment whatever against native fascists.

Merwin K. Hart and Archibald Ewing Stevenson continue to work together. Hart has expanded the scope of the New York State Economic Council and changed the name to National Economic Council, Inc. My belief is that Hart, like Reverend Curran, is being groomed for more festive fascist days.

Rumely's mailing activities continue side by side with his campaign to "Keep America American." Rumely took a hand in the 1942 elections by issuing an unprecedented volume of literature and according to lavish full-page advertisements had established many "cells" of "100 members per congressional district." Rumely wanted to increase the number in each "cell" in order that the Committee might be a "continuing and decisive influence in national affairs." And while Rumely directs the promotion, Frank E. Gannett—esteemed by *Social Justice*—works backstage in Washington in welding farmers' lobbies into a powerful organization hostile to the Administration. Rumely continues scrupulously to avoid publicity while managing the affairs of the Committee.

While in Washington I tried desperately to learn the identity of the mysterious "Cincinnatus," author of the most virulent anti-Semitic book published in America. I tried to see the Washington attorney, George Edward Sullivan who had the answer, but he avoided me. I remembered his description of "Cincinnatus. . . . He is in the vicinity. He is a pretty old man and has a brilliant mind."

B. H. Roberts of Washington was reputed to be the author, but he did not fit the description, and I was convinced that he merely was a distributor of the seditious book, having sold me two copies before Pearl Harbor. Whoever the author, he was well-read for *War, War, War* quoted from Shakespeare,

Anatole France as well as from *The Eighth Crusade* distributed by the *Deutscher Fichte-Bund.*

Whoever the author, I knew he was extremely friendly with Sullivan, for on page 116, he referred to Sullivan as "an eminent and patriotic Washington lawyer." Before going to Washington I obtained from John H. Mullen, Kamp's printer and typesetter of *War, War, War* (Mullen knew but would not tell me the author) the address of another Washington attorney, Arthur Peter. I ascertained through *Who's Who* that Arthur Peter was a member of the Society of the Cincinnati, and by calling on B. H. Roberts a second time I established that he was friendly with Peter.

I traced Arthur Peter to his office in the Washington Loan and Trust Building, not far from Sullivan's law offices. I found him to be an elderly man, in his late sixties, limping on one foot. But his mind was extremely alert and a half-dozen current books lay about in his office. Peter proved to be extremely tight-lipped about himself, but he admitted his friendship with Roberts and Sullivan and professed considerable interest whenever I mentioned *War, War, War.*

I tried to join the Vigilantes founded by Governor Eugene Talmadge after Georgia voters ousted him from office. As I did not know Talmadge, I wrote the Ku Klux Klan with which I had corresponded and on October 27, 1942, I received a letter from F. Lee Evans, Imperial Kligrapp:

. . . You inquired about Vigilantes, Inc. Would suggest that you write Major John Goodman, c/o State Highway Patrol, Atlanta, Georgia. You may tell him you obtained his address through this office.

The Major—who signed his name "John E. Goodwin"—informed me that membership and annual dues were $7.50 and the Vigilantes were "secret Fraternal . . . Benevolent, Social, and Patriotic." I filled out the application blank he sent me and on November 18 I sent $5 in money order. Goodwin then remitted two insistent letters asking for the dues. I mailed him $2.50 on January 6, 1943 and expected to receive my membership card and literature "promptly," as Goodwin indicated. On January 27 I received a letter from Goodwin in which he stated that the Vigilantes were "pretty well organized" in 100 Georgia counties:

. . . and within the next few weeks we will go into Alabama, Florida, Tennessee and Louisiana, as all of these States are interested and have started negotiations. We had a meeting today of the Executive Committee and the entire Committee expressed a desire to get things lined up in New York.

But Goodwin produced no literature and no membership card as he had promised. This, plus his insistent demands for fees had made me restive about my investment of $7.50. I also became suspicious at Goodwin's use of plain paper, instead of the official Vigilante stationery. I did not hesitate to air my suspicions in a letter I wrote Goodwin on February 6. He did not answer it, nor did he answer my follow-up. I wrote Eugene Talmadge and on February 8 Talmadge wrote back:

I am glad you joined the Vigilantes. I have turned your letter over to the President of the Club and he will forward you the membership card in a few days. You should also be receiving *The Statesman*, a weekly paper I am publishing. If you are ever in Atlanta, come around to see us.

I waited patiently, but in the face of complete silence on Goodwin's part I decided to force a showdown and wrote Goodwin a strong letter. A carbon copy went to Talmadge. On February 20 Goodwin refunded the $7.50 I had paid. "It appears you do not have confidence in our organization," he said. Though I did not become a member, I established the collaboration between the Klan, the Vigilantes, Goodwin and Talmadge—symbols of bigotry and hate, tyranny and nativist fascism in-the-making, the next-of-kin to the international brand.

Talmadge's newspaper advertised *The Struggle of the Ages* published by the American Rangers at Atlanta. I obtained a copy and found it to be the most violent anti-Catholic book I had ever seen. A typical passage read: "The Papal Government being bound by Oath to Murder, violates the Constitution, *is illegal* and should *not* be allowed to operate within the United States Government." It called priests "sleek, dog-collared vultures." I reported this new anti-Catholic source to Father Gardiner.

As to Ham Fish's friend, Dennis, he circulated on the anniversary of Pearl Harbor a 16,000-word blueprint for American Fascism entitled *Grand Strategy of the Republican Party Until 1944.* I am sure that no respectable Republican urged Dennis to circulate the blueprint—an ambitious attempt to inoculate gullible Republican leaders with methods for winning the peace the Dennis way. With consummate hypocrisy, the champion of American National-Socialism regarded as "dangerous to Democracy" the present "truce on political opposition" to the war efforts and demanded the return to the "foreign policies of Washington's Farewell Address."

Slyly Dennis hinted at the need for "change in principles, of policy and national objectives," and urged Republican leaders that "win the war" be retained as slogan until the war is won —after which the knifing and the strict withdrawal to the cave of isolationism. Propagating all the typical Goebbels' lies to the effect that the New Deal is Communist and bent on crushing capitalism, Dennis tried to entice Republicans by maintaining that "opposition of principle was always maintained" during other American wars.

So you see, fascism in America is not dead. It has been pretending sleep. And I wish I could say that the America First spirit, and the threat of an American Fascist Third Party movement were over. I recall the evening I spent with James Banahan at the German-American Athletic Club. Hunched over a glass of beer he finished telling me how the Nazi consulate had helped finance the Phalanx, and added:

"Y'know, George, there aren't many of us right now, but we can sure raise plenty of hell. A pinch of salt isn't much, but throw it in your coffee and regardless of how much sugar you put in you'll still taste the salt. We are that salt and we're here to sour up this Democracy. We are the salt of American nationalism!"

I have indicated the salts which threaten to overflow at the "right time" at the peace table after we have won the military war. For if America's fascists who are psychologically courting America's defeat and fear most a democratic victory,

cannot "win the war" their way—the fascist way—they are
determined to "win the peace" at any cost.

At the same time they are determined to *prolong* the conflict in order to intensify their work of dissension and distrust
and justify their proposed leadership at the peace conference.
I am convinced that American Fascists do not want to see,
and are sabotaging with every means at their command, a
quick Allied victory. Such a decisive victory would completely shatter their time table and give Democracy a permanent victory. The keynote of the fascist strategy was set by
Father Coughlin only a few weeks after Pearl Harbor in
Social Justice:

> First things come first. It is necessary, first in time, to win the
> war. But, first in importance, it is necessary to win the peace
> which follows the war. . . . To win the war and lose the peace
> would be a worse defeat for us [Coughlinites] than if we fought
> the war to a draw. . . . Americans, *Social Justice* advises you to
> get into every patriotic organization in America. Join up. Be
> neither a slacker for war nor a slacker for peace.

The prototype of extreme isolationists caused Germany to
win the peace after the last war. That the same symptoms are
recurrent is indicated by brilliant columnist Raymond Clapper:

> . . . The Axis can still win the peace as Germany won it the
> last time. The Axis can get a chance to fight again if the United
> Nations split up, and if the United States again returns to the
> cave. . . . The Axis can win its second-best victory if the United
> States Senate takes the United States back into isolation.

It is conceivable how officials, industrialists and other interests who have championed the nationalist cause may conspire
to lose the democratic peace for America and surrender our
hard-won victory to those who are hostile to the idea of working together with other nations and planning a post-war program of a durable peace based on international accord. Thus
our "victory" would then be tantamount to having stopped
Hitler in Europe, but permitted a species of nativist nationalism to enter America by the back door to plague us again in
the next generation. That was Father Coughlin's vision when

he urged his henchmen to join up all "patriotic organizations" and "win the peace the Father Coughlin way."

And that is the party line being championed by the promoter of reactionary politics, Gerald L. K. Smith. His candidates for President in 1944 include such prophets of appeasement as Lindbergh; Senators Nye, Wheeler, Taft; Congressmen Hoffman, Fish, and Dewey Short. Simultaneously with Smith's efforts and Dennis' attempts to influence extreme right wing Republicans, the America First Committee is being revived. Douglas Gregory, a New York official of the A.F.C., has met with Senator Nye and Lindbergh is reported to have visited Senator Wheeler. In the January, 1943, issue of *The Cross and the Flag* Gerald L. K. Smith wrote:

Some of us have taken steps to organize an America First Party . . . with which and through which to express our independence and our determination to put America First during the war, at the peace table and in time of peace.

In the next issue he announced that he had opened America First Party units in key cities and was "in the midst of a nationwide speaking tour." In Chicago he spoke under the auspices of Earl Southard, secretary of the Citizens Keep America Out of War Committee who, in March, 1941, wrote William Kullgren the following revealing letter:

Our Committee held a mass meeting in Chicago last night addressed by William Griffin, editor of the New York *Enquirer*, and Mr. Lawrence Dennis, editor of the *Weekly Foreign Letter*. The several thousand at this meeting were inspired by the speakers to continue their effort to keep America out of war. . . .

. . . Beg to advise that we received one hundred copies of the March number of *The Beacon Light* and thank you sincerely for your kindness. We have distributed these magazines. . . . I read your paper with considerable interest and feel that it would be a great contribution to the cause of real Americanism.

With Griffin under indictment for sedition and Dennis "too hot to handle," Smith turned to a mutual Dennis friend, Earl Southard, to promote plans for a so-called isolationist victory at the peace table. This is the picture America is facing. And along with Dennis, other henchmen of American Fascism who are not in jail or under indictment are engaged in "winning the peace"—in their usual way: by rumor-mongering, by spreading defeatism, by agitating against unity and by disrupting morale.

At Germantown, Illinois, Edward A. Koch continues to publish a fascist organ even more outspoken than was *Social Justice*. Issued under lay auspices, it declares itself "devoted to the Cause of a Corporate Order" in America, brands Democracy a plague and adulates Hitler for cleaning out the "liberalistic" heresy; and in October, 1942, Koch wrote:

Whatever our country's proper and legitimate objectives in the war may be, we believe that the destruction of Nazism (and "Fascism" generally) should not be among them. . . . Concealing or distorting the good things in Fascism will be detrimental to our country's future.

After his investigation by the F.B.I. in December, 1942, Koch insisted that his "activities are decidedly pro-American" and that the Department of Justice was in the wrong. It is this American Nazi mentality which, while sabotaging Democracy proclaims itself "serving our country's welfare," that is the *insidious enemy-mind* within our country.

Nazi agents will miss no trick to foment discord. The current cries and agitation of the Drys to bring back Prohibition —and with it poison "hootch" and its effect on war morale—is highly pleasing to the Nazis. Their agent in Switzerland, "Dr." Robert Hercod, is secretary of the Nazi-subsidized International Bureau Against Alcoholism. Hercod wormed his way into the confidence of Americans and became correspondent for *The Voice*, organ of the Board of Temperance Union of the Methodist Church; as well as *The American Issue* and *The Union Signal*, official organs of the Anti-Saloon League, and the Women's Christian Temperance Union. Hercod's Nazi propaganda crept into numerous articles he wrote for American consumption.

Quick to take advantage of the sneak attack on Pearl Harbor, Nazi agents spread about the lie that the surprise attack was due to the "fact" that our men were in a drunken stupor —a lie which was believed in and disseminated by some Prohibitionist factions. And bootleg "Americanism" on behalf of Prohibition has been propagated consistently by Kullgren's *Beacon Light*, Garner's *Publicity* and Winrod's *Defender*.

Captain Edward Page Gaston, reserve officer and director of the World Prohibition Federation, helped promote the Dry cause in Washington. I first interviewed Gaston, founder of the Patriot Guard of America in 1940, in New York, and after I had told of my membership in the Mobilizers and the Nationalist Party, he commended me as an "upstanding young American who loves his country." He then offered to speak for the Mobilizers, gratis, or any other "patriotic" group I named. I interviewed him again in Washington in February, 1943, and learned that he was a personal friend of Hercod, whom he had met in Paris, and that among his Congressional supporters were Senator Reynolds (who, according to Gaston, was personally a "wet" but voted Dry) and Senator Wilbert Lee O'Daniel.

Food-hoarding and rumor-mongering about the "shortage of food" are devices urged by Nazis to help disrupt our morale. A member of the Women's Auxiliary of the Christian Front told me: "I put away canned goods not because I have to, my cellar is full right now, but because I want to make some of these women suffer for the things they can't get. It's the only way they'll learn." And I know of an instance of a former official of the Hamburg-American Line who began hoarding immediately before Pearl Harbor, and whose closets, cabinets and cellar bulge with hoarded food.

Wily Nazi propagandists will stop at nothing to sabotage the war and sabotage the peace. If they do not succeed with one method they are determined to succeed with any of a hundred other methods they have devised and tested on the conquered countries. But there are ways loyal Americans can stop them and help Democracy emerge as victor at the peace table.

After more than four years in the Nazi underworld, I've summarized Hitler's program for the subversion of our Democracy and the overthrow of our capitalist order. It includes:

1) Anti-Semitism to serve as a social dissolvent; 2) Redbaiting to serve as a screen for Nazi propaganda; 3) lies or half-truths to gain the support of the politically ignorant;

4) super-patriotism to arouse his disciples emotionally; 5) a perverted brand of nationalism which most frequently utilizes the slogans "America First" and "America for the Americans"; 6) anti-British propaganda to rally German, Irish, Italian, Spanish and nativist sentiment; 7) an attempt to undermine confidence in the Administration in order to facilitate the acceptance of revolutionary doctrines; 8) defamation of Democracy by exaggerating its failings as a device to "soften up" resistance; 10) the systematic cultivation of mass hatred as a means of blinding reason; 11) the pitting of group against group, race against race, religion against religion to break down national unity; 12) encouraging an attitude of ridicule toward the operation of Nazi propaganda in an effort to draw a red herring across its trail; 13) the adulation of Hitler as the deliverer from, and of Nazism as the panacea for, the evils of Communism, Judaism, unemployment, the national debt and anything else you choose to name; finally, 14) agitation for a "Third Party" or a "new leadership," native fascist in sentiment, to set up the American New Order by "Constitutional methods" and ostensibly in order to "preserve the Constitution," but which at the same time would be friendly to, collaborate with, or appease Hitler's New Order.

If and when fascism—by whatever name it may be called—is foisted on America, it may bear little resemblance to the original product conceived by Mussolini and propagated methodically in America under the guise of "patriotism" by a horde of Nazi agents. Of those agents some are in jail, some in hiding, others in disrepute. The Kuhns and Schmuederrichs are through. Their more refined bedfellows, the Vierecks and Auhagens, are (possibly) also through. Their American-born collaborators—the Trues and Edmondsons, having laid their poison eggs—are on the threshold of the political beyond. But they have trained heirs to carry the torch in Park Avenue circles as well as in the side streets. Therein lies the greatest danger to American Democracy, and the winning of the peace.

Ignorance of the true nature of Nazism and the multiple nativist forms it takes; the prejudices and hates it feeds on; the reason-blinding power of its sugary appeals, which to capital promises the suppression of labor, and to labor the suppression of capital; ignorance of its drug-like strategy which works best while Americans suspect it the least (Boston is a tragic example)—against all these manifestations of political ignorance, *truth* is our most potent weapon.

Those who look upon the slightest variance from the status quo as "revolutionary" are ideal fodder of Nazi propagandists who look to yesterday for their future. And those who like Father Coughlin and Seward Collins regard the Middle Ages— the dark period of corruption and feudalism—as the ideal on which to found our future society are organically hostile to institutional Democracy. Fascist-mindedness today is the most dangerous trend in America's political thinking.

I look back upon my years in the Nazi underworld without regrets. It was a dirty job, but I felt that someone had to do it and live to tell about it. They have been gruelling and abnormal years. I operated literally in a sunless world, under conditions which have impaired my health, but I hope that my mission of exposing dangerous undercurrents will help awaken democratic Americans to vigilance on the home front.

This book is a warning to those Americans who respect Democracy and want to preserve it. It is to warn that any political group which adopts the slogan "America First" may go the way of "Germany First" and "France First," for those countries, too, had their nativist Quislings and a smug section of the populace which insisted that it could not happen to *their* country. I wish to remind America that before he took power Hitler had always asserted: "Neither I nor anybody else in the National-Socialist Party advocates proceeding by anything but Constitutional methods."

I am going back to the world I left behind four and a half years ago to renew friendships and live in the sunshine again —if the countless "friends" I met in the Nazi underworld permit me to live. I have written this book in order to help preserve those values which I learned were synonymous with America when I first came here: freedom, individual initiative and enterprise. I believe in these "old-fashioned" precepts.

In case I may be asked why in my reports of investigations, I have said nothing about Communist subversive elements, I can only state that in my opinion Communist propaganda is as undesirable as Nazi propaganda. I tried hard to investigate the Communists along with my work among the Nazis. I failed for two reasons: first, I was geared to the Nazi pattern of "patriotism" and adopted the gestures and language acceptable among fascists, but conspicuous among Communists; the second, and more important cause of my failure was the infinite shrewdness of Communist Party liners who, at the time I tried to bore within, never allowed anyone to enter their ranks without thoroughly investigating him first.

I attended Communist-front meetings. I enrolled in the Worker's School for one semester under the alias John Correa. I went to social affairs and advertised in *The Daily Worker*. I associated with both their male and female members. I tried every means short of Mata Hari tactics to worm my way into their confidence. But inevitably at the crucial point, I'd be questioned, be commanded to produce identification, and provide a list of persons who would vouch for me. I believe it must be easier to join the F.B.I. than the Communist Party.

I agree somewhat with Rex Stout, chairman of the Writer's War Board: "The political ethics of American Communists still are about as low as anything ever observed in these parts, including the Ku Klux Klan." Neither am I a member of any Socialist, Social-Democrat or Trotskyite faction. Never a joiner—except when I went overboard as a "fascist" and became a member of many organizations—I have tried to be an American without any outside trimmings. I would dread to see in America the victory of a force either from the extreme Left or extreme Right. I hope Americans will remain middle-of-the-road Democrats and Republicans, and that these two parties will keep on fighting bitterly at election time and becoming firm friends after the battle.

It so happens that I believe in our democratic-capitalist order. I have no property and no money to speak of, but it is the system under which I have found the greatest measure of happiness and self-expression. And I have written this book as an exposé of those forces which look upon capitalist Democracy as the only remaining obstacle to their international authoritarian schemes, and are determined to crush it at any cost.

It was the spirit of fair play which first struck me when I

came to America twenty-two years ago. I came from a land of oppression, of fear and age-long hatreds. I dread seeing this country, my adopted homeland, swept by those same ancient winds of bitterness and prejudice. I felt the first cold gusts of those winds as I drifted through the shadowy alleys of America's fascist underworld and determined to do my part to check it.

I feel that my debt to America is an eternal debt, a debt timeless, transmittable from father to son to grandson—a debt payable on demand, instantly during national emergency as well as during peacetime, payable so long as this country remains what it started out to be: a haven for the oppressed, granting equality and opportunity, liberty and justice for all who seek it and deserve to have it. May this blessed nation of ours never degenerate to a system of government by some, for some. May it forever remain a government by all, for all. There is no greater privilege at this moment, no greater honor as we look upon skies free of raining death, to a land free from the barbarisms of war, to a future more promising than any on this strife-torn earth, than to serve this, our home, our country.

This is my faith.

INDICES

I. MAIN INDEX

Abed, Mohammed, 64
Ackley, S. A., 209
Action, 31, 87, 200, 268
Adamo, Alfred P., 302, 312-3, 315
Adrian, Edward C., *see* E. Masgalajian
Afansieff, Peter (aliases: Prince Kushubue, Peter Armstrong), 391, 468
African Pioneering Syndicate, Inc., 156
African Progressive Business League, 155
Aftermath, 31
Agaki, Roy H., 48, 64, 219
Agayeff, George, 64, 91
Ahearne, Michael, 144, 222, 224-6, 234
Albert, Heinrich, 473, 474
Alderman, Garland Leo, 289-91, 294-5, 297, 301-2, 304-6, 314-7, 324-33, 335, 351, 403, 506
Allen, C. F., 374-6, 384
Allen, Henry D., 137, 146, 173, 387, 444-5
Allied Patriotic Societies, Inc., 218
Allison, Brant D., 232
Almanac Singers, 245
Alstyne, J. H., 460
America, 57, 505
America First Bulletin, 258, 260
America First Committee, 240-60; backers of, 242-4, 515; Congressmen and, 126, 128-9, 227, 230-1, 244, 254, 256-9, 487-8, 491, 495-8, 515; Coughlinites and, 248-9, 252-3, 279; in Detroit, 291, 306-8, 313, 315-6, 319, 324, 326, 329-32, 335-6; "Jew-controlled," 249, 377; J. E. McWilliams and, 258, 250-2, 254-5; Nazis and, 160, 179, 215, 229, 232, 235, 239, 242, 256-7, 273, 305, 307, 412-3, 415; revival of, 278-81, 483-4, 515; supported by "patriots," 82, 117, 121, 159, 171, 196, 203, 208, 214, 217, 226, 230, 239-42, 248, 253, 255-8, 283, 374, 380, 394-5, 402, 414-5, 461, 472, 475, 506; *also see* photo
America First, Inc., 146, 222, 224
America First Party, 485-6, 508, 515
America in Danger, 141, 342, 387
America, Look at Spain, 456-7, 460
America Preferred, 508
America Speaks, 496
American Bulletin, 85-6, 89, 180
American Charter, 406
American Civil Liberties Union, 142, 144, 220, 499
American Coalition of Patriotic Societies, 130, 140, 149, 196, 217-9, 238, 415, 448, 450, 457, 459
American Defense Society, 204, 225, 228
American Destiny Party, 83-4, 89
American Fascist Party, 38
American Fascists, 149
American Fellowship Forum, 122-3, 463
American Gentile, The (also known as *Gentile Front*), 391, 468
American Guard, 417-8
American Guards, 257
American Immigration Conference Board, 42
American Indian Federation, 218
American Irish Defense Ass'n., 454
American Legion, 188-9, 256, 282, 354, 402, 417, 445
American Mercury, The, 283, 285, 295
American Monthly, 120, 124
American Mothers, 217, 291, 311-2
American National-Socialist League, 134, 180, 198
American Nationalist Confederation, 78, 132-3, 140
American National-Socialist Party, 24-6, 35, 359

523

II. SEDITION TRIAL INDEX

III. SPECIAL SUBJECTS INDEX

IV. CONGRESSIONAL INDEX REPRESENTATIVES

SENATORS

V. GEOGRAPHICAL FEVER CHART